THE
MANSIONS
AND THE
SHANTIES

ILLUSTRATIONS BY

Lula Cardoso Ayres

M. Bandeira

Carlos Leao

and the author

THE
MANSIONS
AND THE
SHANTIES

[SOBRADOS E MUCAMBOS]

The Making of Modern Brazil

BY

Gilberto Freyre

TRANSLATED FROM THE PORTUGUESE AND EDITED BY

HARRIET DE ONÍS

With an Introduction by Frank Tannenbaum

Introduction to the Paperback Edition by

E. BRADFORD BURNS

UNIVERSITY OF CALIFORNIA PRESS
Berkeley   Los Angeles   London

University of California Press
Berkeley and Los Angeles, California

University of California Press, Ltd.
London, England

Copyright © 1986 by The Regents of the University of California

Library of Congress Cataloging in Publication Data

Freyre, Gilberto, 1900–
   The mansions and the shanties.

   Translation of: Sobrados e mucambos.
   Originally published: New York: Knopf, 1963.
   Bibliography: p.
   Includes index.
   1. Brazil—Civilization. 2. Brazil—Social Conditions. 3. Brazil—Race
relations. I. De Onís, Harriet, 1899–   II. Title.
F2510.F75613   1986   981   86-19215
ISBN 0-520-05681-7 (pbk: alk. paper)

Printed in the United States of America

1 2 3 4 5 6 7 8 9

T O

the Memory of My Mother and Father

IN WHOSE STILL SEMI-PATRIARCHAL HOUSE
(SINCE TORN DOWN)
IN THE ESTRADA DOS AFLITOS IN RECIFE,
A GREAT PART OF THIS WORK
WAS WRITTEN

Introduction

A GOOD WAY to begin this introduction is to recall the many Brazilians who will tell you that in the future the history of their country will be chronicled in two parts: that before and that after Gilberto Freyre. The dividing line is *Casa-Grande e Senzala* (*The Masters and the Slaves*), first published in 1933, of which this volume, *The Mansions and the Shanties* (*Sobrados e Mucambos*), first published in 1936, is a continuation. The books describe the emergence and growth of Brazilian civilization from the patriarchal family, Negro slavery, and a single-crop economy—based on sugar. But *The Masters and the Slaves* is a great deal more than just a book—it marks the closing of one epoch and the beginning of another. Brazilians have in fact been carrying on what may be described as a sentimental affair with what has become for them the symbol of a new age. Since 1933, there have been eleven editions of this book in Portuguese, ten in Rio de Janeiro and one is Lisbon. While the English version of *The Mansions and the Shanties* was on press, the Brazilians published a volume celebrating the twenty-fifth anniversary of *The Masters and the Slaves.*[1] Planned in 1958, it was four years in preparation. It is a big book—576 pages of comments, criticism, eulogy, and sheer jubilation over the first appearance of *The Masters and the Slaves.* The volume contains sixty-seven separate essays, written by eminent historians, economists, sociologists, anthropologists, novelists, poets, artists, musicians, architects, city planners, educators, doctors of medi-

---

[1] *Gilberto Freyre: Sua Ciência, Sua Filosofia, Sua Arte.* Ensaios sôbre o autor de *Casa-Grande & Senzala*, e sua influência na moderna cultura do Brasil, comemorativos do 25ª Aniversario da publicaçao desse seu livro. Livraria José Olympio Editora, Rio de Janeiro, 1962.

cine, geographers, linguists, diplomats, public servants, and others.

This is a tribute by the major intellectual figures of the nation to a national event—an epoch in Brazilian history. It is obvious from the subjects dealt with that Gilberto Freyre's influence has touched the nation's life at many points. There are essays about Gilberto Freyre's impact on the study of Hispanic culture in Brazil; the new literary forms in his writing; *The Masters and the Slaves* and the cultural revolution; Gilberto Freyre as seen by a Catholic; his influence on the new generation; his treatment of Brazilian culture; his work as considered by a geographer; his reinterpretation of the mestizo; Freyre as a poet; his influence on the plastic arts; Freyre as a regionalist, as a traditionalist, and as a modernist; his influence on the mural art of Brasilia. There are interpretations of his style; studies of Freyre as an essayist; of Freyre and Brazilian cooking; of his guides to Brazilian cities; his interpretation of Brazilian reality; Freyre as a conservative and as a revolutionary; his treatment of Brazilian rural values; his impact upon Brazilian foreign policy; his influence on Brazilian literature. There are essays about the lyrical quality of his work; his new view of the Portuguese world; Freyre and the architects; his influence on the modern Brazilian novel; Brazilian philosophy in Freyre's work; Portuguese colonization in Brazil and his theory of tropicalism; Freyre as a social scientist; his influence upon history; medicine as depicted in Freyre's work; his treatment of French and English influence; Freyre and the jurists; his influence on the theater; his influence on the training of physicians; his evaluation of the Negro and the Portuguese. In these and many other areas Gilberto Freyre's work has made itself felt.

The Masters and the Slaves and *The Mansions and the Shanties* have acquired a permanent place in Brazil as national classics; other books of his are also widely known. His intellectual energy seems boundless. For, in addition to traveling, teaching, writing a regular column for Brazilian papers—an activity he began while a student— he has found time to write some twenty-five volumes and an equal number of pamphlets. Many of these have gone through more than one edition and been translated into various languages. What Gilberto's friends, followers, and admirers were celebrating, when they published a volume commemorating the first appearance of *The*

Masters and the Slaves, was the work of a major creative scholar, thinker, and literary artist. In its substance and method, Gilberto Freyre's work is that of a sociologist, social historian, anthropologist, and social psychologist. He is all of these and more. He has focused a new light on the hidden recesses of the years gone by. And that light is his sense of the whole—of a culture that is infinitely complex, contradictory, riven and torn by passion, greed, generosity, love, hatred, sex, jealousy, ambition, physical voluptuousness, and the sense of art, color, music, and faith—all of this and a great deal more are part of the sum.

There is a sense of detail, of the importance of all things: the food, the cooking, the dress, the odors about the kitchen, the house, the oxen, the Negro mammy, the naked little children running about the house, the sanitation, the lighting, the window, the veranda, the master, the mistress, the governor, the emperor, the law, the law-breaker, the judge and the criminal, the fugitive, the lash. The ways of young people with one another, the church, the priest, the friar, the school—and ten thousand other matters, all part of the record—are there, concrete and inescapable. Brazil is the unique combination of all of these things, in their tropical setting—and they are all important, equally important perhaps. The Negro slave and his master, the mistress and the colored girls about the house are equally relevant, and the vision of the author encompasses every one of them and passes judgment on none. They are bound together, and Brazil is what it is because of them, because people of many colors, races, and languages mingled, intermingled, absorbed and were absorbed, regardless of theories, views, or notions of superiority or inferiority, of better or worse, of higher or lower. One sees, through Freyre's eyes, a people emerging through time, with all of their foibles, hero-ism, laughter, and tears, as if through a movie camera. The mulatto mistress is carried in a sedan chair down the street by four stalwart Negro slaves, and the wife, her rival, is carried the same way down the same street at the same time. The bishop, the governor, the street urchin, and the peddler pass over the screen, playing their part in the drama and finally exchanging roles. The view is almost Augustinian, and the method infuses with life the compilation of journals, diaries, letters, photographs, newspaper advertisements, official registers, documents, books, pamphlets, songs, poems, verbal and written tradition. Synthesis, analyses, interpretation, logical deduction, and induction have gone into the shaping of this work. It has all of the craft, documentation, and "jargon" that goes by the name of science in the social sciences. But in addition it has something of the Bergsonian intuition, of the poet's insight and the artist's vision. And here form becomes almost as important as substance. The literary style that carries the subject matter of *The Masters and the Slaves* and *The Mansions and the Shanties* is like a flowing stream after a storm; it is full, deep, and sparkling. It is also intimate; it has the sensitivity of sterling verse and at the same time the richness and variety of a mosaic or a tapestry, except that it is alive, changing, appetizing, and tasteful. It reminds one of Proust at his best, but it is more robust, more vivid and all-embracing. It has a wider range and a greater depth. It reveals and embraces an entire culture in formation.

The Mansions and the Shanties, the sequel to *The Masters and the Slaves*, brings the rural patriarchal society to the developing Brazilian city of the middle of the nineteenth century. The environment changes: the big house becomes the mansion, the slave quarters become the shanties, the open spaces are replaced by the city street, the spacious porch becomes the veranda, the old courtyard and its noises are replaced by the street and its sound and clatter. Instead of the familiar peddler on the plantation, there are the street crier and the vender. The splendid spatial isolation of the *Fazenda* gives way, in the mansion, to the irrepressible bombardment of the growing city, with its developing middle class, government officials, university students, books, newspapers, coffee shops, brothels, banks, society balls, and official honors. The plight of the *Fazenda* family, the patriarchate, with its polygamous traditions and authoritarian rule, is acute in this period of transition. The feudal agrarian aristocracy of the old Brazil is teased into an urban, middle-class world and converted, or half-converted, to a social democracy without completely loosing its feudal paternal features.

To complete the story, one should read *Ördem e Progresso*, published in 1959, and *Região e Tradicão*, published in 1941. Together these give an epic view of the growth of Brazilian culture and the Brazilian people.

Clearly, much more could be said about Gilberto Freyre's work and its significance. What his admirers and followers have just written about him in the volume commemorating the twenty-fifth anniversary of the publication of *The Masters and the Slaves* is the start of what will, in time, be a critical review of his work at the hands of many scholars.

My own special interest in Freyre's work is not directly concerned with a critical evaluation of its substance and form. What has long seemed to me the broad significance of his work is that he has succeeded in changing Brazil's image of itself. This is a remarkable accomplishment. In only a few instances can it be said that one man, in his own lifetime, changed a great and populous nation's image of itself. The difference between the twenties and the sixties in Brazil is that today the Brazilians have discovered themselves. They have taken a good look and like what they see. They no longer wish to be Europeans, and their intellectuals no longer escape to Paris to find something to write about. They no longer describe themselves, or are so described by their own intellectuals, as a mongrel race, inferior because it consists of a mixed people. On the contrary, they find their creative freedom, their pride in the present, their confidence in the future precisely in this fact—that they are a mixed, a universal people. The social democracy of Brazil, and the pride Brazilians have discovered in being what they are, has released a font of creative enthusiasm. *The Masters and the Slaves,* published in 1933, was a revelation for the Brazilian intellectuals, artists, novelists, poets, musicians, and architects; they turned their eyes inward and began to sing a song of themselves. Hundreds of books have since been written by Brazilian scholars about Brazilian themes. They have discovered an endless task and find a ceaseless inspiration in being Brazilian and telling themselves and the world about it. This to me is the measure of Gilberto Freyre's achievement. He has given the Brazilian people a quiet pride in being what they are. As a single illustration: Jorge Amado's *Gabriela*[2] could not have been written before *The Masters and the Slaves.*

The only other country in Latin America where a similar develop-

[2] Published in English in 1962 by Alfred A. Knopf.

ment has taken place is Mexico. But there it required a bloody revolution, untold suffering, and the loss of a million lives. In Brazil, it was accomplished by one man and one book.

FRANK TANNENBAUM

Columbia University
New York
December 1962

The English version of *Sobrados e Mucambos* (based on the second edition of the work) departs slightly from the Portuguese original, in that both text and notes have been somewhat abridged, with the author's permission and agreement, for the sake of easier readability. Such of the notes as do not appear in the Portuguese edition, as well as the Brief Outline of the History of Brazil, were prepared by the author at my suggestion to clarify points that might be obscure or unfamiliar to non-Brazilian readers.

HARRIET DE ONÍS

The following are shortened versions of the preface written by Gilberto Freyre for the first edition (Rio de Janeiro, 1936) and his preface to the second edition, published fifteen years later, in 1951. A third edition appeared in 1961.

I am responsible for these abridgements, but in making them I have consulted Harriet de Onís and Frank Tannenbaum, who have approved my text, as has also my friend, Gilberto Freyre.

ALFRED A. KNOPF

Preface to the Second Edition

THIS STUDY, first published in 1936, is the logical rather than the chronological sequel of an earlier work, *The Masters and the Slaves*.

Neither book makes any claim to being chronologically exact. In neither of them are the facts studied between fixed or unchanging time limits. Who would venture to assign to the beginning of patriarchal society itself in Brazil a single, definite date without in some way qualifying it as the economic, or political, or civil beginning? Instead of a single beginning, it would seem to have had various in different places and at different dates. Instead of developing uniformly in time or space, it developed unevenly and contradictorily in both, achieving maturity in certain areas sooner than in others, declining in the North or Northeast when it was just coming to fruition in Southern Brazil. It varied so greatly in content from the far North to the far South that, confronted by this diversity, sociologists have tended to lose the sense of the uniqueness of form and process which was ethnographic, geographic, or economic rather than sociological—herding here, rubber tapping there, in São Paulo coffee, in Minas Gerais gold and diamonds, sugar, tobacco, cotton or cacao in the North. A uniqueness characterized in different regions or epochs by the less patriarchal organization not of the family alone but of the economy, politics, social relationships; by monoculture, latifundism; and by slave or servile labor with all this implies, including techniques of transportation, cooking, sanitation.

Sociology which fails to take into account anthropology, history, or psychology is indeed a precarious discipline. It will always lack the support that comes from the knowledge of the roots which any institution puts down into the earth, into the flesh and spirit of man. For institutions or human groups may be extremely interesting as ethnographic curiosities, yet not as sociological realities. A sociological understanding of the modern Brazilian is impossible without a knowledge of his origins or his development from the sociological point of view. Genetic sociology being principally the sociology of the family, it would be a basic error to omit the study of the house representative of the dominant type of family, and which, in turn, is inseparable from the physical and social conditions of the human group which dwelt in it. We always come back to *oikos*, that is to say, *house*.

This explains the importance I attach to the house in my studies not only of the sociology but of the ecology and the social history of the family, or of the society, in the main of Portuguese or Iberian origin, which has been developing in Brazil since the beginning of the sixteenth century. It grew up around the figure of the pater-familias, the master of the house, which symbolized not so much his masculine authority over women, children, and other men as that of the family which he represented. First came the Big House, rural or semi-rural, with its slave quarters. Later, the urban and semi-urban mansion, and the shanty, the shack, the hut, or the cabin.

Between these extremes intermediate types of characteristically Brazilian dwellings developed: the small one-story house of country and city, which varied in appearance and design. But I feel that I have been right in assigning to these contrasting types of dwelling a strong symbolic value within the basic framework of Brazilian society from the sixteenth to the end of the nineteenth century.

During this time Brazil was a society that lacked almost all forms or expressions of individual or family status except the two extremes: master and slave. The rise, to any considerable degree, of the middle class, the small independent farmer, the tradesman, is so recent among us that during that entire period it can practically be ignored. And the intermediate types of dwelling during those four centuries can, from the sociological point of view, be disregarded too, although they did exist.

When I decided to designate by a single name the type of house diametrically opposed to the *noble house*, I chose the African name *mucambo*. And I did so, not out of any aversion to the Amerindian designation of the same type of habitation, the *tejupaba*, nor because I am unaware of its existence or ignorant of its importance, but because the proletarian or laboring sector of our principal patriarchal cities—Rio de Janeiro, Bahía, Ouro Preto, Recife, São Luis—seemed to me predominantly African in its cultural traits, including its technique of home building, and its ethnic composition. This study, however, is not a history of civil or domestic architecture in Brazil, but an introduction to the history of patriarchal society in Portuguese America. It is a society examined, and perhaps reconstructed and interpreted, in the light of its most sociologically representative or significant types of dwelling. Masters and slaves were, by and large, from time immemorial among us, more "Whites" and "Negroes" than "Whites" and Amerindians, except, for a time, in a few regions such as São Paulo and for a longer period in the far North.

Let me underscore once more the norm which has guided me in my attempt to reconstruct and interpret the patriarchal society of Brazil. It is to study it in the framework of its principal types and styles of dwelling, which reflect different types and styles of life and culture.

Under this system there was considerable communication between the Big House and the slave quarters, between mansions and shanties, and not merely separation and differentiation. There was interdependence of emotions and sentiments, and not merely a conflict of economic interests. There is no other way to explain the hybrid manifestations, not only cultural but physical, which exist among us.

In the cities of Brazil today mansions occupied by wealthy individuals or patriarchal families are rare, whereas collective dwellings abound: hotels, boardinghouses, sanitariums, hospitals, asylums, barracks, boarding schools, apartment houses, workers' housing units. And there is a multitude of middle-sized detached dwellings, neither large nor very small, halfway between the old mansions and the shanties of one or at most two rooms, which are still common. The most noticeable change in the Brazilian panorama is the disappearance of the mansions, the Big Houses.

This marks the final disintegration of the patriarchal society, and its reorganization along new lines, though with patriarchal survivals. This transition coincided with the substitution of a republican form of government for the monarchical, a change which the people of São

Paulo and other states, and principally the Positivists of Maranhão, Rio de Janeiro, and Rio Grande do Sul, had been actively fomenting since 1870.

These Republicans, some of them masters of Big Houses or city mansions, represented the more progressive type of Brazilian, the majority of whom viewed askance a republic that was not prepared to guarantee the order needed for the material progress of the cities, and the mechanization of industry and agriculture, which they so ardently desired. Hence the motto adopted by the Republic on its foundation in 1889—Order and Progress—reflected the aspirations of the majority of our Republicans, even those not ideologically in agreement with Comte's philosophy. It is worth noting that several of the most important leaders of the new Republic—some of them half-breeds with aristocratic blood in their veins, others of humble origin, some of them the sons of recent European immigrants, who had risen in position through education or marriage to the daughter of mansion or plantation owner—were heads of the police force entrusted with the defense of the existing order. In Rio de Janeiro one of these leaders, with the strong, handsome air of a Moorish aristocrat, challenged the *capoeiras*, who were an outward expression of the hatred felt by the free Negro or the poor free mulatto for the rich whites; by natives, for Europeans; by shanty dwellers for those of mansions. The *capoeiras* had rendered the throne yeoman service as a "Black Guard" in the days when the monarchy, rebuffed by many an illustrious plantation or city-mansion owner, high army officer and clergy, some disgruntled at the excesses of the Abolitionists, others at the civilian or royalist exaggerations of the Emperor, found support and sympathy among backwoods badmen, Negroes, and the black boys of the shanties.

When the city mansion succeeded the plantation house as the expression of the domination of the Brazilian scene by the patriarchal system, the decline or loosening of this domination was followed not only by the increase of modest one-story houses, but by the conversion of old distinguished homes into collective dwellings—tenements, brothels, boardinghouses, asylums, etc.—or their transformation into public edifices—legations, consulates, clubs, newspaper offices, Masonic lodges, theaters, warehouses.

Even during the monarchy, and later, with the decline of the political power of the wealthy individual—power which was centered in the patriarchal plantation or city mansion—came the rise of public political power, embodied in the judiciary, law enforcement, and military branches of government. In fact, the bureaucracy was not infrequently installed in what had once been patriarchal dwellings, as in the case of the palaces of Catete and Itamaraty in Rio de Janeiro, which, even today, remind Brazilians and foreigners of what the patrician patriarchy was like in Brazil. These homes were of such opulence, especially in and around Rio de Janeiro, that the leaders of the republic of 1889 found them a better place to house their main offices than the dwellings of the former Emperor and princes. The patriarchal mansion was characterized by its architectural nobility, its adaptation to climate and milieu, which was in marked contrast to the flimsy, uncouth construction of the administrative buildings erected by the republican governments and those put up during the last years of the monarchy.

The Family, in its patriarchal form, was one of the great permanent forces in Brazil. Around it the main development of Portuguese America centered for four centuries, and not around kings or bishops, heads of state or church. Everything would seem to indicate that among Brazilians the family will not easily cease to be, if not the creator, at least the custodian and propagator of the values to which it gave being in its patriarchal phase.

In a new form which makes it possible to resist the pressure of forces stronger than itself today, and to adapt itself to changed living conditions, the family in Brazil, together with the Church, the co-operatives, the labor unions, the school, serves as one of the organs of regeneration and decentralization of power in a society still impregnated with feudal survivals. However, in purely patriarchal form, the vigor of the family, its mission well- or ill-fulfilled, is almost spent.

Its survivals will have, however, a long and perhaps undying life, not so much in the landscape as in the character and even the political life of the Brazilian. The patriarchal tends to prolong itself in the paternalistic, in the sentimental or mystic cult of the Father still identified for Brazilians with the image of the protector, the man of destiny, the man indispensable to the good ordering of society. It tends to take the form of an equally sentimental and mystic cult of the Mother, identified in our minds with images of protective beings or institutions: the Virgin Mary, the Church, the godmother, the mother.

The addiction of the Roman Catholic Brazilian to the cult of Mary, Mother of God, Mother of Men, may perhaps be explained by that maternalism which compensated morally and psychically for the excesses of patriarchalism, excesses identified with the despotism or tyranny of husband over wife, father over son, master over slave, white over black.

Preface to the First Edition

THE ATTEMPT to reconstruct and interpret some of the more intimate aspects of the social history of the family in Brazil, which I began in an earlier study, *The Masters and the Slaves*, is here continued, employing the same criterion and the same technique.

The principal object of this work is to study the processes of subordination, and, at the same time, of accommodation of one race to another, of one class to another, of the fusion of various religions and cultural traditions into a single one, which characterized the transition of Brazilian patriarchy from rural to urban. And especially to trace, from the end of the eighteenth century, its continuation in a less rigid patriarchy; the growth of the cities; the creation of the Empire—in a word, the formation of the Brazilian nation as, for the most part, a patriarchal society.

In the beginning, the most active processes were those of subordination and even coercion. The attorney-general of the state of Maranhão, Manuel Guedes Aranha, in 1654 was as emphatic in the expression of his belief in the subservience of the Indians or the blacks to the white man as any modern champion of Aryan or Western supremacy: "If in civilized countries," his reasoning ran, "the nobility is held in high esteem, with more right the white man should be esteemed in a land of heretics, for the former was suckled with the milk of the Church and the Christian faith." Moreover, "it is a known fact that different men are fitted for different things: we [the whites] are meant to introduce religion among them [Indians and blacks]; and they to serve us, hunt for us, fish for us, work for us."

But alongside advocates of the type and tenor of Guedes Aranha, there had been emerging since the beginning of the seventeenth century those who favored a better adjustment between the races, and who believed that their respective destinies had not been so rigidly foreordained by God. One of these was Father Antonio Vieira [1]—himself the grandson of a Negro woman. In the face of the invasion of the colony by a nation whiter than the Portuguese—the Dutch—the great preacher asked one day, "if we are not as dark compared to them as the Indians to us?" Could there be a "greater lack of understanding, or a greater error of judgment on the part of men than to assume that I am to be your master because I was born farther from the sun, and that you must be my slave because you were born closer to it?" This misgiving impugned the very basis of slavery.

In 1834 Dr. Henrique Felix de Dacia, whether a full-blooded Negro or a mulatto we have been unable to ascertain, but "Graduate in Law and Attorney," with great pride in his degree and even his color, wrote in *O Censor Brazileiro,* inveighing against the prejudice which makes "knowledge and office" the prerogative of the whites, who are determined "that a poor colored man shall be nothing more than a mere artisan"; "who prefer to give him alms rather than open to him the doors of the honors and emoluments due him; I have not rested; I shall always be the victim of the haughty, but I will never be humble toward them."

The cause of this outburst of pride and even arrogance on the part of Dr. Dacia was the fact that he was not allowed to serve on the bench. But in another newspaper of the same period a more authentically Brazilian voice, imbued with the spirit of compromise, can be heard. "I would ask which is more, to be judge, or priest, congressman, senator, minister, army officer, alderman, professor, magistrate, court clerk? It seems to me that all these positions are more important than that of judge. Now we see dark-skinned and black priests (my own vicar in Bahía was a Negro), we see a colored senator, a colored congressman, Rebouças, colored members of the

---

[1] Father Antonio Vieira (1608–1697), famous Jesuit preacher, missionary, and diplomat. Born in Portugal, emigrated while a child to Brazil with his family. Ardent champion of slaves and "New Christians"—which caused him serious difficulties with the Inquisition. Considered by some the greatest of classic Portuguese prose writers.

municipal government, and Mr. Canamerim, of dark color, about to take his seat in the city council of Bahía; we see colored doctors and surgeons, my honored friends and comrades; we see colored professors in the schools of medicine in great numbers; we have seen colored ministers of state; colored men sitting in our courts; colored students studying at our law schools; in all the societies known as secret, colored men are our beloved brothers, and the accident of color is held of no matter, for we have equal rights, we hold positions and posts without other distinction than that of ability and conduct . . . It is necessary, therefore, to dispel prejudice and promote understanding, avoiding unjustified provocation. We are all children of the fatherland; it belongs to all of us; it is our duty to love it, aid it, defend it, and promote its well-being, for this redounds to our benefit; let there be union between our souls . . ." [2]

The reality, however, was not quite so idyllic. The subordination of the colored people was not only that of race but of class. And the passing from one class to another, although far less difficult than in older European or Asiatic countries, was not so easily accomplished, nor could this be expected in a slavocrat, agrarian regime like that of Brazil. In 1835 General José Ignacio de Abreu e Lima pointed out in his *Historical, Political and Literary Outline of Brazil* that our population fell into two large groups, freemen and slaves, which, in turn, were subdivided into groups, or families, as he called them, "as separate and opposed to one another as the two main groups." And he goes on to say: "That we are all enemies and rivals of one another within our respective classes, requires no substantiating proof; all that is needed is for each who reads this study to scrutinize his own conscience and examine his own feelings."

If, on the one hand, these social gulfs narrowed with the decline of the rural patriarchy and the growth of the cities and the development of industry during the nineteenth century, on the other they became accentuated—at least among certain subgroups—due to conditions that developed with the growth of industry in a country formerly exclusively agricultural; with the more frequent and embittered clashes to which the Industrial Revolution gave rise among

---

[2] *Sentinella da Liberdade na Sua Primeira Guarita, Pernambuco, onde Hoje Brada Alerta.*

us. The patriarchal way of life lost many of its traditional characteristics in the cities as well as in the country; the town dwellers, and
the free or runaway slaves living in the city slums, became increasingly antagonistic, and the relationship between them very different
from that which had developed between plantation owners and their
slaves during the long rural patriarchy. The mediator between these
sharp antagonisms, softening, mitigating them, was the most plastic
and, in a sense, the most dynamic element in our formation: the
mulatto.

The focus of interest in my present study of these antagonisms
and of the adjustments that wore down their rough edges remains
the house—the larger house in relation to the smaller, the two in relation to the street, the square, the land, the soil, the jungle, even the
sea.

The Big House–Slave Quarters system, which I dealt with in *The
Masters and the Slaves,* became, in certain aspects, a veritable marvel
of adjustment: of slave to master, of black to white, of son to father,
of wife to husband.

It was when our social environment began to change in the sense
that the plantation manors became city mansions more after the European manner, and the slave quarters were reduced practically to
servants' rooms, that adjustment disintegrated, and new forms of
subordination, new social barriers began to develop between rich
and poor, white and colored, between the big house and the little.
Settlements of shanties and slums sprang up alongside the mansions,
but with almost no communication between them, and African
cults, diverging more from Catholicism than had been the case on
plantations and ranches. A new distribution of power came about,
but still resting for the most part in the hands of white landowners.
Sharper antagonisms arose between the rulers and the ruled, between white children brought up in the house and colored children
brought up in the street, without the old zone of fraternization between the two that was common on the plantations, and between
the mistress of the mansion and the women of the street. There was
a greater economic gap between the two extremes.

Only gradually did there begin to emerge moments of fraternization between these social extremes: the religious procession, the
church festival, carnival revelries. For the parks, the so-called public

promenades, the squares shaded by spreading *gameleira* trees and, for many years, encircled by iron railings similar to those which were taking the place of walls around the most fashionable houses, were limited to the use and enjoyment of the wearers of high shoes, silk hat, cravat, sunshade—insignia of race, but principally of class. They were for the use and enjoyment of the man of a certain social position, but only for the man. The women and children stayed inside the house, or in the grounds to the rear—at most, on the verandah, at the gate, by the hitching rail, by the garden wall. The boy who went out to fly his kite or spin his top in the street was looked upon as a vagabond. A lady who went into the street to shop ran the risk of being taken for a streetwalker. Mme Durocher—a virago, who wore a Prince Albert and men's shoes—was one of the first ladies to walk about the streets of Rio de Janeiro, and she created a scandal.

By the beginning of the nineteenth century the street was ceasing to be the drain for the dirty water of the city houses, through which the well-shod foot of the respectable citizen had to pick its way, and was taking on dignity and social importance. By night it was no longer a dark passage which citizens crossed, preceded by a slave bearing a lantern, but was lighted by street lamps burning fish oil and hung from wires on high posts. This was the beginning of public lighting, the first gleam of dignity of the street, previously so neglected that it depended for its illumination on that of private houses and the candles burning in the saints' niches.

At about this time the municipality began to defend the street against the abuses of the mansion, which had moved into the cities bringing with it the same highhanded ways, almost the same arrogance of its plantation and ranch days, making of the street a place to chop wood, a dump for dead animals, refuse, dirty water, at times even chamber pots. The very architecture of the town mansion developed on the basis of the street as its adjunct: the drain pipes emptying their flood of rain water into the streets; doors and shutters opening on to the street; and windows—when windows came to take the place of jalousies—which made it convenient for men to expectorate into the street.

City ordinances at the beginning of the nineteenth century were for the most part directed toward restraining these abuses and toward establishing the importance, dignity, rights of the street which had been so disregarded and flouted. Flouted by the landowners; flouted in Rio de Janeiro by the Jesuits who appropriated many small farms and farmhouses, and outlying dwellings. Some of these formed part of the city's land grant, and were enlarged or exploited against the public interest. Father Cepeda,[3] in a famous allegation, refers to "the distinguished thieves in the school"—the Jesuit school of Rio de Janeiro.

For many years the municipal councils, the judges, even royal edicts were practically helpless against such powerful individuals. The feudal shadow of the rich plantation owner or the Jesuits lay athwart the cities. The streets were footpaths that served the homes of the wealthy.

But beginning with the nineteenth century certain abuses were decreed illegal, such as the drains which arrogantly poured their flood of water into the street; the pigs raised in the street. Only pigs "with a triangular wooden yoke and a ring in the nose" might run loose in the streets, the Municipal Council of Olinda ruled in 1834. Sheep and goats, too, all had to wear yokes.

The Negro shanty dwellers were forbidden by ordinance to wash clothes at the public fountain in the middle of the city, and were ordered to do this in the streams outside the gates.

Other restrictions on individual liberties followed, such as forbidding the mansion owners to whip their slaves after the church bell, which played such an important role in the domestic and even the public life of Brazilian cities before clocks became common, had solemnly rung nine at night.

Still other ordinances were designed to make the street respected by the backwoodsman who came down from the hills, the backlands, or the plantations, riding high in the saddle or in his oxcart. He was ordered to dismount and lead his animal by bridle or reins, failure to do so carrying a penalty of twenty-four hours in jail; in the case of Negro slaves, two dozen lashes. And nobody was any longer to show such disrespect as to enter the city in shirt and draw-

---

[3] A priest who severely criticized the Jesuits and their school in Rio during the final phase of the colonial period.

ers, or cantering or galloping through the streets down which, since the end of the eighteenth century, vehicles had begun to roll, coaches, chaises, buggies, at first, then cabriolets, cabs, tilburies, gigs, all jolting over cobblestones and potholes.

The builders and owners of urban property were also being made to respect the street. They had to build their houses in a straight line along it and not at random or hit-or-miss as before. They had to fill in the holes and mud puddles in front of them. They had to observe a similar alignment in the promenades and sidewalks, doing away with the constant ups-and-downs from one strip of pavement to another, laid when each houseowner followed his own whim and thought only of what suited him best.

Thus the street was becoming emancipated from the absolute dominion of the "villa," the "manor," the mansion. The street urchin—that vivid expression of the Brazilian street—was showing a growing lack of respect for the great house as he defaced walls and fences with scrawls that were often obscene. Not to mention relieving himself on the doorstep of illustrious portals and even on the stair landing in the halls of the mansion itself.

Yet, though losing face to the street and diminished in its patriarchal functions (which it preserved even in the heart of certain cities) by the cathedral, the factory, the school, the hotel, the laboratory, the drugstore, the house of the nineteenth century continued to exert more influence than any other factor on the social formation of the urban Brazilian. The mansion, more European, produced one social type; the shanty, more African or Indian, produced another. And the street, the square, the church festival, the market, the school, the carnival, all contributed to the communication between classes, the intermingling of races, and the working out of a Brazilian solution for coming to terms with different ways of life, different cultural patterns.

The "corner house" or "the house with a door on the street" represents the maximum approximation between declining patriarchalism and the rise of the street. It marks the end of the phase of an almost prophylactic distance between the two, of shutters instead of glass windows, of walls and hedges of thorns that separated the house from the street.

Of the strictly patriarchal dwelling, represented among us by the plantation house or the country house in general, Gustav Schmoller [4] has said, in pages that have become classic, that its architecture bred our men, customs, work habits, styles of comfort. Spengler is almost repeating Schmoller when he pays tribute to the influence of the patriarchal *atrium*, when he opposes the influence of the house, with all that it stands for in the way of "economy," to the influence of race, and its capacity for enduring under diverse forms of habitation, living conditions, and climate.

By reason of his deep-rooted patriarchal formation, the Brazilian reflects the influence of the house both ecologically and economically. Nothing is more in the forefront of the poor man's thoughts than the idea of buying *his* shanty, or in the rich man's than, after making his fortune, to erect a fine mansion in full view of the street. The preference for hotel, boardinghouse, apartment—which is still the house—is as yet limited to Rio de Janeiro. In the rest of Brazil it is

> *My house, my little house,*
> *There is no other house like mine.*

Most modern Brazilians are still dominated by a patriarchal or semi-patriarchal sense of property.

This study, which is the continuation of *The Masters and the Slaves*, is the fruit of the same investigation. The main sources utilized in this work are listed as precisely as possible whenever they are drawn on for the first time. The reader will quickly see that I have used in large part manuscripts in public and private archives, and newspaper advertisements, virgin, or almost virgin material.

Like its predecessor, the present study has faults in the distribution of the material, repetitions; the contents of one chapter sometimes run over into another. I have found it necessary to come back to certain matters already touched upon, but focused now from a different angle, considered in relation to other social and psychological situations.

The near absence of conclusions, however, in no wise signifies a

---

[4] German social and economic historian of the second half of the nineteenth century.

disclaimer of intellectual responsibility for what may be unorthodox in these pages, for that which diverges from the established, the accepted, the recognized. For I have assembled and developed and interpreted my material with all possible objectivity.

The time has come for us to attempt to discern in the formation of the Brazilians a series of deep maladjustments, as well as the adjustments and balances. And to see them in their totality, laying aside narrow points of view and the attempt to reach satisfying conclusions. The human being can only be understood—in so far as he can be understood—in his total human aspect; and understanding involves the sacrifice of a greater or lesser degree of objectivity. For in dealing with the human past, room must be allowed for doubt, and even for mystery. The history of an institution, when undertaken or attempted in keeping with a sociological criterion which includes the psychological, inevitably carries us into zones of mystery where it would be ridiculous for us to feel satisfied with Marxist interpretations or Behaviorist or Paretist explanations, or with mere descriptions similar to those of natural history.

"Humility in the face of the evidence," to use a term recently employed by a master critic, together with a more human and less doctrinaire awareness, is making itself felt with increasing force among the new scholars and social scientists who are endeavoring to save the truths of history both from stratification into dogmas as well as from swift dissolution into short-lived absurdities.

Brief Outline of the Social and Cultural History of Brazil

1500 Official discovery by the Portuguese. The land was first called Vera Cruz, then Santa Cruz, and finally Brazil because of the abundance of red dyewood—brazilwood—found there.

1533 Division of Brazil by the King of Portugal, Dom João III, into hereditary captaincies so that, in keeping with the feudal system, the grantees would colonize their lands without expense to the royal exchequer. Outstanding among these captains was Duarte Coelho, who was accompanied by his wife, Dona Brites, and by numerous families, who set up sugar plantations and sugar mills in the northeast and imported large numbers of slaves from Africa. Sugar cane had been brought to Brazil around 1520 from Madeira or São Thomé; the first sugar mills were established in São Vicente (São Paulo) and Pernambuco. One of the early settlers in Pernambuco, Bento Teixeira Pinto, wrote a poem, *Prosopopeia*, which is considered the beginning of Brazilian literature.

1549 Arrival of the first governor-general, who founded the city of Salvador (Bahía). He was accompanied by the first

Jesuits, who at once set about converting the natives and establishing schools for whites and Indians. As early as the sixteenth century there was a school of university level in Bahía.

1554   The government of the captaincy of New Lusitania (Pernambuco), at the time the most important in Brazil, was taken over by Dona Brites, the widow of the grantee Duarte Coelho. She was the first woman governor of a state on the American continent.

1555   Arrival in Rio de Janeiro of French Calvinists, who undertook the first Protestant educational and missionary activities in America.

1575   Beginnings of the theater in Brazil, with Jorge de Albuquerque, governor of Pernambuco, and the Jesuits. Olinda, the capital of Pernambuco, consisted at the time of seven hundred houses of stone and mortar, several of them more than one story high, various churches and convents, and a splendid Jesuit school, with faculties in the humanities.

1580   Brazil, together with Portugal, came under the rule of Spain for sixty years. During this time a number of Spaniards settled in Brazil, some of whom became the founders of patriarchal families.

1615–19 French invaders entered Maranhão in northern Brazil.

1624   Dutch invasion of northern Brazil, at the time the country's most important area and its largest producer of sugar. After first attacking Bahía, the Dutch established the capital of their domain in Recife, Pernambuco, which they held for thirty years. During this time many Dutch settlers and, under their protection, a number of Sephardic Jews moved to Brazil. The descendants of both Dutch and Jews who became converted to Catholicism still live in Brazil today, as perfect Brazilians. Those Jews who remained faithful to their religion moved to New Amsterdam and other parts of America after the Portuguese reconquered Brazil. It was in Brazil, in the early seventeenth century, that Jewish literature in the American continent began, with a poem written in Recife by Aboab da Fonseca, a brilliant Sephardic scholar.

1641   A nativist movement arose among the inhabitants of São Paulo, who had already distinguished themselves as *bandeirantes*, conquerors of new lands for Brazil, and pioneers in the discovery of mines.

1654   Withdrawal of the Dutch after their defeat at the hands of the Portuguese, the Spaniards, and, above all, the settlers loyal to Portugal and staunch in their Catholic faith—whites and Negroes, native-born and immigrants, half-breeds and Amerindians. This war was in the main a guerrilla war. During the Dutch occupation of northern Brazil, a remarkable governor, Count Maurice of Nassau, distinguished himself, like the princes of the Renaissance, by his tolerance toward the Catholic and Jewish religions, and by his far-sighted civic planning in Recife. He brought out from Europe artists such as Post, the first painter of the American landscape in the Dutch manner, and scientists such as Piso and Marcgraf, the founders of the scientific study of the Indians, plants, animals, and tropical diseases of America. It should not be forgotten that colonial Brazil was under Spanish rule until 1640.

1693   Minas Gerais became the scene of a gold and diamond "rush." Cities began to spring up, with fine houses which rivaled those in the cities of the sugar region, such as Salvador, Olinda, Recife.

1697   Destruction of Palmares, the fortified settlement of runaway Negro slaves.

1697   Death of Father Antonio Vieira, who through his sermons and his missionary and diplomatic activities had exerted great influence on the social and cultural formation of Brazil.

1710   The Peddlers' War, a clash between the residents of Olinda and Recife over municipal rights. Recife was victorious.

1720   Revolt in Minas Gerais against the governor, led by retired General Vieiga Cabral. The uprising was quickly put down.

1727   Introduction of coffee, first in Pará, then in Maranhão in 1732, and in Rio de Janeiro in 1762, where its first cultivators were the Franciscan friars of the convent of St.

Anthony. The first proponent of its cultivation in Brazil was the botanist Fray José Mariano da Conceicão Veloso. From Rio de Janeiro the cultivation of coffee spread in the first half of the nineteenth century to São Paulo and Minas Gerais, where by the second half it had displaced sugar as the chief product of Brazil. It gave rise to a new aristocracy, owners of lands and slaves, who, like the sugar aristocrats, lived in the Big Houses of their plantations and in their city mansions.

1763   Transfer of the capital of Brazil from Salvador da Bahía to Rio de Janeiro. The governor-general was known, from the time of the Marquis of Montalvão (1640), as viceroy.

1769–79 The third viceroy of Brazil, the Count of Azambuja, distinguishing himself as a sort of city planner, made a number of improvements in the capital, including paving of the streets.

1789   The famous *Inconfidencia Mineira*, one of Brazil's early attempts to shake off Portuguese rule, developed in Vila Rica, the capital of Minas Gerais, where the gold mines were being exploited by the Portuguese mainly for the benefit of the Crown. It began in 1786, and the conspirators, among whom were some of the most important inhabitants of the region, looked to a republic along the lines of the North American colonies. In 1789 Tiradentes (as one of the leaders, a dentist, Joaquim José da Silva Xavier, was nicknamed) and the rest of the conspirators were betrayed to the governor of Minas Gerais. Tiradentes was sent to the gallows, and the others were exiled.

1808   Removal of the royal family of Portugal to Brazil after the invasion of the mother country by Napoleon's troops. With the queen came Prince Dom João, later King Dom João VI, who, with a large entourage of nobles and a considerable part of the royal patrimony, established the court in Rio de Janeiro.

1808   Opening of Brazilian ports to all friendly nations. This resulted in increased commercial, social, and cultural contacts between Brazil and Europe and the United States; also in increased urbanization.

1808   Manufacturing, forbidden until then, was permitted. In the same year the Royal Press was founded, and the Royal Library was established in Rio de Janeiro with books brought from Portugal.

1808–21   The erection in Rio de Janeiro of imposing public buildings, among them the Customs House, the Institute of Fine Arts (later known as the Imperial Academy of Fine Arts), the Lyric Theater, the National Museum.

1815   Elevation of Brazil, until then a colony governed by viceroys, to the status of kingdom, united to that of Portugal and the Algarve.

1817   Arrival in Brazil of Princess Leopoldina of Austria, future Empress of Brazil, among whose retinue was a band of musicians.

1818   First land grants to Swiss and German settlers.

1820   Founding of the colony of New Friburg (Rio de Janeiro) by Swiss settlers. This marked the beginning of a systematic policy of non-Iberian European immigration, consisting mainly (in the nineteenth century) of Irish (Rio de Janeiro, Bahía), Germans (Rio Grande do Sul, Santa Catarina, Paraná, São Paulo, Pernambuco, Espirito Santo), Italians (São Paulo and Rio Grande do Sul).

1822   Independence of Brazil from Portugal. The new American nation, in contrast to all the others, kept the monarchical form of government, naming as its first ruler the heir to the throne of Portugal, the Brazilianized Dom Pedro, son of King João VI, and giving him the title of Emperor. The distinguished statesman, José Bonifacio de Andrada e Silva, who was also a great naturalist, was largely responsible for this development.

1825   Separation of the Cisplatine province, which since 1821 had formed a part of Brazil, while the latter was still politically linked to Portugal. Upon its separation it took the name of the Republic of Uruguay.

1827   Founding of the law schools of Olinda (later Recife) and São Paulo. For nearly a century, these were the university centers where Brazilians received their training in diplomacy, politics, administration, and teaching.

1831   Abdication of Dom Pedro I, who retired to Europe. As guardian of his son, Dom Pedro II, the future second Emperor of Brazil, he left a native-born Brazilian, the scholar José Bonifacio de Andrada e Silva.

1831   The composer Francisco Manoel da Silva, the first director of the Royal Conservatory of Music in Rio de Janeiro, wrote the music of the Brazilian national anthem.

1840   Coronation of Pedro II, the son of Pedro I, at the age of fifteen. His long reign was characterized by stability and by well-oriented policies, in contrast to the frequent upheavals in the neighboring Spanish-American republics. Consolidation of a social and political aristocracy with agrarian roots, which even accepted mulattoes. Some of them, by their personal integrity and intellectual superiority, won national esteem.

1849   Ruy Barbosa was born in Bahía. At a very early age he became a power in national politics and distinguished himself by his advanced liberalism.

1850   Selling slaves or bringing them into the Empire was forbidden.

1851   The first steamship line between Brazil and Europe was inaugurated in Rio de Janeiro.

1854   The first railroad was inaugurated.

1857   Beginning of the Indianist trend in literature—rediscovery of native Brazilian cultural values—with the publication of the novel *O Guarani* by José de Alencar.

1860–71 Period of activity of the poet Castro Alves, who played an important role in abolition.

1864   War of the Brazilian Empire against the dictator Francisco Solano López, who had made of Paraguay a highly militarized and aggressive nation. Brazil was victorious, at the cost, however, of numerous lives. The indemnity that the Paraguayans were ordered to pay was never collected.

1870   The composer Carlos Gomes wrote the music for the opera *Il Guarany*, based on José de Alencar's novel *O Guarani*. It won universal acclaim at La Scala in Milan. By this time, some of the most famous opera singers of Europe were visiting the theaters of Brazil.

1870–1908 Literary activity of the mulatto Machado de Assis, author of numerous novels and short stories in which he skillfully analyzed the Brazilian society of his day, especially as typified in the aristocratic Brazilian of the Empire.

1872 Religious conflict between the Catholic clergy, represented principally by the Bishop of Olinda, and the Imperial government.

1872 Law of the Free Womb: first severe blow to the system of slave labor. It was largely the work of the Viscount of Rio Branco, considered by some the Empire's greatest statesman.

1874 Inauguration of the transatlantic cable.

1879–89 Period of Joaquim Nabuco's great efforts on behalf of abolition and social reform.

1881 Publication of the novel *O Mulato* by Aluizio Azevedo, which dealt with the struggle of the educated mulatto in the face of class and color prejudices.

1888 Abolition of slavery in Brazil by a law to which Princess Isabel, regent at the time, gave her name. As a result, the sugar industry and the social order based upon it suffered a mortal blow. In the coffee industry, however, due to the foresight of the statesmen of São Paulo, slaves had already been replaced by Italian laborers.

1889 Proclamation of the republic, organized along Anglo-American lines.

Author's Preface to the Paperback Edition

THE MANSIONS AND THE SHANTIES is so closely linked to *The Masters and the Slaves* that if one reads the earlier book without reading the other he will fail to understand essentials in the process of Brazil's social formation within the perspective initiated by that first book. Although initiated by the first book, the perspective is developed in the second in such a way that the design for revealing the process, which was barely started in *The Masters and the Slaves*, takes on major significance.

Three of the author's books, *The Masters and the Slaves*, *The Mansions and the Shanties*, and *Order and Progress*, have been said to form a trilogy, consisting as they do of three inseparable parts. It is plain they were viewed in this light by a London publisher who published the three together as a monumental history of Brazilian civilization.

The Mansions and the Shanties is considered by its author to be a work in various aspects superior to *The Masters and the Slaves*, but especially in its organization and presentation of a wealth of material derived from sources up to that time quite overlooked or even unknown—yes, completely unknown.

The theme ceases to be predominantly Brazil's rural, telluric, strictly patriarchal origins in its attempt to fix the definite beginnings of a complex urbanization of modes of existence that were initially rural. This complex urbanization included the revival of European and Europeanizing influences that had been in large part Brazilianized during the period dominated by the Big Houses in conjunction with their slave quarters and chapels; the Brazilianization of such influences was furthered by an ecology that is partly tropical.

Hence the special importance of the book *The Mansions and the Shanties*. It opens up a new vision of the process of social formation in Brazil, which with the renewal of European influences has come to be remarkably heterogeneous. The predominating Iberian influences, Portuguese in particular, have been succeeded by other Europeanizing impacts like the British and the French, with some Italian influence in the field of music.

The city mansions, remaining to some extent patriarchal, have come to constitute in an obvious manner new, significant presences in Brazilian life. Those kept as residences have been joined by ones destined for other important functions: bureaus and doctors' offices; houses of ladies of easy virtue, from expensive to reasonably priced. Hotels have sprung up in some mansions, an innovation by no means without significance in the Brazilian social structure, inasmuch as in the days of the all-dominant Big Houses certain duties were laid upon their noble, patriarchal hospitality—not of a commercial nature, however. Restaurants appeared in the mansions. Associations of various sorts were installed in them: Masonic lodges, for example. And they began to house deposits of patriarchal savings, a step toward their use as banks.

Yet the colonial days were not completely without their urban mansions, at least in certain parts of Brazil, especially in Recife during the period of Dutch rule. When the Dutch made Recife their capital instead of Olinda, they constructed streets of houses patterned on the north European model, with steeply sloping roofs as if in expectation of a heavy load of snow. The architecture indicated a lack of creativeness on the part of those mercantile Europeans when faced by the challenge of a tropical climate or ecology. Be that as it may, given the Dutch presence, the Recife streets were verticalized for better utilization of space, something new in Brazil.

The Portuguese or their descendants, in erecting their two-story town houses, had an inclination to create an urban architecture, as it were, ugly and substantial: solid, sturdy walls, and, in place of glass windows, Moorish-style balconies [*abalcoadas*].

Owing to the English influence, so strong in Brazil after we achieved independence from Portugal, those good old *abalcoadas* were replaced by wrought-iron verandas (iron coming from England) and glass windows (glass likewise coming from England). We see, then, that the city mansions had become a new presence in Brazilian life, not only socially but also by reason of their urbanizing and architectonic impact.

Socially they came to represent an intercourse between residences and public spaces, a development that was possible only in cities. The streets too, together with the mansions, began to create new relations between residences and public spaces; this sociological subject has been one of those treated with especial originality by the author of *The Mansions and the Shanties*, a book peculiarly sensitive to such challenges. The streets, it might be said, began to compromise the dignity and decency of the residences.

Coinciding with the appearance of elegant town houses in the Brazilian landscape, one may discern the appearance of a new social elite made up of distinguished occupants of those urban residences, including not only well-to-do merchants but also young doctors and lawyers, just out of school, whose professional practice would be favored perhaps by urbanization, perhaps by a revived Europeanism. Then on the ground floors of city mansions, warehouses and shops, whose operations ranged from heavy trade to light commerce in wearing apparel, shoes, barbershops, drugstores, and the like, began to appear. With increased Europeanization there came a flood of imported cosmetics, razors, soaps, remedies, children's toys. Golden-haired dolls led to the idealization of red-haired women—a type of Aryanism.

The city mansions, although creating new relations between the well-to-do and the streets, were still set off by fences enclosing abundant open spaces. The streets were in part, or totally, filthy. The residents of the elegant town houses strove to excel in cleanliness: they defecated in chamber pots whose contents were carried to the beaches in so-called tigers. The beaches, consequently, were foul.

A common expression among residents of stately mansions was "to wash one's hands of the street." Before learning the ways of city living even residents with clean hands had to wash their "hands of the street." One must remember the poor sanitary conditions of urban Brazil from its earliest days.

In this particular British and French influences were considerably beneficial to the Brazil of city mansions. Among the French influences was that of the famous engineer Vauthier, who, being also an architect, endowed Recife with a handsome neoclassical theater.

British and French influences spread to various sectors of urban Brazil. One French influence, it is understood, was the importation, by proprietors of certain well-known fashionable shops, of young French women as clerks whom, according to the oral tradition, they also employed for their own sexual purposes: nice little clerks who were mistresses on the side. The same oral tradition tells of Portuguese owners of warehouses and stores who are supposed to have instituted the same traffic with respect to young boys who were hired as clerks; nevertheless, their mustachioed bosses, either for economic reasons or from sexual preference, proceeded to make use of them as if they were women. Depending on the success of the relationship, such male clerks might achieve commercial triumphs.

The age of *City Mansions and Shanties* witnessed some good adjustments, but there were also surprising contrasts, with the shanties being at times nauseous.

It was the residential practice to place town houses in urban strongholds of the socially elite, whose standards of living presented a strong contrast to those of shanty dwellers, who were almost without exception coarse and low class. On the other hand, the town houses added to their residential functions other functions of a public nature, which included certain types of intimate relations that were possible only in an urbanized Brazil.

And yet the patriarchal families of the big plantation houses would not have lacked intimate relationships, especially those facilitated by endogamy within the families, through marriages of cousins with cousins, uncles with nieces. In the cities a new relationship was created for town house residents both through neighborhood living and through attendance at the same Catholic churches. In this particular, it should be remembered that some of the more spacious city mansions, with a few adaptations or because a use of the sort had been part of the initial plan, were turned into theaters.

One should also take note of more amplitude in conjugal unions among the occupants of Big Houses, formerly so inclined to be endogamous. The elite of the town houses proved to be less endogamous.

It is also certain that town house residents favored relationships, including the conjugal one, between Brazilians and foreigners. And with these relationships came crossbreeding of cultural influences of diverse origins, which in turn created preferences for different types of furniture, although there may be evidence that the taste of the rural Big Houses for jacaranda and vinhatico furniture, and for

Portuguese plate, had been transmitted to the occupants of the city mansions. A detail should be added, however: the occupants of the city houses were favored by a greater facility in obtaining fine china from the Orient, china that came to be characteristic of Olinda's and Recife's city mansions. Moreover, they were better able to obtain silk, including the silks for judicial robes ordered from the Orient by bachelors of law.

One can easily believe that the cuisine in the town houses took on Gallicisms and Anglicisms not known in the Big Houses. And this explains what happened more especially with wines and cordials; Brazilian rum came to be universally despised as a vulgar, low-class drink. Among their vices, town house residents held in high regard the snuff and tobacco brought from Bahia.

Nor should one forget the city mansions' affinity for new modes of transportation: sedan chairs, being considered old-fashioned, were replaced by horse-drawn carriages of elegant English make.

It should be noted that, from a certain point on, residence on a suburban estate entered into competition with residence in a city mansion of the noble type. This change is attributed to the influence exerted on Brazilians by Englishmen fearful of so-called tropical ills and fevers. Even with the preference for suburban estates, it was found that the architecture of city mansions, long old-style in Olinda, has extended to the suburbs. Also in Olinda, from a certain period, those blessed with having good, old residences acquired a taste for sea bathing—saltwater bathing—signifying a certain connection between the town house and open-air living; walking, physical exercise, replaced the horseback riding that had prevailed at the patriarchal Big Houses.

Recife   Gilberto Freyre
1986

Introduction to the Paperback Edition

FEW HAVE MADE more original contributions to the study of the Brazilian past than Gilberto Freyre, a historian of broad vision and challenging interpretations. Living in Recife, the preeminent city of Brazil's northeast, he has written prolifically. His production, now spanning more than half a century, has influenced generations of intellectuals, not only in Brazil but internationally.

Freyre catapulted to prominence in 1933 with the publication of *The Masters and the Slaves*. In this social study of Brazil's long colonial past, he concentrated on the emergence of a unique Brazilian civilization created by the amalgamation of European, African, and Amerindian contributions. The races and the cultures mingled and mixed in the shadow of the great plantation houses dominated by omnipotent patriarchs. Freyre's thesis attracted global attention. Historians have since pursued that intriguing theme as a fundamental starting point for the study of Brazil. At the same time, Freyre's claims of the relative mildness of the Luso-Brazilian institution of slavery and of a pervasive Brazilian racial democracy sparked a lively controversy which also continues into the present. Clearly Freyre had torn the veil concealing Amerindian and, particularly, African participation in the historical process. His boldness and success continue to enrich our understanding of the South American giant.

An impressive testimony to Freyre's contributions, *Gilberto Freyre: Sua Ciência, Sua Filosofia, Sua Arte,* was published by José Olmypio in 1962 to commemorate the silver anniversary of *The Masters and the Slaves*. In its more than five hundred pages, Brazil's leading intellectuals paid eloquent homage to their peer and to his impact on Brazilian self-perception. Their essays reveal the extent to which

Freyre's ideas have altered Brazilian historiography. Not only were there new themes to consider, but Freyre also introduced novel sources for historians to examine: riddles, folktales, popular poetry, recipes, children's toys, the vernacular vocabulary, and so forth. The list is as long as it is innovative. He literally moved historical research out of the archives and into the streets. In doing so, he allied the historian with the anthropologist, the sociologist, and the folklorist.

Freyre followed his multidisciplinary study of the colonial past with *The Mansions and the Shanties* (1936), an interpretation of the nineteenth century, which politically extended from the arrival of the Portuguese monarch in Rio de Janeiro (1808) to the overthrow of the Brazilian emperor (1889). Interpretive studies of that transitional but formative century had been few. Historians had contented themselves with narrative accounts whose numbing details blurred rather than clarified the meaning of the past. With his usual panache, Freyre banished boredom in his fascinating sweep across the century, although the emphasis falls on the first half. He shifted the locale in this volume from the plantation to the city in order to highlight significant changes in attitudes, life-styles, and ideas. From such changes "modern" Brazil emerged.

With his customary broad vision of the past, Freyre selects some challenging themes: the decline of patriarchal domination, the rise of the mulatto, a conflict of cultures, the re-Europeanization of society, the growth of the city, the emergence of an urban middle class, and the centralization of political power. These themes tightly intertwine. Although they inescapably have political and economic dimensions, Freyre, true to the patterns established in *The Masters and the Slaves*, adheres primarily to their social implications. In doing so, he continues to introduce his readers to a gratifying variety of novel sources, widening and enriching our vision and perception of Brazil's past.

During the first two centuries of Portuguese colonization, the city manifested neither the vigor nor the importance of its counterpart in Spanish America. The discovery of gold in Minas Gerias in 1695 challenged that pattern. Mining, unlike agriculture, promoted urban living. The eighteenth century witnessed an impressive urban expansion. Whereas in the seventeenth century only four cities and thirty-seven towns were founded, the eighteenth century witnessed the creation of three cities and 118 towns. Freyre provides ample evidence that the trend gained momentum during the nineteenth century. Rio de Janeiro certainly demonstrated impressive urban growth. On the eve of the arrival of the Portuguese court, the viceregal capital counted 50,000 inhabitants. After the overthrow of the monarchy and the establishment of the republic, the population of the capital was 552,651, an elevenfold increase in about eight decades.

Freyre correctly emphasizes that the cities, ever larger, more important, and more receptive to change, steadily eroded the influence of the rural aristocracy, thereby diminishing patriarchal authority. The landowners themselves began to build impressive residences in the cities and, furthermore, to spend considerable time in them. Thus they lent prestige and authority to the city, enhancing its position. The government bureaus, export agencies, and banks, rooted in the cities, branched out to exert economic control in the countryside, a trend that accelerated impressively throughout the nineteenth century. The landowner could make fewer decisions within the confines of the *fazenda*. He had to visit the city to consult his banker or his agent; he had to petition a government official for a favor. If his children were to receive a higher education, they had to remain in the cities, where the sons of the new middle class— Freyre associates that class with the rise of the mulattoes to greater prominence—as well as of the plantation aristocracy enrolled in ever larger numbers in law, medical, engineering, and military schools. Upon graduation they pursued urban careers, contributing their numbers and their ability to strengthen the city. After 1870, larger currents of European immigration flowed into Brazil. A high percentage of these foreigners chose to settle in the cities, where their differing customs and thoughts helped to alter the urban milieu. Rio de Janeiro well illustrated the growing presence of foreigners. In 1836 about 7 percent of the capital's population was foreign-born; in 1856, it had leapt to 35 percent; and in 1890, the figure stood at 30 percent.

European influences entered into the city and from there penetrated the interior, albeit at a much more leisurely pace. The innovation of steamship service with Europe—in 1851 the Royal English Mail Line established regular routes to South American ports—the submarine cable (1874), increasing commerce with Europe, and the travels of the elite to the Old World as well as the visits of curious Europeans to Brazil brought the empire into ever wider contact with the outside world.

France contributed mightily to shape Brazil's intellectual, social, and cultural life. Three French cultural missions, the first in 1816 and the last in 1840, succeeded in strengthening a preference for Parisian values. The educated classes embraced French as a second language. The English visitor Maria Graham related, in her *Journal of a Voyage to Brazil and Residence There during Parts of the Years 1821, 1822, 1823*, that she conversed with ladies of high society in French. French literature eclipsed Brazilian, or any other for that matter. The educated animatedly discussed the novels of Gustave Flaubert, Honoré de Balzac, and Emile Zola. Their works dominated the bookstores. In the shops of the major cities, every Parisian luxury could be found. Ouvidor Street, one of Rio's principal shopping areas, was almost exclusively French. The ladies vied with one another to copy the latest Parisian styles.

English influences were no less dominant, particularly in commerce, banking, and politics. Although Brazil's parliamentary monarchy was sui generis, it found a model in the British system whose order, stability, and exclusivity appealed to the aristocrats. Britain wielded overwhelming economic power within Brazil.

The emerging urban middle class adopted the elite's preferences. To the fullest extent possible it, too, copied European models, thereby deprecating traditional Brazilian ways, mores, and culture. Joaquim Manoel de Macedo offered convincing evidence of these and other characteristics of that incipient class in his *A Moreninha* (1844), the most popular Brazilian novel of the nineteenth century. Through the students, merchants, court bureaucrats, physicians, lawyers, and members of their families populating its pages emerged a profile of the new bourgeois society of the first years of the Second Empire. Their conversations, indeed their thoughts, to which the reader is privy, all seem limited to themselves, their routines, and their ambitions. Although they may have kept one eye on their fellow citizens, the second, nonetheless, was turned toward Europe.

This renewed attention to Europe, this growing influence and dominance of Europe, constituted what Freyre terms the "re-Europeanization of society." His reference is to the Portuguese impact on Brazil in the sixteenth century, followed by an amalgamation of European, Amerindian, and African cultures into a unique, fascinating Brazilian civilization. Europe's renewed and growing influence after 1807 challenged Brazilian values. It set in motion a reshaping of society to make it conform more closely to English and French patterns. Freyre highlights "the intensive re-Europeanization of Brazilian society at the beginning of the nineteenth century, which coincided with the decline of the patriarchal system in its traditional rural areas" (p. 301).

The "re-Europeanization" detonated a "conflict of cultures," a significant theme weaving in and out of the Freyre text. It merits future study. For one thing, it is paramount in understanding nationalism, specifically a popular nationalism. Large segments of ordinary people partial to Brazilian ways struggled with those determined to modernize the nation according to European patterns. For another, cultural conflict in many ways provides transcendental meaning to the course of nineteenth-century Brazilian history. Students of the Brazilian past are just now beginning to explore the theme. The rich historical veins of messianic movements and backland banditry have hardly been mined. The dimensions of popular rebellion, such as the War of the Cabanos, the physical confrontations between the expanding coffee planters and the small farmers of the Paraíba Valley, or the Quebra-Quilo Revolt, have barely been suggested. They reveal two Brazils in conflict. Cultural loyalties separated the two.

By the end of the century it was abundantly clear that the modernizers had won. Perhaps, in 1897, the defeat of the religious followers of Antônio Conselheiro in the backlands of Bahia by government troops symbolized that victory. A witness to the eradication of the followers of Antônio Conselheiro at Canudos, the brilliant intellectual Euclides da Cunha mused, "We are condemned to civilization. Either we shall progress or we shall perish. So much is certain, and our choice is clear." At Canudos, the cannons of the army apparently had opened the vast interior to "civilization."

What was the clear choice indicated by da Cunha? Politically it was a republic whose constitution echoed that of the United States; economically it was capitalism. The rise of the city coupled with the boom of coffee exports foretold both choices.

Much of the modernization, urbanization, and industrialization floated on a sea of coffee prosperity. In the nineteenth century coffee production, and consequently prosperity, centered in Rio de Janeiro, Minas Gerais, and São Paulo, the focal point of Brazil's economic growth. By the time of independence (1822) coffee was already accounting for a fifth of Brazil's exports, about 190,000 bags. That figure rose to 5,600,000 bags, approximately two-thirds of total exports, by the time of the fall of the monarchy in 1889. As early as 1841 Pedro II paid tribute to the producers of the empire's new wealth when he first elevated a coffee planter to the nobility. With each passing decade thereafter, the coffee class figured ever more prominently among the new nobility. Some representatives of this new nobility enjoyed vast wealth. They dominated society, at least in the dynamic southeast. They built residences in the capital to rival the royal palace. In fact, the *palácio* of one coffee baron, the Barão de Nova Friburgo, became the residence of the president of Brazil after the proclamation of the republic.

On many levels the coffee boom, burgeoning cities, and a proud new republic doomed institutions linked with the colonial past: patriarchal society, slavery, and the monarchy. Freyre's account concentrates on their demise. Paradoxically, and this aspect receives less attention in *The Mansions and the Shanties*, change also strengthened some long familiar institutions, thus ensuring a continuity with the past—elite control of politics and the economy, the prevalence of the large estate, the dominance of the export sector, and monoculture—as well as the inevitable consequence of dependency, both economic and cultural.

The centers of the large cities pretentiously replicated Europe. A modest industrialization was under way. Railroads and steamships challenged the impressive distances that characterized Brazil. As Freyre concludes, "The coffee boom represents the transition from the patriarchal to the industrial economy" (p. 131). The new coffee class prospered, and to a much more limited extent so did the urban middle class. In the eyes of some, progress had triumphed.

Yet a major question arises: What benefits accrued to the majority? Those Brazilians seemed to suffer a stagnant or declining quality of life. Access to land diminished; food production failed to keep pace with population growth; inequities of income distribution widened; the acquisitive power of working-class salaries declined. In his novel of the urban proletariat, *A Brazilian Tenement* (1890), Aluízio Azevedo depicts a Rio de Janeiro festering with prostitution, drunkenness, misery, exploitation, street crime, and insanity. The themes of pervasive poverty and limited social mobility dominate the novel. Clearly re-Europeanization and whatever progress might have accompanied it did not favor the poor in nineteenth-century Brazil, and the overwhelming majority was impoverished.

Examining the nineteenth century for signs of economic development—the use of a nation's potential for the greatest good of the largest number—the researcher will be disappointed. The economy grew. Changes occurred. Yet dependency and poverty remained dominant. The Brazilian writer Graça Aranha concluded in his novel *Canaan* (1902) that Brazil was a colony of the Europeans: "'You gentlemen speak of independence,' observed the municipal judge caustically, 'but I don't see it. Brazil is, and always has been, a colony. Our regime is not a free one. We are a protectorate.'" A decade later, the eloquent nationalist Alberto Torres advised, "We cannot be free if we do not control our own sources of wealth. . . . In order to maintain the independence of a nation, it must preserve the vital organs of its nationality, among them its principal resources." Obviously, the mansions of the cities brought no more solutions to Brazil's legacy of underdevelopment than had the plantation houses of the rural past.

Los Angeles, California   E. Bradford Burns
September 1986

Contents

Illustrations

*Suburban patriarchal mansion in the second half of the
nineteenth century. (Drawing by L. Cardoso Ayres)*

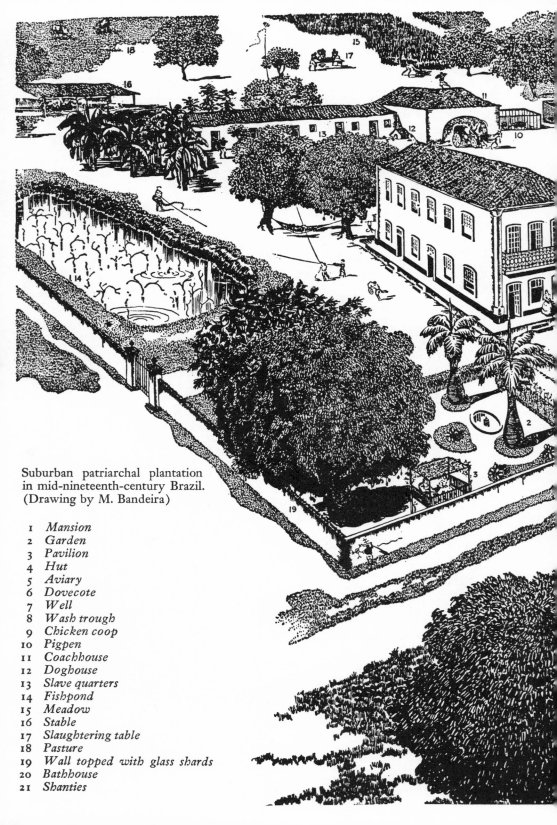

Suburban patriarchal plantation
in mid-nineteenth-century Brazil.
(Drawing by M. Bandeira)

1   Mansion
2   Garden
3   Pavilion
4   Hut
5   Aviary
6   Dovecote
7   Well
8   Wash trough
9   Chicken coop
10 Pigpen
11 Coachhouse
12 Doghouse
13 Slave quarters
14 Fishpond
15 Meadow
16 Stable
17 Slaughtering table
18 Pasture
19 Wall topped with glass shards
20 Bathhouse
21 Shanties

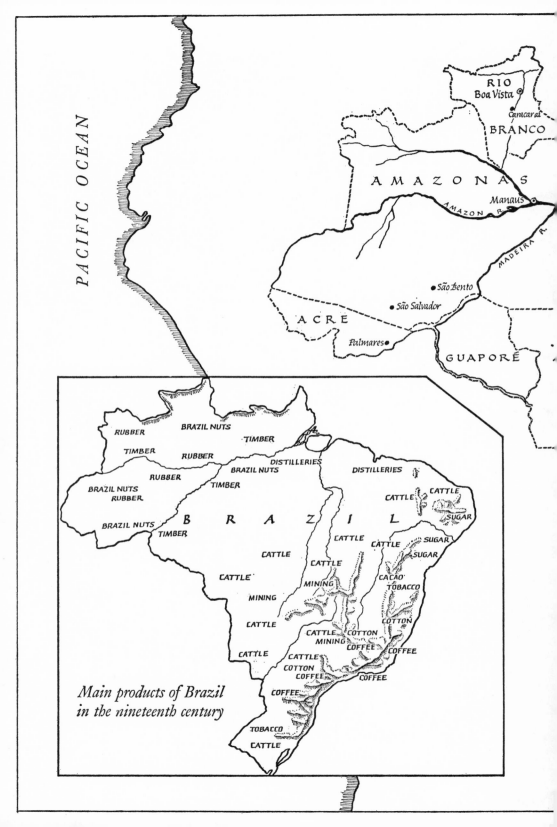

PACIFIC OCEAN

RIO
Boa Vista ⊙
Caracaraí ●
BRANCO

A M A Z O N A S

Manaus ⊙
AMAZON R.
MADEIRA R.

São Bento ●
São Salvador ●

A C R E

Palmares ●

GUAPORÉ

RUBBER
BRAZIL NUTS
TIMBER
TIMBER
RUBBER
DISTILLERIES
DISTILLERIES
RUBBER
BRAZIL NUTS
CATTLE
CATTLE
BRAZIL NUTS
RUBBER
TIMBER
CATTLE
SUGAR
B R A Z I L
BRAZIL NUTS
CATTLE
SUGAR
TIMBER
CATTLE
CATTLE
SUGAR
CATTLE
CACAO
TOBACCO
MINING
CATTLE
MINING
COTTON
CATTLE
COTTON
COFFEE
COFFEE
CATTLE
MINING
COFFEE
CATTLE
COTTON
COFFEE
COFFEE
COFFEE
TOBACCO
CATTLE

*Main products of Brazil
in the nineteenth century*

ATLANTIC OCEAN

Miles

0   500

MARACÁ I.

AMAPÁ

CAVIANA I.

AMAZON R.

MARAJÓ I.

Belém
(Pará)

Barbacena

XINGÚ R.

São Luís do Maranhão

Rosario

PARÁ

TOCANTINS R.

MARANHÃO

Fortaleza (Ceará)

Teresina

Madalena

Aracati

CEARÁ

Mossoró

PARNAÍBA R.

RIO GRANDE
DO NORTE

Natal

PIAUI

Sousa

PARAIBA

João Pessoa (Paraíba)

Triunfo

Monteiro

Itamaracá

PERNAMBUCO

Olinda

Recife

Bonito

SÃO FRANCISCO R.

ALAGOAS

Maceió

Pilar

MATO GROSSO

TOCANTINS R.

SERGIPE

São Cristovão

Maruí

G
O
Y
A
Z

Paraná

BAHÍA

Rio Pardo

Cachoeira

Salvador (Bahía)
de Todos os Santos

Praia Rica

Cuiabá

Goias

Goyania

Paracatú

JEQUITINHONHA R.

Minas
Nova

Mucuri

MINAS

Serro Frio

URUGUAY R.

Pitanguí

Belo Horizonte

Sabará

Guapé

Ouro Preto

GERAIS

ESPÍRITO SANTO

Espírito Santo

PARANÁ R.

SÃO PAULO

Paraiba do Sul

São Pedro

Itu

RIO DE
JANEIRO

Sorocaba

Jundiaí

Piratininga

São Paulo

Paraibuna

Rio de Janeiro

PARANÁ

Santos

São Vicente

Iguaçú

IGUAÇÚ R.

Curitiba

SANTA CATARINA

Florianapolis

SANTA CATARINA I.

RIO GRANDE
DO SUL

Porto Alegre

Viamão

URUGUAY R.

Mostardas

Pelotas

(URUGUAY)

Santa Lucía

O DE LA PLATA

BRAZIL

in the nineteenth century,

with the addition of
states and territories acquired
subsequently. The cities
are those that flourished
in the nineteenth century

THE
MANSIONS
AND THE
SHANTIES

CHAPTER I

THE CHANGE IN THE SOCIAL LANDSCAPE OF PATRIARCHAL BRAZIL DURING THE EIGHTEENTH CENTURY AND THE FIRST HALF OF THE NINETEENTH

WITH THE ARRIVAL of Dom João VI in Rio de Janeiro in 1808, the rural patriarchy, firmly established in its plantations and ranch houses—the plump ladies in the kitchen making sweets, the men puffed up with their titles and privileges of sergeant-major or captain-major, their silver goblets, spurs, and daggers, their many legitimate children and by-blows scattered about the house and the slave quarters—began to lose its grandeur of colonial days. A grandeur which the discovery of the gold mines was already undermining. From that moment the interest of the Crown in its American colony began to grow. Brazil ceased to be the land of brazilwood, at which the King looked a little down his nose, to become Portugal's best colony—the pompous, church-serving Portugal of Dom João V—and for that reason the most exploited, the most jealously guarded, the most sternly ruled.

The presence in Rio de Janeiro of a prince with royal powers; a prince of bourgeois tastes, slovenly, flabby, his fingers sticky with chicken gravy, but the wearer of the crown, bringing with him the queen, the court, nobles to kiss his fat but prudent hand, soldiers to parade in front of his palace, foreign diplomats, doctors, musicians, and royal palms in whose shade the first secondary schools sprang up, the first library, the first bank. The mere presence of a monarch in a land as republic-minded as Brazil, with its rebellious Rochellas,[1] its people of Minas Gerais and São Paulo who refused obedience to the far-off king whom they despised, and arrested and even expelled the Crown representatives (as did the landholders of Pernambuco with the Xumbergas), a land so anti-monarchical in its tendencies toward regional and even feudal autonomy, brought about a profound change in colonial society, modifying its most typical traits.

A series of influences, economic for the most part, some prior to the arrival of His Royal Highness but only subsequently defined and apparent, began to affect the structure of the colony in the sense of strengthening the power of the Crown. And not only of the Crown, which became stronger even in Dom João's flabby hands, but also that of the cities of industry and urban activities.

The more direct intervention of the Crown in the affairs of Brazil, which was to give rise to the revolt of 1720 in Vila Rica and the *Inconfidencia* rebellion, had for some time been paving the way for a greater centralization of government and the strengthening of the royal power. The independence of the planters, the Paulistas, the Mineiros, and the ranchers was no longer the same as in the eighteenth century, nor their arrogance so great.

In Pernambuco the lines were drawn up between the "backwoods" aristocracy and the bourgeoisie of the mansions of Recife—the latter supported by the King, now at odds with the plantation owners, his former allies, and the former by the higher clergy—in a civil war known as the "Peddlers' War." The war ended in the victory, although only partial and fragmentary, of the urban interests over the privileges of the rural nobility, so strong and entrenched in the

---

[1] Those "Paulistas," some of them mestizos, who in the sixteenth and seventeenth centuries became famous for their independent attitude toward the Portuguese Crown and the Catholic Church. They contributed greatly to the territorial expansion of Brazil.

captaincy of the Albuquerques.[2] There, as in Minas Gerais as a result
of the discovery of gold, conditions of urban life, both industrial and
commercial, sprang up which ran counter to those privileges. In
Pernambuco this situation developed mainly as a consequence of
Dutch domination, which threatened at one and the same time the
power of the plantation owners and that of the church of Rome.

Under Dutch rule, and with the presence in Brazil of Count Maurice of Nassau, far more princely in his bearing and actions than the
husband of Dona Carlota Joaquina—although Dom João was not,
as the historian Oliveira Lima has already proved, the nincompoop he
was generally considered—Recife, a simple fishing village around
a church, completely overshadowed by the feudal and ecclesiastical
preeminence of Olinda, developed into the finest city of the colony
and perhaps of the entire continent. Four-story town houses. Royal
palaces. Bridges. Canals. A botanical garden. A zoological garden.
An observatory. Calvinist churches. A synagogue. Many Jews. Foreigners of the most diverse origins. Prostitutes. Shops, warehouses,
offices. All the conditions for sharply vertical urbanization.

This was the Portuguese-American colony's first great adventure
in freedom, its first broad contact with the world, with modern
Europe—middle-class and industrial—for until that moment it
had been kept in an almost virgin state. A rustic virginity, barely
scratched by the attacks of French and English pirates, or by dissensions due to proximity and kinship (not always conducive to good
relations) with the neighboring Spaniards. But in no wise wounded
or even seriously affected in its basic way of life or even its fundamental values; its agricultural routine, its uniformly Catholic faith,
and its peninsular morality were quite unperturbed, except for slight
divergences. There were Jews who in the privacy of their homes
scoffed at Our Lord, Negro witch doctors, converted Indians. But
neither the Jews nor the Negroes really showed hostility toward the
Catholic faith; great diplomats or compromisers, as is the case with
peoples, and the more intelligent women and children, who suffer
oppression, for the most part they effected a kind of substitution or

---

[2] The first feudal lord of Pernambuco, in the sixteenth century, Duarte
Coelho, was married to an Albuquerque. His brother-in-law, Jeronymo, became famous for his numerous descendants, bearing the name of Albuquerque.

transfer, conferring on their saints or rites Catholic names and outward attributes though they remained inwardly different.

The great Pernambuco adventure did not suffice to destroy the
seemingly loose, but in fact sturdy, homogeneity of the emerging
Luso-Catholic "collective conscience" which had been developing
among the settlers of Brazil, under that uniformity of faith and morality maintained by the inflexible orthodoxy of the Jesuit fathers,
even though this worked *pro domo sua* and not in the interests of
the integration of the Brazils into a single Brazil. This developed
thanks to the similarity of methods of economic production and
work, made possible, or rather, stimulated by the similarity of climate and soil conditions: a monoculture based on latifundism and
slavery. And intensified by the endogamy in general practice among
the various colonizing groups, even though they did not disdain contacts with the so-called "native Negro women" and even with those
brought in from Africa, nor were marriages with foreigners rare—
Felipe Cavalcanti and Gaspar van der Lei in Pernambuco, John Whit-
all in São Vicente, were accepted as sons-in-law by rich patriarchal
families of Portuguese and Catholic origin. A manuscript recently
acquired by the National Library, "Journal of a Residence in Brazil
written by Cuthbert Pudsey during the years 1629–1640," gives evidence that marriages between the Dutch and the daughters of planters and other rural nabobs were frequent.

After the thirty years of Dutch domination, the North returned
to its agricultural routine and Catholic uniformity, to the leisurely
process of social integration in the Portuguese, Catholic manner.
That adventure in differentiation became a memory almost like a
dream; "the time of the Flemings," a phrase the country folk still use
in referring to something unusual, extraordinary, marvelous, almost
diabolical, a piece of engineering or art which seems to them beyond
the technical ability of a Portuguese or a native son. Something like
"the time of the Moors" in Portugal.

Nevertheless, the "time of the Flemings" left in the Brazilian of
the North, principally in the tenant farmer—insignificant in fact
but potentially important, who was neither master nor slave but the
first glimmer of the populace and the petty bourgeoisie among us—a
taste, a liking for the experience of something different from the drab
monotony of his hard life in the shadow of the Big House. The taste

for city life, not the old cities of the sixteenth and early seventeenth century, which were prolongations of the plantations, centers where the gentry came to spend the holidays, gathering there for horse races and banquets, but for the city with a life of its own, independent of the great landowners. Probably the "time of the Flemings" also left in the populace-in-the-making, which at the time was nothing but a conglomeration of independent mestizos, artisans, and traders of European origin, a taste for the material well-being enjoyed under the administration of the Dutch, who in this respect were more efficient than the majority of the Portuguese. The "Fleming," who was the product of an urban rather than a rural civilization, brought to this colony of backwoodsmen—with the exception of near-metropolitan Bahía—novelties of almost magic effects, the knowledge and resources of new European techniques, in other words, middle-class industrialism.

The conflict in 1710 between Olinda, an ecclesiastical and plantation-owner city, and Recife, until that moment a middle-class, artisan city which in the seventeenth century had the most heterogeneous population of the colony, was not merely the nativist reaction which the history books teach: native-born Brazilians against Portuguese of the mother country. It must have been mainly a clash between rural and urban interests, which political and, in a vague way, racial antagonisms further dramatized.

Everything leads us to believe that in 1710 there must have been a definitely aristocratic, and somewhat anti-monarchical movement against the King of Portugal, rural and anti-urban, with the national interests ostensibly identified with those of the agrarian squirearchy. It was the prominent families, land and slave owners, who stood to gain by a minimal intervention of the King and the legislative chambers controlled by the Portuguese, or influenced by the artisan class, in the affairs of the colony. If these rural patriarchs had their way, municipal legislation would be according to their dictates or in their favor, like the royal edicts which had forbidden writs of attachment or foreclosures against plantation owners. Rural debtors would be protected from their city creditors, feudal agrarian interests from the capitalists.

This aspiration, however, received a severe blow with the discovery of the mines and the development in the cities of a wealthy bourgeoisie whose power the kings could pit against the arrogance of the great landholders and slaveowners. As had happened earlier in Portugal, the Portuguese kings of Brazil threw their weight on the side of middle-class, urban interests, without, however, openly antagonizing the rural and provincial.

Minas Gerais was another colonial area where the discrepancy between city and country quickly manifested itself. Colonized by bold settlers from São Paulo, some of them perhaps descendants of Jews, the first generations, dauntless and independent, became the lucky prospectors and the developers of cities which played a highly important role in the formation of our nation. These cities, with their tradesmen, business agents, experts in the cutting and polishing of precious stones and the coining of counterfeit money, their mechanics and artisans, seemed divided—in moments of crisis, at any rate—into two warring halves. But, by and large, the dominant power was in the hands of the mineowners, the autocrats of mansions erected in the cities—noble houses which cast their shadow over the lesser dwellings. They were an extension of the rural and semi-rural plantation houses, in which some of these magnates indulged themselves, too. Nothing gave them more satisfaction, as Saint-Hilaire pointed out in one of his well-known comments on Minas Gerais, than to call themselves planters,[3] proof that the mystique of social prestige then prevalent was still the patriarchal-rural, even though its bases were already being undermined.

The interests represented in the first revolt of Vila Rica, that of 1720, against the abuses of the Crown's fiscal agents, and in the second, that of 1789, led by Tiradentes, which had more popular support, were those of these older magnates. They used the demagogue Felipe dos Santos as a stalking horse, though apparently at the eleventh hour they denied him. Nevertheless, the presence of the new patriarchs, urban rather than rural, can be sensed in the movement.

Brazilian documents of the eighteenth century give evidence of the existence of a new class, thirsting for power, members of the middle class and rich merchants bent upon destroying the preponderance of privileged families of landowners in the legislative assemblies or senates. Adventurers, some of them Portuguese, derisively called "lead-

---

[3] Auguste de Saint-Hilaire: *Voyages dans l'Intérieur du Brésil, Partie I. Les Provinces de Rio de Janeiro et de Minas Geraes* (Paris, 1830).

feet," who had struck it rich in the mines or had made good in business, and wound up as "mansion merchants." These were the new white, or near-white, elements who were hungry for power. The planters and ranchers held them in contempt, and often lumped them together with the greengrocers and cottage dwellers, looking on them all as peddlers. But they made a display of their fine urban, or semi-urban, residences, such as those used by the richest of the rural gentry when, in the rainy season, they moved into the cities with their families.

Even though the antagonism between the burgeoning colonial cities and the great plantations and ranches was already beginning to manifest itself in the seventeenth century, and the power of the cities continued to grow, the rural gentry still preserved almost intact, until the end of the nineteenth, certain of their privileges, and, above all, the outward trappings of their social preeminence.

The greatest ambition of the tradesman or Portuguese immigrant of humble origin and of the lucky prospector, once he had made money, was to enter the ranks of the rural gentry or imitate their way of living, buying a plantation and raising sugar cane or coffee. This was the case, in the eighteenth century, of the Portuguese Lourenço Gomes Ferraz, who, after making a fortune in Recife as a merchant, became a plantation owner, an alderman of Olinda, and one of the bitterest enemies of the peddlers. Or, in the nineteenth century, of Bento José da Costa, a rich merchant and importer of slaves in Pernambuco. Marriage was the ladder by which various of these successful businessmen, of lower-class origin, made their way into "country" society; achieved the right to wear a religious habit, and the title of sergeant- or captain-major in colonial days, and of baron or viscount under the Empire.

The most perfect example is perhaps that of João Fernandez Vieira, the hero of the war against the Dutch. In spite of being from the Azores, and in spite of the "certificate of whiteness" by which he attempted to establish himself as pure white, Vieira was a mulatto and a person of low extraction; he had worked in a slaughterhouse and as a clerk in a store. Nevertheless, he wound up as one of the most outstanding and aggressive representatives of the nobility of Pernambuco, eclipsing, for all his beginnings as an adventurer, the figure of Antonio Cavalcanti, another of the leaders in the war against the Dutch, who was in all probability white and much closer connected with the rural gentry by birth and blood. Vieira became a member of the class from which everything would seem to have barred him by virtue of his marriage to the daughter of Francisco Berenguer de Andrade, a wealthy rural landowner.

The social ascent of elements from the town mansions, and even from humble dwellings or shacks to the manor houses of the large plantation owners was to become more frequent in the nineteenth century. It came about as the result of the growing prestige of the cities; the emergence of a new and brilliant class—the lawyers and doctors, some of them sons of artisans or shopkeepers by Negro or mulatto women; the growing dependence of the plantation owners on their commission merchants and agents for dealings in slaves, sugar, and coffee, which continued in force until the development of railway communications, almost at the close of the Empire. But only to give way to another: the dependence of agriculture on the banks, which did even more to undermine the prestige of the landowners, who were often in debt or needed loans.

As a result of the sociologically feudal conditions under which the agrarian colonization of Brazil had begun, the landowners were accustomed to bearing little responsibility, and often none, for the financing of their crops. In this they were for a long time favored by the Crown, which was interested in seeing them prosper, and needed them and their half-breed retainers and bow-and-arrow Indian fighters to protect the colony against foreigners' attempts at invasion.

In spite of the risks involved, the financing of the great colonial enterprise—sugar—from the beginning attracted moneylenders, who would seem also to have dealt in the importation of slaves for the plantations. There are indications that among these dealers there was a preponderance of Jews, in whom the spirit of commercial adventure is keener than in any other race. Perhaps this is the reason certain historians, among them Sombart,[4] emphasize the role of the Jews in the establishment of the sugar industry in Brazil.

The prosperity of the colonial cities would appear to have been due to these intermediaries. The capacity for development shown by

---

[4] Werner Sombart, famous nineteenth and early twentieth century German sociologist, who studied the role of the Jews in the history of capitalism, including the development of the sugar industry in colonial Brazil.

these cities, which grew from simple warehouse and embarkation terminals into independent centers, with the owners of the luxurious mansions taking a high and mighty attitude toward the rural plantation owners—canceling debts in consideration of a marriage between a merchant's daughter and the son of a plantation owner, or between the son of a merchant, or the merchant himself and the refined "missy" of the plantation—would seem to have come about as the result, in large measure, of the fortunes amassed by the moneylenders and brokers.

The indebtedness of the landowners of the North is mentioned in the earliest chronicles, such as that of Father Cardim,[5] who, moreover, suggests the connection between this state of affairs and the cornerstone of colonial wealth—the slave. A wealth, to be sure, that was extremely precarious, for it crumbled away at the touch of smallpox or cholera.

Therefore the moneylender—whose chief dealing was in slaves—could not fail to play an important role in the unhealthy system of patriarchal economy. He was essential to it because of the two running sores of monoculture and slavery, two wide-open mouths that clamored for money and for blacks. The moneylender lived like the doctor who exploits a patient by keeping his wounds open. And the cities began to grow at the expense of the owners of lands and slaves who were thus exploited.

João Lucio de Azevedo, the Portuguese historian, in a masterly study [6] rejects the thesis put forward by Sombart and by Jewish historians, more or less apologists for their race, that the sugar industry in Brazil was exclusively or mainly the work of Jews, or that they were the founders of the plantations and mills established here in the sixteenth century, which flooded the European market with their sugar to the point of arousing the cupidity of the Dutch. In Azevedo's opinion, "as considerable capital was needed to set up a mill" it is difficult to believe that immigrants of "Jewish origin, for the most part fugitives from the Inquisition, exiles, and those whose poverty made them envisage the hope of a happier lot across the sea," could have brought this capital with them. A point certainly worthy of consideration.

---

[5] Sixteenth-century Jesuit who wrote on social conditions.
[6] João Lucio de Azevedo: *Epocas de Portugal Economico* (Lisbon, 1929).

Inner courtyard of a mansion in Minas Gerais
in the nineteenth century.

But it must also be borne in mind that among those of Hebrew origin, scattered throughout various countries and engaged in all of them in different, but related, forms of trade and moneylending, there existed then—as, up to a point, today—a kind of Freemasonry. A kind of secret society of commercial interests, linked to those of a persecuted religion or race, that functioned with special efficacy in moments of great adversity.

Abbé Raynal, who was of the opinion that the Jews were the first to cultivate cane and manufacture sugar in America, points out that "many of them found loving relatives, faithful friends; others, whose ability and honesty were well-known, obtained funds from brokers of different nationalities with whom they had business dealings. With this aid these men were in a position to undertake the cultivation of sugar cane, the first of which was brought from the island of Madeira." [7] This statement somewhat weakens Azevedo's contention.

It is very probable that when they were expelled from Portugal the Jews who set out for the "Land of the Blessed Cross" were assisted by their brethren in prosperous communities. This was the

[7] Abbé Raynal: *Histoire Philosophique et Politique des Établissements & du Commerce des Européens, dans les deux Indes* (Geneva, 1725).

source of their capital, not precisely for agricultural enterprises—
which here, as everywhere, probably was repulsive to their traditional and "canonical" (the phrase is Max Weber's) horror of the
land and to their calculated policy of commercial speculation in
countries whose soil they felt did not belong to them—but for the
underwriting of agriculture and industry then springing up in Brazil,
and which called for money and Negroes. It was probably in these
two activities that the economic genius of the Jewish immigrants specialized in Brazil, providing that agriculture and that industry with
the necessities for their development. Without the Jewish moneylender, it is almost certain that Brazil would not have acquired such a
swift and complete monopoly of the European sugar market so that
the output of the plantations of Pernambuco, Itamaracá, and Paraiba
at the beginning of the seventeenth century yielded more revenue
to the Crown than the entire trade of India with all the glitter of its
rubies and rustle of its silks.

The traces to be found of the presence of the Jew here in the early
days of the cultivation of cane and the manufacture of sugar make
possible an attempt at the reconstruction of his role. It was not that
of a great creator of wealth and of a national or subnational form of
life comparable in any way with that of the Portuguese during this
first phase in the formation of Brazil, Portuguese like Duarte Coelho
and his tenants who opened vast clearings in the jungle and laid out
plantations, built blockhouses, fortresses; who put down roots in the
earth, even though homesickness for Portugal was always like an
itching—not wholly unpleasant—around the heart (that heart
which, if the Portuguese could, he would spend his life voluptuously
scratching); who erected manor houses of stone, and, inside or
beside them, chapels or churches with a space set aside for their
graves; who brought their families from Portugal, or took wives
among the natives and recognized the children of such unions in their
wills. The figure of the Jew did not have this creative grandeur. On
the contrary, he lived in the shadow of the patriarchal Portuguese.
And nearly always mobile and transient wherever he went. So much
so that many Israelites who made their fortunes in Brazil moved to
other parts of America.

But the Jew in colonial Brazil was not in any sense a parasite who
only sucked off the wealth of another: the "Old Christian" land-

owner and sugar planter, and between them the strength of the Negro, the one who worked hardest in this new society. Or of the Indian, who was used to transport persons and chattels.

It is clear that the Jews came to Brazil with sufficient funds, if not to set themselves up as producers of sugar, at least to lend the plantation owners money for the harvest and the replacement of slaves. Azevedo himself, after describing the exiled Jews as being too poor to establish plantations for the production of sugar, admits later on that "advancing supplies or money, but mainly slaves, to the plantation owners, who were always in difficulties," certain Hebrews "in this way came to own lands and refineries." [8] This would indicate that they were not church-mouse poor, but men of some means. It does not matter that they employed this capital with the ability those of their race had developed over the centuries to acquire, as Azevedo says somewhat rhetorically, "for next to nothing, the flotsam of the wreckage." The wrecks were not of the sea, but of the land: plantations that foundered for lack of Negroes and money for the harvest. They were not responsible for such failures.

In the opinion of this Portuguese historian it was the Jews Brandonio had in mind when he spoke to Alviano about certain men in eighteenth-century Brazil who became enormously rich "by buying merchandise from small merchants in towns or cities, and peddling it on remote ranches and plantations, often making a hundred per cent on such transactions." Brandonio also refers in the *Dialogos* to instances of Jews or city sharpers who took merciless advantage of country folk—a practice which was later to become so frequent in dealings in sugar, gold, and coffee—where a shrewd dealer bought "a lot of slaves from Guinea for a certain sum in cash, and then turned around, without even taking possession of the slaves," and sold them to a planter "on credit for a term which never exceeded a year at a profit of more than eighty-five per cent."

But it was not only among the squires of the sugar-growing captaincies that such brokerage and moneylending activities were carried on. It also occurred in Minas Gerais when the bulk of the slave

[8] Azevedo: Op. cit. See also Robert Simonsen: *Historia Economica do Brasil*, I, 1500–1820 (São Paulo, 1937); and Caio Prado Junior: *Formação do Brasil Contemporaneo* (São Paulo, 1942).

trade began to shift toward the gold mines and diamond fields. "Conveyancer" was the name applied in the mining area to this bogeyman, not of children but of grown-ups; this hobgoblin, not of the forest but of the city, for whom the miners developed the same horror as the child for those fearsome figures. A historian of the diamond mines defines the "conveyancer" as "the Jewish usurer . . . a fetid vampire," though the word "Jew" was here used as pure rhetoric, not as an ethnic description. The miner feared him, fled him, but in the end "necessity or new hopes forced him into his talons." [9]

An older chronicler has left interesting details about the figure of the conveyancer. And not only his figure, but his subtle technique as moneylender and man-seller. He bought slaves at the port of entry at one hundred milreis, the best at one hundred and twenty; duty and transportation came to around twenty. He sold them to the miners and to the backland planters in the state of Rio, on two years' credit for one hundred and eighty or two-hundred eighths of an ounce of gold dust, in a single payment or "in two equal installments each year." This was the same profit which Brandonio considered illicit on the part of slave traders in Pernambuco in the seventeenth century: the one hundred per cent profit on materials and merchandise from the cities sold to the plantations. "All the information they ask," says the chronicler of the mines, "is whether the prospective purchaser of a slave can at least meet the next payment; and if the next two, still better." [1]

In the eighteenth century and all through the nineteenth the power of the middleman, which had begun in the seventeenth century, grew. His status was dignified by his development into agent, commission merchant of sugar or coffee, and then banker. A city aristocrat, with a gold chain about his neck, silk hat, a tiled mansion, a luxurious carriage, eating imported delicacies, raisins, figs, prunes, drinking Port wine, his daughters ravishingly attired in dresses copied from Parisian fashion books when they attended the *premières* of Italian divas at the opera house. All this often at the expense of

---

[9] "Exposição Manuscrita sobre o Estado das Minas por José da Costa Sousa Rebello," in J. Felicio dos Santos: "Memorias do Distrito Diamantino," *Revista do Arquivo Público Mineiro*, XV (Belo Horizonte, 1910), pp. 65–6.

[1] Ibid., p. 66.

the Cinderellas in the country, stoking the fire box of the sugar mill, grinding cane, refining sugar, distilling rum; or planting their coffee or digging their mines. Finding their amusement in the local dances and the chatter of the Negroes of the sugar mill or the field hands or the coffee pickers. Often, eating nothing but jerked meat and drinking genipap wine or drowning their troubles in rum. And not always able to send off to study in Coimbra, or Paris, São Paulo, or Olinda the son who had to stay home and took to going with the black boys, then ruffians, then colored wenches.

"The old rancher or plantation owner," wrote Joaquim Nabuco in 1884, recalling the life of the old-time landowner, "worked for the dealer who supplied him with slaves as those of today work for the agent . . ."[2] For the agent or for the bank—another city institution which with the coming of Dom João VI made its appearance in Brazil. It brought about a change in the social landscape in the sense of urbanizing it. It sped the gravitation of wealth and energy to the capitals, especially to the Court. To the capitals and the capitalists, one might say, without fear of falsifying the truth with this easy play on words.

It should be repeated that agriculture in Brazil during the early days—principally in that marvelous sixteenth century which represents the zenith of the creative activity of the Portuguese settlers in America—enjoyed exceptional favors. Favors with which the Crown rewarded the initiative of the grant-holders, conferring on them great political and economic privileges. The clearers of the jungle, the pioneers of the backlands, the establishers of great plantations were for two centuries the recipients of privileges which gave them political control of the legislative bodies. And along with this control went contracts, tax collections, public works. At the same time they were protected from the insolent demands of impatient creditors.

But with the development of the mining industry, with the growth of cities and towns, the King's love for the country gentry cooled. Their aristocratic privileges began to dwindle as a result of the new prestige with which the captains-general, the magistrates, the in-

---

[2] Joaquim Nabuco: "Conferencia a 22 de junho de 1884 no Teatro Politeama" (Rio de Janeiro, 1884).

tendants, the bishops, the viceroy were invested. Certain of these captains-general, like Count Valladares in Minas Gerais, appointed mulattoes and Negroes regimental officers, thus disparaging the native whites.[3]

The captains sent out to Minas came as though they were entering conquered territories, arrogant, domineering, checking everything with a censorious eye, even the friars' weaknesses of the flesh. The hallowed privilege of the great landowners of administering justice on their own estates was set aside in Minas Gerais in the eighteenth century. The Count of Assumar ordered a certain General Macedo, who had killed his wife, arrested, not on the plantation of John Nobody, but on that of Field Marshal Paschoal da Silva Guimarães, the owner of Ouro Podre, proprietor of the richest mines in the world, master of two thousand men, countless horses, and two vast plantations. Moreover, the prestige of certain noblemen of the colony was dealt a blow as the result of an edict of April 25, 1719, which ordered their resignation from their posts as officers where there was no organized army corps.[4] This clipped their wings and put them on almost the same level as plebeians, mulattoes, and peddlers. And as though this were not enough, ranches and plantations were invaded by the police, thus violating the most sacred taboo of the rural aristocracy.

It was in the southern region, São Paulo, and Minas, that from the beginning of the eighteenth century the pressure of Portuguese imperialism fell hardest, now the mere exploiter of the wealth which in the first two centuries it had helped discover. It found it to its interest to ally itself with the populace of the city against the rural magnates; with the tradesmen against the nobles; with the rich merchants of the coast against the inland plantation owners; even with the mulattoes against the whites of the interior.

This new policy of the metropolis, let us point out again, was unmistakably evidenced on the occasion of the conflict between the rural gentry of Pernambuco and the city of Recife. And even more clearly in Minas Gerais under the rule of Count Assumar,

---

[3] "Relatorio do Marquez de Lavradio," *Rev. do Inst. Hist. e Geog. Br.*, No. 16 (Rio de Janeiro, 1843), p. 419.

[4] Ms. in Public Archives of Minas Gerais, codex 11, formerly 10.

who did not hesitate to attack the oligarchy of the legislative chambers.

However, when in 1670 the captain-general of Pernambuco, Bernardo de Miranda Henriques, ordered the arrest of the president of the Council of Iguaracú—one of the many councils controlled by the sugar aristocracy—he was rebuked by a stern and solemn royal letter. Four years earlier, when the Council of Olinda deposed Captain-General Jeronymo de Mendonça Furtado, the viceroy approved this insolent act. And it is hardly necessary to recall the series of acts and expressions of barefaced insolence on the part of the Council of São Paulo in the seventeenth century.

The economic policy of Portugal, which from the eighteenth century had been to relegate large-scale agriculture to a secondary position, and favor the cities and the merchants, and even the small businessman, was continued by Dom João VI. Or, to be more exact, by those who influenced him, urban- rather than rural-minded, capitalist rather than feudal.

Under Dom João the prestige of the rural aristocracy declined still further. The benevolence of the King toward debtors always in arrears disappeared. The legislative bodies ceased to be the private domain of the great landowners. "Crushing taxes" and "exorbitant interest rates," in the words of a historian of the mid-nineteenth century, became a constant vexation for the landowners. For "if the neglected agriculturist cannot meet his payments because of a bad year," the return on his crops not sufficing to cover "the exorbitant surcharges on the supplies he has had to buy," he could give himself up as lost.

With the city magnates of the nineteenth century lending money to the planters at 9 per cent, and a mortgage for double the amount loaned, the planters felt themselves without protection of any sort. And the banks set inexorable time limits on their debts, whereas the merchants, already well-off, now enjoyed the benefits of moratoriums. In spite of all this, said an apologist for the planters, trade "resorted to contraband and fraud."

The early colonial days had been good ones for agriculture, when the plantation owners enjoyed privileges that went almost to the point of favoring swindle when practiced by certain of them.

"Everybody robs the unwary farmer," wrote old Mello Moraes in 1870.[5] The collecting of debts through agents sent out by the banks to the great plantations seemed to this historian one more step in the downfall of the planters' prestige. But this was less an abuse than the regularizing of the relationship between creditor and debtor, which formerly had been completely arbitrary, the planter paying almost no attention to the claims of his urban creditors.

The plantations, formerly hallowed spots approached hat in hand to ask for something—asylum, votes, a daughter's hand, a contribution for a religious festival, food—were now being invaded by debt collectors, representatives of an arrogant city institution, the bank, almost as lacking in respect for the majesty of the plantation house as the police of Count Assumar in Minas or President Chichorro da Gama in Pernambuco.

According to Mello Moraes, the debt collector discredited "the agriculturist from every point of view, making him lose face in the very place where he lived, thus causing the ruin of families, for many engagements have been broken off in our rural areas because of the discredit spread by these collectors, forcing certain proud men to the desperate measures they have taken on occasion in the interior of Brazil." These "desperate measures" were less often suicide than murder. Not a few of the agents were ambushed by plantation ruffians and stabbed to death along the backland roads.

The attitude of the moneyed men of the cities toward the plantation owners had a strong quality of redress about it. At times it was a case of sons and grandsons avenging humiliations of which their fathers or grandfathers had been the victims.

The younger generation of sons of the plantation, lads educated in Europe, in Bahía, São Paulo, Olinda, Rio de Janeiro, were gradually becoming, in a certain sense, deserters from an aristocracy whose way of living, style of politics, morality, sense of justice were no longer in keeping with the tastes and attitudes of these university graduates, these doctors and lawyers with their European training.

The law-school or university graduate—magistrate, governor of

---

[5] A. J. Mello Moraes: *O Brasil Social e Politico. O que fomos e o que somos* (Rio de Janeiro, 1872).

the province, minister, chief of police—was to become the ally of
the government against his own father or grandfather in this
struggle almost to the death between the King's justice and that of
the rural paterfamilias. The doctor was to bring about the discredit of home remedies, the dispensing of which was one of the
pleasantest forms of matriarchal authority exercised by his mother
or grandmother, the plantation mistress.

Moreover, university graduates and doctors rarely returned to the
patriarchal acres when they had completed their studies. Their ability
and training went to enrich the Court, add luster to the cities, leaving the countryside deserted. Diplomacy, politics, the liberal professions, at times business management, absorbed them.

The cities took from the plantations their most illustrious sons, including those who chose the priesthood or a military career. The
poorer-endowed, or those without the desire to leave, were the ones
who, in the majority of cases, succeeded their forebears in the
management of the rural properties, which shrank in importance
and size, becoming divided up among distant heirs who were not
interested in farming and were rooted in the cities. Cases like that of
Antonio de Moraes Silva were rare. After completing his university
studies, he moved with all his learning, his books, his Greek, his
Latin, from the Court to the plantation of Muribeca, to devote
himself not only to the tremendous task of compiling his Dictionary,
a classic today, but also to improving the methods of cane growing
and sugar refining in Pernambuco. This scholar, who received
visitors like Father Souza Caldas on his plantation, and from his
Big House kept up a correspondence with the outstanding Portuguese philologists of his day, nevertheless maintained a town house in
Recife, with windows on the street and a view of the sea.

But nobody should get the idea that the great landowners, so
prosperous in the early years of the colony, all wound up as
Lears, betrayed by their learned sons and by their daughters (married to university graduates) who deserted the Big Houses of the
plantations and ranches like rats a sinking ship; betrayed by the King
who once had favored and indulged them; betrayed by the Church
which had formerly fawned upon them. The drama of the decay of
the power, for a time almost absolute, of the rural paterfamilias of
Brazil was not that simple, nor the rise of the bourgeoisie so swift.

There were planters who, crushed by debts and mortgages, found a helping hand in son or son-in-law, congressman, minister, public official, and not merely a "house-proud" merchant. The State proved "the great asylum for the bankrupt fortunes of slavery," as Joaquim Nabuco puts it.[6]

There were those for whom the factor or agent turned out to be an honest friend who conserved and even augmented the fortune of his slipshod employer, who had no idea even of the extent or boundaries of his property or the volume of its production. A perfect hidalgo in his country manor, he was a dead-beat in the full sense of the word, and not the victim of the Jews of the city. Instead of being plucked in the city, it was he who was the swindler in his shipments of sugar or coffee. In brief, many a rascal and sharper hidden behind patriarchal beard got the better of factors, debt collectors, and even gypsy horse traders with his tricks.

In the sale of sugar, wrote Frederico Burlamaqui in 1833, referring to the tricky plantation owners, "they mixed in several inferior qualities and a certain amount of dirt and sand and sold it as first quality."[7] A law of February 28, 1688, attempted to control the adulteration of products carried on not only by the middlemen but by the producers as well. It alluded to the "bad reputation" in which the sugar of Brazil was held "because of the defects in its preparation, as the producers were free to adulterate it . . ." "And in the event of sugar being adulterated, the owner of the mill will at once be exiled for a space of two years to one of the captaincies of that state and fined forty thousand milreis, and the bookkeeper of the mill will pay the same fine and be exiled to Angola for two years . . ."[8] But it was difficult to enforce the measure in a land that was still, to a degree, feudal.

It is worth mentioning that on April 27, 1840, a correspondent of the *Diario de Pernambuco,* calling attention to the alarming adulteration of the principal articles of food in Pernambuco, included among the adulterated products sugar mixed with lime and manioc flour. Adulteration in which the producer had a hand, as in

---

[6] Op. cit., p. 12.

[7] Frederico L. C. Burlamaqui: *Analytica acerca do Commercio d'Escravos e acerca da Escravidão Domestica* (Rio de Janeiro, 1837), p. 81.

[8] *Informaçoes sobre o Estado da Lavoura* (Rio de Janeiro, 1874), pp. 47–8.

colonial times, although the chief villain was now the city merchant.

The story is still told in Pernambuco of a wily rural squire who did not give his slaves names, but numbers—Ten, Fifteen, Twenty. When the broker's representative visited him, the sly gentleman, who owned ten or twelve scrawny slaves, would assume an air of great opulence, calling out to the overseer: "Put Ten on this job," "Fifteen on that one," "Twenty on the other." In this way, it is said, he maintained his credit.

Undoubtedly the anecdote is an exaggeration. But it was by the number of his slaves that the planter's standing was gauged. It was a precarious basis, demanding such volume in the slave population that the only way to impress the agent was by doing as this rascal did, calling each slave "Ten" or "Twenty" or "Thirty." "A plantation owner," wrote Burlamaqui in 1833, "with a capital investment of six to eight hundred thousand cruzados in slaves, land, and machinery can at most count on an income of twelve to fifteen thousand cruzados a year, which barely covers expenses and at times fails to meet them." [9] The major item of expense was slaves; the least, land and machinery. The land was subjected to brutal treatment: the primitive method of burning over and axe. No fertilizing, forethought, or care; when it ceased to produce, it was abandoned, especially in the regions of less stable plantation residences, where the houses of mud and wattles did not link the owner as closely to the land as did those of stone and mortar.

Throughout patriarchal Brazil agriculture which exhausted the land to a greater or lesser degree prevailed. Very particularly in the North, in Maranhão, in Pará; in certain regions of Pernambuco and Bahía; in Minas, in Rio de Janeiro, in São Paulo. In São Paulo, in the eighteenth century, when the expansionist fever abated and the more typically agricultural phase set in, Louis Antonio de Sousa, writing to the King of Portugal (in 1767), was amazed at the "poor system" of cultivation: "they plant only in the cleared forest because of the small effort it involves, and because of their unwillingness to undertake the harder work of cultivating the land as they do in our kingdom." And in 1781 José da Silva Lisboa wrote from Bahía to Lisbon, complaining that even with the high market

[9] Op. cit., p. 82.

price of sugar the owner of lands and slaves showed little profit.[1] As for Minas, its president, Antonio Paulino Limpo de Abreu, lamented in a report of 1835 that the ease with which lands can be acquired keeps their owners "from remembering the time-proven methods of making them productive." The problem came not only from the ease in acquiring lands and the ease in exploiting them by slave labor; it lay in the fact that the very basis of wealth and rural credit under our patriarchal system was less the land than the slave.

If the slave system, the basis of wealth and credit, made the use of machines and expensive fertilizers dispensable for the planter, on the other hand, it meant not ten, but fifty mouths to feed, fifty bodies to be clothed, even if only in cotton or flannelette, and often fifty wounds to be treated. If there were planters who calculated the value of the slaves in terms of their maximum production, killing them with hard labor, making ten do the work of thirty, the majority did not have this overwhelming lust for gain, nor this industrial concept of agriculture, and most of what they made on their cane and coffee went into the upkeep of their Negroes. Moreover, there were many Negroes who preferred to let their feet rot, infested with parasites, for the sake of not working, while others ran away; and many sickened.

During this period Brazilian society became consolidated around a stronger government, the law courts were freer from the pressures of powerful individuals, and the Church also, with priests of a higher moral caliber, grew more independent of regional oligarchies. The Church, through its bishops, raised its voice louder and stronger than formerly, to the point of protesting, as did Dom Vital,[2] against the excesses of His Majesty's own government, and not merely against those of religious brotherhoods and sodalities, manifestations of the power of the rich, the educated, even the artisans.

On the other hand, this was a period of deep differentiation—

---

[1] *Carta muita interesante do advogado José da Silva Lisboa para o Dr. Domingos Vandelli, Director do Real Jardim Botanica de Lisboa* (Bahía, October 18, 1781). Ms. Arquivo Historico Colonial de Lisboa, antigo da Marinha e Ultramar, 10, 319, Inventario Castro e Almeida, Rio de Janeiro, 1914, II.

[2] Extremely orthodox bishop of Olinda who was appointed to this high post as a young man in the second half of the nineteenth century. His vigorous opposition to the Masons, then very powerful among Brazilian political leaders, caused him to be imprisoned.

there was less patriarchalism, less domination of the son by the father, of the wife by the husband, of the individual by the family, of the family by its head, of the slave by the owner—and greater individualism—of the woman, the child, the Negro; and there was more prostitution, more poverty, more suffering, more old people cast off. An epoch of transition. Patriarchalism becoming urbanized.

Mauá [3] and the English were to modernize the techniques of transportation. City services—lighting, paving, and, finally, sanitation—were improved: city ways of living. Life became freer from domestic routine. The street, once only for Negroes, peddlers, urchins, acquired status.

And in the cities, factories were making soap, candles, the cloth once woven in the house, on the plantations, in leisurely, patriarchal fashion. Foreigners of various origins and professions—cabinet-makers, hairdressers, apothecaries, tinsmiths, blacksmiths, dressmakers, cheesemakers—were setting themselves up in workshops, foundries, stores. The more fashionable ladies no longer wore their hair in the Portuguese, almost the Oriental, fashion, but in the French manner, and were dressing in French style, going to the theater to listen to operas sung by Italian divas, to whom the students sent flowers, addressed speeches, wrote sonnets. The children were being educated in schools—some of them directed by foreigners—and academies, and not at home by the priest or the chaplain, nor only in schools of the religious orders.

It was a period of balance between the two tendencies—the collective and the individual—in which some of the most engaging features of the moral make-up of Brazilians were emphasized. The political gift for compromise. The juridical gift for reaching agreement. The ability to imitate the foreigner and to assimilate from him the finer cultural traits and not merely the superficial. By and large, the typical Brazilian lost the sharp edges of the Paulista or Pernambucan to acquire in politics the suaveness, urbanity, and even courtliness of the Bahian.

To be sure, the die-hards of the first half of the nineteenth century could see in the new generation nothing but shortcomings, ridiculous aping of Europeans, lack of respect for their elders. "Where," asked

---

[3] Baron of Mauá (João Evangelista de Souza), pioneer of industrialism and modern transportation under the Empire.

a chronicler of the most representative period of rural-patriarchal orthodoxy in the face of the European and urban innovations and novelties, "are the captains-general of the times of the kings of Portugal," men of the background and experience of "that famous Franco de Almeida," who in their day governed with such profound good sense the captaincies, now provinces ungoverned "by young whippersnappers just out of law school?" [4] He had in mind, when he made his contemptuous reference to "whippersnappers," the generation of João Alfredo, Alfredo de Taunay, Sancho de Barros Pimentel, Alencar, Caio Prado, Lucena,[5] university graduates who, it is true, began to govern the country when they were little more than boys, whose mustaches and beards looked false.

And Father Lopes Gama—a priest who was also a severe social critic—was outraged at the sight all around him of fops wearing "coats down to the groin," "beards and mustaches like Moors," "fancy vests"; young squirts who no longer ask their elders for their blessing because "such usages smell to them of Gothic times and are degrading to the noble pride of a youth for whom a mere nod of the head, like a lizard, suffices"; coxcombs who during the celebration of the mass turn their backs on the altar to ogle the ladies.[6]

Father Lopes Gama was unyielding in his antipathy for these new ways. His taste was for the type of life he had known as a child, that of the eighteenth century, still rustic and patriarchal in its most typical aspects. An epoch of decent people, of children who respected their parents, of upright, strong men who lived to "a ripe old age," of diligent housewives, of mouth-watering sweets and loins of veal that came to the table sizzling in the pan—the days of his late grandmother, who had brought him up. A Brazil without horse-drawn carriages racing through the streets, without English machinists operating mysterious machines, without French dressmakers, or doctors trained in France or Germany, or Italian operas, or youths taking the place of their elders.

---

[4] Mello Moraes: Op. cit., I, p. 20. Cf. also his *Corographia Historica, Chronologica, Genealogica, Nobiliaria e Politica do Brasil,* V (Rio de Janeiro, 1863), p. 320.

[5] Political leaders during the Empire.

[6] Miguel do Sacramento Lopes Gama: *O Carapuceiro* (Recife, 1839), No. 4.

CHAPTER II

THE PLANTATION AND
THE CITY SQUARE

THE HOUSE AND THE STREET

THE CITY SQUARE triumphed over the sugar plantation, but gradually. And for the most part respecting certain qualities and idiosyncrasies of the defeated, trying to imitate, at times even glorifying and exaggerating them, in that aping of "superiors" by "inferiors." At other times jeering at the rich backwoodsmen, the wealthy planters, more old-fashioned in their ways of speech and dress, the boastful and even quixotic squires, the yokels, the "hillbillies." Holding up to ridicule their defects of speech, their being years, even centuries, behind the times in the way they lived and their methods of travel, their outmoded morality and manners. This backwardness varied from region to region, giving the country a picturesque, at times even dramatic, variety of styles and stages of culture. And not only from region to region; it varied also from sex to sex, from race to race, from class to class.

When in the preceding chapter I pointed out the decline of the rural patriarchy, especially in Pernambuco and Bahía, where, since the sixteenth century, it had centered about the Big House of plantation or ranch and came to dominate the landscape of colonial Brazil,

I was attempting merely to call attention to a predominant trait, and not implying that the dominion of the Big House had until that time been absolute. The Paulista, for example, who dramatized like no one else the landscape of the backlands during the first two centuries of colonization, leaving on it the stamp of his creation, left no large, stable house of stone and mortar in his wake, but the thatched hut similar to that of the Indian, the shack almost like that of the gypsy, the cabin almost like that of the Negro. Only toward the close of the eighteenth century, a relatively sedentary epoch for those nomads, did these become Europeanized into an urban dwelling of mud and wattle, "that is to say," one writer remarks, "of mud," and "plastered over with colored clay."

In 1720, in a letter to Bartholomeu de Souza Mexia, Count Assumar, complaining about Domingos Rodrigues do Prado," a native of the region of São Paulo, a contentious, overbearing man," stated that he had decided to settle Pitanguí by bringing in Portuguese the better to work the mines, for it was a site occupied until then by Paulistas, "whose dwellings always are of mean appearance because their manner of life and their natural inclination to wander about the forests make their settlements impermanent . . ." [1]

In a country as far-flung as ours, and with such a marked diversity, not so much of climate or of methods of production and work—for work was pretty much the same everywhere: the enslavement first of the Indian and then of the Negro—as of contacts with other peoples and other cultures, which varied greatly during the period of Brazil's formation, it was natural that the process of social and national integration should have varied, as it did, from region to region. Integration, moreover, is not yet completed.

It was only well into the eighteenth century that in the region of Minas families began settling on the land in considerable numbers. Until then the gold region was less marked by villages and plantations than by bands of adventurers without sanctioned family ties. They lived in movable camps, seeking mines and slaves, their settle-

---

[1] Letter of the Count of Assumar to Bartholomeu de Souza Mexia, dated February 9, 1720. Ms. codex 11, formerly 10, Colonial Section of Public Archives of Minas, Letters, Orders, Dispatches and Proclamations of the Count of Assumar.

ments disappearing and reappearing like shifting scenery on a fair-time stage.

It is understandable that among people on the move like these no type of stable or better-class dwelling should have developed. The adventurous settlers were content with shack, mud hut, or shanty, with a type of life, shelter, and food similar to that of the Indians, and with the natives' system of transportation, fishing, hunting, and even working. Their cultural contacts with Europe almost disappeared as they pushed inland from the seacoast, whereas their ties with the native culture were strengthened.

And as these shanty or mud-hut dwellers were, for the most part, unmarried, it was easier for them to turn into nomads. The King, who already saw the political advantage of the settlers' marrying and leading a normal family life, enjoined this upon Dom Lourenço de Almeida in a letter saying: "In this way they will more readily obey my royal commands, and the children born of such marriages will make them even more obedient, and you will advise me whether it would be desirable for me to order that only married men may hold a seat on the municipal councils, and if there are enough of them to carry out such an order . . ." To which Dom Lourenço replied: ". . . Our experience has shown us that the few married settlers in this region are much better workers in the old mines than the unmarried ones, who spend all their time in wanton living". . .[2]

There may have been an injustice, and a great one, to the unmarried men in this judgment of Dom Lourenço's. It was they who discovered the mines, hacked their way through the jungle, cut roads, and were probably more effective during this almost military phase of the colonization than the married men. Naturally, when life had become less hazardous, and all the dangers overcome, with nothing to do but work the mines, set up the government agencies, regularize and give the relations between the sexes benefit of clergy, these romantic figures became outmoded and a nuisance, not fitting comfortably into a society sleek with quiet and peace. Unless, like Jeronymo de Albuquerque in Pernambuco, they married, after years of a free, even dissolute, but not on this account useless life.

---

[2] Letters quoted by Feu de Carvalho in "Primeiras Aulas e Escolas de Minas Gerais, 1721–1860," in *Revista do Arquivo Público Mineiro*, XXIV (Belo Horizonte, 1933), pp. 350–1.

There is no need to deny all worth to the unmarried nomad to recognize the enormous importance of the married man and, above all, of the woman, the mother, the stable center in our formation.

The noble type of dwelling which continued to be known as the "Big House" developed in the region of the sugar plantations, and centered less around the figure of the man than around the imposing bulk of the Portuguese matron of the sixteenth century, the Dona Brites, the Dona Genebras, the Dona Franciscas, the Dona Teresas, the Dona Marias, women who had come out to Brazil with their husbands.

Where they established themselves, fat and slow-moving, with their knowledge of the culinary arts and the hygiene of the home, with their European and Christian manner of caring for children and the sick, there European civilization sent down its deepest roots and achieved its greatest permanence.

This explains, in great measure, the regional differences in the style of living in Portuguese America: the greater predominance of European patterns of culture in the areas colonized by married men, and the lesser in those regions colonized by men who were, for the most part, unmarried, or simply cohabited with native women.

Prince Maximilian of Neuwied, traveling in the interior of Brazil in the early nineteenth century, found in São Salvador dos Campos dos Goitacases rich planters living the same slovenly life of two hundred years earlier. Men who were the owners of a thousand or fifteen hundred head of cattle, and sent to the nearest city mule trains carrying produce, were living in houses inferior to those of the poorest German peasants.[3] Mud hovels that were not even white-washed. Veritable shanties. Probably what was lacking among these settlers was the hand of the Portuguese woman.

In São Vicente, in Reconcavo da Bahía, in Pernambuco, the earliest areas of Portuguese colonization in Brazil, the presence of European women accounted for the aristocratic tone of living. And together with this, the relative stabilization of an economy which, while patriarchal in its main features, had, nevertheless, a matriarchal quality: the creative maternalism which from the first cen-

---

[3] Prince Maximilian Neuwied: *Travels in Brazil in 1815, 1816 and 1817* (London, 1920), p. 53. See also Ribeiro Lamego: *O Homen e O Brejo* (Rio de Janeiro, 1945).

tury of colonization stood out as typical in the formation of Brazil.

At the end of the sixteenth century, Father Cardim was amazed to find "great ladies" in Pernambuco. And men and women dressed in the same fashion as in Lisbon; who feasted on the delicacies and wines of Portugal; slept in beds canopied in silk finer than those of the princes of the realm.[4]

The presence of European women in greater numbers is perhaps the element most actively responsible for the development, in Pernambuco, Bahía, São Vicente, in the sixteenth century and later on, in Minas Gerais, Maranhaõ, Pará, Santa Catarina, Rio Grande do Sul, of a nobler type of dwelling than those of other areas of Portuguese and Spanish colonization in America. This first took shape in the Big House of the plantation and later became perfected in the several-storied Big House of the city. The architecture of the elegant colonial residence and the type of domestic life that went with it were linked, in the development of Brazil, to the dominion of Portuguese women.

Brazilian patriarchalism, when it moved from the plantation to the town house, did not at once come to terms with the street; for a long time they were almost enemies, the house and the street. And the greatest struggle was that which was joined over the woman, whom the street enticed, but whom the paterfamilias tried his best to keep shut up in her room among the slave girls, just as on the plantation, not allowing her out even to go shopping but only to mass on the four festivals of the year—Christmas, Easter, Corpus Christi, the Assumption—and, even then, in a sedan chair, and later, in a closed carriage.

Consequently the life of the daughter of the city mansion was limited to the house. She amused herself with the chatter of the parrots calling her "Darling," "Love," "Missy," as a substitute for the deep masculine voice her ears longed to hear, with the caresses of marmosets and monkeys instead of the strong hands of a man. And with the aphrodisiac head-rubbing by the slave maid which perhaps made her think of herself as the "enchanted Mooress," with some charm hidden in her hair, as in the tales told by the old Negro women.

---

[4] Fernão Cardim: *Tratados da Terra e Gente do Brasil,* 2nd ed. (Rio de Janeiro, 1931).

The shops sent to the mansions their parasols, their bombazine shoes, ribbons, their "ivory combs to dislodge and remove lice," their hair ornaments, their tulles, their satins, and the young ladies, in corset cover and petticoat, their hair loose, as happy as a sick child surrounded in bed by toys, selected what they liked, spreading out, as they did in the inland cities almost until our own times, the merchandise on carpet or sofa.

When they did not order the merchandise brought in from a shop, they sent for the peddler. The pink trunks and the pasteboard boxes of the peddlers were opened under their covetous eyes. The trunks began to spill out over the dining tables of rosewood or the rush carpets their contents of satins, ribbons, bottles of perfume, sometimes dresses already made, and it became a sort of holiday in the gloomy houses.

These peddlers visited the plantation houses, too, carrying their trunks on muleback. D'Assier was struck by the contrast between the peddler in the interior of Brazil—living like a lord, enjoying the hospitality of the plantation, riding a donkey or a mule—and the *colporteur* of the Alps and the Pyrenees, with his pack on his back, climbing and descending the hills on foot.[5] But in the Brazil of slaveholding days barbers, blacksmiths, carpenters, house painters all had this air of importance; they owned slaves who carried their tools and mixed their paints; the masters in three-cornered hat and frock coat hardly soiled their fingers. Not a few foreigners were surprised to see that even beggars had the manners of lords; some of them begged alms from a hammock carried on the shoulders of two slaves. Others on horseback.

In the interior the peddlers, many of them Jews from Alsace and the Rhineland, though the earliest were Levantines or Portuguese, continued during the nineteenth century to practice their sharp dealings. In the middle of the nineteenth century this new breed of peddlers really struck it rich. Profits of a hundred per cent, or better. Rings bought in Europe for a hundred francs were sold to plantation owners for eight hundred thousand milreis, cash on the barrelhead. If on credit, the planter signed a note for one million milreis, that is to say, twenty-five hundred francs—more than six hundred dollars

---

[5] Adolphe d'Assier: *Le Brésil Contemporain* (Paris, 1867), p. 190.

—and provided hospitality for the peddler. Some of them specialized in the sale of jewelry; others, the French, in perfumes; the Italians, in images of saints for the chapels of the Big House, the oratories of the city mansion.[6] In certain regions they were called "gringos," either because they were light of complexion like the English, or because in their methods they resembled the gypsies, who were also called "gringos" in Brazil.

For all their sharp dealing and even swindling, these peddlers played a useful role vis-à-vis the downtrodden sex, enlivening the ladies' dull existence with their jewelry, their fabrics, their bottles of perfume, their rosy-cheeked Saint Anthonys, which were sometimes exchanged for rolls of fine lace made by the women and their maids. These pretty images then became objects of fervent devotion and, in certain cases, of practices of sexual fetishism.

But it was not only the peddlers who broke the monotony of life in the Big House and the aristocratic city mansions, bringing into these semi-convents a little of the bustle of the street and the novelty of the market place. Negro women also came to sell needles and pins, candy and pastries to the "missies." It was said that certain of these venders carried messages from lovelorn swains to the young ladies; the older ones seem to have made a specialty of carrying gossip from house to house, making trouble and spreading tittle-tattle and lies. Father Lopes Gama tells that he knew a "worthy matron" who went into raptures over these venders. A Negro woman had no more than set foot in the house with her boxes or trays than the lady began to ask her questions: "In front of her own daughters she began to pry into the life of her masters, and that of the young ladies of the family, trying to find out who was courting them, what men came to the house, etc., etc."—which the priest regarded as "vulgar curiosity." [7]

But what were the poor city ladies to do, at times more lonely and isolated than those of the plantation? There was only one field in which they could assert their initiative: inventing dishes. Everything

---

[6] Ibid., pp. 261–2. See also M. H. L. Seris: *A travers les provinces du Brésil* (Limoges, n.d.), p. 19; and N. Bruzzi: *Casimiro de Abreu* (Rio de Janeiro, 1949).

[7] Miguel do Sacramento Lopes Gama: *O Carapuceiro* (Recife, 1839).

else was the drab routine of a woman's life under the patriarchal system.

Some of them concocted dishes, sweets, preserves out of native fruits and tubers. Fritters of manioc "delicious, wholesome, and easily digested," "a dish enjoyed by the finest people," "invented by the Portuguese women, for the populace did not use them," says Gabriel Soares, a planter of the sixteenth century.[8]

And not only manioc; the cashew, too, was brought into the European culinary family by the mistress of the plantation. It did not take her long to make out of Brazil nuts all the "sweetmeats usually made of almonds, which are agreeable in their smoothness and favor." The juice "of fine aroma and flavor" of the cashew fruit was made into the sweet wine which became the official drink of the Big House, almost its symbol of hospitality. From the pulp, jelly was made, preserves, and the sweetmeats which Gabriel Soares praises so highly, "when cooked in sugar and sprinkled with cinnamon they have no equal." And the plantation mistress used the cashew in the morning "for it gives a sweet breath to those who eat them." All this was done by the women in Brazil utilizing the sugar their husbands milled, and the fruits which the Indian servants, and later the black boys, gathered in the woods or on the plantation.

And there were not only the manioc fritters, manioc couscous, the cashew sweets and wines; there was the plantain "cooked in syrup with cinnamon"; yams stewed with meat; corn cakes made with eggs, sugar, and bread; water-ground cornmeal to be eaten with meat, fish, or chicken broth— "which tastes better than rice," according to Gabriel Soares, who must have been the greatest gourmet among the plantation owners of his day. The plantation housewife smoked corn "so it would not spoil," and in this way kept it from one year to another. In the Big Houses and in the early town mansions smoke took the place of ice in the preservation of certain articles which the housewives used the year around in the preparation of preserves and delicacies.

What they did with the cashew, the banana, and the yam, they

---

[8] Gabriel Soares de Sousa: *Tratado Descritivo do Brasil em 1587*, 3rd. ed., I (São Paulo, 1928).

did with the genipap, the azarole, the papaya, the guava, the passion fruit, the quince, and, later, with the mango, the soursop, the breadfruit, the coconut. Mixed with molasses, sugar, cinnamon, clove, Brazil nuts, these fruits were converted into syrups, preserves, butter, marmalade, jelly, thus enriching the desserts of the Big Houses and the city residences with a variety of new and tropical flavors. They were even shipped to Portugal in cans and boxes. It would seem that the word "marmalade" itself, in such common use in English today, is of Brazilian origin.

In the city mansions and even in the Big Houses of suburban estates the kitchen never assumed the importance it held in the plantation houses, nor did the board acquire the dimensions of a convent refectory table as on the plantations, where whoever happened by sat down to any or all three meals. Travelers, peddlers, not to mention the friends and self-invited hangers-on who were never missing, the poor relatives, the agent, the overseer, the chaplain, visitors spending the day—whole families who came from other plantations by oxcart. The tables were of rosewood sometimes six, eight yards long, such as we still knew in the Big House—a huge rural mansion—of the Noruega plantation.

Not that in the country houses and town residences the tables (nearly always of rosewood, too, which became established as the quality wood of the Big Houses as of the churches) were not long enough to accommodate the numerous members of the family, father, mother, children, grandchildren, relatives, guests, friends. But in the cities and the suburbs life was, in a way, more withdrawn and less open to guests than on the plantations. On the plantations the laws of Brazilian hospitality made it incumbent to receive the traveler at any hour with silver washbasin, linen towel, to provide him with a place at the table and a bed or hammock in which to sleep. All the work was done by the skillful servants, but under the direction of the mistress of the plantation or the lady of the house, who rarely showed herself before anyone who was not a close relative by blood or compaternity.

The arrival of a strange man in the house was immediately followed by the rustle of departing skirts, the scurry of girls hiding or running up the stairs. And this was the case in the city mansions as well as on the plantations. By the nineteenth century São Paulo was already a center of some importance, with various imposing mansions, a branch of the Bank of Brazil, a theater, handsome suburban estates, shops as well stocked as those of the capital. But just as in Minas Gerais, when a male visitor was announced the city ladies disappeared into the darkened bedroom or among the plants or palms of the gardens behind the living rooms or in the center of the house, places where the women could enjoy the air without being seen from the street or by strangers and which were taboo to outsiders.

Saint-Hilaire complains fretfully of not having seen ladies in the homes of São Paulo, of nobody having asked him to dinner. One day when he went to call on a city aristocrat he found him about to sit down to table and was invited to dine, but neither wife nor daughters appeared. In Vila Rica he went to a dance in the palace of Dom Manuel de Castro e Portugal, and there he danced with a number of distinguished ladies. But during the entire time he spent in the city of Minas he did not lay eyes again on a single one of these ladies with whom he had danced at the noble's ball. He visited the husbands of many of them, but the lady of the house never appeared.[9] Tollenare in Recife, early in the nineteenth century, had the same experience as Saint-Hilaire in the cities of the South: as he entered the house of a certain important resident of the city, the women disappeared, leaving their embroidery and needles on the table. In the residence of Lieutenant Machado in São Nicolau, Saint-Hilaire was more fortunate: he was able to see the girls of the family spinning cotton and making lace. Proof that not all of them spent the day with their hair loose and their head resting in the lap of some maid skilled at head-rubbing.

It was in Rio de Janeiro, the Court, first of the viceroys, then of the regent, the King, and finally, of the Emperor, that women began to appear before strangers. But only gradually. In 1832 a traveler still complained about the houses "with high walls, small windows, and even narrower doors" which were difficult of access to strangers because "inside jealous, brutal husbands held sway."[1]

---

[9] Auguste de Saint-Hilaire: *Voyages dans l'Intérieur du Brésil*, I (Paris, 1830), p. 210.

[1] C. S. Stewart: *Brazil and La Plata: The Personal Record of a Cruise* (New York, 1856), p. 148.

Maria Graham had observed some years earlier that unmarried girls were not present even at wedding festivities. And Commander La Salle looked in vain for society women in the promenades and streets of Rio de Janeiro.[2] They were beginning to appear with face uncovered in dances and at the theater.

The only women encountered in the streets were Negro slaves and mulatto girls, with whom, after dark, the old sports of Recife philandered on the Boa Vista bridge. La Salle says that men did not go out of the house much either. This was true of Rio de Janeiro at this time, but in Recife as well as in São Luis do Maranhão tradition has it that they spent most of the afternoon in the street. In Recife, flirting with the mulatto girls, or discussing the government and other people's affairs seated on the benches along the bridge, placidly making business deals under the *gameleira* trees that lined the piers. These were often important deals, transactions involving thousands of dollars. The rich bourgeoisie in those cities of northern Brazil were men of the market place or street, as the Greeks had been of the agora, in contrast to those of Rio de Janeiro and Bahía who rarely emerged from their residences. It must have been with this in mind that Doctor Lima Santos wrote in 1855 in his "Health Rules" published in the *Diario de Pernambuco* of August 18:

"I have observed that Brazilians, whether by reason of temperament or climate, do not take sufficient exercise to develop their physical and spiritual energies. Confining themselves to the house, and sitting most of the time, leading a completely sedentary life, it is not long before they fall into a state of fatal laziness. The truth is that the great sign of nobility, importance, and distinction is to go out in the street as little as possible, and to avoid contact with that part of the population which the grandees call the populace, and which they so despise. To be sure, we are not making a sweeping statement; there are many who do not have this deplorable monomania, as for example, in Pernambuco; but in certain other provinces, Bahía, for example, a large proportion of the men (we are not speaking of the ladies, for these live like nocturnal birds, coming out only at nightfall) do not go out in the street, not only because of laziness, but as a mark of rank and dignity. These are harmful

---

[2] For De la Salle's comments on Brazil, see C. de Mello Leitão: *Visitantes do Primeiro Imperio* (São Paulo, 1934), p. 84.

and deplorable examples, and the wise man should eschew them, not to afflict his body and his life with such a detestable habit. To avoid such handicaps, which give rise to a decline of health, which undermine strength and energy, a strong will is needed which, disregarding the climate and the heat, casts aside bad habits and examples, taking the necessary exercise, moderated and regulated by hygienic principles; for strength of character has always been the great weapon in the victorious fight against the climate of a warm country and indolent habits." And the hygienist concludes: "From the point of view of general hygiene, it must be admitted that Brazil has made some progress in the last twenty-five years, but this is confined to the large cities. It is lamentable that the sewage system is still in a primitive state when the health of the cities depends upon it. Personal hygiene, too, is still very backward."

To go out on a dark night in the early nineteenth-century Brazilian cities was something of an adventure. Pitch black, narrow alleys; mud puddles; chamber pots emptied into the middle of the street; dead animals. In Bahía, in Vila Rica, in Olinda, slopes on which a person whose foot slipped ran the risk of bruising himself on the stones and even of going over a cliff. The sensible thing was to go out with a slave carrying a whale-oil lantern to illuminate the road, the street full of holes, the dirty alley.

It would seem that in the older cities of Brazil the streets preserved a kind of medieval-guild quality; in some, certain artisans had their place of business, if not exclusively, by preference; in others, dealers in certain articles, such as meat or fish. Or certain races: Jews or gypsies. There was the Street of the Coopers. Blacksmiths Alley. Street of the Fishmongers. Jew Street. Goldsmiths Street. Street of the Gypsies.

The location of trades and industrial and commercial activities was, in the main, due to the layout of the city, but also to hygienic considerations. It was with the latter in mind that the City Council of Recife, in the early years of the Empire, limited the sale of salt meats and dried fish to the Rua da Praia; and that the City Council of Olinda forbade washing clothes or any dirty object at the fountains Poço do Conselho, Baldo, and Varadouro, under penalty of a two thousand milreis fine or four days' imprisonment, and at the same time ordered leather workers to leave skins to dry only on the beach of San Francisco and along the wall of São Bento. The City Council of Salvador forbade tanners to salt hides and make glue in the city and settlements within its limits.[3]

The city, for all its shortcomings, was showing improvement over the rural areas, if not in the sanitation of the houses, in certain prophylactic measures and medical resources which made it possible for it to come to the assistance of the plantation or ranch dwellers and of settlements of the interior when they suffered epidemics of smallpox or other devastating diseases. The panegyrists of the rural life are wrong in accusing our nineteenth-century cities of being foci of epidemics, and giving a clean bill of health to ranches, plantations, and country settlements, where at times terrible epidemics, such as smallpox or the bubonic plague, wrought havoc. They were better combated in the cities. It was the city which, in alliance with the Church, introduced in Brazil not only hospitals, asylums, orphanages, charity hospitals, the activities of Third Orders and brotherhoods, but also public medicine, for the most part scorned by the patriarchal family.

The latter was also indifferent to good roads, which could have been built through the joint efforts of several of the great landowners. Instead, they limited themselves to producing for the most part only what they needed for their own use, and displayed no concern about expanding their production or facilitating communication. They were content with simple trails over which to get out their coffee and sugar during certain months of the year. This attitude, rather than any political design on the part of captains-major to impede solidarity among the settlers, seems to me the explanation of the slow development of communications in Brazil. It was patriarchalism itself, creating economic autonomy, or near-autonomy, stimulating the individualism of the landholders and the self-sufficiency of the families, that weakened the desire for solidarity. This desire is still weak in the Brazilian of rural origin, who feels only the ties of immediate kinship and religion. When in the *Diario do Rio de Janeiro* for March 6, 1822, the inhabitants of Maruí requested the "heirs of the plantation of Murundu" to cut down the

[3] Livro Ms. da Camara do Recife, 1828; Livro Ms. da Camara de Olinda, Section Mss., Biblioteca Estado de Pernambuco; Posturas da Camara de Salvador, 1844.

woods and clear the part of the road that ran through their lands, "so there may be free transit for all the inhabitants of that village, for it is now impassable not only because of the thick growth of trees and briars, but because of the shelter it affords to lawless deserters and runaway slaves," they spoke for hundreds, thousands of inhabitants of cities, towns, villages, who suffered losses to their person and property as a result of the selfishness of the great patriarchal families.

With the exception of the Catholic sodalities, it was through the Negro slaves that there came into being in Brazil a sense of solidarity more extensive than that of the family in the form of a feeling of race and, at the same time, of class. A capacity for frankly co-operative association, with a sense of ethnic brotherhood and of militant defense of the rights of the worker. Not to mention the near-socialist form of life and work which the settlement of Negroes in Palmares assumed. Rather than a simple revolt of runaway slaves, this republic of shacks would seem to have been a real attempt at independence based on the extension of a parasocialist type of culture.

The Negroes who had come together at Palmares [4] under a para-socialist dictatorship, which, according to the historians,[5] stored the crops in the community granary, pooled the product of the work in clearing the land, on the ranches, at the mills; and carried out in the street, in the market place, the distribution of food supplies among the inhabitants of the shacks, were able to hold out for half a century against the attacks of the plantation owners assisted by the authorities. A city of straw shacks arose by itself, in the midst of the forest, in opposition to the Big Houses and the stone mansions of all the North of Brazil. And it was with difficulty that the Big Houses,

---

[4] Palmares was founded in 1631 by Negroes who fled from plantations with weapons and tools to the interior of Alagoas. There they set up a "republic" under a dictator. They were joined by other Negro and mulatto runaway slaves. Their capital was a fortified stronghold in a palm grove; from time to time they raided some of the Dutch and Portuguese settlements. Their number grew and it required the combined efforts of troops from several of the captaincies to destroy this Negro "state" after seventy-six years of existence. Some of the inhabitants committed suicide rather than return to their former state of servitude.

[5] See Edson Carneiro: *O Quilombo dos Palmares* (Rio de Janeiro, 1947).

the mansions, and the colonial government finally managed to over-power it.

It was the first city to rise up against the plantation, this para-socialist city of Negroes; just as its technique of working the land was a forerunner of the diversification of crops in contrast to the predominant monoculture of the white planters.

Another example of co-operativism was given by the Negroes in Ouro Preto, who systematically joined forces for the purposes of se-curing slaves' freedom and living independently. Led by a Negro by the name of Francisco, a large number of slaves in the mines of Ouro Preto bought their freedom with their work, first the older man, who then bought his son's freedom, then father and son to-gether that of a stranger, and in this way dozens of Negroes be-came emancipated. And the free Negroes wound up as the owners of Encardideira Mine, also known as Palacio Velho.

The resemblance to Christian socialism, which Diogo de Vascon-cellos discerns in this admirable co-operative effort,[6] lies in the form rather than the essence of this organization of free Negroes of Ouro Preto, which was religious, but not Catholic. The Negroes organized themselves even better than the white merchants and artisans into a brotherhood, that of Saint Iphigenia. And they built a church, that of Rosario. There, on the Feast of the Magi, they celebrated with great merrymaking their festival, more African than Catholic, pre-sided over by the old leader dressed as a king. To be sure, there was a high mass; but the main feature was the dancing to the sound of African instruments. Dances in the street in front of the church, Negro dances. Long before Professor Nina Rodriguez, Mansfield had observed[7] that the Negroes in Brazil, instead of adopting the Catholic saints and forgetting or deserting their own, substituted the African by the Portuguese, exaggerating the points of resemblance between the two, at times practically creating new saints out of elements of the two religious traditions—mestizo saints, so to speak.

It was religion that gave a holiday air and excitement to the

---

[6] A. Teixeira Duarte: "Catecismo da Cooperação," in *Rev. Arq. Pub. Min.*, XVIII (Belo Horizonte, 1914), note to pp. 341–2.

[7] Charles B. Mansfield: *Paraguay, Brazil, and the Plate* (Cambridge, 1856), p. 91. See also A. Ramos: *A Aculturação Negra no Brazil* (São Paulo, 1942).

streets of the old cities of Brazil. The religion of the blacks with their dances; that of the whites, with their processions and Holy Weeks.

The rich folk came from their plantations and ranches to accompany the processions through the streets of the episcopal cities, dressed in black and purple. Fat ladies watched from the verandahs of the city mansions the passing of the Crucified. Others walked beside the float dressed as in bygone days. The many-storied mansions and the humbler homes decked themselves out for the occasion. In an official notice published in the *Diario do Rio de Janeiro* of January 18, 1825, one reads that the Municipal Council of Rio de Janeiro notified the inhabitants of the city that, in the streets through which the procession of St. Sebastian was to pass, "they should whitewash the fronts of the houses and adorn them with draperies, and bestrew the part of the street before their residences with sand and leaves."

The brotherhoods, the sodalities, the Third Orders paraded through the streets strewn with sand and leaves, between houses adorned with hangings from India. A gallimaufry of habits and surplices; bands of musicians; penitents naked from the waist up, slashing themselves with pieces of broken glass. The floats of the saints. The governor, the bishop, the state officials, officers with glittering epaulettes. Some of the ladies were dressed in the height of fashion; others in antiquated garments. At the head of them all went the buffoon, with a kind of sack over his body, two holes for his eyes, and a whip in his hand. And the street urchins pelted him with cashew nuts.

At times there was a Negro who had been slashed by a razor, some black boy with his intestines hanging out who was carried off in a white hammock (the red ones were for the wounded; the white for the dead). For these processions with bands of music were the meeting place of the *capoeiras*, a curious type of urban Negro or mulatto, whose counterpart was the *capangas* and *cabras*, the hired gunmen of the plantations. The specialty of the *capoeira* was his razor or sharp-pointed knife; his trademark, the kinky hair combed in the shape of a turban, the light sandals on his feet, which were almost those of a dancer, and his loose-jointed gait. His art included, in addition to all this, a variety of difficult steps and movements of incredible agility, in which the street vagabonds were initiated almost as in a Masonic rite. We shall return to the figure of the *capoeira*.

The celebrations in the churchyard and the street processions were also occasions for courting; the "saint's followers" were almost scandalous, with the girls singing quatrains to St. Gonzalo which sounded shocking to Lopes Gama. After the tragic days of the scenes of the Passion, the sermons, people weeping aloud at the sufferings of Our Lord, women dressed in black, men in deep mourning, Holy Week concluded with gay dinners of fish, fried crabs, shrimp gumbo, manioc and fish stew, red snapper cooked with manioc mush.

Some of these sights must have scandalized the plantation dwellers who came to the city and returned to their Big Houses full of wonder, their eyes dazed by the churches resplendent with gold and silver, dazzled by the gold of the altars and the beauty of the saints.

Those who saw the Royal Chapel in Rio de Janeiro in the days of Dom João VI must forever have kept the memory of the royal pew hung with silk and fringed with gold where the prince heard mass; the sweetness of the organ music played by the hands of a European musician, the orchestra led by Marcos Portugal. If we are to believe certain historians, church music reached such heights in the cities of colonial Brazil that Rio de Janeiro indulged itself in the luxury of having its *castrati*.

Profane music, too, flourished in the city mansions. In 1850 anyone passing through the streets of Rio de Janeiro would have heard, instead of the sound of guitar or harp, pianos played by the young ladies of the house for the exclusive enjoyment of the whites of the upper class, and instead of the plangent *modinhas*, French and Italian airs. Mello Moraes, who had known the Brazil of the first half of the nineteenth century, voiced indignation at the decline of the *modinha* in the colonial Big Houses and mansions. ". . . Aping foreign music, the Brazilians are ashamed to sing our enchanting *modinhas* even at family gatherings." [8] And Father Lopes Gama remarked that in colonial days they played and sang in Brazil, not arias of Rossini or Bellini, "but duets of *modinhas* accompanied by

---

[8] A. J. Mello Moraes: Op. cit., p. 102.

zither or guitar," such as "My adored Nise," or "Maiden, Maiden, my Beloved." [9]

It should be noted that these *modinhas*, for a long time the mellifluous expression of the romantic idealization of the fair sex, were turning, in the first half of the nineteenth century, into the expression of a mild feminine protest against man's faithlessness echoed by composers who sought to voice the changing sentimental relations between the two sexes.

Wetherell in his book on Bahía—the Bahía he knew in the first half of the nineteenth century—reproduces a curious *modinha* which timidly expresses woman's protest against man's despotism, at first "a lamb," who turns into a "sly wolf." Other examples of the change in feelings are to be found in Almir de Andrade's collection of nineteenth-century Brazilian *modinhas*.

There were also plantations that had their black choir boys, their musicians, their grand pianos. As early as the sixteenth century a rich planter of Bahía had his orchestra of Negroes directed by a Frenchman from Marseilles. In the nineteenth century a North American missionary traveling in Brazil was astounded at the music he heard in the mansion of a baron of the Empire at the Soledade plantation near Paraibuna in Minas Gerais. When the master of the house suggested a little music, the North American thought it would be some country air, "a wheezy plantation fiddle, a fife, and a drum." He was wrong. To his astonishment, what he heard that afternoon was an orchestra tuning up. Violin, flute, clarinet. When he saw the orchestra, it was made up entirely of Negroes, one seated at the organ, and a chorus of boys, the score gleaming white in their black hands. The first number was an operatic overture. The next, the *Stabat Mater* sung in Latin. The March of La Fayette.[1]

But these ultra-refined Big Houses, with Negroes playing opera airs and singing in Latin, were not typical of the rural aristocracy, which, a world to itself, surrounding itself only with inferiors, always laid more stress on the quantity than the quality of its claims to greatness: the size of its coffee groves, of its acreage, the

---

[9] Lopes Gama: Op. cit.

[1] D. P. Kidder and J. C. Fletcher: *Brazil and the Brazilians* (Boston, 1879), p. 356.

number of its slaves and cattle, of its rooms. In the eyes of the majority of the Brazilians of the patriarchal era, still predominantly rural, it was this that constituted grandeur. The country planter, grown uncouth in his isolation, disdained everything in exchange for the pleasure of issuing orders to his many slaves, and of talking at the top of his lungs to everyone, separated not only socially, but physically, from his wife, his children, his Negroes, in an enormous house, with huge rooms where people almost never came together. Even at mealtime, to make himself heard at the other end of the dining table, often eight yards long, the master of the house had to bellow. As for music, the more rustic planters were satisfied with that of the birds, hung in cages all about the house, in the corridors, the dining room, the verandah. Many country houses had an aviary filled with little birds. In some of the suburban mansions there must have been a conflict between the woodland warblers and the grand pianos imported from England. A conflict between art and nature which reflected the conflict between the city and the country.

Mansfield, an Englishman traveling in Brazil around the middle of the nineteenth century, no longer felt as distant from Europe when he was visiting the Big Houses as his compatriot Luccock fifty years earlier. Some of the plantation mansions reminded him of third-rate country estates in England. And if in Carauna the mistress of the house did not come down to eat with the visitors, she did appear and serve tea to the Englishmen. This was a compromise between the patriarchal old style, where the woman never appeared before strangers, and that of middle-class Europe, where she presided at meals and took part in men's conversations.

On the Macujé plantation in Pernambuco, Mansfield had an even stronger feeling of being in England and in nineteenth-century Europe. "The service in this house is almost the same as in the best English country houses," he observed.[2] And the mistress of the house, "a lady of beautiful character," and her three daughters came out to meet the foreign visitor and shared the meal with him. The house was not as luxurious as that of Carauna. Perhaps it had the same cuspidors, so disgusting to an Englishman, which Mansfield

---

[2] Mansfield: Op. cit., p. 98.

found in all the Big Houses he visited in Brazil. But life no longer had the old musty Mohammedan tang. The tone in everything was more European, and even English, than Oriental. And the cuspidors, to judge by those advertised in the newspapers of the period, had their dignity, like the one offered in the *Diario do Rio de Janeiro* of November 15, 1821: ". . . antique silver cuspidor with lid and handle." Noble cuspidors, which were handed down from generation to generation.

As we shall have occasion to point out later, the contact with English fashions, which increased after the arrival of Dom João VI, was to exert a marked influence on the customs and even the domestic architecture of Brazil, contributing to the taste for country residences surrounded by trees, for tea served by the mistress of the house, for the vogue of beer and bread, for cleaner streets and more sanitary houses. This influence would seem to have become more pronounced in the first half of the nineteenth century in Pernambuco, in Bahía, and in Rio de Janeiro, before it made itself felt in São Paulo, in Minas Gerais, and Rio Grande do Sul. What attracted Englishmen to Brazil at that time was the wealth of the plantation aristocracy of those regions, ennobled by sugar.

In the second half of the nineteenth century, with coffee taking preponderance over sugar, the houses of the North began to be superseded in comfort and luxury by those of the South. The streets of Rio de Janeiro, with Dom João's arrival, were becoming the most elegant of the entire Empire. The Rua do Ouvidor became the street of the luxury trade and French fashions. But, for all this, the house remained the house, and the street, the street—enemies.

"For Sale: a black girl, well brought up, very diligent in all household duties, sixteen years old, who has been raised without going into the street," reads an advertisement published in the *Diario do Rio de Janeiro*, January 28, 1821. The wording is significant; it indicates the sharp differentiation between the house slave and the street slave, which lasted throughout the first half of the nineteenth century. As late as the middle of the century slaves were advertised for "all indoor domestic duties," as in the *Diario de Pernambuco* of February 19, 1842, just as others were advertised in the same paper for "selling in the street." The former in contact with the white folks of the Big House, like a member of the family; the latter, less

one of the household than an individual exposed to the degrading influences of the street.

More than one European received the impression that the street
slaves of Rio de Janeiro were gay and much given to the dance and
music, and it seemed to them that they were better off than the
plantation hands.[3] This generalization is open to question, unless by
plantation hands one refers to field hands under hard-driving overseers. Or if one compares prosperous cities with rural areas in
decline like the sugar-producing North in the second half of the
nineteenth century.

On the majority of the plantations of the North, Coelho Rodrigues stated at the Agricultural Congress of 1878, such luxury as
still existed "was as nothing compared to the style of living on the
great ranches in the South." Many of the plantation owners of the
North had no furniture except in their parlors, and "for most of
them, such furnishings do not exceed a few tables, benches, and
stools of local manufacture." And their normal fare at dinner was
"dried beef or codfish, grudgingly supplied by the broker to keep the
mill running," and on Sundays "a bit of meat bought on Saturday
in the village market." Breakfast was a cup of coffee with tapioca,
sweet potato, cassava "when they had time to plant it." And supper
the same. Bread and crackers were a rare luxury except on the most
opulent Big House tables.[4]

The relative ease of life in the sugar-growing region, already
affected by the discovery of the mines, declined still further with the
rise of coffee. In the cities the fine residences of the more im-
provident sugar planters were degenerating into big "barns" in need
of paint, where the rosewood furniture was no longer lacquered or
varnished. Rats, bats, ghosts were taking over the neglected houses.
Slaves, imports such as raisins, canned peas, English pianos, French
wines were all going up in price, beyond the reach of the rural sugar
barons, who were now being eclipsed by the coffee planters. The

---

[3] Andrew Grant: *History of Brazil* (London, 1809), p. 145.

[4] For a long time wheat bread was a luxury in Brazil, so general was the use
of manioc meal, plain or in the form of cakes, couscous, or tapioca. The
Brazilians served rice with many kinds of meat, thus eliminating the need for
bread.

Big Houses of the interior were becoming overshadowed by the city mansions.

And bank rates became steadily more stringent for the planters, while the price of slaves skyrocketed. "Illegal slave trade," said one political writer of the epoch, Antonio Pedro de Figueiredo, was stimulating poverty, definitively enslaving agriculture "to business and the city capitalists." [5] Interest rose to 24 per cent and even higher, and the sugar industry seemed to many threatened by "paralysis and death." For such planters as did not have the means to import their own slaves, or the daring to steal them from their neighbors, the acquisition of slaves for the plantations became a tragic problem, with the English and the Imperial government itself redoubling their vigilance against the slave-runners. The ranches of the South began to absorb the Negroes from the North, which was gradually left without slaves to cultivate cane. It was then that the stealing of slaves became an outrage and a scandal in the streets of the cities of the North. These thefts were a kind of revenge of the plantation Don Quixotes against the Sancho Panzas of the cities. The revenge of a romantic type of agriculture, not given to systematically exploiting the slave and the rural proletariat, against business, the banks, city methods of financing, which were far greater exploiters of human beings and, indirectly, of the land itself. A vengeance of the House against the Street, which seemed to be beautifying itself at the former's cost. The newspapers of the first half of the nineteenth century cite cases of poor women, robbed of their Negroes in the capital itself, insinuating that the thieves were acting under the protection of powerful persons in the North, planters or ranchers. But it was toward the middle of the century that the slave thieves threw off all pretense, and there were organized gangs for the stealing of Negroes in the cities. These gangs apparently had their customers beforehand on some of the most illustrious plantations of the day.

---

[5] Antonio Pedro de Figueiredo was for some years editor of the magazine *O Progresso,* published in Recife in the first half of the nineteenth century. He wrote some of the best critical studies of the period on the patriarchal economy and society. See also Sergio Bagu: *Economía de la Sociedad Colonial, Ensayo de Historia Comparada de la América Latina* (Buenos Aires, 1949).

On May 7, 1828, the *Diario de Pernambuco* published the following information concerning the stealing of slaves: "It is public knowledge that slave-stealing goes on in this city almost daily, and that there are men who make a business of this. Some entice and lure the Negroes and Negresses they encounter in the street, others take them into their homes and hide them there until they can be put aboard ship or got out of the city; others make a deal with the first ones they come across, and take them to some distant place to sell them; and others buy them for their own service . . ." But it was apparent that the public turned a blind eye on these crimes: "The theft of Negroes, of horses, and still more serious crimes, even when there is indisputable proof, does not prevent the circumvention of writs with bail, not put up by the criminal himself, but by some bondsman, pledging a small surety which the criminal repays when he is freed . . ." Whereas in Rio de Janeiro there was strict vigilance by the police over the thieves of slaves—as evidenced by the *Diario do Rio de Janeiro* of February 12, 1830—in Pernambuco and the provinces during the first half of the nineteenth century, still predominantly rural and patriarchal, it seems that such thieves were never apprehended.

In most of the provinces the agrarian interests still controlled the government, the courts, and the police. This explains the benevolence toward the gangs of slave-stealers in provinces like Pernambuco. The criminal records of the Municipal Councils, such as that of 1838 of the capital of the province in question, reveal the extent of such thefts, and at times there appear among the suspects distinguished names of the region, such as Carneiro d'Albuquerque e Mora, for example, or Gusmão e Moura. And in newspapers of the day members of some of the best families among the gentry are accused of slave-running, and, competing with them in other types of smuggling or fraud, wealthy residents of the Court, like the one whose title of nobility had the initials N.F., which were interpreted by the wags of the day as: *No Funds*.

Probably, or rather, certainly, many of the Negroes advertised as "runaway slaves" during the days of the Empire had been stolen in the cities for sale on plantations. But the slaves themselves sometimes slipped away from one plantation to another, and it is hardly necessary to remark that it was from the smaller to the larger ones, to planters having closer connections with the political authorities of the capital and the province. It is possible that in certain cases of large landowners accused of taking in or buying runaway slaves, they had simply given asylum to Negroes who, of their own free will and not decoyed by anybody, had left the poor plantation whose owner worked them to death, or the widow who earned her living selling sweets and who made her one slave do the work of three, or the bakeries where the working hours were long and hard, for the big plantations known for the kindly treatment of their slaves, plantations that had many slaves, and an abundance of manioc and corn, heartening rum, and where on occasion they could dance the samba all night long.

In 1846 Father Lopes Gama in his *O Sete de Setembro* accused some of the most illustrious members of the Rego Barros and Caval-canti families of slave-stealing. "It is common knowledge that . . . he has been stealing slaves for many years, utilizing as his principal agent in this activity a relative of his . . ." Not that there were not "capable and upright men" in these families, the priest continues. But under cover of the families' influence in the politics of the Empire, or, at any rate, their name, there were those who engaged in illicit slave trading. "What does it matter," he asks, "that Baron Bôa Vista on the one hand fosters public works, and encourages the theater and the ballet, if at the same time smuggling is rife in the North and the South; if forged identification papers can be procured without difficulty, and if the public works in question are a gold mine for certain individuals, and if relatives of the baron himself rob and kill wholesale, and murder has increased to the point where President Thomaz Xavier, addressing the provincial legislature in his report on the state of the country during the past two years, went so far as to say we were turning into a nation of barbarous Ishmael-ites?"

The scions of the first families of the rural aristocracy did not all, or perhaps even the majority of them, always behave in matters having to do with the public good and the political morality of the Empire in the chivalrous manner attributed to them by the rapturous admirers of our lords of lands and slaves. The high-handed measures of the "shore patrol" of Chichorro da Gama, which in Pernambuco invaded plantations, surrounded and bombarded "certain feudal castles . . . where they had runaway slaves hidden," even pursuing a close relative of the Baron of Bôa Vista, were motivated in part by the hatred of Praia Street for the Big Houses of the interior, and undoubtedly represented a reaction, even vengeance, of the City against the Plantation, against the "backwoods," against the countryside. One might almost say, of the Peddlers against the Planters; the creditors against the debtors; the owners of city mansions against the masters of the rural Big Houses.

But not because of this can we absolve the planters, painting them as Nature's noblemen in contrast to the hard-boiled inhabitants of the cities, centers, to be sure, of usury, counterfeiting, the adulteration of food products, but which produced some of the outstanding reformers in the field of political administration, hygiene, and our religious and intellectual life. Revolutionists who were practical, constructive idealists, and not simply street demagogues, of the type generally associated with the city, in contrast to the sound "good sense" of the ranchers, or the "enlightened liberalism" of the planters.

It would, however, be foolish to reduce the problem to a college-debate level, something like "Rome vs. Carthage," and deny the creative contribution of plantation- and ranch-bred men to our political, administrative, and even literary life. Contributions not only of a conservative nature, but of a liberal and revolutionary stripe, and in such cases the physical risk was greater for the planter than for the men of a coastal city.

Southey, the English poet and scholar, who wrote a history of Brazil, attributes to the Pernambucan planters who in 1710 revolted against the Portuguese, "separatist and republican intentions." [6] It was from the plantations, eager to free themselves from the "planned economy" of His Majesty's captains-general, that "the first sparks of independence and democracy" arose in Brazil. They were also the point of origin of the glorious campaign against the Dutch and the Jews in the seventeenth century, even though their relations with the invaders were not entirely those of men defending their native soil

---

[6] Like other historians, Robert Southey attributed republican aims to the rebels of 1710. See Mario Mello: *A Guerra dos Mascates como Afirmação Nacionalista* (Recife, 1941).

from the grasp of the foreigner: they were also those of remiss debtors against pressing creditors.

The brothers Francisco de Paula, Luiz Francisco de Paula, and José Francisco de Paula Cavalcanti de Albuquerque, all of them planters, the first the owner of Suassuna plantation, were accused at the beginning of the nineteenth century of one of the most romantic conspiracies to occur in Brazil: that of the independence of Pernambuco under the protection of Napoleon Bonaparte. This was plotted not in some city mansion, but on a Brazilian plantation of colonial days, the "academy" or "areopagus" which, in the words of Father Muñiz quoted by Oliveira Lima,[7] was a democratic school where "adepts and neophytes, not only of the province and the country in general, but even foreigners, found light, hospitality, and support."

It is impossible to generalize in the case of Brazil, as has been done in sociological studies dealing with other countries, and say that the rural gentry, consolidated principally, until the middle of the nineteenth century, on the big sugar plantations, and only secondarily on the coffee plantations or cattle ranches, always stood for the conservative interests and the *status quo*, while the cities, the residences of the rich middle class, the streets themselves, were always the storm center of democratic uprisings and liberal movements. The economic pressures, great or small—the intervention of the mother country through the viceroy or the captain-general in private economy and on behalf of the common man—must have strongly influenced the political attitudes of the landholders in the eighteenth and the first half of the nineteenth century. Attitudes which were often those of resentment and insubordination, in contrast to the passivity of the coastal cities, which for many years were almost devoid of a lower class, with only a fickle rabble or street mob, dominated by merchants who were even more interested than the planters in maintaining government stability, first that of the Portuguese and then that of the Empire.

True, during one period of the Empire, the sugar planters, and especially the coffee planters, effectively joined forces with certain

---

[7] Oliveira Lima, historian and diplomat, author of *Dom João VI no Brasil*, a historical and sociological work.

conservative interests against the demagoguery of the cities, that is
to say, of the streets, the market place, the shanties. But even during
this phase of their closer union with the Empire, the planters at
times stood up to the Emperor, the chief of police of the capital,
the bishop of the diocese, with the same hostile air of colonial days,
when their parlors and dining rooms, hung with bird cages, with
naked pickaninnies crawling around on the floor and the straw
mats, with Negroes and Negresses on every hand awaiting the
orders of the whites, were transformed into "areopagi" where the
masters, together with priests, friars, and even foreigners—French
and English—plotted with Masonic secrecy and Brazilian intrep-
idness to bring about independence, liberty, and, to a degree,
democracy in the land of Brazil.

Referring to the influence of the socialist engineer L. L. Vauthier
in the still-patriarchal Brazil of the first half of the nineteenth
century, João Peretti recently pointed out that it was not only the
intellectuals of Recife who were influenced by the revolutionary
doctrines of the young Frenchman: "Moreover, all the aristocracy
of the province, with the Baron of Bõa Vista at their head, followed
Vauthier without clearly sensing where he was leading them
with his dangerous theories." [8] Vauthier was received at some of the
richest plantations of the period—that of Viscount Camaragibe
and the Marquis of Recife—and he was also on friendly terms with
aristocrats of the bar such as Nabuco de Araujo, who was his
lawyer, and with social lights of the city like Maciel Monteiro. And
also with mestizos who had achieved status thanks to their intelligence and education like Nascimento Feitosa [9] and A. P. de Figueiredo,[1] as well as with agitators like Borges da Fonseca,[2] and with
men known for their efforts on behalf of order, like Figueira de

---

[8] "Vauthier et la Gentry Pernambucane," *Asociação de Cultura Franco-
Brasileira do Recife, Bulletin d'Outubro,* 1949. See also Gilberto Freyre: *Um
Engenheiro Frances no Brazil* (Rio de Janeiro, 1937); and *Diario Intimo do
Engenheiro Vauthier,* annotated by Gilberto Freyre (Rio de Janeiro, 1940).

[9] A political leader of Negro origin under the Empire; noted for his liberalism.

[1] A talented mulatto publicist who during the first half of the nineteenth
century wrote on social problems with great objectivity.

[2] A political agitator in the first half of the nineteenth century.

Mello.[3] But the point we are trying to bring out is that this French revolutionary enjoyed the esteem of the apparently reactionary conservatives of the patriarchal plantations and city mansions. In some of them it seems that he instilled a curiosity about socialist ideas. Certain of these aristocrats are known to have been subscribers to French socialist reviews such as *Phalange Socialiste* and *Democratie*. Therefore it is not surprising that some of the insurgents who participated in what is known as the Praieira Revolt had been influenced by French socialism of the first half of the nineteenth century. Included among them were men from the interior, with their roots firmly sunk there.

In a series of articles entitled "Agriculture and Colonization," published in *O Liberal Pernambucano* of April 4, 1856, the editor of this paper, which was almost socialist in its orientation, said: ". . . Nobody leaves his native hearth for a foreign country to submit to a feudal system without guarantees . . ." If in the South of the Empire—where there was known to have been in Saí (Santa Catarina) a frankly socialist community—certain colonies have flourished, it is because there "the habits, the climate, and other circumstances afford advantages which neither Pernambuco nor other provinces of the North can offer." In his article of April 5 of that same year, this critic points out the need of a "rural code of law" in Brazil. He hoped in this way to break the grip of a "feudal system without guarantees."

This series of articles constitutes an outstanding expression of the social, and not merely political, ferment that was active or latent in Pernambuco from the time of the ill-fated Praieira Revolt (in reality, from the riots of 1823, which twenty-five years later culminated in that revolt). While socialism was a living reality in Santa Catarina, in Pernambuco the fight for socialist ideas was carried on in the press and the streets.

"Even as we are writing these lines," said the journal published in 1846 by the mulatto A. P. de Figueiredo, one of the "rioters" of 1823, whom study had converted into a socialist in 1840, "there

---

[3] Author of a book on the "Praia" movement: a revolutionary local movement.

is without doubt more than one person looking for work, more than one dismissed employee, more than one workman without a job, who dreams of revolutions, etc., etc." It considered "out of all bounds the number of our tailors, cobblers, masons, carpenters, etc." suffering "from competition that ruins them"—that of foreigners—and "often . . . without employment." The solution of "small farms" did not seem the answer. The big landowners refused to sell land that would be appropriate for small farmers; in Pernambuco, or in a large sector of the North, these were precisely the lands "given over to sugar plantations." These observations of one who felt that the atmosphere was charged not merely with political but with social revolution appeared in *O Progresso* (Recife) in the study entitled "The Colonization of Brazil." [4]

In 1858 it was José Ignacio de Abreu e Lima [5]—a Brazilian who fought with the Spanish Americans in their wars for independence —who, in an article in the *Jornal do Commercio* of Rio de Janeiro, May 14, 1858, stated that the reason for the high cost of living in various provinces of the Empire was due to the imbalance between large- and small-scale farming, including "the prejudices of the great landholders against the cultivation of cereals." In this article Abreu e Lima gave further consideration to a problem he had set forth years earlier, especially in a study in *A Barca de São Pedro* on "the colonization Brazil needs": the problem of the abuses of the large landowners in our country. The connection between these abuses and the colonization of the Empire was a topic which ever since the memorandum of Raymundo José da Cunha Mattos published in *O Auxiliador da Industria Nacional* [6] had been a matter of special concern to men in public office and political thinkers of the Empire. It had led certain of the latter to consider the possibility of the intervention of the government on behalf of the working man and the curtailment of the feudal power of the large landowners, not only in the number of slaves, but in the lands they had equally enslaved.

---

[4] Vol. II, 1846.

[5] Publicist and man of action of the first half of the nineteenth century, noted for his liberal ideas in politics and religion. He participated in liberation movements in Spanish America.

[6] Rio de Janeiro, 1837, Nos. II-V.

As late as the year 1856, the lawyer Nascimento Feitosa, in a polemic with Professor Pedro Autran da Matta Albuquerque, went even farther than Abreu e Lima. He defended the direct intervention of the State in the economic life of the country: "What is government's mission? To decide rightly and justly all disputes between the governed; to protect the weak against the strong in a manner that re-establishes equality or mutual respect. And this protection refers to persons or property, and more to the former than to the latter." This article, entitled "The government should intervene in the provisioning of flour and meat," [7] is one of the most interesting in the history of the development of socialist ideology in Brazil, a development more stressed in the middle of the nineteenth century in Pernambuco than in any other province, even after the failure of the Praieira Revolt had discouraged certain partisans of phalansterianism.

On January 5, 1856, the *Diario de Pernambuco*, after publishing news of the arrival in the port of Recife of "several shiploads of salt cod," pointed out the fact that "this article was still scarce," due to the "avarice of certain speculators" and "the lack of punitive measures." The conservative newspaper thus accepted, in the somewhat oversimplified form of "punitive measures," the intervention of the State in economic matters, the intervention demanded by socialists nurtured on French ideas like Figueiredo and near-socialists like Feitosa, both, moreover, colored men who had reached the position of intellectual leaders through their intelligence and knowledge. They were the continuators of the French-influenced mulattoes who had taken part in the conspiracy of Bahía in 1798, and not merely of the revolting Negroes and mulattoes of Recife in 1823, for whom the enemy was the white man and whose inspiration was King Henri-Christophe of Haiti.

It was to the same Antonio P. de Figueiredo that Professor Autran addressed an article on August 7, 1852, accusing socialism—and lamenting the fact that Figueiredo was of this school—of having proclaimed that women were to become "community property," an article to which Figueiredo replied in the *Diaro de Pernambuco* of the twelfth of that month: "Socialism is not a doctrine; as yet it

---

[7] *O Liberal Pernambucano*, January 26, 1856.

is no more than an aspiration, but this aspiration has as its goal the reform of the present state in the direction of bettering the moral and material condition of all the members of society." Including, he might have added, that of women, who were "community property" under the patriarchal system still in force in Brazil: patriarchal and polygamous.

CHAPTER III

FATHERS AND SONS

Towner points out that in primitive societies boy and man are nearly equal. Not so under the patriarchal system; an immense social gulf separates children from grown-ups. As wide as that between the sexes: the "strong" and the "weak," the "noble" and the "fair." As wide as that between classes: the rulers and the servitors, dissimulated at times under the race or caste classification of "superior" and "inferior."

It is true that in patriarchal societies childhood is short. The angel's wings are quickly clipped. Thus the antagonism between child and man, father and son, is attenuated. In periods of patriarchal decadence, such as that we are studying here, this antagonism does not disappear; it becomes transmuted or, rather, prolonged into a rivalry between the young men and the old.

So great is the prestige of the mature man in patriarchal societies that the child, ashamed of being a child, tends to ripen prematurely. He takes pride in a precocity which relieves him of the humiliation of being a child, of the inferiority of youth.

So great is the prestige of ripe, advanced age in such societies that from adolescence the youth imitates the old man. He attempts to conceal behind bushy whiskers and glasses, or, at least, by a stern expression, all the glow of youth, the joy of adolescence, all the traces of childhood which still dance in his eyes or animate his gestures.

In the Brazil of patriarchal days, the child, as long as he was looked upon as such, was always kept far from the man. At a great distance from the human element, one might add.

Up to a certain age, he was idealized to the point of exaggeration. Identified with the angels. Raised like an angel—going about the house naked like an infant Jesus.

If he died at this angelic age, the child became an object of adoration. The mother rejoiced over the death of the angel, like the one Luccock saw in Rio de Janeiro, weeping with delight because the Lord had carried away her fifth child. There were now five angels awaiting her in Heaven.[1]

Du Petit-Thouars saw in Santa Catarina in 1825 a dead child who was openly worshipped: ". . . I saw at the rear of the room a platform on which an infant was arranged on an altar, surrounded by lilies and vases of flowers; its face was uncovered and it was richly dressed, with a crown of forget-me-nots on its head and a cluster of them in its hand." Around the altar where the dead child rested there were mats, and, kneeling on the mats, women in holiday attire, singing. Afterwards there were even gay dances.[2]

This voluptuous pleasure in connection with the death of a child may perhaps, as I suggested in an earlier study,[3] be a legacy of the Jesuits, of their eagerness to counteract the anger of the Indians against the whites, and particularly the Jesuits themselves, as a result of the high mortality of infants which followed the first contacts of the European conquerors with the native population. This mortality, which also occurred among European families or families of European origin, was sublimated among them, too, in a kind of rejoicing one might call theological, fostered by the Jesuits, over the death of children. A morbid rejoicing, developed as a consolation for the mothers in a period of the most anti-hygienic living conditions.

But this adoration of the child antedated his reaching the theologi-

---

[1] John Luccock: *Notes on Rio and the Southern Parts of Brazil, taken during a residence of ten years in that country from 1808–1818* (London, 1820), p. 192.

[2] Abel du Petit-Thouars, in C. de Mello Leitão: *Visitantes do Primeiro Imperio* (São Paulo, 1934), Chap. X. See also Wetherell: *Stray Notes from Bahía*, p. 85.

[3] Gilberto Freyre: *The Masters and the Slaves* (New York, 1946).

cal age of reason. Between his sixth or seventh and tenth year, he turned into the child-devil. A "foreign body" who neither ate at the table nor shared in any way in the conversation of the grown-ups. Treated like something superfluous. His head shaved, the curls of his angelic days put away by his sentimental mother in the bottom of a dresser drawer or donated to the church to make hair for the figures of the religious processions.

And because he was looked upon as an alien being, sinful by nature, of a lazy, wicked bent, his body was the most sorely punished of all the household—after that of the slave, naturally. After that of the black whipping boy, who sometimes caught it for himself and the white boy. But the white boy got his share, too. He was punished by his father, his mother, his grandfather, his grandmother, his godfather, his godmother, his uncle, his maiden aunt, his tutor, his schoolmaster. Punished by a society of adults in whom the habit of absolute command, as well as responsibility, over the slave had developed an inclination to mistreat children. And the system of the Big House continued to prevail, in slightly attenuated form, in the city mansions.

In patriarchal Brazil the authority of the father over a minor son— and even one who was of age—was carried to its logical conclusion: the right to kill. The patriarch had absolute power in the administration of justice in the family, some fathers reproducing, in the shade of the cashew grove, the severest acts of classic patriarchalism: killing and ordering killed, not only Negroes, but white boys and girls, their own children.

Even Solomon's famous ruling is said to have been carried out by one of the old planters, harsh old men to whom passing judgment and executing justice on their own family was one of the sad but inevitable duties of the patriarch's authority. This was the case of the one known as the Old Man of the Wall, the feudal lord of Pitanguí, in the captaincy of Minas, who at the beginning of the eighteenth century built his mud and wattle house on the peak of a hill, and from there exercised his rule over the entire area. It is told that a young Portuguese who had come out to Brazil married one of the Old Man's daughters, called Margarida. One day, who should unexpectedly come to Pitanguí but the Portuguese wife of the patriarch's son-in-law. (It seems that cases of bigamy were frequent in regions such as Minas, with its floating population, and constituted a difficult problem for the bishops of Mariana, as well as being a nightmare for the old-fashioned fathers with unmarried daughters.) When the Old Man of the Wall, tradition says, had to decide the question, he put into effect the order of the Hebrew king and with his own hand—so they tell in Minas—chopped the body of the young man in two down the middle, giving one half to his daughter and the other to the woman who had come out from Portugal looking for her husband.

The administration of justice by the patriarch to his own family, the authority exercised by the adult over the child, really or ostensibly in the interests of the child's education and upbringing, undoubtedly took on at times a frankly sadistic character. A sadism which was very slightly modified when the patriarchal system of the Big House was transferred to the city mansion, where the old men continued their almost absolute rule over the young.

With the decay of the rural patriarchy, this sadistic pedagogy, exercised at home by the patriarch, the tutor, the chaplain, took on a new and terrible lease of life in the religious and State schools. The parents delegated to teachers and priests the authority to punish with quince switch and ferule.

Throughout this cruel procedure of teaching the child Latin, grammar, religion, good manners, the social gulf between man and boy was carefully perpetuated. The religious schools stressed the principle that childhood, from the age of six to ten or twelve, was a foul age from the theological standpoint, during which the child, lacking the painstakingly acquired virtues of the adult, could be tolerated only thanks to servile manners, self-effacement, and abject respect for his elders. He was tolerated, but on condition that he keep his distance, not speak unless he was spoken to, nor answer pertly. He was not to raise his voice even to those who shouted at him almost as they did at the slaves; he was to disappear from the parlor when the grown-ups were talking, and play without making a noise. In a word, to conduct himself toward his elders as though he were a being of a lower order.

And if the child did not behave thus of his own accord, he was made to do so by every means, even the most cruel. By punishments and humiliations, of which our folklore preserves dramatic instances, as well as the records found in autobiographies and memoirs. Men who from infancy suffered like slaves at the hands of those in authority, and became stammerers as a result of the despotism of fathers or tutors, stepfather or stepmother, and at school, of teachers. The advertisements for runaway slaves in many cases mention the fact that they stutter, which may perhaps be due to the terrorism, or despotism, and at times even the sadism, of old men toward the pickaninnies.

The religious school, nearly always occupying a huge building, is one of the landmarks in Brazil's social landscape which, from the opening of the eighteenth century, indicates the decadence of the all-powerful patriarchalism of the Big House. During the first century of colonization the Jesuit school, in cities like Salvador, was already vying in importance with the plantation houses and the city mansions in its authority over children, women, slaves. As far as authority over the child was concerned, the Jesuits in Brazil early became rivals of the patriarch as they had done with regard to the enslaved Indians.

But the education of the Jesuits, even though it might diminish the authority of the master of the Big House over the child, employed the same methods of domination, although pursuing different ends. There was the same determination to break down the individuality of the child, with a view to making passive and subservient adults. Passive vis-à-vis the Lord of Heaven and Earth and the Holy Mother Church, and not so much toward the flesh-and-blood father and mother.

Whence the terrible, though subtle, tactics of the Jesuit teachers in persuading the Indians to give them their young ones, the white settlers to entrust them with their children, to educate them all in their boarding schools in the fear of God and the Mother Church, and later to launch the children, educated in this fashion, against their own parents. Making them more the children of themselves, the Jesuits and the Church, than of the chieftains and the mestizo mothers, than of the lords and ladies of the plantation or the city.

It was in the great barracks of stone and cement, in which the first schools of the Jesuits were established, that the first educated men of Brazil were trained, those who were to become the first university graduates, the first magistrates, priests, judges, men of the city rather than of the country or the backwoods. The literary culture which made its precocious appearance in colonial Brazil is deeply indebted to them.

The organizers or consolidators of civil and intellectual life in Brazil, the revolutionists of Bahía and Vila Rica, the poets, orators, writers of colonial days had nearly all studied with the Jesuits. The desire for the bachelor's degree was early awakened in the Brazilian youth by the Jesuits.

The judge's robe gave a nobility of its own to the pale adolescent who came from the Jesuit "playing fields." It foreshadowed the university graduate of the nineteenth century who was to bring about abolition and the republic, with the support of even bishops, generals, and barons of the Empire, all of them somewhat bedazzled by the brilliance of an academic title.

But all that precocious and somewhat melancholy learning emphasizes once more the fact that the Jesuits imposed it on the more intelligent children of the colonists and the little ones wrested from the Indian settlements by stern discipline and a policy of "spare the rod and spoil the child," a tradition that remained in force in the religious schools until the end of the nineteenth century.

The Jesuits, it must be repeated, in the sixteenth century gave exaggerated importance to the intelligent child with a literary bent, metamorphosing him into an almost sacred being in the eyes of his elders, who were filled with admiration for those sons so brilliant, so gifted at speaking, so superior to themselves in attainments. But this artificial status was achieved by sacrificing the child's childhood, stifling his spontaneity, drying up the wellsprings of his youth. And it was with punishment and privations that, later on, other religious orders, which also took over the teaching of children, made their schools even more gloomy than those of the Jesuits. The Jesuits failed in part in their valiant opposition to the patriarchal system of the Big House, to the excessive domination of the son by the father, of the individual by the family. But these other schools coincided with the very moment of the decline of the paternal authority in Brazil. Or of its disintegration to the benefit of the greater power of the Church.

Caraça became a sinister landmark in the social panorama of Brazil during the early years of the Empire, snatching children from the plantations (where, though they were treated like pariahs by the grown-ups of the Big House, they were monarchs of the sugar mill, the stables, lording it over the young Negroes, the chickens, sheep, horses, oxen), the remote ranches, the suburban estates, the city dwellings. They were turned into boarding pupils of a great lugubrious school, off in the mountains, with damp classrooms whose walls were covered with pictures of St. Luis Gonzaga, with gentle feminine eyes, a stalk of lilies in his hand, with images of St. Anthony, St. Joseph, the Virgin, and St. Vincent in all the study halls. These rooms resembled sacristies, the air heavy with incense and withered flowers. And above all, the fathers, the fearsome friars, who, instead of the stalk of lilies St. Luis carried in his girlish hand, carried locust ferules and quince switches.

"Caraça!" "I'm going to send you to Caraça!" Old residents of Minas Gerais, of Rio de Janeiro, and the North tell that it was a name that made the bravest youngsters quake. "Caraça," a historian recalled some years ago who was making a survey of the students who had studied in the school at the time of its greatest prestige, which was also that of the greatest severity of the fathers, "was an execrated name." [4]

But it was not alone to the sadism of the brutal teachers that the child was exposed in the convent schools or in seminaries or boarding schools of which Caraça became the symbol. They ate badly in these religious schools, there was much fasting, and the boys were always hungry. It is apparent that more than one director of a religious school found theological grounds to economize on the students' food.

It seems that the situation improved, in certain hygienic aspects, in state schools like the Pedro II Secondary School of Rio de Janeiro, and certain private ones. Schools with the names of saints—St. Luis Gonzaga, Saint Genevieve, St. Joseph—but without the air of seminaries, and situated in the most important cities of the Empire and not in the isolation of the hills. So it was easier to introduce improvements made possible by urban development: sanitary facilities and bathtubs, for example. In Saint Genevieve in Recife in the middle of the nineteenth century the students were obliged to take a bath once

---

[4] *Rev. Arq. Pub. Min.*, XII (Belo Horizonte, 1907), p. 249.

a week and wash their feet every night. They dressed like men; on holidays, a frock coat and black trousers; for daily wear, a black jacket and white trousers.

Nevertheless, the importance of the seminaries and Jesuit schools in Brazilian society during its most difficult epochs of integration can never be sufficiently stressed; the sixteenth and seventeenth centuries along the entire seaboard, the eighteenth century in the inland region. These were centuries given to excesses, uprisings, revolts, the preponderance of material over spiritual values, and of the interests of the family, or the head of the family, over the general welfare. One of the most powerful factors in that integration was the influence of these schools upon the sons of the rich and the young mestizos, and through them on the more refractory social and cultural elements of the population.

The students who had studied in these religious schools brought an element of civility and universality to a medium powerfully influenced by the autocrats of the Big Houses and the more patriarchal mansions of the city or inland towns. In their attire and mode of living they represented the growing tendency toward the prevalence of European ideas and city manners as against the rustic or turbulently rural ambiance, often personified in their own fathers, or in the whiter elements of the population, full of prejudices about purity of lineage and color. Many of the pupils of such religious schools were mestizos of various origins—bastards and orphans whom the friars often took in, or the Portuguese state of the colonial epoch, in this a forerunner of ultra-modern ideas, turned over to worthy families, paying them a certain allowance for the children's upbringing, as attested by old documents preserved in the Public Archives of Minas Gerais. Orphans raised by such families were often later educated by the friars.

The number of illustrious figures of the colonial period and the early years of the Empire who received their primary and secondary education in religious schools far exceeded that of those who had been educated at home by chaplains and resident priests. They represented something subtly urban, ecclesiastical, and universal—the Church, Latin, the classics, Europe, the awareness of another life beyond that dominated by the stern regard of the master of the house from his eyrie, a house so exclusively his that he changed the patron saints of the family chapel at will.

The Marquis of Recife was educated at home, and probably most of his forebears, members of the rustic gentry, the sugar barons, the Paes Barretos, and many of the Albuquerques and Cavalcantis, who when they reached adolescence went almost straight from their backwoods plantations to Coimbra or French, German, English universities, where a number of them studied philosophy, mathematics, law, and medicine. Of Joaquim Caetano da Silva,[5] from the southernmost part of Brazil, it is said that he was known in Montpellier as "the infant prodigy." Joaquim Nabuco, too, received his early education at home, under the supervision of his godmother, the mistress of Massangana plantation.

But it was in the religious schools that the majority of the outstanding figures in politics, literature, and science of colonial and First-Empire Brazil received their education.

The influence of the religious schools, as well as of the private teaching of chaplains, resident priests, plantation bookkeepers, was of maximum importance in restraining the marked differentiation between the language of Brazil and Portugal. This differentiation took on alarming proportions in the agrarian zones, not only the more outlying, but also the more patriarchal, where the Negro slave lived in the house, a member of the family. Even today members of certain illustrious plantation families can be identified by special defects of pronunciation which they picked up from the Negro house servants. In other regions the manner of speaking is characterized by a peculiar intonation, nearly always slow, but without tenderness, a nasal, complaining drawl. A manner of speaking "wearisome and somniferous," as Father Lopes Gama observed with regard to "the language of the ignorant" used by many of our people.

Naturally, the priest-tutor was almost a purist, aiming at a language in the Big House or city mansion which should not have a trace of the speech of the Negro. Uncontaminated by the slave quarters or the shanties. Identical with that of Portugal. However slight our sympathy for the purism of language, with its sacrifice of spon-

---

[5] Nineteenth-century Brazilian historian and scholar.

taneity, it does inspire a touch of horror to think of the lengths to which the corruption of Portuguese would have gone in the patriarchal country houses and city dwellings, if the protection of the purity of the language and, consequently, its unity, and the unity of Brazilian culture as a whole, had not been carried on by the Jesuits in their schools since the sixteenth century. It was mainly through their teaching that this strand of integration was kept strong and alive.

The unifying action of the language—unifying and at the same time purifying, urbanizing, Europeanizing—was carried on in the religious schools in the most intelligent manner. At least in those of which the Seminary of Mariana, in the center of the country, was representative. Saint-Hilaire remarked, at the beginning of the nineteenth century, that it had gentled the habits of the people of Minas Gerais, coarsened by their avidity for gold.[6] And in the North, the seminary, which was also the College of Pernambuco, founded in the city of Olinda by Bishop Azeredo Coutinho, performed the same duty.

This was a type of school which was no longer that of the Jesuits, with their excessive emphasis on the teaching of rhetoric, literature, and religion, a teaching, in a sense, almost anti-Brazilian. On the contrary, Azeredo Coutinho brought to the teaching not only of small and adolescent boys in the Seminary of Olinda, but of little girls and young ladies in the Academy of Our Lady of Glory, in the city of Recife, a new attitude, much gentler than that of the fathers of the Company of Jesus and the State teachers. Far more human in its understanding of the Brazilian milieu, of the defects to be corrected and the virtues to be fostered.

It is surprising to find in a priest of the eighteenth century, even though he be Azeredo Coutinho, the descendant of an illustrious family of Paraiba do Sul, and educated in Coimbra, ideas so far in advance of his time regarding the relations between adults and children. In a period when the accepted rule was to treat the child as though he were a devil, once the phase of adoring him as an angel was over, Azeredo Coutinho pleaded on behalf of the little ones that they be regarded simply as human beings. With regard to inquisitive

---

[6] Auguste Saint-Hilaire: *Voyage dans l'Intérieur du Brésil*, I (Paris, 1830), pp. 163–4.

children, for example—probably the ones who suffered most under the patriarchal system, as well as that of the Jesuits, who saw in their curiosity not only a lack of respect for their elders, but the undermining of what to the Jesuits was the supreme angelic attribute: memory —the Bishop of Pernambuco urged that under no circumstances should the adult give the impression that he considered the child's many questions importunate, "but, on the contrary, it is advisable to show him that it gives pleasure to answer them."

But it is even more extraordinary to see Dom José Joaquim da Cunha de Azeredo Coutinho recommending an almost psychoanalytical approach to teachers dealing with nervous girls who wept over the least trifle or were frightened or homesick: "Certain girls display fear over the slightest thing, or indescribable timidity, which often seem characteristics of their sex when they are nothing but the effects of the education they have received, instilling fear in them from a tender age to hush them up or keep them quiet." The remedy was to make them aware of their error, "until they could laugh at their own timidity." [7]

It may fittingly be recalled that the bishop gave to the teaching in the Seminary of Olinda—"later considered the best secondary school in Brazil," says Oliveira Lima—a character that was almost scandalous in its day. Instead of teaching only religion and rhetoric, grammar and Latin, it began to give instruction in applied sciences, which made the pupils better fitted to meet the problems of their milieu, where the transition from agrarian patriarchalism to a more urban and more industrial way of life called for trained technicians and not merely Negro and mulatto mechanics and artisans who carried on the peninsular tradition of the Moors, or the African of their forefathers. The state of flux also called for the study of the economic problems to which mining, industrialization, the decline of an economy based on a monoculture or monopoly gave rise—another aspect of the Brazilian situation which Azeredo Coutinho seems to have grasped admirably.

Tollenare found a certain resemblance between the Seminary of

---

[7] "Estatutos do Recohlimento da Nossa Senhora da Gloria, Recife," in A. do Carmo Baretta: *Um Grande Sabio, Um Grande Patriota, Um Grande Bispo* (Pernambuco, 1921).

Olinda and the French *lycées* of the provinces, with students not being prepared for the clergy but for other professions; boys who wished to study the humanities; and studying not only Latin and philosophy, but mathematics, physics, drawing. This was the orientation given by Azeredo Coutinho, who in this way broke with the lingering Jesuit tradition in colonial teaching.

This was not the case of the schools which during this same period —the close of the eighteenth century and the beginning of the nineteenth—were taking the place of the former Jesuit schools in Rio de Janeiro. Luccock, at any rate, had a poor impression of the Seminary of St. Joaquin. And one of the things that impressed him most was its backwardness in the field of science; its teaching was still literary and ecclesiastic. Jesuitically literary. Another thing which horrified him was the sadness of the children. Silent, sickly, sunken-eyed children.

It was their precocity. It was the pressure of a sadistic pedagogy on the orphan, the rejected, the pupil whose father was still living but allied with the teacher in the endeavor to oppress the child. Both of them, father and teacher, enemies of the child and desirous of turning him into a man as quickly as possible. The child himself was his own enemy, wanting to be a man before his time.

The nickname the natives of Rio de Janeiro gave to the pupils of St. Joaquin is very expressive: sheep. Little sheep. Silent, sad-eyed, without a will of their own, they were indeed veritable sheep. And the uniform they wore heightened the resemblance: a white cassock with a red cross on the breast and a belt of black braid.

In the days of the Empire, when the cassock as a school uniform had disappeared, the scholars continued to be sad children, now dressed in a black frock coat, like men, some of them already habitual smokers, and even takers of snuff, according to Father Gama. The school curriculum had become less religious, but life there was still sad. And the pedagogical trend of colonial days still prevailed, which was to hasten the child's maturity and encourage precocity. Dom Pedro II himself was an example of such precocity; at the age of fifteen he was already Emperor, surrounded by middle-aged ministers with flowing beards, among whom he, too, as soon as it was possible, appeared with a thick golden beard covering his breast.

A deserter from childhood, which he seems to have left without any regrets, Pedro II was, nevertheless, the champion of Youth against Age in the struggle between the rural patriarchy and the rising generations of college and university graduates which characterized his reign. Between the elders of the Big House, accustomed to imposing their authority by reason of an almost mystical prestige of age, and the young men just graduated from the academies of São Paulo and Olinda, or from Paris, Coimbra, Montpellier. Young men to whom learning, the humanities, science with its keys to the future, were beginning to lend new prestige in Brazilian society.

As yet this curious aspect of the Second Empire has not been examined, the sudden valuation of the youth of twenty, pale with study, like a Talmudic scholar. A valuation encouraged by the young Emperor in a kind of solidarity of generation and culture. To which must be added the fact that the young men represented a new social and juridical approach, of which the Emperor was a symbol, toward the powerful interests of the rural patriarchy, at times rebellious and separatist, anti-national and anti-juridical.

It is true that in the closing days of the colony the motherland, in open conflict with the oligarchies represented in the legislative bodies, with the great plantation owners, with the magnates of the mines, was sending out as governors of the more overweening captaincies young men, some twenty or thirty years old, such as the Count of Valladares. Men whose youth scandalized the elders of the Big Houses, whose pride they were coming to lay low, whose prestige, based partly on age, they were coming to destroy. But it was with Pedro II that this tendency became manifest, and that young men systematically began to occupy posts which had previously been entrusted to old men with long experience of life. To be sure, these youths, once in the saddle, imitated their elders in every way, and disguised their lack of years as best they could.

Even so, their ascent of the social and political ladder was not achieved without the hostility or, at least, the resistance of the older generation. They were imposed on it by the will of the Emperor, who perhaps saw in the men of his generation and of his own cultural and juridical formation his natural allies in his policy of urbanization and centralization, of order and peace, of tolerance and justice. A policy which ran counter to the abuses of turbulent individualism and the predominance of the clan, and, consequently, to the most cherished interests of the agrarian oligarchy which still dominated our social landscape at the beginning of Dom Pedro's somewhat anti-patriarchal reign.

If Pedro II began his reign in the shadow of certain renowned elder statesmen from colonial days and from the inland plantations, it was not long before this blond adolescent, born and brought up in the city instead of a rustic palace, and eager to take the reins of government in his own hands, showed himself as one of the firmest rulers who had yet governed Brazil. He had little fear of the plantation oligarchs. What he feared more was what Europeans thought about him. Europeans who lived in mansions in Paris and London.

Schooling and book learning developed in Brazil at the cost of the well-rounded development of the individual. And it is worth pointing out that the young men who during the reign of Pedro II assumed such importance in politics, letters, public administration, law, were characterized by an almost romantic note of delicate health.

It was not only that they were sickly; they took a voluptuous delight in their ailments. The older men took on the stature of giants compared with the frail youths, victims of "gastritis, encephalitis, bronchitis, pneumonia, spleenitis, pericarditis, colitis, cephalagra, hypertrophy, cardialgia, and the whole gamut of nervous disorders," which as early as 1839 Father Lopes Gama was ridiculing. "A young man in other days," he wrote, alarmed at the sight of so many hollow-eyed fellows, so many sickly youths, "was a Hercules; what fine color, what strength, what agility, what liveliness, what health! Now what one sees are young men who can hardly be distinguished from an Egyptian mummy." [8]

It became so elegant to "enjoy" poor health that young ladies of fashion of the early nineteenth century spent their time leeching themselves, eating nothing but chicken broth and sago porridge. And the young men tried to look like the conventional Jesus of the scenes of the Crucifixion.

Father Gama was greatly concerned about the young men of his time. At sixteen they already had side whiskers "fit to frighten people (excepting the young ladies); by the time they reached twenty-five they were suffering from a multitude of ailments and many of them were dying of old age by the time they were thirty."

---

[8] Lopes Gama: *Op. cit.*

It became almost as pleasant to die at twenty, or thirty, as to die an angel, before reaching seven. To die old was for the bourgeoisie, for the rich planters, for the obese vicars, for the favorite plantation slaves. "Geniuses" died young and, if possible, of tuberculosis. Health was not for them. Nor vigor, nor to be well-fleshed. And the "geniuses" collaborated in their own demise. They consumed quantities of brandy. They associated with prostitutes. They picked up syphilis in their cheap orgies. As Sylvio Romero remarked, "they had their program," the first article of which was plenty of cognac, and the second, libertinism in general.[9]

Romantically ailing though they were, or dying in their twenties or thirties—or, like José de Alencar and Gonçalves, at the age of forty—young men were replacing the healthy old men and filling the most important posts in the administration, government, courts, and diplomacy of the Second Empire.

It seems indisputable that the public administration of Brazil suffered as a result of the appointment by the Emperor of young men as provincial governors, without other preparation than their university background and their book learning. Brilliant and cultivated though they were, they lacked that down-to-earth common sense, that balance, that stability, the perspective which experience alone can give, that profound political realism with which the majority of the captains-general the Portuguese government sent out to its American colony were endowed. Many of these colonial administrators were of a stature that ranked with the greatest England or France were later to produce. Statesmen of rare astuteness, such as the Count of Assumar in Minas Gerais, Dom Thomaz de Mello in Pernambuco, the Count of Arcos in Bahía, the Count of Cunha in Rio de Janeiro.

By 1838, when the young men of Olinda and São Paulo, with their "juridical romanticism," were taking over the posts formerly held by those old realistic politicians, some whose eyes were weary with all they had seen but who did not let themselves be deceived by appearances, whose ears were growing deaf with all they had heard but who never let themselves be taken in by words of intrigue or plot, João

---

[9] Sylvio Romero: *Historia da literatura brasileira,* 4th ed., III (Rio de Janeiro, 1949), p. 376. See also T. H. Montenegro: *Tuberculose e Literatura* (Rio de Janeiro, 1950).

Gualberto dos Santos Reis was already asking where "were those so-called old fogies," renowned "for their strength of character, their good sense, their mettle?" The old captains, magistrates, judges, the good men and true.[1]

They were leaving the stage. The triumph of the young was becoming pronounced and accelerated. The Church itself was bestowing the bishop's crosier on priests and friars who still had the appearance of novitiates.

With the social and political rise of these young men, respect for age, which until the beginnings of the nineteenth century had been almost a religious cult, began to wane. This marked the decline of patriarchalism, the discredit of the fearsome grandfathers, the discredit of the "Sir Father," who was becoming simply "Father" or "Papa." It was the emancipation of the child from the tyranny of the adult, of the student from the tyranny of the teacher. The son was rebelling against the father, the grandchild against the grandsire. It was the beginning of what Joaquim Nabuco called the "neocracy": "the abdication of fathers to sons, of maturity to adolescence . . ." A phenomenon which he regarded as "exclusively ours," [2] when it would seem, with all its excesses, to be typical of every transition from patriarchalism to individualism.

---

[1] A. J. de Mello Moraes: Op. cit.; also *A Independencia e o Imperio do Brasil* (Rio de Janeiro, 1877).

[2] Joaquim Nabuco: "O dever dos Monarquistas. Carta ao Almirante Jaceguay" (Rio de Janeiro, 1895), pp. 18–19.

CHAPTER IV

WOMAN AND MAN

I<small>T WAS ALSO</small> characteristic of the patriarchal regime for man to make of woman a being as different from himself as possible. He, the strong, she, the weak; he the noble, she, the beautiful. But the beauty he prized was a somewhat morbid beauty. The delicate, almost sickly girl. Or the plump, soft, domestic, motherly woman, ample of hips and buttocks. Without a trace of masculine vigor and agility, with the greatest possible differentiation in figure and dress between the two sexes.

Perhaps the psychological reasons for preferring this type of soft, plump woman had economic roots, principally the desire (concealed, naturally) of eliminating possible competition by women for the economic and political control wielded by men in patriarchal societies.

The exploitation of woman by man, characteristic of other types of society or social organization too, but notably of the patriarchal-agrarian type which prevailed for a long time in Brazil, is favored by marked specialization or differentiation of the sexes. This justifies a double standard of morality, permitting man complete freedom in the pleasures of carnal love and only permitting the woman to go to bed with her husband when he feels like procreating. And for the woman this pleasure goes hand in hand with the obligation to conceive, give birth to, and raise the child.

This double standard of morality allows the man every opportunity for initiative, social intercourse, contacts of many sorts, while it limits those of the woman to domestic duties and activities, to contacts with her children, relatives, nurses, old women, slaves. And from time to time, in a Catholic society such as that of Brazil, with her confessor.

In the light of certain more generally accepted findings of psychoanalysis, the confessional in patriarchal society, where the reclusion or oppression of woman is the norm, may be credited with serving a useful hygienic function, or, to be more exact, one of mental therapy. Through it many anxieties, many repressed desires find their outlet, which otherwise would fester within the oppressed and repressed person.

Many a Brazilian woman was probably saved from insanity, which seems to have had a higher incidence among the women of the Puritan colonies in North America than among us, thanks to the confessional. Pyrard, who visited Brazil in the seventeenth century, was struck in Bahía by the number of women who went to confession, and deduced from this that sin must flourish among them. Their sinning was neither greater nor more frequent than among European women of the same period, only more toxic for the poor sinners, condemned to a more recluded and segregated existence than those of Western Europe, who were by this time frankly bourgeois. Confession was a way of relieving, purging themselves. It was a cathartic for their nerves, and not merely for their souls, longing for heaven, where their little angel children were awaiting them.

Thus the plantation or ranch mistress, and even the lady of the town house in Brazil, became an artificial, morbid being. A sickly person, deformed by her role of servant to her men and doll of flesh and blood to her husband.

Nevertheless, there were magnificent examples of extremely able women in town mansion as well as in plantation house. As I have already pointed out, it is to the early plantation mistresses who had come out from Portugal that the Brazilians owe a series of comforts in their way of living, of happy assimilations and adaptations, of ancillary cultural values. These assimilations, adaptations, and combinations of values were later to distinguish the areas colonized by married folk from those in which the Portuguese established themselves alone, unmarried, or, at least, without the company of white women. What happened was that in the rugged early days of the settlement of the coast, when men and women were confronted with an awe-inspiring virgin land waiting to be conquered, women enjoyed greater freedom of action. And this greater freedom of action took the form of a variety of creative activities. It was during this period of relative nondifferentiation that one of the important captaincies—New Lusitania—was governed by an illustrious matron, Dona Brites, the wife of Duarte Coelho.

But throughout the entire patriarchal period—when delicate women spent their days indoors, sewing, lolling in the hammock, tasting and passing opinion on preserves and jellies, calling for their slave girls, playing with their lapdogs, watching male visitors through the crack of the door, smoking cigarettes and sometimes cigars, bearing children and dying in childbirth—there were also women, especially plantation mistresses, with a fund not merely of domestic but of social energy greater than that of most men. The energy to run a plantation, as did Dona Joaquina do Pompeu; to direct the political activities of the family throughout an entire region, like Dona Francisca de Rio Formoso; martial energy, such as that the matrons of Pernambuco displayed during the war with the Dutch, not only on the two marches on Alagoas and Bahía, through the jungle and across deep rivers, but also in Tejucupapo,[1] where tradition has it that they fought bravely against the heretics.

Langsdorff, early in the nineteenth century, visited a plantation in Mato Grosso where the man of the house was a woman. An enormous matron, five foot eight inches tall, with a body proportionate to her height, wearing a gold chain about her neck. Though in her fifties she went everywhere, on foot or horseback, bellowing orders to her men, managing the sugar mill, the cane fields, the herds, the slaves.[2] Compared to her, her brother the priest was almost like a girl.

Plantation mistresses of this Amazon stripe, though rare, were not unusual in the days of the Empire. Several families preserve the tradi-

---

[1] Site of a battle in the seventeenth century between Portuguese Brazilians and Dutch, in which women are said to have taken an active part.

[2] A. d'Escragnolle Taunay: "A Expedição do Consul Langsdorff ao Interior do Brasil," *Rev. Inst. Hist. Geog. Br.*, Rio de Janeiro, XXXVIII, p. 337; H. Florence: "Viagem de Langsdorff," XXXVIII, p. 231.

tion of grandmothers who were virtual queens and who managed plantations almost the size of kingdoms; widows who preserved and often increased their wealth; matriarchs who had their armed retainers, executed their own justice, were "conservatives" or "liberals."

There are instances of sons who took the surname of their mothers, not only because they were of more illustrious family than their fathers and enjoyed the prestige of greater wealth, but also because of their capacity for action.

The complex of sweet and amiable traits attributed exclusively to the feminine sex was like the complex of passive and inferior qualities of the Negro, similarly ascribed to the physical or psychological factor of race under the regime of slavery, and even today. The truth of the matter is that the "typing" of woman in the role of a frail, neurotic, sensual, religious, romantic being, or a fat, practical housewife in patriarchal and slaveholding societies, was largely due to economic factors or, earlier, to social and cultural factors, which repressed her, deformed her, widening her hips, narrowing her waist, rounding her figure in keeping with the taste of the dominant sex in a society organized on the basis of exclusive domination by one class, one race, and one sex.

It is not true that sex alone determines the division of labors, assigning to man the extra-domestic activities, and to woman, the domestic. Thus, among the Amerindian societies found by the Portuguese on their arrival in Brazil, the activities of the woman were far from being limited to her domestic tasks; on the contrary, there came within her province social activities generally regarded as masculine.

In primitive societies of this sort, in contrast to those of patriarchal structure, there is a physical resemblance between man and woman, a tendency of the two sexes to become integrated in a single figure, which did not pass unnoticed by some of the early chroniclers and observers of the Amerindian population, whose observations were to be confirmed by investigators of the nineteenth century and our own day. Ave-Lallemant says, referring to our Botocudos,[3] that men and women did not exist among them but men-women and women-men. Professor Colini collected interesting data, in this connection, which

---

[3] Tribe of Indians of eastern Brazil. The name first appeared in the writings of Prince Maximilian von Neuwied. A few have become civilized, but the bulk, between 12,000 and 14,000, are still the wildest of savages.

appear in his study on the Caduveos.[4] And certain of Von den Stein-en's remarks on the Bororos [5] are also pertinent.[6]

Mathias and Mathilde Vaërting state in their thoughtful study, *Die weibliche Eigenart in Männerstaat und die mannliche Eigenart in Frauenstaat* (Karlsruhe, 1923), that not only among certain punitive societies, but among the Laplanders as well, traces may be found of a period when domestic labors were performed by men and the extra-domestic tasks by women. The women were lean and angular; the men fat, voluptuous, and curved. It must have been a period of a somewhat Amazonian organization, with the female politically dom-inant over the male. Almost a matriarchal system, without being strictly a matriarchy, such as that brought to Brazil by certain of the African slaves who were not always easily adaptable to the division of labor on the basis of sex.

Even though the indication or suggestion of an Amazonian organi-zation among certain primitive societies, matronymic rather than ma-triarchal, is questionable, it is clear, as more than one anthropologist has pointed out, that women appear to be physically stronger than men in certain African societies where the harder tasks are performed by women and the lighter by men.

Among the majority of the Indians of Brazil, the situation must have been similar: the woman almost the equal of the man in physical attributes. For, inasmuch as the agricultural labors fell to her, her physique was not that of the anemic, housebound woman of the pa-triarchal regime.

Under a regime in which one sex is dominated by the other, this tendency toward the single or common type of woman-man or man-woman, so characteristic of primitive societies, disappears. The dif-ference between the sexes is so accentuated under a patriarchal sys-tem that it becomes shameful for a man to resemble a woman and

---

[4] Indian tribe that inhabits border area between Brazil and Paraguay on the west bank of the Paraguay River. They are famous for their painted pottery. The faces and sometimes the entire body of men and women are elaborately tattooed.

[5] Tribe of Indians of unknown origin in the states of Matto Grosso and Goyaz in eastern Brazil. They are semi-nomads and hunters.

[6] Ave-Lallemant: *Reise durch Nord-Brazilien in Jahre 1859* (Leipzig, 1860). See also Von den Steinen: *Entre os Aborigenes do Brasil Central* (São Paulo, 1940), Chap. 17.

unseemly for a woman to resemble a man. The same thing probably held true of the matriarchal regime, if it ever existed, complete and orthodox, as some believe.

But a whole series of facts justifies us in deducing that the artificiality or unhealthiness of the type of fragile or languid woman created by the patriarchal system of society in Brazil engendered not only an exaggerated code of etiquette, but also a profoundly erotic literature, with its Elviras, Clarices, Dolores, Idalinas, at times idealized beyond belief, at others extolled for the attributes of their bodies for physical love. For their delicate feet. For their dainty hands. Their tiny waist. Their high, round breasts. For all that conveyed or accentuated their physical contrast to men; their quality of a living doll to be fondled by man, by the imagination of the poet and the hands of the male.

The cult of woman, reflected in this etiquette and this literature, as well as in an equally erotic art—cloyingly sweet music, romantic painting, sculpture whose only interest was its prettiness or nudity (not the pure, but the suggestive); this cult of woman, examined a little more closely, is perhaps a form of narcissism on the part of the patriarchal man, of the dominant sex, who makes use of his woman— her feet, her hands, her hair, her throat, her legs, her breasts—as of something warm and sweet which soothes him, excites him, and stimulates his voluptuousness and pleasure. He approaches this soft, delicate creature, pretending to adore her, but in reality to affirm himself.

The feet of Brazilian ladies of the upper classes were often deformed in their anxiety to keep them small, in contrast to those of the Negresses, as a rule large, wide, coarse. Woman's waist, which, in an epoch not far removed from our own, was narrowed even in Europe by artificial means, among us was laced in to the point of exaggeration. Hair, worn in braids, coils, loose, in the most elaborate coiffures of a complication and size beyond belief, held or adorned by combs, was another sex symbol which Brazilian women carried to a ridiculous degree. Men wore flowing mustaches and whiskers. These were fashions almost as typical of Brazilian patriarchalism as they had been of the Chinese, the Hebrew, the Arabian. In Rio de Janeiro the first leading man to appear on the stage without beard or mustache—and this was at the close of the Second Empire—was loudly booed. That was not a man—that was a transvestite!

The woman of the patriarchal era in Brazil—mainly of the city mansion—even though she went about the house in chemise and bedroom slippers, without stockings, took great pains with her attire when she appeared before men on festive occasions or at church, emphasizing her difference, not only from the opposite sex, but from women of another class or race, by the excess of adornments, ruffles, lace, feathers, ribbons, jewelry. Gabriel Soares had already noted in the sixteenth century how the wives of rich Brazilians overdid the use of silks and fine fabrics; the author of the *Dialogues*, a chronicle of the seventeenth century, remarked how they painted their faces; and Father Cardim spoke of the excessive use by the ladies of Pernambuco of silks, velvets, jewels. The art of lacemaking was highly developed, and the use of feathers to trim ladies' hats; of gold charms, bracelets, rings, earrings, eardrops. There was no lack of craftsmen in these fields during the period of splendor, and even decline, of the patriarchal regime, and the work of some of them was admired by foreigners who were capable of distinguishing between our confused aesthetic values.

These crafts, before they became industrialized around the middle of the nineteenth century, were, with the exception of the goldsmith's art, domestic crafts with which the so-called "ringed hands," the hands of refined ladies in their long and boring hours of isolation, busied themselves.

The Vaërtings are of the opinion that idleness stimulates eroticism in woman. And that, in the man's absence, eroticism, thus encouraged, finds an outlet in or is sublimated by exaggerated self-ornamentation.[7]

Andrew Grant, after commenting on the luxury displayed in public by men of standing in colonial Brazil, says: "Such is their love of shew and finery, that the sumptuary laws for the regulation of dress are wholly evaded . . . At home most of them wear either a thin night-gown or a jacket, while others go about in shirt and drawers." He then goes on to say of the women of the same class: "The hair, which is suffered to grow to a great length, is fastened in a knot on the crown of the head, and loaded with powder of tapioca . . .

---

[7] M. and M. Vaërting: *The Dominant Sex. A Study in Sociology of Sex Differentiation* (London, 1923).

Their chief ornament consists of a gold chain, passed two or three times round the neck, and hanging down the bosom . . . The superior workmanship of these chains, and the number and value of the ornaments attached to them, indicate the rank of the wearer."

Wetherell, in his *Stray Notes*, observes that in Bahía during the first half of the nineteenth century the colored women for the most part wore their hair short and covered with a turban, a fashion which seemed to him a manifestation of cleanliness in a country where the hair of even aristocratic ladies was full of lice, but which they nevertheless let grow as long as possible as a mark of their social standing. The native-born Negresses and the mestizas, as a rule, let their hair grow, as though to show that they were of higher rank than those who used a turban.

The Brazilian-born Negroes, in contrast to those of Africa, whose hair was usually cropped short, took great pride in "parting their hair." In parting their hair, which they allowed to grow, and in wearing shoes often as expensive as those used by whites or, at least, carrying them in their hand. If they did not wear them all the time, it was because they hurt their feet.

DeGabriac recalled, in his *Promenade à travers l'Amérique du Sud* (Paris, 1868), having seen many Africans in Belem do Pará, some of them slaves of the fine city residences and the beautiful nearby country estates. There were some, however, who were free, and they could be distinguished, says the European observer, by their shoes, "which they alone have the right to wear and which they never fail to proudly display." As we shall see in the next chapter, well-cared-for hair and well-shod feet were, in patriarchal Brazil, the vainglory of the white race or the upper class—or, at least, the free class—more than of the fair sex.

The lady of the city mansion or the Big House spared nothing in the way of adornment to distinguish her attire from that of the women of the lower classes, and, above all, from that of the male, which in turn was heavily ornamented when, lord and master of other men, he appeared in the street or at some celebration. Content to walk about indoors in bedroom attire, in the street he displayed his decorations and insignia of rank. As well as those typical of the "stronger sex," such as spurs, sword, gold-headed cane. The first newspapers published in Brazil carried frequent advertisements of such accessories: epaulettes, uniforms, feathers, judge's robes "richly embroidered from China," "cocked hats for Knights of the Order of Christ," "elegant canes of Indian bamboo with head, ferrule, and chain of gold" for gentlemen, "court swords" for nobles.

The superadornment of the rich city dweller consisted mainly in the use of charms attached to his watch chain, of rings on most of his fingers, of gold-headed canes or sunshades, and, at times, dagger, of fancy haircuts and whiskers, of perfume on his hair, whiskers, handkerchief. At the same time, Negroes and slaves of either sex were forbidden the use of gold jewelry or charms.[8] Those female house slaves who went well dressed and covered with jewels were in the nature of an alter ego of their white mistresses when they displayed themselves in church festivities or on the street.

The free Negroes, the mestizos, and free mulattoes almost equaled the whites in their concern over having the hair well combed and shining with coconut oil. Men took as much pride in this as women; the schoolboy almost as much as the judge. Even runaway slaves are mentioned in advertisements as having "French haircut," "Nazarene beard." These must have been privileged characters.

Setting himself apart from women by certain manifestations of virility in attire, manners, voice, while at the same time setting himself apart from the slave by the almost feminine excess of ornament which marked his status of master, that is to say, a person of idleness or leisure, the patriarch, with his Moorish beard and his delicate hands covered with rings, was a combination of masculine aggressiveness and effeminate languor. In the nineteenth century—an era of bourgeois mansions rather than of plantation houses, which were still rustic fortresses—the Brazilian aristocrat, lacking heretics to combat or runaway slave settlements to destroy, became less the stronger than the noble sex. Or merely the privileged.

Exaggerating a little what certain modern sociologists call "the power relation" between the sexes, it might be said, in the words of a gaucho orator, that in rural patriarchal Brazil, in spite of sexual differentiation, man was, in certain aspects, a woman on horseback. Al-

---

[8] A typical ban forbidding slaves to use adornments or jewelry is contained in the Royal Edict of February 7, 1690. Ms Arquivo Nacional Rio de Janeiro, "Officios para os Vice-Reis do Brasil."

most as delicate as a woman, and debilitated almost as much as she by idleness and a sluggish life. And it is a curious fact that during the orthodox period of the patriarchal system—which was also that of chivalry in the purest, almost literal sense of the word—women were denied, or, at least, hampered in the use of the horse, which was looked upon as the animal of the dominant and, strictly speaking, chivalrous sex. The woman, when she left the house, almost always traveled in a curtained hammock, a palanquin, a litter, an oxcart. Rarely on horseback. It was only when rural patriarchalism began to decline that the Amazons of the plantation made their appearance: but they rode sidesaddle, almost never astride like a man.

The substitution of English and, principally, French styles for women during patriarchal days was, in part, a by-product of the influence of the young Brazilians who went abroad to study. They returned with newfangled ideas, some of which they passed on to the women.

In *O Carapuceiro* Father Lopes Gama says that "during peaceful colonial days" few Pernambucans crossed the Atlantic; and these were for the most part young men who were sent to European schools, principally Coimbra. And he added: "It was through these travelers and educated fools that the impious doctrines of the French philosophists made their way into Brazil." Doctrines and fashions. For the French influence included feminine fashions: "Our ladies, young and old, no longer want to be called anything but *Madame* and *Mademoiselle*. In attire, usages, fashions, manners, only what is French meets with approval; the result is that we now have not a single custom, a practice, anything of which we can say: this is truly Brazilian."

It has been observed in modern societies, less sociologically feudal than ours, that this divergence between the sexes during the patriarchal epoch, depends up to a point on biological factors or limitations (limitations which only a fanatical feminism or a certain Communist-Marxist mystique would try to deny) and not merely on circumstances of social formation which differ for the two sexes.

The social fact of this divergence between the sexes, the one more militant, the other more stable, undoubtedly is related to the physical make-up of the woman-mother, who leads a more sedentary existence. The tendency to depart from the norm seems to certain authorities on the subject, such as Havelock Ellis, greater in the man than in the woman, just as it seems to certain anthropologists greater in the white race than in the black. Woman, in her conservative, conformist, and collectivist tendencies, would seem to be closer to the black race —the "ladylike" race, to use the expression of the North American sociologist Park; whereas man, by reason of his individualism, his tendency to diverge from the norm, either in the sense of genius or moron, his capacity and taste for differentiation, would seem to correspond to the white race.

In Brazil these two individualistic tendencies, of race and sex, met in the patriarchal man, the creator or organizer of our social or national differentiation. This creator was for the most part the white colonist, or one with only a touch of Indian or African blood.

In patriarchal and even bourgeois Europe, fashion tended to exaggerate to a marked degree a specialization of woman's body: the broad, fecund, maternal hips and the very small waist. Topinard was perhaps the first to observe with the eyes of an anthropologist this accentuation of the difference between the bodies of man and woman with the advance of "human progress," or what he considered human progress.[1]

Not only the form of the human body became altered, but the tone and vigor of the person and his appurtenances, such as chairs and beds. Formerly there was less "gastritis," "enteritis," "pneumonitis"; and the daughters of the household, observes Lopes Gama, "were rarely visited by a doctor; when they were ailing they had mother, grandmother, aunt, or godmother, who applied potato or bugloss poultices, or pepper enemas, or camomile tea, or fern with wild honey, and with such treatments they got well and lived to a ripe old age." There were no false teeth nor cosmetics nor bustles for women; older people did not dance or go to dances.

With urbanization, the defects or the excesses of figure incompatible with Paris or London styles were corrected by means of lotions, cosmetics, false teeth and hair, bustles, hair dyes, stays. Stays which were widely advertised in the Brazilian newspapers from early in the nineteenth century, as well as lotions, "waters," "milks" for eruptions, chafing, irritations of the skin. Many of these skin irritations

---

[1] Paul Topinard: *Eléments d'Anthropologie Générale* (Paris, 1885).

were probably the result of the immoderate use by the fashionable
city dwellers of fabrics, hats, stockings, underwear made in Europe
and intended for a climate which only that of the extreme southern
part of Brazil resembled.

If the women of the city residences suffered more from such skin
irritations than the men, it was because the life they led was even less
hygienic. These differences in their way of living may have been
responsible for more important differences between the sexes which
are attributed, like racial differences, to inherent biological factors.

That mental differences having to do with creative capacity and
the predisposition toward certain forms of activity or sensibility exist between the sexes would seem as indisputable as that similar differences exist between races. The school of Professor Boas has not
claimed, as some of its more hasty interpreters or superficial critics
assume, that differences between races are nonexistent, and that their
diversity is merely of a picturesque nature, such as the color of the
skin and the form of the body. What his followers stressed was the
error of equating racial differences with superiority or inferiority,
and, above all, the failure to take into account historic-cultural criteria in the analysis of the supposed superiority and inferiority of races.

The same historic-cultural criteria may be applied, as a number of
scholars have done, in the field of sex sociology—which should not be
confused with genetics—to the study of the supposed superiority of
man over woman.[2] But one should not try to escape one mystique by
falling into another, confusing the differences that exist between the
sexes, as do those who would deny the differences between races.

In studying the political and literary history of Brazil during the
patriarchal phase, one outstanding trait in members of the ruling class
—or the majority of them, at any rate—is the preponderance of a
subjective approach, an approach which in general is weak and mediocre. We find it in literature as well as in politics, and particularly
under the Empire. Hand in hand with this flabby subjectivity goes a
marked lack of interest in concrete, immediate, local problems. This
almost total lack of objectivity may in part be attributed to the slight
or nonexistent part played by women in artistic and political activity.

---

[2] Viola Klein: *The Feminine Character, History of an Ideology* (New
York, 1949), p. 171.

That is, if we accept, even with qualifications, the thesis of Ellis and other sexologists, that, by and large, women have a greater sense "of practical reality" than do men, as a result of predispositions engendered by what the English psychologist calls "affectability," an "affectability" possibly caused by menstruation and which expresses itself psychologically in woman's tact and capacity to adapt herself more easily than man to unforeseen circumstances.

In the English colonies of North America, the interest in concrete problems and objectivity in facing them was far greater than in Brazil, and in this attitude the collaboration of women, even though indirect, made itself felt. With George Washington, one recalls the name of Martha Washington. Such collaboration was almost entirely lacking in our statesmen and intellectuals of the patriarchal era. Almost nobody in Brazil knows the name of the wife of such prominent statesmen as José Bonifacio or Pedro de Araujo Lima.[3] The voice of the wife of an outstanding man was never heard in the drawing room when men of affairs were talking, except to ask for a new dress, to sing the fashionable air of the day, or to pray for the men. Almost never advising or suggesting anything outside the domestic sphere; almost never entering upon what was considered man's province. Very exceptional were women like Dona Veridianas da Silva Prado,[4] whose intervention in political matters surpassed that of both her husbands, even while they were still living; the few to be found— nearly all toward the close of the Empire—were, so to speak, outside the pale of patriarchal orthodoxy.

As a result, matters of general interest were dealt with, not only from the purely masculine point of view, but also from an almost exclusively masculine psychological approach, that is to say, with the predominance of the subjective over the objective. It might be observed in passing that a study of the casuistry of the Jesuit Fathers, their dealing with cases of conscience, reveals feminine mental and psychic processes which contributed to the strength and efficacy of their activity in Brazil.

The life of Brazil, its politics, literature, education, social welfare,

---

[3] A political leader of the Empire, later ennobled with the title of Marquis of Olinda.

[4] A very wealthy and intelligent woman of São Paulo who lived in the second half of the nineteenth century.

and other fields suffered from the lack of the feminine touch during the splendor and principally during the decline of the patriarchal system. Only little by little did there emerge from the purely domestic confines a type of woman who had received a little more education—the rudiments of literature, music, French, a smattering of science—to take the place of the ignorant mother whose influence on her children was almost wholly sentimental.

In letters, late in the nineteenth century, a Narcisa Amalia [5] appeared. After her, a Carmen Dolores.[6] And even later, a Julia Lopes de Almeida.[7] Before them, there was almost nothing but an occasional mediocre "blue stocking," pedantic or naïve spinsters, a few women of French background, some of them contributors to the *Almanack de Lembranças Luso-Brasileiro* (*Almanac of Luso-Brazilian Recollections*). And even so, they were rare. Nisia Floresta's [8] appearance was a startling exception: a real Amazon among the languorous ladies of the mid-nineteenth century. In a milieu where the men held as their preserve all extra-domestic activities, in which baronesses and viscountesses could barely write, and ladies of the upper classes could with difficulty spell out their books of devotion and the simplest novels, Nisia is an amazing figure. Like the Marchioness of Santos [9] or Dona Francisca do Rio Formoso [1] or Dona Joaquina do Pompeu.[2]

I have often quoted Father Lopes Gama because of his keen criticism of the habits of the town magnates. He thundered against the ladies of the early nineteenth century, who, as the result of French influence, read their innocent novels, as though they were hardened sinners. In his opinion, the good mother should not concern herself with anything but the management of her house, arising early to put the servants to their tasks, see that wood was chopped, the kitchen fire started, a fat hen killed for soup; to get the preparation of the

---

[5] A poetess of the same period.

[6] A writer of the early twentieth century.

[7] A novelist of the same period.

[8] A Brazilian woman of the mid-nineteenth century distinguished for her intellectual attainments; she lived for some time in Europe and was a friend of Auguste Comte and other European intellectuals.

[9] A lady of São Paulo who was the mistress of the Emperor Pedro I.

[1] The very able mistress of a large sugar plantation.

[2] The capable owner of a ranch in Minas Gerais.

dinner, which was served at four o'clock, underway, and supervise the sewing of the housemaids and young Negro girls, who patched, darned, made over, prepared the clothing of the household, and also made soap, candles, wine, liqueurs, preserves, jellies. But everything supervised by the white mistress, often with whip in hand.

Father Lopes Gama protested that this type of lady of the house was disappearing in the city mansions and even in some plantation houses, and was being replaced by one who was less submissive and more worldly. She got up late, after having attended the theater or a dance; she read novels; looked out at the street from her window or verandah; spent two hours at her dressing table "on her complicated coiffure"; an equal number practicing at the piano and still others at her French or dancing lesson. Far less on her devotions than in former days. Less time in the confessional. Less talk with the housemaids. Less time listening to old wives' tales. And more on novels. The family doctor had become more important than the confessor. The theater attracted the ladies of fashion more than the church. "Ladies of quality" even attended masked balls.

One of the innovations of nineteenth-century Brazil was the masked ball during carnival, in a public theater and not in a private house, or in a semi-private, semi-public center like "the country residence of Senhor Brito," where in 1846 a "country carnival was held," which was reported by the *Diario de Pernambuco* of February 19. "A country carnival" attended only by members of the household, invited guests, and their families. The atmosphere was still patriarchal and with the rustic flavor of the Big House.

The first truly public dance for persons of the upper class would seem to have been that held in the Theater of St. Peter of Alcantara in Rio de Janeiro in 1844. In 1845 the other theaters of the capital held their own masked balls, the most sumptuous being those given in the two theaters of João Caetano, that of Praia Grande and that of St. Francis of Paul. The fashion had been launched, and the aristocratic Brazilian carnival of the city, with its tradition of merrymaking, which would seem to have been of Oriental or Indian origin, gave way to the masked ball in the French or Italian manner.

In 1848 Recife made preparations to hold a grandiose masked ball, encouraged by the *Diario de Pernambuco* of February 18 in words which reflect the spirit of the new epoch: "Pernambuco, whose capi-

tal rivals the Imperial court in luxury and refinement, should not remain the victim of the prejudices of the eighteenth century, when
our windows were covered with close-woven blinds, our doors with
screens," etc., etc.

Accordingly, the Pernambucans, so that Recife should not take a
back seat to the Court, built a great pavilion or pagoda—a lingering
Oriental touch—in the capital for the masked ball of 1848. A huge
edifice, with rows of chairs on the right for the ladies, on the left for
the gentlemen. Only those wearing masks were permitted to dance.
All who came unmasked, or not "in fancy dress," occupied boxes as
mere spectators. The mask was considered sacred. No intoxicating
liquors were allowed. Nor was smoking permitted.

To be sure, this refined, fashionable silent carnival, with its silken
elegance, did not do away with the other, the common, noisy, plebeian celebration, with its opportunities for the young to give rein to
their youth, the Negroes to their Africanism (normally somewhat
repressed), for blacks, slaves, children to shout, dance, and cavort as
though they did not belong to a race, class, sex, and age oppressed by
the lords of the manor. In spite of the rule of silence, the carnival in
the public theater gave an opportunity for release to other repressed
classes in their fancy dress and beneath the masks considered "sacred."
It gave transvestites the opportunity to don woman's attire; women
of masculine inclinations, the opportunity to dress themselves as
men; men, who because of their calling or social standing were condemned to an almost funereal solemnity, the opportunity to disport
themselves, capering and dancing as though they were law students.

In a society so full of repressions, oppressions, overprotectiveness,
the carnival served, as did the confessional on a higher level, as an
outlet for repressions suffered by men, women, children, slaves, Negroes, Indians, which would otherwise have burdened many of them
beyond endurance with resentments and phobias. The masked balls
joined hands with the street revelry to effect a psychic release, as well
as a lowering of social barriers for a part of the population bound on
workdays by norms of behavior which often smothered their instinctive tendencies toward noisy diversions and sensual dances.

In the semi-patriarchal and more mundane life of the mansion
dwellers, the social horizons of many a well-born Brazilian young
lady were broadened by a variety of contacts with life beyond the

house walls. There was the theater, novels, the open windows, classes in dancing, music, French.

But the avenues of expression for the still patriarchal, and even bourgeoise woman, her opportunities for taking part in extra-domestic activities, continued minimal in the Brazil of the first half of the nineteenth century, even in those areas which anticipated the urbanization of the patriarchal system. She was still limited to graceful forms, graceful and innocuous.

In a country like Brazil at the time of the Empire, beset with problems demanding maximum objectivity, it is impossible to overstress the useful and constructive part which women who were halfway educated might have exercised through their husbands if they had been admitted to intellectual intimacy, if their qualities of tact, intuition, realism had been utilized, even indirectly, in the interpretation and solution of general problems. For many of these were psychological problems of conflict and maladjustment, and not merely economic. The activity of women like Dona Leonor Porto, Princess Isabel, Dona Olegarinha,[3] the gentle but energetic wife of José Mariano, in political causes, principally that of the abolition of slavery, cannot be considered the fullest employment of those feminine qualities.

The most common type of Brazilian woman during the Empire continued to be that of Dona Manuela de Castro, the wife of Baron de Goiana. Very kind, very generous, very devout, but happy only among her kinfolk, her close friends, her household servants, the saints of her chapel; morbidly attached to her home and family; completely indifferent to her husband's political activities and friends, even when she was invited to take part in their conversations. At most, merely brushing the sentimental fringes of patriotism and literature. Alien to the world beyond the walls of her house—family, chapel, slaves, the poor tenants of the plantation, the Negroes in the nearby shanties.

The absence of woman, not as a source of inspiration, but as the collaborator of husband, son, brother, lover, reveals itself in the aridity, the incompleteness, and even perversion to be found in certain of

---

[3] Leonor Porto and Dona Olegarinha—the latter a Brazilian aristocrat—participated actively in the movement for the abolition of slavery. Leonor Porto encouraged society women to contribute to the movement; Dona Olegarinha, it is said, sold her family jewels to help finance it.

the most important men of patriarchal and semi-patriarchal Brazil. Men like Fagundes Varela,[4] Feijo,[5] Gonçalves Dias, Tobias Barreto,[6] Raul Pompeia.[7] Men in whom the lack of a woman's intelligent collaboration or deep feminine sympathy for their labors or person seems to have given rise to a narcissism or monosexualism in intellectual and even personal aspects that bordered on the morbid.

The purely sentimental repercussion of the woman on the man was always strong in the semi-patriarchal days of the city mansions as it had been during patriarchal times on the plantation. The mother was the ally of the son against the excessively stern discipline of the father, at times so harsh in the exercise of his authority. She was his comforter, his nurse, his first love. It was she who indulged him, who sang him to sleep at night.

The influence that was lacking in the formation of the child or growing boy was that of the mother who understood the world toward which he was moving blindly and without guidance. Correa de Azevedo, in 1872, laid the blame principally at the door of "the indolent, ignorant mother," "the slave nurse," and the "immoral housemaid" for the fact that the young Brazilian became depraved so early: "syphilis in his body, debauchery in his soul . . ." "Feeding him, dressing him, putting him to bed, seeing that he gets exercise are things which these commonplace, ignorant mothers leave almost wholly to the child's whim." [8] But how could she do otherwise when she did not even know how to dress or feed herself properly, nor was she free to dress or feed herself except in keeping with the whim or will of men?

"Our boys' schools teach a great deal of French, a great deal of philosophy, but do not explain the Lord's Prayer," wrote Father Pinto de Campos in 1861. "And the situation is even more serious in girls' schools," he went on. "Woman can and should be the great re-

---

[4] A Romantic poet.

[5] Diogo Antonio Feijo, a priest and political leader of the first half of the nineteenth century, noted for his liberal ideas.

[6] Professor, writer, and poet of the nineteenth century, of Negro origin, noted for his enthusiasm for German rather than French culture.

[7] Writer of the nineteenth century, author of *O Ateneu*, a novel of social criticism.

[8] Luiz Correa de Azevedo: "A Mulher Perante o Medico," *Annaes Brasilienses de Medicina*, XXIV (Rio de Janeiro, August 1872), p. 93.

forming force; but for this there must be a change in her present position of fettered idol or reproductive machine. A nation is a congregation of families; woman is the hearth." And he concludes: "The new education for women today is exclusively that of dances, receptions, display, and those who live outside the cities, or are not wealthy, vegetate in ignorance due to the concept that woman *per se* is nothing." [9]

Accepting the differences between the sexes and the limitations of each, it would be unfair not to emphasize the responsibility of the economic regime which prevailed in Brazil for the pigeonholing of the women of city mansion and plantation house as "the fair sex" and "the weaker sex." Limiting them to the spheres of domestic duties or religious devotions. Imposing on them a humiliating physical specialization: first the frail young virgin, "pale virgin of my dreams," in the words of more than one poet. Then after marriage, "the plump, pretty woman." Or simply plump, domestic, and reproductive.

This artificial situation, whose aim was the greater social preeminence of man and his increased sexual pleasure, was brought about by means of a special system of nutrition and way of life. For the pale virgin, chicken broth, rice gruel, sweetmeats, warm baths. For the plump and pretty matron, a fattening diet, with an abundance of molasses, guava paste, cakes, jellies, pastries, chocolate, a whole gamut of dainties which the society reporters of the epoch described as being copiously consumed by Brazilian ladies. It may be that for some of them this overeating was a kind of compensation for the disappointments and frustrations of their sexual life. In both cases it was an unsound and deficient diet, which produced narrow-chested children, fourteen- and fifteen-year-old girls with deep, sunken romantic eyes, whom twenty-five- and thirty-year-old university graduates courted strolling the street in front of their houses, their eyes fixed on the verandah as on a niche or altar. Or mothers of eighteen and twenty, with a soft, puffy, unhealthy obesity. Women who died old at the age of twenty-five, at the birth of their eighth or ninth child, whose only intimacy with their husbands had been that of the marriage bed.

In 1882 Baron Torres Homem, one of the foremost doctors of the Empire, wrote that in the richest, the most illustrious mansions of Rio

---

[9] J. Pinto de Campos: *Carta (que dirigiu) ao Excelentissimo Senhor Ministro dos Negocios Eclesiasticos* (Rio de Janeiro, 1861), p. 20.

de Janeiro pulmonary tuberculosis among young girls was frequent, "one of whose causes is an inadequate diet." And he goes on to say: "As a rule in such cases the physician has to contend with the caprices of girls between fifteen and twenty who eat nothing but knickknacks all day, fruit, candy, pastries, who look with disgust at a juicy beefsteak, who cannot bear the sight of a piece of rare roast meat, and who care for nothing but tidbits which contain little nourishment and are often harmful." [1]

But the fault was not theirs. The fault lay principally with a system that imbued the unmarried girl with a sense of shame at eating hearty food. The danger she wanted to avert was not that of putting on weight, but of becoming robust, like a man. This vigor was becoming only in Negress slaves. Or at most in less worldly matrons, with their idyllic days behind them and concerned only with housekeeping and the upbringing of their children. Or for widows who had to take the place of their husbands in managing their plantations. But not for girls seeking a husband, young ladies of fashion.

Correa de Azevedo, a doctor of the middle of the nineteenth century, who was deeply concerned over problems of hygiene and education, and who openly denounced the shortcomings of the social organization of the Brazil of his day, regarded women as slaves under this regime, "a slave who has not yet received, nor will in the near future, the benefits of emancipation." She was not even a human being: "a doll from the most elegant workshop of Paris would not be adorned with more ruffles, flounces, sequins, ribbons, and colors than this pathetic creature whom they indoctrinate from a tender age with the idea that woman should be a slave of dress and outward show so she may more easily become the slave of man." [2]

These social influences, together with the inadequate diet, made themselves felt with the greatest intensity on the little girl of the city mansion. At eleven she was already a young lady, with strict "proper behavior" forced upon her which deprived her, even more than her

---

[1] J. V. Torres Homem: *Elementos de Clínica Medica* (Rio de Janeiro, 1870).

[2] Correa de Azevedo: "Concorrera o Modo por que são dirigidos entre nos a Educação e Instrucação da Mocidade para o Benefico Desenvolvimiento Fisico e Moral do Homem?" *Annaes Brasilenses de Medicina*, XXIII, 11 (Rio de Janiero, April 1872), pp. 416–40.

brother, of all freedom to run, jump, climb trees, play in the back yard, in the open air. From the time she was thirteen she was dressed like a woman, smothered in silks, ruffles, laces, wearing décolleté dresses when she went to the theater or a dance. The result of all this was consumptives, and sufferers from anemia; also the many mothers of stillborn infants—"angels"—the many who died in childbirth.

In the opinion of Correa de Azevedo, the Brazilian girl child, from the time "she was nursed at the breast of an African or Indian wet nurse, women who, as a rule, suffered from chronic irritations of the skin, hereditary or not," grew up among enemies, who, instead of shielding her, did her harm in the form "of petting, kissing, and an excess of affection which was enervating." She grew up "enveloped in tight clothing, which prevent the proper development of her internal organs, and affect the uterus, an organ which above all needs care in the early stages of a woman's development." [3] The anti-hygienic clothing continued when the girl was sent to boarding or day school, and accentuated when she became a matron or young society lady frequenting theaters and dances, or, at least, attending mass and church festivals.

As early as 1798, the doctors called upon to explain the insalubrity of the city of Rio de Janeiro mentioned the anti-hygienic life of women, more confined than men to living quarters, to boudoir, to bedroom; more sedentary, for the ladies of the city mansions rarely took any exercise; more shut in, for the house was almost Moorish or Oriental; weakened by the daily warm bath, which further enervated these already languid women. It was inevitable that tuberculosis, as well as other infirmities, should have taken such a strong grip on this well-born sector of the population.

I have already mentioned the confessional as one of the means whereby the women of patriarchal Brazil could relieve their conscience and free themselves to some degree from the pressure of father, grandfather, or husband on their personality. The supremacy of the doctor over the confessor in Brazilian family life, which began to make itself felt in the early decades of the nineteenth century, marked a new phase in the position of woman, as well as in her relations to men who were neither relatives nor husband.

---

[3] Ibid., p. 420.

The woman of the city house began to find in the doctor a distinguished masculine figure to whom she could confide, instead of to husband or priest, her ailments, her sufferings, her bodily intimacies. It is worth mentioning that in the stories of deceived husbands—relatively rare in orthodox patriarchal days in Brazil—the figure of the priestly Don Juan came to be replaced by the doctor. Tales of adultery committed on patriarchal sofas and beds were told of more than one doctor. Also the terrible surgical punishments inflicted on the doctors, and not merely on priests or friars, from whom on more than one occasion, in patriarchal days, the wrath of father or husband exacted barbarous penalties for the offense to his honor as owner of women.

The absolutism of the paterfamilias in Brazilian life—the paterfamilias who, in his purest avatar, was the plantation or ranch owner —began to fade as other masculine figures acquired prestige in the slave-based society: the doctor, for example, the priest; the director of a school; the provincial president; the chief of police, the judge; the business agent. Other institutions grew up around the Big House, diminishing its importance, overshadowing it, opposing counterbalances to its influence. There was the Church, speaking with the more independent voice of its bishops, the Government, the Bank, the School, the Factory, the Office, the Shop. With the rise of these figures and these institutions, woman, in turn, began to free herself from the excessive patriarchal authority, and together with the child and the slave achieved a higher juridical and moral status. There was also the factor of marriage of the poor university graduate, sometimes a mulatto, or the soldier of lower-class origins to the wealthy white girl, the daughter of a planter or city magnate, and this at times enhanced the wife's influence, giving rise among us to a kind of matrilinear lineage: children who took the illustrious and sonorous name of their mother—Castello Branco, Albuquerque e Mello, Rocha Wanderley, Hollanda Cavalcanti, Silva Prado, Argollo, Osorio—and not that of the father. In such cases, the element of social prestige could not fail to have moral or psychological effects favorable to the wife.

The Church, which fought so tenaciously to exercise authority over the family through the Jesuits in the first century of the colony, and was forced to capitulate in the second, defeated by the monarchs of the Big Houses, later recovered certain of its supposed rights and part of the spiritual and moral prestige it had lost as a result of the almost complete subservience of the family chaplain to the paterfamilias. But without achieving the complete domination to which it aspired over the woman and child, who, having freed themselves from the excessive oppression of the master of the house, were being affected by the new influences of doctor, school, theater, profane literature, and not only that bearing the stamp of approval of bishops and vicars.

But the Church must be listed—the Church of bishops and the Internuncio—among the forces which contributed to the decline of the patriarchalism of both plantation house and city mansion, many of which, as can be seen from newspaper advertisements of the first half of the nineteenth century, had their own oratory or chapel.

In 1886 it was the Internuncio himself, the Archbishop of Otranto, who sent a letter to the bishops on this matter, which marked an epoch in the life of the Church in Brazil; and which at the same time marked, if not the end—for the letter was held to be void by the Archbishop of Otranto's successor—certainly the decline of the era when the chaplain subordinated himself to the patriarch and hardly heeded his prelate, and the beginning of a new type of relationship between the patriarchal establishment and the Church, and between priest and bishop. Sanctions were issued against the celebration of the mass in private homes, in family oratories, and infractions were to be punished by the suspension of *ad celebratione Missae*.[4]

The forbidding of the celebration of the mass in the private chapels of ranches, plantations, country homes, and city mansions, which was a direct blow at patriarchal authority, must have been particularly hard on the more sedentary women, the mothers of families who almost never left the house. But it should be pointed out that private chapels existed not only on isolated plantation manors, but in suburban mansions, almost inside the cities, as well as in certain city dwellings of Rio de Janeiro, Bahía, Recife that were only a step from churches and even cathedrals.

When the Church yielded, as late as 1886, on the matter of private

---

[4] Raymondo Trinidade: *Arquidiocese de Mariana. Subsidios para sua Historia,* I (São Paulo, 1928), p. 502.

chapels, it must have made this concession principally because of the women, who, since the beginning of the century, had constituted, together with children and slaves, the most conservative element of the faith, for the men leaned toward liberalism and Freemasonry. There were city houses which, instead of maintaining a chapel or oratory, were even turning into a kind of Masonic temple, adorned, like the house of Gonçalves da Cruz in Recife, with portraits of French and North American revolutionaries instead of saints and martyrs of the Church.

Pereira da Costa [5] is of the opinion that Freemasonry was introduced in Brazil in 1801, and, judging from the remarks of the English traveler Lindley,[6] there was already in the early eighteen hundreds a Masonic lodge in Bahía, which would seem to have been established in the previous century. These lodges, like the secret societies—"academies," "areopagi," "universities," "offices"—which were springing up during the same epoch in areas more under European influence, played a role in our patriarchal society similar to that of secret societies of men in primitive societies. Associations forbidden to women, who were not allowed to view the sacred objects even from a distance. The Masonic secrecy of the liberal conspiracies—conspiracies which, however, for many "liberators" presupposed the exclusion of women, Negroes, and mulattoes from the democratic regimes so fervently pursued—contributed to the already existing antagonism between the conservative and the innovating sex.

It is possible that certain of the liberal conspirators were, with relation to wife and children, the sternest of husbands and fathers. Supporters of democracy, they wished to see the colony free from the yoke of Portugal, while at the same time they maintained their monosexual manner of being democratic and liberal.

Early in the eighteenth century the Governor of Minas Gerais, Dom Lourenço de Almeida, said that, in spite of the large number of unmarried men in the captaincy, many girls were forced by their tyrannical fathers to enter a convent, where some of them pined away in sad virginity. Some of the fathers wanted the honor of having a daughter a nun; others, it would seem, wanted to avoid having

---

[5] A historian of the late nineteenth and early twentieth century who wrote extensively about Brazil's past.

[6] Thomas Lindley: *Narrative of a Voyage to Brazil* . . . (London, 1805).

to select a son-in-law from among men whose whiteness might be open to doubt. Particularly in a region like Minas, notorious during the colonial era for its miscegenation. Antonio de Oliveira, for example, stabbed his own daughter to death, suspecting that she was having a love affair with a young man of low extraction. Some fathers sought out members of illustrious families from the older captaincies, or Portuguese, who all too often in Portugal "were the offscourings and despised by decent people, and once they found themselves in a broad and free land grew insolent, and all want to be 'hidalgos.' "[7] It was these spurious hidalgos whom the patriarchs of the older families endeavored to sort out from the true, just as they were determined to separate the dubious whites from the pure. This concern of the patriarchs with the nobility and whiteness of their sons-in-law made marriage a problem in regions of more haphazard development, such as Minas Gerais.

In Pernambuco, in São Paulo, in Reconcavo da Bahía the problem was settled more smoothly by marriage between cousins, or uncles and nieces: patriarchal endogamy. Marriages which gradually fused the various families of the first settlers practically into one, and which, by marking so clearly the limits of matrimonial unions, made it extremely difficult for Portuguese adventurers and native mulattoes to win a wife among the gentry families. Nevertheless, there were cases of mulattoes and adventurers from the hinterland who, even in the seventeenth century, made their way by marriage into the highest aristocracy of Pernambuco, becoming as good hidalgos as their fathers-in-law.

De Freycinet describes the shelters for girls whose purpose was to make impossible the marriage of well-born girls to adventurers. Some of them were really colleges or schools—and among those should be included the Gloria, founded in Recife by Bishop Azeredo Coutinho; others were houses of correction or convents "for the reclusion of women and girls, not necessarily prostitutes, but who gave their fathers or husbands serious grounds for complaint." It should be added that these serious grounds for complaint did not always exist; at times it was merely the suspicion that the girl was

---

[7] "Governo de Dom Lourenço de Almeida," *Rev. Arq. Pub. Min.*, VI (Belo Horizonte, 1901).

having a love affair. And for some husbands, not even that. "It is a known fact," wrote a German traveler, Hermann Burmeister, "that many Brazilians, for no valid reason, shut their women up for years in a convent, simply so they can live more to their taste in their home with a mistress. The law contributes to such an abuse; anyone who wants to free himself from his wife goes to the police and has her taken to the convent by the officials, provided he is willing to pay her expenses." [8]

Under the semi-patriarchal system of city life, the woman continued to be the victim of father and husband. Less so, however, than in the Big Houses of the ranch and plantation. In the city mansion the greatest victim of decadent patriarchalism (with the middle-class capitalist no longer willing to spend as much as the planter on his unmarried daughters) was perhaps the spinster. She was the victim not only of the men, but of the women. It was she who, every day and even on holidays, stayed at home, half-governess, half poor-relation, looking after the children, keeping the slave girls at their work, sewing, darning, while the matrons and marriageable girls went to the theater or to church. At birthday parties or baptisms she was rarely seen by the guests; she stayed in the kitchen, in the pantry, helping to decorate the dishes, preparing the desserts, bathing the children and getting them ready for the party. It was she who took most of the care of the saints—adorning with jewels and bangles the Infant Jesus, St. Anthony, Our Lord. Her position of complete economic dependency made her the most obedient member of the household, obeying even the children and hesitating to reprimand a housemaid.

In the France of Liberty and Equality, whose democratic ideas had been arousing echoes in Brazil since the end of the eighteenth century; in the France of 1807, Portalis could still write in his *Exposé de motifs* of the Civil Code: "Woman has need of protection because she is the weaker vessel; man is freer because he is the stronger . . . The obedience of woman is a homage paid to the power that protects her . . ."

It is not surprising that, among us, jurists of the conservative rather

---

[8] Hermann Burmeister: *Reise nach Brazilian. Durch die Provinzen von Rio de Janeiro und Minas Geraes* (Berlin, 1852).

Mid-nineteenth-century Brazilian matron.

than the liberal slant of Trigo de Loureiro should remain, in mid-nineteenth century, advocates of the subservience of woman to her patriarchal lord, or that spinsters should be little more than slaves in the city mansion household. The restrictions of a juridical and social nature—the reflection, for the most part, of economic motives—which rested so heavily on the Brazilian woman during the patriarchal era explain much of the inferiority which seemed due to her sex.

We Brazilians liberated ourselves more quickly from racial prejudices than from those of sex. In the very first century of the colonization of Brazil by the Portuguese the severest taboos against the Indians were broken; and in the seventeenth century the King's voice was raised on behalf of the mulattoes. The sexual taboos were more tenacious. "The inferiority of woman" took the place of "the inferiority of race," making our culture less similar to that of North America, with half of its values crushed or repressed because of differences of race and color, than to the Oriental cultures, with many of their richest elements crushed and denied expression because of the taboo of sex. The weaker sex; the fair sex; the domestic sex; the sex kept in a completely artificial situation for the pleasure and convenience of man, the unchallenged master of this half-dead society.

The argument put forward by Proudhon that woman did not invent even the distaff lacks the importance it would seem to have at first glance to justify the premise of inferiority of the feminine sex; it stands up no better under examination than the theories of the inferiority of the Negroes or other colored races. It can be explained, in great measure, by the constraint under which women lived during the epoch of home industries, which corresponds to patriarchalism. Man, by reason of his command of the culture accumulated under systems of masculine civilization enjoyed, as the anthropologists and sociologists point out, better opportunities for cultural expression and accomplishment. Much the same as in the case of races considered superior, whose greater richness of expression or cultural achievement is conditioned, up to a point, at any rate, by better opportunities for contacts, imitation, assimilation.

In the patriarchal formation of Brazil, the social differences between the sexes, which were favorable to the man, were at times in conflict with the social differences between the races, which were favorable to the white. When white, well-born women fell in love with mulattoes, these differences were upset. But this happened infrequently.

The distance, not social alone but mainly psychic, between the white woman and the black slave, was always greater in Brazil than between the white man and the black slave woman. On the other hand, as I shall point out in the next chapter, it was, in large measure, the white woman of good family, responding to the physical attraction and the sexual allure of the mulatto—apparently stronger, more alert, more exotic (a reaction against endogamy), perhaps more ardent than the white man—who, as patriarchalism declined, made possible the rise of the light mulatto or the poor university graduate or soldier to the highest ranks of Brazilian society. The aristocratic parents, in the majority of cases, would not hear of marriage except between ethnic, social, and economic equals. And the equals were nearly always cousins, or close relatives. The daughters, however, the young ladies of the city mansion, of the Big House of the plantation, who allowed themselves to be carried off by low-class or colored Don Juans, upset, to no small degree, since the beginning of the nineteenth century, the patriarchal and endogamic criterion of marriage.

These abductions dramatically point up the decline of the patriarchal family and the beginning of an unstable and romantic period. Arrogant patriarchs found themselves in a position similar to that of King Lear. The rise of the mulatto and the university graduate, which we shall be examining, was favored by such abductions; but that of the woman as well. Her right to love, independently of considerations of class and race, of family and blood. Her courage in defying father and family to respond to the call of sex, or heart, or "true love."

Quite rightly, in 1885 Dona Anna Ribeiro de Goes Bettencourt, a distinguished contributor to the *Almanack de Lembranças Brasileiro* (*Almanac of Luso-Brazilian Recollections*), alarmed by the romantic tendencies of the rising generation, above all, by girls eloping with their sweethearts, wrote that it was the duty of the parents to keep their young daughters away from bad influences, such as the bad theater, the bad novels. The novels of José de Alencar,[9] for example, "with certain rather crude scenes" and "certain portraits of proud, capricious women . . . which may lead an innocent young girl astray, inducing her to try to imitate these undesirable examples in real life."

Even more dissolute novels were appearing, even more dangerous writers were publishing books, some of them going so far as to suggest that "the union of a man and woman sponsored only by love is as holy and pure as that blessed by religion and society." And, as though that were not enough, "they even excused adultery

---

[9] Nineteenth-century novelist whose works dealt largely with the Indians. A kind of Brazilian James Fenimore Cooper.

on the part of the woman." To counteract such influences, Dona
Anna Ribeiro recommended the novels of Pérez Escrich [1] and those
she herself wrote: *Jephthah's Daughter* and *The Forgiving Angel*.

A complex system such as the patriarchal in Brazil had to be, as it
was, a system in which the biological basis was overridden by the
sociological structure. A system under which on more than one occasion the woman became, sociologically, a man as far as the effects
of managing a house, directing a family, and running a plantation
were concerned. A system in which the mestizo, by his position, became for all social purposes, including the political, white. In which
the godchild, or nephew, likewise became the son. Even children of
priests suffered no loss of social opportunity when they were per-
functorily designated godsons or nephews. In which the son-in-law
at times outstripped the son in social privileges. In which the godfather or godmother took precedence over the father or mother, in
which in more than one instance the godson or goddaughter not only
became the complete substitute for the son or daughter of the
childless couple, but also the substitute for the absent or dead husband. This was the case of Joaquim Nabuco, who was raised as an
only child by his godmother, Dona Ana Rosa, a widow, who tried to
change his family name to that of Carvalho, the name of her dead
husband. Such cases were frequent in the history of Brazilian
patriarchal, or tutelary, society, which was characterized by a complex of protectiveness.

With the transfer of patriarchal power from the Big House of the
interior to the city residences there came a curtailment of the distance
not only physical but social between the gentry and the artisans,
tradesmen and industrialists who were appearing in these same cities
relatively independent of the mansion dwellers, though, chiefly, for
their service and convenience. Including the service and convenience
of the women.

There began to appear in the Brazilian cities of the nineteenth
century—at times alongside the mansions or in shops belonging to
them—cabinetmakers and carpenters who built not only the furniture for the houses, but also coffins and biers; apothecary shops

---

[1] A Spanish novelist of the early nineteenth century, widely read in Brazil
in his day.

where drugs imported from Europe and the United States were sold, against which the old home remedies held out for a long time —even today; ice-cream shops where cakes, cookies, shrimp patties, spongecake, Italian and French sweetmeats were also found, which the Negresses of the patriarchal houses did not know how to make, even though their prestige remained unchallenged, almost sacred. Livery stables where the more modest houseowners, who did not own their own carriage, could hire carriages for outings, marriages, baptisms, the graduation of sons or godsons. Shops selling notions and hardware, and stores where, among other European and North American novelties for bourgeois comfort or adornment, were to be found Belgian kerosene lamps and, instead of the old-fashioned, evil-smelling, smoking fish oil, "Diamond Light, guaranteed against explosion, smoking, and bad smell." Bathhouses where the middle-class patriarch, tired of his tin or wooden tub, or of rustic river bathing, could enjoy the novelty of shower baths, warm or cold, which were later installed in the more modern private houses. Doctors who could be summoned at any hour of the day or night to visit the sick or attend the labor of the mistress of the mansion. Music stores which sold pianos and where there was a large assortment of foreign music for the young ladies of the house (where *modinhas* were no longer sung nor the guitar played). Schools where the children of the wealthy could learn to read and write while they played with other children who were their social equals and not only with the Negro urchins of the sugar mill. Watchmakers whose grandiose quarters at times occupied a whole house, from whose roof big clocks, like the "Marine Regulator" of Recife, informed the city of the correct time, thus discrediting the bells of the church or convent towers. Banks where one could deposit money or keep one's savings, which had formerly been entrusted to friars to be safeguarded in their convents or warily buried, together with jewelry, in the grounds or in the walls of the house. Cafés where, in the second half of the century, there appeared as rivals to the genipap and cashew wines painstakingly brewed at home by the ladies of the house, liqueurs and cognacs imported from Europe. Other cafés were fascinating the city gentlemen with the hubbub of "electrical devices" for the milling and roasting of coffee, which had so long been done in both the city and country houses in a pleasantly rustic fashion by the patient hands of Negress slaves. Tobacconists where, in addition to cigars for gentlemen, there were "dainty little cheroots" for the ladies, some of whom enjoyed a good cigar as much as the men, or cigarettes, which by 1870 were advertised "as exquisite and very appropriate for the entertainment of ladies who know how good, useful, pleasant, and healthful smoking is." Painters who offered their services to make "faithful portraits in oils, or miniatures" of the outstanding figures of the day, and "if the likeness was not satisfactory" they would "receive no pay." Shops selling sunshades, canes, men's hats. Tailors; railway stations; modern theaters with Italian, French, Spanish, Portuguese companies, even though among the operettas there began to appear, from the middle of the century, numbers which glorified the girls of "Bahía" and the "yellow girls," as highly esteemed by many of the fine gentlemen in the audience as the blondes, and rivaling the blondes in the applause they received from the spectators, whose Europeanization did not go so far as to destroy their taste for mulatto girls.

Also, mainly for the benefit of the daily growing population of the town mansions, who had to go out at night to the theater, the confectioners, the festivals in the churchyard, and not only to mass in the morning or to make an occasional call in the afternoon, the street lighting, at least that of the better streets and squares, became vastly improved. With this, the frequency of holdups in the main streets declined, as well as apparitions of souls in torment, werewolves, headless mules.

From what we can gather, it was in the theaters that gaslight won its great triumph around the middle of the century. From there it spread to the homes of the well-to-do, bringing new luster to their rosewood and sandalwood furniture, their mirrors, their marbles, crystal, porcelain, silver. On January 28, 1847, it was the director of the Public Theater of Recife—one of the best of its day —who, in the *Diario de Pernambuco*, in connection with the complete illumination of the theater by gas installed by one Mr. Chardon, spoke of "the imaginary dangers" of such a system, advising the inhabitants of the city to give up the "old methods of oily combustibles" and avail themselves of "the gaslights which, besides giving a splendid light, are absolutely clean." Not only theaters but the rich mansions began to install gas light, oil being relegated to the modest homes, shacks, country dwellings.[2]

A Brazilian who had been educated in Paris, Soares d'Azevedo, began to clamor in the *Jornal do Recife* of June 4, 1859, for a "public promenade" for the city, now that "the brilliance of hydrogen gas has come to take the place of the wan light of castor oil." A "public promenade" already existed in Rio de Janeiro, though without "hydrogen gas." What still predominated were the private gardens—converted from vegetable garden and orchard—on nearby country estates that were veritable parks, so large that processions were held in them. These private parks, like the houses, were affected by the re-Europeanization which so visibly changed the form and colors of the urban, suburban, and even rural landscape of the Brazilian seaboard during the first half of the nineteenth century. Re-Europeanization in the sense of English and French, not Portuguese. On the contrary, it meant, almost invariably, anti-Portuguese, as though in the opinion of the more ardent Anglophiles and Francophiles the Portuguese tradition were only seemingly European.

Wetherell observed in Bahía, where he lived during the first half of the nineteenth century, that in the old city the garden surrounding the house had become fashionable. Where previously only a few plants were to be seen, pineapples and an occasional rosebush, gardens in the French manner began to spring up. Gardeners had come out from France with European and exotic plants, principally roses. Some people had been importing delicate camellias planted in baskets from Portugal. But the tropical orchids, which the Englishman found so beautiful, had few cultivators or collectors. All enthusiasm was lavished on European plants.[3]

Naturally, only the owners of city mansions or Big Houses could

---

[2] C. J. Dunlop recalls in his *Apontamentos para a Historia da Iluminação a Cidade do Rio de Janeiro* (Rio de Janeiro, 1949, p. 2) that in 1763 when Rio became the seat of the viceroys, instead of Salvador, the lighting consisted of "chandeliers in front of certain religious buildings and the niches and oratories on the street corners before which an oil lamp or candle was lighted at night. . . . Only in 1794, when the Count of Rezende became viceroy, was lighting made a public service."

[3] Wetherell: Op. cit., p. 149.

afford these delicate and expensive imported plants. Naturally, too, the display of such plants, beside or in front of the houses, was a mark of ostentation by the upper classes, principally its women. The shacks and shanties had to be content with those native or African or Asiatic plants which played a part in the household economy or pharmacopeia, many of which, in the new atmosphere of re-Europeanization, were held in contempt. Plants of "common people," plants "of Negroes," "Voodoo plants," "shanty plants." The Portuguese custom of the vegetable garden combined with the flower garden was disappearing too, with its cummin, anise, saffron alongside the tuberose, carnation, madonna lily.

Social distinction on the basis of animals was less marked than on the basis of garden plants. But nevertheless it existed. The thoroughbred dog—large, fierce, loud-barking, sleek, well-fed—was typically an animal of the city mansion, the living and operative expression, so to speak, of the porcelain lions and dragons beside the doorway of the elegant houses. The cat, too. The dairy cow instead of the goat, the horse instead of the mule. And the peacock, whose brilliant spreading tail became as typical of the noble house as the plumed crest of the royal palm. Peacock and pigeon acquired the reputation of being birds "that bring bad luck to a house." This may have been due to the fact that they were typical of the establishments of the well-born or rich, establishments which in Brazil were, as a rule, of transient glory and opulence.

Rare was the city mansion which did not preserve the custom inherited from the Big Houses of cages of songbirds—the hobby, for the most part, of the gentleman of the house as the flowers or garden plants were of the lady. The newspapers carried advertisements of "fine rollers from Angola," "imperial canaries," "banguelinhas." And other good songsters: "finches," "grassquits of Parahyba," "seedeaters." Rare birds, expensive birds, aristocratic birds, which, nevertheless, at times were to be seen hanging in cages in shanties or modest homes, bringing happiness to the life of the poor, who were so fond of their canaries and gamecocks that they would not sell them to the rich. As a boy, I knew an old tinker who had been born in the days of the Regency and who boasted that he had gone hungry in his hovel rather than sell his grassquit to a rich baron who coveted it more than a jewel.

CHAPTER V

THE MANSION AND THE SHANTY

THE HOUSE, the type of dwelling, is known to be one of the most powerful social forces of human experience. It acts upon everyone, but very specially on the woman, who is almost always more sedentary and home-loving. This was particularly true under the Brazilian patriarchal system, which frowned upon the street and even the highway, in so far as these represented outside contacts for the woman.

This influence was exercised in a decisive fashion upon the patriarchal family by the Big House of the sugar plantation. Certain extreme features of this isolation were corrected by the city mansion, which emphasized others. As for the country place—the *chacara*, as it is called from Bahía southward—it represents the transition from the rural dwelling of the gentry to the urban. Three different forms but a single house: the patriarchal with slave quarters, chapel, bedrooms, a kitchen as big as that of a convent, pigsties, carriage-house, hitching rail, vegetable and flower garden. The plantation house and the country house facing roads that were practically impassable, or rivers; the town house, facing dirty streets, filthy hillsides where the only passers-by were Negroes on their way to work, street urchins flying their kites, or prostitutes. A child of the wealthy house who played in the street ran the risk of becoming a delinquent; a young lady who went out in the street alone was sus-

pected of immoral habits. The place for the well-bred child to play
was in his own yard; the street was for the urchins. The place for
the young lady was her room or, at most, the window, the verandah,
or the carriage step.

Little by little, however, the "noble house" of the city, aristocratic rather than middle-class, was diminishing in size and com-
plexity. The slave quarters were smaller than on the plantations,
and were known as "servants' rooms" or "annexes."

But as the slave quarters became smaller, settlements grew up
near the city mansions and country places, filled with shanties and
shacks. They began to spread over the poorest areas of the cities.

As a result of the pressure brought to bear on the rural patriarchy
by a powerful combination of circumstances unfavorable to the
continuance of its latifundian and feudal character, it began to break
up physically as well as socially. The Big House–Slave Quarters system was almost ended, the component elements scattering pretty
much everywhere and serving each other badly in the resulting antagonisms between European and African or native culture. Antagonisms which had formerly been kept in balance in the shadow of
the big plantations and ranches.

The growing urbanization of the country intensified these antagonisms; the relationship between the whites of the city mansions
and the blacks, mestizos, and free mulattoes of the shanties could not
be the same as between the white folks of the plantation house and
the Negroes of the slave quarters. It is true that, while antagonisms
grew, opportunities for social betterment increased in the cities for
those slaves and children of slaves who happened to be endowed
with exceptional artistic or intellectual capacity, or outstanding
sexual attraction. And miscegenation, as frequent in the cities as on
the plantations, softened, in its own way, the antagonisms between
opposites.

When the era of rural patriarchalism had come to an end, when
the old-style sugar plantations, which were almost a world to themselves, were its last outposts in the North, and their counterparts in
the South, the coffee plantations and cattle ranches of more artisto-
cratic type; and with the beginning of the industrial epoch of large
factories, and of plantations and even ranches, run more often by
city corporations than by families, even in the rural areas the op-

posite poles—master and slave—which once formed a single complementary economic or social unit, became opposing halves of what had once been a whole. In any case, they grew indifferent to each other's fate. The slave quarters shrank, and free workers, without the help, the supervision, and the protection of the Big Houses, came to swell the population of huts, caves, or shanties.

With the separation of the masters from the slaves, who had been so intimate under the completely patriarchal system, and the growth of shanty settlements where non-European styles of living and morality prevailed, a profound change came about in sexual relations. It was in one of these settlements that a Capuchin friar discovered to his horror that the men calmly engaged in the practice of trading wives, in a true sexual communism. The friars in Brazil were in the habit of looking indulgently on polygamy in the Big Houses, on the woman being taken advantage of by the master; on the idea of the woman as the property of the wealthy man. But that open sexual communism of the lower orders astounded the Italian Capuchin.[1]

The Big House in Brazil may be said to have become a type of domestic architecture designed for an almost Freudian purpose: to safeguard women and valuables. The women behind grilles, lattices, screens, shutters, or, at most, allowed into the backyard or inner court or garden, pining among the immortelles or jasmin; the jewelry and money, hidden underground or in the thick walls.

A significant instance of reciprocal effect was the way in which this type of house came to reflect new social tendencies that originated in the street, and, at the same time, exerted an influence on them and on the street, somewhat after the fashion of the relationship established between vehicle and highway. The city mansion retained, as far as possible, the role of the plantation house: safeguarding women and valuables. This explains the walls topped with shards of glass, intended not alone to discourage thieves but Don Juans as well. This explains the shutters, so forbidding in appearance, which separated the house from the street as though from an enemy.

It was by way of the hitching rail or the pergola or the corner of

---

[1] Placido de Messina: "Officio ao Presidente de Pernambuco Barão de Boa Vista," Nov. 26, 1842. Ms in Arquivo do Instituto Arqueologico, Historico e Geografico Pernambucano.

wall overlooking the road in the country place, and in the city home by way of the verandah, the shutter, the window looking out on the street, that the de-Orientalization of the women, their Europeanization or re-Europeanization was accelerated.

The verandah and the pergola represent one of woman's triumphs over the male's sexual jealousy and one of the concessions of the patriarchal system to the anti-patriarchal city. Jealousy which expressed itself so unmistakably in the almost conventual construction of the Big House. With the verandah and the pergola came the flirtation of ladies of the upper class, not merely with cousins, but with strangers. A timid flirtation, to be sure, employing the language of handkerchief and fan. But enough to romanticize love and make it exogamous. When the shutters were forcibly removed from the mansions of Rio de Janeiro in the time of Dom João, and from the imposing residences of Recife and the richest cities of the colony, which was now almost independent of Portugal, it may be said that a new phase in the relations between the sexes had begun.

And, at the same time, in the relations between the house and the street. From its early days, in the sixteenth century, Salvador had that "very long, very broad street, full of dwellings" which Gabriel Soares speaks of. But they were dwellings closed to the street, set in "their yards . . . full of palms laden with coconuts, date palms, orange trees and other thorny trees, figs, pomegranates, and pears . . ." [2]

In Recife, a city which was socially an island and geographically halfway between an island and a peninsula, the almost gardenless city house was the prevalent type due to lack of space. The house closed in upon itself, sometimes facing, sometimes with its back to the river, was the type of dwelling imposed by circumstances. A narrow, vertical building. The traditions of Dutch architecture, under which Recife developed, seem to have collaborated with ecological conditions to produce that lean and narrow house, as though to harmonize with the leaner and narrower type of the Bahían.

Morales de los Rios is of the opinion that Dutch architecture in Recife, whose influence can be detected even today—according to

---

[2] Gabriel Soares de Sousa: *Noticia do Brasil*. Introduction, comments, and notes by Piraja da Silva, I (São Paulo, n.d.), Chap. 7.

this authority—in the "gabled side walls of the buildings," [3] took very little inspiration from its surroundings. The Dutch superimposed on the tropical city the type of house designed for Northern cold. Even today, in the oldest houses of Recife, which have been preserved for the sake of tradition, the Flemish influence is so strong that it would surprise nobody to see snow slipping down the roofs, some of which slope almost vertically.

Nor is this to be wondered at. Lacking the plastic sense of the Portuguese, that unique gift of theirs for compromise, for adaptation, for creating new and special living conditions, the Dutch lived a highly artificial life in Brazil, importing all their foodstuffs from Holland: butter, cheese, ham, dried meats, codfish, rye flour, wheat flour, dried peas; and wine, beer, oil, vinegar, bread, bacon. And it was not only food; they practically transported their houses from Europe. They brought in lime, dressed stone, bricks, wire, beams, canvas, metal trim, everything. [4]

It is well to take a glance at the topographical and soil conditions of Recife; they were not the same as those of Bahía or Rio, to mention only the chief seaboard cities. They demanded different treatment of the problems of man's relations to the urban area; of the house to the street; of the mansion to the shanty; of the house to the water. They imposed upon the city a different ecological configuration.

During his eight years of rule, Count Maurice of Nassau was bent upon giving Recife the wisest type of city planning, and he turned the task over to one of his best technicians, Peter Post. One of the greatest benefits he conferred on the city was the many bridges he built, probably, in their day, the most technically advanced in tropical America. Thanks to them, a part of the population could move from the peninsula of Recife to the island of Antonio Vaz, where previously there had been only a monastery and a few fishermen's huts.

---

[3] Morales de los Rios: "Resumo monografico da Evolução da Arquitetura do Brasil," in *Livro de Ouro Comemorativo do Centenario da Independencia e da Exposição International do Rio de Janeiro* (Rio de Janeiro, 1922).

[4] Hermann Wätjen: *Das Hollandische Kolonialreich in Brasilien* (Gotha, 1921), p. 306. See also J. H. Rodrigues and J. Ribeiro: *Civilização Holandesca no Brasil* (São Paulo, 1940).

The housing problem, without this outlet, would have become un-bearable. Narrow, cramped houses, filled to overflowing with peo-ple. Eight persons at times sleeping in a single room. Veritable tenements—the first tenements in Brazil.

Even so, at the beginning of 1640, there was no place for people arriving from Europe. Count Maurice and his advisers made every effort to have houses built for the new arrivals in Antonio Vaz; but "certain of the more influential," buying up lands in the areas that were slated for development into suburbs, took advantage of the situation to profit from the lack of housing and the limitation of space. And the rent of houses and rooms reached unbelievable figures. Two bedrooms and a small living room brought as much as 120 florins a month.[5]

With the richer burghers moving out to houses that were in the nature of country places on the outskirts of Antonio Vaz, the peninsula of Recife became the business center and the living area of Jews, minor government officials, and employees of the West Indies Company, artisans, workmen, soldiers, sailors, prostitutes. Some of these lived in veritable pigsties, among dirty water-front taverns and "the filthiest brothels in the world." "God help the young man who strays in there. He faces certain and irremediable ruin!" says a Dutch report of the period.[6] And these words were fully confirmed by a French observer of the same epoch.[7] Many were the youths swallowed up by this Sodom of Jews and mulatto wenches, of Portuguese and Negro women, of soldiers and sailors from the four quarters of the earth.

Recife, with its tenements and houses of ill-fame was one of the main centers of syphilis in all Brazil, and syphilis was frequent, says Piso,[8] among the Dutch as well as the Portuguese. The "port prosti-tutes" became terrible spreaders of the disease. It was not only the Negro, mulatto, or half-breed women who excited the desire for

---

[5] Wätjen: Op. cit., p. 191.

[6] J. A. Gonsalves de Melo: *Tempo dos Flamengos* (Rio de Janeiro, 1947).

[7] Pierre Moreau: *Histoire des Derniers Troubles du Brésil entre les Hol-landois et les Portugais* (Paris, 1651), p. 52. See also J. Nieuhof: *Voyages and Travels into Brazil and the East Indies* (London, 1732).

[8] Guilherme Piso: *Historia Natural do Brasil Ilustrada.* Tr. and comments by A. Correia (São Paulo, 1948), Book II, Chap. 19.

exotic pleasures of the blond men, including even ministers of the Reformed Church, one of whom became notorious for the immoral life he led. Recife filled up with Dutch prostitutes, too. Whole cargoes of red-haired or blond trollops arrived. For some of the Flemings, everything had to be the same as in the motherland: house, food, women. In 1636, however, one of the more levelheaded of the Dutch councilmen of Recife requested the authorities in Holland to end this shameful state of affairs. The company directors were the first to recommend, the councilor pointed out, that offenses of a sexual nature be severely punished; and yet they allowed great levies of "those bearers of calamity" to come out to the colony.

New Holland, the first attempt at urban settlement in Brazil, where the mansions were more numerous than the modest houses or the shanties, outdid New Lusitania in offenses of a sexual nature, in moral irregularities of every kind. For the student of our history, Pernambuco provides the perfect example for an analysis and evaluation of the influences of two types of colonization, the urban and the rural. The predominantly capitalist, the predominantly feudal. The Dutch and the Portuguese. That based upon the Big House of the plantation, rounded out by the slave quarters, and that which grew up for the most part around the city mansion, at times degenerating into tenement. And this gives rise to considerations which complete, in certain aspects, what was lightly touched upon in the preceding chapter: the antagonism between the city and the rural areas in the social formation of the Brazilians.

It would be hard to conclude that the Dutch colonizers were superior to the Portuguese, or the urban type of civilization to the rural, on the basis of race or national culture. The colonizing activities of the Dutch were not carried out with racial and cultural elements that were exclusively Dutch, or even North European; more than anyone else in America, they made use of the Jews, and tried to utilize the Portuguese, the Negro, the Indian, the German, the French, the English, all the flotsam and jetsam which the tropical venture washed up on our shores.

The moral life in New Holland was in no way superior to that of rural and Portuguese Brazil. Even though the punishment for women who committed adultery was severe, there were frequent cases of unfaithful wives, especially those of soldiers. From the records of the Ecclesiastical Council, one sees that many were hung by a pulley in the market place of Recife. There were also numerous instances of bigamy. Frequent, too, as Moreau points out, were cases of sodomy and crimes against nature, a notorious sodomite being a certain Dutch captain who was sent first to Fernando de Noronha and later to the prisons of Amsterdam.[9] Although dueling was forbidden, encounters between enemies became a struggle to the death, filling the streets of the city with pools of blood. As for syphilis, as we have already seen, it was most widespread in this first commercial urban region of Brazil. Dysentery and grippe, undoubtedly the result of polluted water and unsanitary living conditions in the wealthy homes as well as in the tenements of Recife, were also rife.[1]

The city of Recife may be regarded as the first of a series of small Sodoms and Gomorrahs which flourished on the confines of the patriarchal system of Brazil. Many were the mansion dwellers there, as in the mining centers and the cities of Salvador and Rio de Janeiro, who forswore their patriarchal destiny, their family sense disrupted, and their Christianity undermined by excesses of libertinism. This is not surprising inasmuch as the Big Houses of plantation and ranch were often turned into brothels or seraglios by masters who had departed from their principal duty of fathering a legitimate family, and whose right to add natural children to the number of the legitimate was always accepted. And not only the Big Houses; even the churches. In 1733 Father Francisco da Silva, who was living in Olinda, was suspended from orders because he had been taking advantage of the confessional to seduce young penitents. And cases of this sort are not infrequently listed in confessions and accusations assembled by the Inquisition in colonial Brazil.[2] Friar Bastos in Bahía was as renowned for his licentiousness as for his eloquence.[3] In Rio de Janeiro another friar, also a sacred orator,

---

[9] Moreau: Op. cit., p. 53.

[1] Wätjen: Op. cit., p. 192.

[2] Denunciações de Pernambuco, Primeira Visitação do Santo Oficio as Partes do Brasil (São Paulo, 1929), p. 356.

[3] Pires de Almeida: *Homossexualismo* (*A Libertinagem no Rio de Janeiro*) (Rio de Janeiro, 1906).

known as "Missy," won dubious fame not as the seductor of young women, but as an effeminate who enjoyed being seduced.

In 1798 the surgeon-general, Bernardino Antonio Gomes, in answer to the questionnaire addressed to the doctors by the Senate of Rio de Janeiro, pointed out that "prostitution existed on a larger scale in Brazil than in Europe," as "the inevitable result of idleness and wealth come by without work" and "encouraged by the example of slaves . . ."[4] Dr. Pires de Almeida estimated that, at the close of the eighteenth century, there were in Rio de Janeiro around 255 of what were known as "window women," that is to say, public prostitutes, without counting the slaves who plied their trade in secret, of which there must have been many.[5]

In the first half of the nineteenth century the number of prostitutes was to increase enormously. Dr. Lassance Cunha wrote in 1845 that the capital of the Empire had at the time three classes of prostitutes: (*a*) "the aristocratic" (in fine houses); (*b*) those living in poor houses, and the "window women"; and (*c*) the "offscourings."[6] The offscourings comprised women from hovels and shanties, and it was they who, for the most part, used the so-called "pass houses" or "zungus," "stinking rooms which belonged to Negro street venders," or the "back rooms of barbershops, which were rented out for a reasonable price for this purpose by free Negroes." In Rio de Janeiro there were also "dressmakers' houses," "hotels" in Botafogo and in the Botanical Garden, and, by the middle of the nineteenth century, the brothels of "Barbada." There the rich countrymen, the sons of planters or ranchers, the well-to-do city youth found not only foreign women but pretty domestics or young mulatto girls, some still in short dresses, teen-agers and younger.

Pederasty took on considerable proportions in Rio de Janeiro during the first half of the nineteenth century, especially among the small shopkeepers, mainly Portuguese who lived for the most part to themselves and who, for the sake of economy, used clerks instead of

---

[4] "Resposta ao Inquerito da Camara do Rio de Janeiro" (1798), *Annaes Brasilenses de Medicina*, II, 5 (Rio de Janeiro, 1846).

[5] Almeida: Op. cit., p. 46.

[6] H. A. Lassance Cunha: *A Prostituição, em particular na Cidade do Rio de Janeiro* (Rio de Janeiro, 1845), p. 19.

women to satisfy their sexual impulses. It was to do away with or reduce male prostitution among the petty tradesmen of Rio de Janeiro that the Consul of Portugal, Baron de Moreira, fostered, in 1846, the importation of women from the Azores. These were followed by Polish and French women.

The annals of the period indicate that coachmen and coaches suddenly assumed an important role in the libertine or philandering life of the Brazilian cities, and the use of these vehicles became most widespread in Rio de Janeiro and Recife. In Recife there was still to be seen in my own day, among the relics of one of the oldest livery stables of the city, alongside an outmoded bishop's coupé and the victoria with silver lamps in which the Marquis de Herval rolled triumphantly through the main streets, the closed carriage which we were told had been the scene of the amorous adventures of a beautiful young society lady. The slave coachman had been the panderer. The elegant coach was at times a kind of ambulatory bedroom. Some of those advertised in the newspapers had a whiff of sin about them that was hardly in keeping with their luxurious dignity. For example, this which appeared in the *Jornal do Commercio* of Rio de Janeiro, June 27, 1849: "A sumptuous Wurst coupé . . . lined with cherry-colored damask, with mirrors, and wheel frames of silver, etc."

Pandering was also plied by Negroes or slaves following trades even more typical of urban intimacy than the coachman: sellers of sweetmeats and flowers, for example, whose calling gave them entry to the homes of the rich. Around the middle of the nineteenth century there was a well-known *marchand de fleurs* of whom a journalist wrote that he was "an uppity young Negro who, as he had worked as butler in a French home, gabbled the language fairly fluently . . ." And there was also in the Rua da Carioca a Frenchman, by name Chahomme, set up in a fine house with a wooden balcony, surmounted by a stuffed monkey.[7] These panderers, or go-betweens, their real activities concealed behind flowers, sweetmeats, stuffed monkeys, placed advertisements in the newspapers in which they offered to libertines who knew how to read between the lines black or yellow women of alluring figures. There also ap-

---

[7] Almeida: Op. cit., pp. 70–1.

peared in these advertisements "midwives" who knew what to do in the cases of ladies whose bellies became rounded out by an illicit or unconfessable love affair. "Makers of angels," was the name by which they were known.[8]

Many cures for venereal diseases were also advertised in the newspapers of the Imperial era. The use and the abuse of mercury in treating them dated from colonial days. Mercury, and young black virgins, in whom the syphilitic gentry cleansed their blood.

Drink was another vice which took on alarming proportions in Recife during the Dutch occupation—probably because of the greater predisposition of people of the North toward alcohol—and in the eighteenth century in the mining area. In 1667 the missionaries Fray Michel Angelo de Gattina and Fray Dionisio de Carli de Piacenza were amazed, as they passed through Recife, to see how disinclined to the use of wine the inhabitants were; nearly everyone drank water.[9] It was the Negroes and the half-breeds who were fond of their rum.

Dutch Recife, on the contrary, was a city of topers. Persons of the best classes were to be seen drunk in the streets. The Dutch themselves were amazed at the contrast between their own people and the Luso-Brazilians. The latter almost always drank only water, flavored at times with sugar and fruit juices; a cooling drink or lightly fermented.[1]

But it must not be assumed that in the rural areas and among those Luso-Brazilians who were completely free of Nordic influence, alcoholism did not exist. It was in the rural areas—which preserved, to be sure, reminiscences of an early urban colonization—that Burton found, in the middle of the nineteenth century, evidence of such heavy use of rum and brandy that he had no hesitation in

---

[8] Cf. A. Nascimento: *O Centenario da Academia Nacional de Medicina de Rio de Janeiro. Primordios e Evolução da Medicina no Brasil* (Rio de Janeiro, 1929).

[9] Fray Miguel Angelo de Gattina and Fray Dionisio de Piacenza were in Brazil in 1667 enroute to the Congo. Their observations may be found in Affonso de E. Taunay: *Non Ducor, Duco* (São Paulo, 1924).

[1] An English traveler of the period remarked: "Drunkenness is almost unknown among native Brazilians who have any shred of respectability left. . . . Our national character does not stand high in this respect there." (*Brazil: Its History, People, Natural Productions, etc.* [London, 1860], p. 176.)

comparing the people of inland Brazil with those of Scotland: "The consumption of ardent spirits exceeds, I believe, that of Scotland." He confessed his surprise that earlier travelers to Brazil, Saint-Hilaire and Gardner in particular, claimed that they had rarely encountered drunken persons in Brazil.[2] Burton came upon them frequently. And, also in the nineteenth century, in his inland travels, Prince Maximilian had seen many a drunken backwoodsman.

Those of Minas Gerais, Burton pointed out, could not vaunt their moral superiority over the English, as the other Brazilians did, of not being such "tosspots." It was difficult to encounter a herder or boatman, freeman or slave, who did not begin the day with rum, to "scare off the Devil" or "as a hair of the dog"; who at night did not foregather with his comrades to play the guitar and empty demijohns of rum. When foreigners were shocked at the huge amount of rum consumed in the inland areas of the Empire, the Brazilians reminded them that a great part of it was used for bathing purposes.

Contrary to what might have been expected, it was in the coastal cities that the temperance of the Brazilians, so highly praised by Gardner, could be observed. But even in the cities, this was a trait of the upper classes rather than of the inhabitants in general, and more typical of the bourgeoisie of the mansions than of the proletariat of shanties and tenements. "The Brazilian drinks almost only water," observed the Capuchin friars in Pernambuco in the seventeenth century, and Tollenare, in the nineteenth; Denis had the same impression of Rio de Janeiro in the early days of the Empire.[3] But their observations were evidently confined to the nobility or the bourgeoisie of the town mansions. Nearly all of these drank their Port, their homemade cashew liqueurs, their "Immaculate Conception" swig of rum the first thing in the morning to fortify them-

---

[2] A. Saint-Hilaire: *Voyage dans l'Intérieur du Brésil*, I (Paris, 1830), p. 212. Also George Gardner: *Travels in the Interior of Brazil, Principally through the North Provinces* (London, 1846).

[3] Tollenare: "Notas Dominicais Tomadas durante um Viagem em Portugal e no Brazil em 1816, 1817 e 1818" (Section dealing with Pernambuco translated from unpublished French ms. by Alfredo de Carvalho), in *Revista do Instituto da Arqueologia, Historia, e Geographia*, XI, 61 (Pernambuco). F. Denis: *Brésil* (Paris, 1829), p. 125.

selves for their river bath or to whet their appetite for black beans or neat's foot. But they rarely drank to excess. Going beyond the limits happened only on very rare occasions: when goblets were shattered after the famous singing toasts at the banquets of the Big Houses and the patriarchal city mansions.

At the banquets of the wealthiest or most ostentatious planters —who since the sixteenth century had amazed Europeans by the lavishness of their entertainment—the wine flowed freely. Food was so abundant that it went to waste; at the end came the musical toasts. And wine everywhere, on the tablecloth, on the floor, a display of conspicuous waste. Old Major Santos Dias of Jundiá was one of the last of the planters who was renowned for his bountiful board. There was no lack of wine there, and of the finest. English lords who came out to Pernambuco to hunt cougars in the plantation forests were guests at Jundiá, making the acquaintance of the Brazilian cuisine. The Portuguese admiral, Ferreira do Amaral, who was entertained at the old Escada plantation, formerly the property of the Albuquerque Mellos, with such an abundance of food and drink, wrote in his official report to his government that the old major had a "veritable mania for hospitality."

But we must not generalize, confusing these luxurious city mansions and plantation houses of Pernambuco, Minas, Rio de Janeiro, and the Reconcavo with those where the normal fare was cassava, dried meat, manioc meal, hardtack, salt codfish, genipap or cashew wine. Houses where there was not enough money for ham, canned peas, prunes, raisins, or the French wines advertised by the shops of Rio de Janeiro, Recife, Salvador. Nor for the Port which guests were served in the better houses.

The table wine of the wealthy plantation houses and, for the most part, of similar city homes had been brought from Europe since the sixteenth century. As it was shipped direct to the consumer, it underwent none of the adulterations at which the importers of less aristocratic drinks were so skilled. The judge of the Court of Appeals, Camara, for example, could boast of the purity of the wines in his cellar of porous rock; but the poor man who, for once in his life, wanted a change from home-brewed rum had to be satisfied with wine that was not only cheap but adulterated. "Many of the poorer classes and nearly all the slaves of the city are given to alcoholic drinks," wrote Antonio José de Souza in 1851 in his study of living conditions among the poor and the slaves in the city of Rio de Janeiro, "and such beverages, if they are table wines, are almost always adulterated." [4] About this same time Francisco Fernandes Padilha observed that the liquids, "wines, vinegar, etc.," consumed by the poor of Rio de Janeiro were all adulterated.

The same adulteration of wine took place in Bahía, whose diet was the object of a study by Eduardo Ferreira Franca.[5] And probably in Recife and the other cities with a large underprivileged population, which, during the Empire, was freely exploited by the importers of liquors and foodstuffs. The gentry were free from such exploitation, inasmuch as they imported their wine, vinegar, and olive oil directly; butchered their own sheep, goats, pigs; raised and fattened their own turkeys, chickens; and often had their own milk goats and cows.

As a result, little thought was given to the diet of the city poor, the whites, the mulattoes, the free Negroes living in the tenements, the shanty dwellers, and even those of the less important decent houses, often the children and grandchildren of some great planter whose death had suddenly left the widow and children like castaways to take refuge in a rented house.

In contrast to the house slaves of the city residences, who shared, as on the Big House of the plantation, the patriarchal diet, the free poor, from colonial times, had to content themselves with salt cod, dried meat, meal, and the sweet potatoes not too far gone which they could buy from market or street vender. And with an occasional morsel of fresh meat. The slaughter of beef cattle in Rio de Janeiro in 1785, when the number of mouths to be fed was around 50,000, had reached the figure of 21,871 head per year; 59 kilos 60 grams per year per person, or 165 grams a day; under the Empire,

---

[4] Antonio José de Souza: *Do Regimen das Classes Pobres e dos Escravos na Cidade do Rio de Janeiro em seus Alimentos e Bebidas.* Thesis presented to the Faculty of Medicine of Rio de Janeiro (Rio de Janeiro, 1822). See also J. L. Pereira Junior: *Algumas Considerações sobre . . . o Regime das Classes Abastadas do Rio de Janeiro em seus Alimentos e Bebidas.* Thesis presented to the Faculty of Medicine of Rio de Janeiro (Rio de Janeiro, 1850).

[5] E. Ferreira Franca: *A Influencia dos Alimentos e das Bebidas sobre o Moral do Homem* (Bahía, 1834).

when the population had increased, this figure dropped. In 1789 the population of the capital consumed, according to the figures of a hygienist of the time, and using his own terminology, 9,447,-553 kilograms of fatty foods, 184,934,553 kilograms of cereals, and 19,162,500 kilograms of butcher's meat. However, he included in "butcher's meat" all kinds of salted meats, tripe, tongue, sausage, and even dried meat, which was used mostly by the poorer and more numerous members of the population. And among the cereals he included dried legumes, and fruits, wheat flour and other starches, crackers, tubers, tea, sugar, onions, garlic, cinnamon, sweet potatoes. Even so, the ration amounted to 140 grams of meat, or even less, a day, after discounting the nonedible parts of the products included under the heading of "meat" and that which was consumed by the domestic animals, which were so numerous in the patriarchal city homes and even in the tenements and shanties.[6]

We know from the letters of the Jesuits that in the cities during the first century of the colony there were almost no slaughterhouses, and the fathers had to raise their own cattle to feed their novitiates, seminarians, and boarding pupils. And the minutes of the meetings of the municipal council of the city of São Paulo, where the problem of food supplies was perhaps less acute than in the North of Brazil and in Minas, inasmuch as the single-crop system had never been so complete there, at least during colonial times, nor mining so all-engrossing, reveal that there were continual shortages of fresh meat.

Moreover, on the day when the poor or the person in moderate circumstances, who did not have a fish hatchery of his own, wanted to enjoy the luxury of eating fresh fish as a change from the salted variety, he had to deal, not with just one middleman, but with a whole series. And these middlemen were neither Jews nor gypsies—the whipping boys of every dishonest deal. They were pure-blooded old Christians, members of noble families, and even army officers who possessed some of the most chivalrous traits of the upper classes. Vilhena in the eighteenth century, lamenting the fact that fresh fish

---

[6] On the consumption of meat in Rio de Janeiro, see A. Martins de Azevedo Pimentel: *Subsidios para o Estudo da Hygiene no Rio de Janeiro* (Rio de Janeiro, 1890).

should be so expensive in Salvador de Todos os Santos, at the time the most important city of the colony, wrote that the high price was inevitable: the fish passes "through four or five hands before reaching those of the customer who is to eat it . . ." And he went on: ". . . Everybody is aware of this state of affairs, but nobody does anything about correcting it, for this business is practically a monopoly of female workers who belong or belonged to wealthy and so-called noble families, with whom nobody wants to interfere. The workers sell the fish to other Negro women, who resell it, and this transaction is known as 'carom.' "[7]

Much the same was the case with fresh meat and with vegetables. Indeed, with all food articles, which the poor city dweller had to buy at exorbitant prices, less because of problems of production than because of the producers—the owners of latifundia and land grants given them in the early days of the colony and which in the eighteenth century continued to be "dens of jaguars and pumas on the very outskirts of the cities."[8] These fallow lands could very well have been used to raise cattle to supply the urban population with meat. Salvador de Todos os Santos, with all its outlying fertile land, depended for its meat on the cattle of Piauí, which were cornered in the most shameless fashion by army officers, who were the greatest profiteers in colonial days.

The imbalance between the city population and the foodstuffs of rural European origin which had existed in Brazil from the earliest colonial days, as a result, in the main, of the latifundarian mono-culture, was aggravated by the gold fever, the exclusive concern for mining in the seventeenth century.

The mining cities grew in size, with the poorest among their population suffering from the lack of foodstuffs and from high prices. The lucky adventurers were rising in the social scale, becoming planters or owners of city mansions, which, like the Big Houses of the sugar plantations, had their own self-sufficient private economy. They butchered their own hogs and turkeys, and fattened their own dairy cows. The rest of the population had to make out as best it could.

---

[7] Luiz Santos Vilhena: *Recompilação de Noticias Soteropolitanas e Bra-sílicas (ano de 1802)*, I (Bahía, 1921), p. 328.

[8] Ibid., p. 350.

And just as in the North there were army officers who shamelessly cornered the market in meat, growing rich at the expense of the city poor, in the cities of Minas Gerais the speculators in food supplies were not the Jews, nor the gypsies, nor the "gringos," but the friars. One of them was Fray Francisco de Menezes of the order of the Blessed Trinity.

At first the supply of livestock to the slaughterhouses in the diamond region was in the hands of Francisco do Amaral, a rich merchant who was given this concession by the government. The contract, signed in 1701, was for a term of five years, but the business was so lucrative that the magnate did everything in his power to have it extended, including bribing government officials—justifying his petition, says one historian, on the grounds of "the sacrifices he had made, his meager profits, and the public welfare." But Amaral's pretension was disputed by the Paulistas, "who never engaged in trade . . . occupying themselves with their farming." Farming, it should be pointed out, which was almost like that of the Indians, without the relative stability of the sugar cultivation in Bahía, Pernambuco, Paraiba do Sul.

Taking advantage of this conflict between Amaral and those nomadic farmers, and of Don Fernando Mascarenhas's dilatoriness in settling it, Fray Francisco de Menezes appeared on the scene at the head of one of the biggest business ventures that had ever been organized in Brazil up to that time. His objective was to control the supply of meat to the mining population. He had powerful allies: another friar, Fray Firmo; Manuel Nunes Vianna, the owner of big cattle ranches; Sebastião Pereira de Aguilar, another rancher.

But the Paulistas would not yield their claims. There was a dramatic tug of war between the two groups. The profiteers and shady dealers won out. Their victory almost cost the governor his post. And it marked clearly the predominance of private over public economy, of special interests over the general good.

In these clashes between the general interest of the population of the cities and that of the profiteers and monopolists, it is worth bearing in mind that the colonial governors were nearly always on the side of the people. In Rio de Janeiro, Luiz Vahia Monteiro defied the rascally friars; sent the Abbot of St. Benedict himself into exile. So resolute were his measures that he was finally defeated and deposed by the city council. The Count of Cunha was another who, as a result of his public-spiritedness and his valiant defense of the general against the private interests, aroused the big city merchants of Rio de Janeiro, the profiteers, the smugglers against his government.[9]

Toward the close of the eighteenth century the Governor of Pernambuco, Dom Thomaz de Mello, wrote the Court that when he took possession of the government of the captaincy in 1787 he found in Recife "a great shortage of articles of first necessity," including manioc meal.

"The little that there was had been cornered by individuals of reprehensible conduct," the captain-general reported. As a result, Dom Thomaz was obliged to "take stern measures against the monopolists." And, repeating the action of Count Maurice of Nassau in the preceding century, "he ordered the planting of manioc encouraged by every available means," a crop which had been neglected by the farmers who at that moment were carried away by the high price of cotton, as formerly—and again in the nineteenth century—by that of sugar.

"Prompt steps also had to be taken," Dom Thomaz continues in his report,[1] one of various documents which reveal the political acumen of certain of the Portuguese governors during the colonial period, "with regard to fresh and salt meat, of which there had been a great scarcity in previous years; I informed myself of the reason for this by listening to the opinion of persons who were in a position to know; and they agreed that in the ports of Assú and Mossoró, from which the herds could travel on foot to the market here and in that way assure a supply of fresh meat, there were various establishments where they salted and dried meat, slaughtering the cattle from the nearby ranges and then shipping the meat to other captaincies, leaving this one not more than three or four boatloads for its annual consumption. I ordered the work of these establishments in the aforesaid ports suspended, communicating to Her Majesty by the Secretary for Overseas Affairs that this would

---

[9] Delgado de Carvalho: *Historia da Cidade do Rio de Janeiro* (Rio de Janeiro, 1926).

[1] Pereira da Costa: *Dom Thomaz José de Melo em Pernambuco*. Ms. in Mss. Section of Library of the State of Pernambuco.

be in effect until Her Majesty ordered differently. Moreover, I ordered that the vessels engaged in this operation were to carry on their commerce from Aracati northward, and that they were to drop anchor and enter Recife so that I could see that enough was left here for the needs of the city and the sugar plantations, and the people of the region who for the most part eat nothing else; for I am of the opinion that one should not leave one's own hungry to provide outsiders with abundance . . ."

These measures, which today would be called "planned economy," of the admirable Dom Thomaz did not meet with the approval of persons of great influence and powerful groups in Pernambuco (as in Bahía, Minas, and Rio de Janeiro) who were dedicated to the bold-faced exploitation of the business of supplying the colonists with meal and fresh meat, and principally that sector of the population which, concentrated in the cities, could not slaughter its own meat at home and had no land on which to plant manioc. But it was not only the poor city dwellers who suffered; as can be seen from the report, it was the sugar plantations, too, which certain lyric poets fondly imagine to have been autarchic, producing all the necessities, and even the superfluities, of their diet.

"Nevertheless, I did not escape," Dom Thomaz continues, "the malevolence of certain individuals, who, thinking only of their own interests and seeking unlimited freedom to do as they liked, dared to attack all these efforts of mine on behalf of the public welfare with the specious argument of the harm suffered by the creditors most closely connected with the establishments that had been closed down . . ." After admitting this harm, the great Portuguese ad-ministrator did not hesitate to oppose the private interests of "three or four men who had enriched themselves twenty or thirty thou-sandfold, and were now raising a hue and cry about the great harm that was being done to them . . ." [2]

It was governors of this sort, with this courage and this clarity of vision, rather than the chambers of representatives or the senates, who defended the population of the captaincies, especially the poorer people of the cities, against the exploitation of profiteers, middlemen, and monopolists in the trade in meat and meal. Middle-

---

[2] Ms in Mss. Section of Library of the State of Pernambuco.

men who were often in the service of the great land and slave owners.

The chambers of representatives, in so far as the food supply of the cities was concerned, were more than once on the side of private as against public interests. And if among the governors and royal officials there were those who accepted bribes, who turned a blind eye on the illegal dealings of the rich, and even profited by them, one must not forget the attitude of those who, even at the risk of their lives, employed against the special privileges and monopolies all their power and authority as agents of the Crown.

The situation was very much the same with regard to fish, which at first glance would seem to be an easily available source of food for the poor people of the city. But the business of supplying fish also became controlled by the big landholders, the owners, in the northeast, of the fishing grounds and reefs along the shore, or of private fish ponds, by the middlemen, and by the rich burghers of the cities. Pernambuco, in particular, at the beginning of the nineteenth century, decreed that fishing was not to be carried on on the high seas nor with tackle: fish was either to be caught from rafts, or in fishing garths formed between the shore and the reefs "with traps driven into the bottom, woven of withes and tied with lianas"; and "having three divisions or sections: the first, which fishermen called the parlor, spacious, allowing the fish to go in and out easily; the second, known as the middle stall, narrower, but still allowing the fish to go in and out; and the third, or the 'death stall,' constructed in such a fashion that once the fish are in they cannot get out. In addition to these divisions, there was the lattice or breastwork, many of them forty, fifty, a hundred fathoms wide, which serve to herd the schools of fish into the fishing grounds . . ." These big fisheries belonged as a rule to landholders who rented them to the fishermen together with a plot of coconut grove. There the fishermen erected their shanties, paying a rental of twelve *vintens* (or twelve pennies) a year per foot of land. At times, the rental of the fishing grounds was separate, the usual price being ten thousand milreis, which, however, varied according to the yield of the spot.

Finally a royal decree of July 17, 1815, ruled that "all payment demanded for the use of the sea and shores was unjust and abusive." Meanwhile, the fishermen had revolted against the landowners;

they decided not only not to pay rent for the fishing grounds, but not even for their plots of ground. It was perhaps one of the earliest revolts of the shanty or cabin dwellers against the city mansions; but it was so unorganized that the exploiting system was restored, though a little less oppressively. In the Cabanagem uprising[3] the protest was more determined and represented a genuine revolt of the shack and cabin dwellers against their exploiters. This was also true of the Balaiada and Praieira revolts.

With the achievement of independence, and the disappearance of the viceroy or captain-general—who so often, during the eighteenth century, had combated the arrogance of the rich businessmen and of the municipal councils who served them—the means of subsistence of the poor, especially those living in city shacks and tenements, became even more precarious.

In 1823 we find the Municipal Council of Recife complaining about the provisioning of fresh meats: ". . . in the hands of a single man, to the exclusion of the freedom which we are all entitled to enjoy." The system was so bad that "in cities which have no contract they receive better and cheaper meats." And in 1824, on the eve of the uprising which counted Fray Caneca[4] among its martyrs, the Senate of Recife went on record as "distressed to the bottom of its heart at the evils which this unfortunate province suffers, deprived of the most basic provisions . . ." Especially the shortage of fish, and the high prices it brought, was making the population of the city suffer greatly.[5]

In the face of all these abuses, "the municipal corporation is helpless." But in 1824 the Senate of Recife requested the president of the *pro tem* governing council to take immediate measures against the "wicked bloodsuckers." In the opinion of the Senate, one of the reasons for the high cost of fish was the laziness of the fishermen, "who are satisfied with the catch of a single day, earning what they need for meat and meal for the next day, and spending the rest of the

---

[3] A political-social movement of the first half of the nineteenth century, a revolt of the people of the interior against the more urbanized population.

[4] A Carmelite friar who became an active liberal political writer and leader and was executed because of his radical attitudes.

[5] Book of the Council of Recife, 1823. Mss. Section of Library of the State of Pernambuco.

week playing cards, strumming the guitar on the beach, etc., etc."
But the root of the trouble was probably the economic system, with
the rich planters and bourgeoisie extending their power over the
sea, controlling this industry just as they did that of fresh meat,
cereals, legumes, milk, or even drinking water, which certain of the
Big Houses of the suburbs sold at so much a pail to the poor of the
shacks and shanties.

Andrew Grant [6] writes of the fishing boats along the coast of
Bahía in colonial days, "that they were the property of a few
comparatively wealthy men." The fish, when not sold for money,
was traded by these "comparatively wealthy" in the capital for
articles of food and clothing, which they then resold to such of the
poor as were able to pay for them. However, in general, the diet of
the inhabtitants of Bahía consisted mostly of fish and manioc meal.
To this, some could add fruits which in Europe, as the Englishman
points out, were luxuries for the rich: oranges, bananas, coconuts.
But this was in rural areas that were less affected by the single-crop
system, and in suburban areas where the fruits from the orchards
of the Big Houses exceeded the needs of the owners and their
slaves.

With growing urbanization, the situation became worse. The
soaring cost of meat, vegetables and milk created a problem which
greatly alarmed the economists of the day, and which they attributed
to the most varied causes. Some, vaguely, to "the falling-off of production and the increase of consumption." Others, to the shortage
of labor as a result of the ending of the slave trade and the high
mortality of slaves in a cholera epidemic. Sebastião Ferreira
Soares,[7] even though he emphasized the cornering of the market by
food speculators as the main cause, had an inkling of the one which
today impresses us as being the most fundamental of all: the over-
riding concentration of labor in the cultivation of food for export
—sugar and, later, coffee—to the neglect of that for home consumption: "Labor . . . has of late been exclusively employed in big-
scale farming . . ." From the end of the eighteenth century, cof-

---

[6] Andrew Grant: *History of Brazil* (London, 1809), p. 177.

[7] Sebastião Ferreira Soares: *Notas Estatísticas sobre a Produção Agrícola e
Carestia dos Generos Alimenticios no Imperio do Brasil* (Rio de Janeiro,
1860).

fee, even more than sugar, began to aggravate this situation, which was absurd in an agrarian society which, little by little, was becoming urban at the expense of what Professor Normano has called "king products,"[8] without assuring the rural bases of its diet.

But the monoculture of coffee was merely an extension of that of sugar. It was precisely in the large monocultural provinces that in the middle of the nineteenth century the high cost of living became most acute. There and in the most urban areas, in Rio de Janeiro, Bahía, Pernambuco. In general, wrote Soares in 1860, "the terrible effects of this scourge for the moment are most keenly felt in the maritime provinces most occupied in trade." Pernambuco and Bahía were given over almost exclusively to the production of sugar. The province of Rio de Janeiro and part of São Paulo, to that of coffee. And the main cities—Rio de Janeiro, Recife, Salvador, São Paulo—were living not off the nearby rural areas, but the remote: Rio Grande do Sul, Santa Catarina, Mato Grosso, Piauí. Not to mention the products imported from abroad, such as tea, cheese, wine, oil, which were used more than the native products by some of the plantation houses and many city mansions. For the poor, salt cod was imported from Europe, and dried meat from Montevideo and Buenos Aires. Dried meat as well as salt cod and wheat flour, however much the import duties on them were reduced, were still expensive due to the speculation and profiteering of the dealers under the Empire. There was no instance of any head of a province or ministry risking his future by opposing the meat profiteers with the determination of Dom Thomaz de Mello in the days of the "old kings"; nor any municipal council distinguishing itself for the vigor of its action against the meat and other foods monopolists like that of Salvador, in the seventeenth century. The abuses of monoculture were most keenly felt under the economic liberalism of the Empire, to the greater disadvantage of those regions where the monoculturists were almost the only ones to benefit from the profits of "exportable products," at the cost of production of food for home consumption.

In 1865 Dr. Manoel da Gama Lobo[9] pointed out that the diet

[8] J. F. Normano: *A Study of Economic Types* (Chapel Hill, 1935).

[9] Manoel da Gama Lobo: "Ophtalmia Brasiliana," *Annaes Brasilenses de Medicina*, XXX (Rio de Janeiro, 1865), p. 16.

of the slaves—and he could have added to a lesser degree that of the masters—varied not only between the cities and the ranches, but between the sugar- and coffee-growing regions and those producing a relative variety of products, such as Rio Grande do Sul, Mato Grosso, Pará, Amazonas. In the monocultural provinces, whose inhabitants—especially the shanty dwellers—rarely ate meat or fish, miscarriages were more frequent; chronic ulcers and night blindness were common. In those where a fair amount of fruit formed part of the Negroes' diet, such ailments would seem to have been rare, the birth rate was higher, and longevity greater.

There are many who believe the diet of the Big Houses was always better than that of the city homes. But this was not the case. Many city homes received from Europe a variety of delicacies which were lacking on the table of the less prosperous plantations and ranches. And to these products there were added fruits and vegetables raised in their own yards or suburban estates, which were also consumed by their Negro slaves.

The indications are that, just as on the plantations or ranches, slaves enjoyed a more regular and abundant diet than the tenement, shanty, and cottage dwellers of the cities; and even than the apparently free population of plantations and ranches. By and large, this was the case; but we must not forget that there were ranches and plantations whose owners were just beginning to get rich, men who were seeking quick profits. Ranches or plantations where the slaves were brutally exploited, the last drop of work squeezed out of them. And the same thing happened on the poorer plantations, whose owners, lacking other resources, tried to get the highest interest they could on their human capital. There all the slaves got to eat was mush, a bit of salt pork, boiled pumpkin or squash; and with these meager rations, those in the coffee regions had to get up at three in the morning and work until nine or ten at night, with only five or six hours' sleep. Even in the rainy season, the Negroes on the coffee plantations had to gather the coffee at night. "The excessive work, the insufficient diet, the rigorous corporal punishments," wrote Dr. David Jardim, an observer of the system of slave labor on the coffee plantations, "made of these miserable beings veritable money-making machines . . . without the slightest act of kindness to attach them to the land . . ." [1]

The coffee boom represents the transition from the patriarchal to the industrial economy, with the slave less a member of the family than a mere worker or "money-making machine." Dr. Jardim asked a planter, one of those who represented the spirit of this industrial type of slavery that was growing up in the South, why so many of his Negroes got sick and died, and was amazed at his answer: "He quickly replied that, on the contrary, the death rate did not represent any loss, for when he bought a slave it was with the intention of using him for a year, longer than which few could survive, but that he got enough work out of him not only to repay his initial investment, but even to show a good profit.[2]

This same industrial phase of slave labor is referred to by Sebastião Ferreira Soares: "I have been told that the planter who bought one hundred slaves calculated that at the end of three years he would have twenty-five left." The others would have died or run away. The horror of the slaves of the pleasantly patriarchal northeast, or even of the Reconcavo da Bahía, when their masters threatened on the days of their blackest anger that they would sell them to the coffee plantations of São Paulo, to the mines, to the distilleries of Maranhão and Pará, is proof of the fear the Negroes had of the system of industrial slavery, of working for poor masters or those who were in the process of making their fortune.

There were slaves who ran away from the plantations of poor or niggardly masters to those of better-situated planters, living in Big Houses, men who were almost always more kindly in their dealings with slaves and more humane in their demands than the poorer ones. On such plantations the work was divided among more hands and therefore less burdensome.

But Negroes and, above all, mulattoes ran away from the plantations to the cities more probably to pass themselves off as free. Those who had a trade—tinsmith, cabinetmaker, blacksmith—

---

[1] David Gomes Jardim: *Algumas Considerações sobre a Hygiene dos Escravos.* Thesis presented to the Faculty of Medicine of Rio de Janeiro (Rio de Janeiro, 1842), p. 10.

[2] Ibid., p. 12.

sometimes gained by this not only their freedom but professional and social advancement. The more attractive and able mulatto and Negro women became the mistresses of Portuguese or Italians who had recently emigrated from Europe, and were willing to take up with colored women who could help them with their earnings as laundresses, cakemakers, street venders. And some of these colored women, who were faithful to these first lovers of theirs, wound up as the wives of wealthy merchants and even of gentlemen high in the social scale, owners of fine mansions.

If they were not lucky at their trade or love affairs, the fate of these mulattoes, men or women, was no better than that of the plantation slaves in their quarters, many of them of stone and mortar, with window and verandah, houses that were better than those of farm workers in France, as Tollenare pointed out in Pernambuco,[3] where the food might be monotonous, but was never lacking. Neither food, nor sugar, nor rum.

Freedom alone was not enough to make the life of the runaway slave who merely managed to pass as free in the cities more palatable, at least from the physical point of view. Swallowed up in the proletariat of shanty or tenement, his patterns of living and diet suffered. His means of subsistence became irregular and precarious. Many a former slave, degraded by freedom and the living conditions of the town became a street idler, ruffian, thief, prostitute, and even murderer—the terror of the bourgeoisie of the mansions.

Dr. Antonio Correa de Sousa Costa, who made a study around the middle of the nineteenth century of the living conditions and diet of the proletariat of Rio de Janeiro—from the minor public employees to the laborers—has left us moving details about the housing of the lower middle class. This was made up, for the most part, of artisans or small businessmen recently arrived from Europe, of whites of the better class who had become impoverished, and colored people who had prospered in their trade or manual crafts. The houses were those from which dead "angels" were always being carried out, that is to say, infants, young children. And everything would seem to indicate that they were dirtier and darker than the shanties and huts of the poorer people. "As a rule small, low, at

---

[3] Tollenare: Loc. cit., p. 118.

street level, and with a minimum of windows; often they have no floor and only a roof to protect them." But these were the better and more decent houses, where the more fortunate of this class lived. In the others, made of clay, the floor was a thing of horror: the bare earth, damp, black, sticky; the roof, a sheet of tin, "ignoring every rule of hygiene in its construction." And the situation in these small houses was made even worse "by the crowding in these cramped quarters." [4]

Unquestionably the inhabitants of many of the shanties were better-housed. Some of these had as roof two or three layers of sapé grass, like the first primitive Indian huts discovered by the Portuguese along the shore. This afforded good protection against the rain and even against the heat. This detail did not go unnoticed by the Portuguese, who were always more ready than other Europeans to learn from the natives. And the tradition is still observed by the builders of the most typical huts.

The native cabin was later influenced by the shanty of African origin. To the African, especially the runaway slave, the fugitive who had taken to the woods, the Negroes of the colony of Palmares, may be attributed the use of coconut-palm fronds, later on so extensively employed in the building of rural cabins along the coast, and even in the city in the North, as well as the wax palm in an extensive zone of the same region.[5]

As time passed, the differentiation between persons of the upper classes and the poor was evidenced by the durability of the materials which had gone into the construction of their respective houses. And also in the case of the city mansion, by the height of the building; in its expanse, in that of the Big House. Koster, when traveling through the North, from Pernambuco to Maranhão, learned to distinguish the social position of the inhabitants by the materials of which their houses were built, which varied from stone and mortar to straw.

With the growing urbanization of the country came the tenement

[4] Antonio Correa de Sousa Costa: *Qual a Alimentação de que vive a Classe Pobre do Rio de Janeiro e a sua Influencia sobre a Mesma Classe.* Thesis presented to the Faculty of Medicine of Rio de Janeiro (Rio de Janeiro, 1865), p. 29.

[5] Gilberto Freyre: *Mucambos de Nordeste* (Rio de Janeiro, 1937).

house, which the lower classes used to a more European way of life preferred to the shanties. Its origin is perhaps to be found in Dutch Recife, the first place in colonial Brazil where a modern city developed. Business interests and the topography of the area prevailed over military considerations, and the population was crowded into high, narrow houses. This situation was, however, attenuated in its anti-hygenic aspects by the presence of two large rivers, which laved and supplied water to the city, which was completely flat and devoid of hills, which form the natural bases for social distinctions. The water supply was also assured by the dams built in accordance with the engineer Post's plans, and there was room to expand, thanks to the bridges Maurice of Nassau ordered built.

In Rio de Janeiro and, it would seem, to a degree, in the capital of Bahía, in Ouro Preto, in Olinda, at first the homes of the poor were built at the foot of the hills. The wealthy, the Jesuits, and the friars quickly took possession of the hills to build their mansions, their churches, and their convents. The ascent was no serious problem, with so many slaves at the service of the houses and convents. To the poor were left stinking mudholes, mangrove swamps, marshes. And so shanties and shacks sprang up, in the low, foul parts of the city. Only after these swamps and marshes had been filled in, less through any systematic effort on the part of the government than by the succession of hovels built on them, did the rich begin to come down from the hills and take over the lower parts of the city as well. It was then that the crowding of the poor into areas not only unhealthy but cramped began.

In Rio de Janeiro, what with the Jesuits, the friars, and the rich owning veritable plantations within the city, the poor were forced to live in the limited space that the others disdained. As a result, tenements began to spring up so fast that in 1869 there were 642 of them, with 21,929 people housed in 9,671 rooms: 13,535 males and 8,374 females; 16,852 adults and 5,077 children. The tenements represented 3.10 per cent of the total housing, accommodating 9.65 per cent of the population; by 1888 the ratio had become 3.96 to 11.72.

The contrast between the homes of rich and poor in Brazil was not absolute, with all the advantages on the side of the mansion and all the defects on the side of the shanty or hut. It is even possible that the person who lived in a shanty built on a dry, well-drained spot, with a double roof to protect him from the rain, was and is more hygienically housed in the tropics than the rich man and, especially, the rich woman of the old-fashioned mansion. Or than the lower middle-class resident of a single-story house.

The old-fashioned city mansion was nearly always the most unhygienic type of dwelling that existed, less because of the material used in its construction, and still less because of its architectural design, than because of the conventions of the patriarchal way of life, which protected, to the point of exaggeration, the man, the woman, and, above all, the young girl, from the street, the air, and the sun.

As for the materials employed, these depended on (1) the means of the owners; (2) their degree of contact with European civilization; and (3), most important of all, the terrain of the region where they settled. Gabriel Soares says that the settlers of Bahía used oyster shells for the lime they needed in the building of the first big houses.[6] Martius, at the beginning of the nineteenth century, found that there were suitable materials in Brazil for the construction of fine and lasting houses, and Roy Nash was surprised to find Penedo (Alagoas), as well as Diamantina (Minas Gerais), cities with large and small houses of stone.[7] He found that, contrary to the situation of the fellah of the Nile delta, who has no durable materials with which to build his home, the Brazilian always had at his disposal an abundance of stone, wood, and lime; and of charcoal to bake bricks. Therefore, the poverty reflected in the shanty or hut of straw or adobe, and thatched with grass, still to be seen today, is not due to any lack of building materials, but to the inhabitants. The reason this type of house is so widespread is the result of the poverty or the social mobility of great masses of the population in a land rich in stone, lime, wood. All of it, however, in the hands of such a small minority that at the end of the nineteenth century millions of Brazilians did not possess one foot of land, in contrast to the few thousand owners of factories, ranches, rubber plantations, coffee

---

[6] Soares de Sousa: *Noticia do Brasil*, I, p. 256.
[7] Roy Nash: *The Conquest of Brazil* (New York, 1926).

groves, cane fields, some of them the owners of groups of tenements, of whole settlements of shanties, or dozens of hovels. The
case of those rich country people whom Prince Maximilian found
living in tumbledown houses, devoid of all comfort, can be explained
by the lack of almost all contact with Europe, and the consequent
predominance among them of native or semi-native ways of life.

There have been many discussions as to which was the first European type of house built in Brazil. There are those who suppose it
to have been the Carioca house. It is believed that in 1504 Gonçalo
Coelho built a house beside a brook, perhaps in a small settlement,
to which the natives gave the name of "the white man's house." [8]

The French Protestants later attempted to establish themselves in
the vicinity of the Portuguese settlement, and in a more bourgeois
manner.[9] In "white man's houses," where they could continue the
same style of life as in the villages of France and Switzerland
and where the mistress of the house had come over from Europe. No
Indian or Negro woman was to live here; the "white man's house"
was to be the house of the white woman as well.

By 1575 there were already seven hundred stone and mortar
houses in Olinda, and it is probable that there, as in Salvador, a typical coastal city, with its streets and the houses themselves open wide
to the sea, some of the houses with terraces giving on the water, lime
was made from the shells of molluscs. Duarte Coelho, who built
Olinda, gave New Lusitania that semi-urban character it was to preserve for a long time, with many of the plantation owners spending half the year in their mansions in the town. He brought workmen from Europe, who helped build the "white man's houses" and
churches, as well as set up the sugar mills. These workmen must
have been paid almost as high wages as the master builders who
came to Bahía from Portugal and built there the "noble houses"
of which Gabriel Soares speaks. The cost of a "well-ordered house"

---

[8] See Gastão Cruls: *Aparencia do Rio de Janeiro* (Rio de Janeiro, 1949),
p. 105. Mello Moraes states in his *Cronica Geral e Minuciosa do
Imperio do Brasil* (Rio de Janeiro, 1879, p. 69) that "the first house of stone
and mortar built within the confines of the bay of Rio de Janeiro was on the
Sapateiro beach, after that of Flamengo, near the Carioca River. . . ."

[9] For French attempts to establish themselves in Rio de Janeiro, see Paul
Gaffarel: *Histoire du Brésil Française au seizième siecle* (Paris, 1878).

was no trifling matter; to indulge it, the rich settler of the sixteenth century had to open his purse wide.

For such a house, stone from Lisbon, which had been brought by ships as ballast, was frequently employed. In Rio de Janeiro, abundant use was made of the granite from the neighboring hills, with mortar made of mollusc shells mixed with sand and clay. In the inland cities, clay seems to have been the main ingredient of the mortar. In the first buildings of the city of Piratininga the white clay known as "tabatinga" was used, for the most part, and stone from the "site later known as Morro da Força."

Travelers who visited the early Brazilian cities, those of the sixteenth and seventeenth centuries, mention the sturdiness of the houses. Froger's admiration was not limited to the fortresses, the public buildings, and the Jesuit college which he saw in Salvador, but included the private homes as well.[1] They were large and several stories high. Quite different from those in the remote interior of which Father Mancilla speaks: "houses of mud and wattle," which, "wherever they happen to go, they can duplicate." For that reason, "leaving their houses does not matter to them at all . . ."

At about this same time Frézier, who was French, and the Englishman William Dampier were in the capital. Both remarked on the number of houses there, close to two thousand. Poorly furnished houses, says Dampier; with bare walls, the living rooms without the comfort which for the English bourgeoisie was the hallmark of civilization. Whereas the city houses of Salvador, two or three stories high, gave the visitor the impression of solidity and even of distinction of design and material. Façades of dressed stone; wide balconies; thick walls; tiled roofs; and set in the midst of fruit trees and shrubs, some native, others imported from India or Africa.[2]

The Scandinavian Johan Brelin, who visited Rio de Janeiro in the middle of the eighteenth century, found well-built houses there, too: "houses of stone in the Spanish or Portuguese manner, with

[1] Froger: *Rélation du Voyage fait en 1695, 1696, et 1697 aux Côtes d'Afrique, Détroit de Magellan, Brésil, Cayenne & les Isles Antilles par une Escadre des Vaisseaux du Roi commandée par Monsieur des Gennes* (Paris, 1700), p. 123.

[2] Frézier: *Rélation du Voyage de la Mer du Sud aux Côtes du Chily et du Pérou, fait pendant les années 1712, 1713, et 1714* (Paris, 1716), p. 89.

balconies in front of the window shutters, which are enclosed by grilles, because glass is very expensive there and is used only in the most important buildings, such as churches or convents.[3]

Salvador would seem to have preserved in the seventeenth and eighteenth centuries that rustic air which Gabriel Soares described. Johan Brelin himself saw charming gardens between the houses. And woods within the city. The mansions of the wealthy rivalled those of the plantations not only in the patriarchal expanse of the building but also in the space given over to the cultivation of manioc and fruits, and the raising of animals for the table. The residents of these mansions needed to be sure that they would not lack the most important staples, and produced as many as they could at home. Crackers, cheese, and dried fish came by boat, and even butter, cookies, wine, hats, English stockings; some houses even received their Negroes directly from Europe, Africa, or the Canary Islands at their private wharfs. The sea provided whale oil to strengthen the mortar used in building, fish oil for illumination, fresh fish for the table, mollusc shells for lime. The Brazilian cities could not have depended more on the sea and less on the land.

Thus, the Big House represents not only the center of a rural system of economy and family life, but also a type of patriarchal dwelling which existed, in modified forms on the outskirts of the cities, or within those along the coast. In the advertisements of houses for sale in the newspapers of the nineteenth century, the country places and even the patriarchal mansions of the cities still are referred to as "Big Houses." "For Rent: a country place in the locality of Piranga, with a fine Big House of stone and mortar, with horse block, good drinking water, many bearing fruit trees, and land for roses or whatever else is desired, for everything does well, as the aforesaid country place is in a cool spot," runs an advertisement in the *Diario de Pernambuco* of September 17, 1835. In other advertisements, instead of Big House or mansion, the term used is "country dwelling" or "noble house" or "country dwelling or fine residence house," as in the *Jornal do Commercio* of December 7, 1827,

[3] Johan Brelin: *Beskrifning ofver en Afventyrlig Resa til och ifran Ost-Indien, Sodra America, och en del Af Europa, Aren 1755, 56 och 57* (Upsala, 1758), pp. 88–100.

with many orange trees, a large coffee grove, the grounds completely encircled by lemon trees, a big grape arbor, and a natural spring. Another country residence advertised in the *Jornal do Com-*

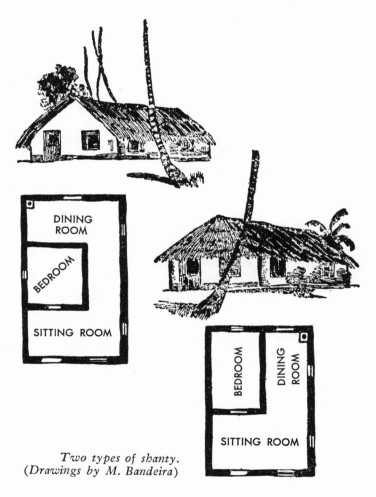

Two types of shanty.
(Drawings by M. Bandeira)

mercio of January 10, 1828, was "of stone and mortar, with glass windows," a view on the sea, slave quarters, warehouse, sixty thousand young coffee bushes beginning to bear, virgin forest. A veritable plantation close to the city, almost within the city limits, almost on the shore.

This explains, in part at least, the spreading out of the cities. In

cities like Recife, whose topography made it more difficult for the
population to spread out or the houses to grow horizontally,
urbanization proceeded vertically. The homes of Rio de Janeiro,
an English traveler wrote at the beginning of the nineteenth century, were generally two stories high; but "there were some of three;
they were well built, of granite or brick, covered with shell
lime . . ." [4] Von Spix and Martius saw in Bahía residences of three
and even five floors, "as a rule, built of stone." [5] These residences of
the early nineteenth century were faithful to the tradition, to the old
fondness for the view on the sea: "facing the sea, wide verandahs of
wood," the Germans observed. And surrounding the houses, banana
and orange groves, and walled enclosures. No crowding, as in the
case of the smaller houses, which even today in the inland villages in
Brazil tend to huddle together.

Roy Nash, explained this as a protest against the oppressive silence
of the vast expanses between the cities, a reaction against the enormous distances that separated one settlement from the other,
especially in the interior. [6]

In São Paulo the city residences—for the most part two stories
high and almost always of adobe, in contrast to those of Bahía,
Recife, and Rio de Janeiro—never seem to have had the social prestige of the country residences. It was in their country places that
the wealthier Paulistas preferred to live. These were single-story
houses, whitewashed, surrounded by *jaboticaba*, lemon and orange
trees. Their residents, even more withdrawn than those who lived
in the city, hardly ever left their homes except to go to mass or
religious festivals. The more sociable may have also gone to the
theater, where plays such as *The Miser* were performed by mulatto
actors. And nearly all of them certainly left home to watch from

---

[4] *Description of a View of the City of St. Sebastian and the Bay of Rio de
Janeiro, Now Exhibiting in the Panorama, Leicester Square. Painted by the
Proprietor Robert Burford from Drawings Taken in the Year 1823* (London,
1827).

[5] Joh. Bapt. von Spix and C. F. Phil. von Martius: *Travels in Brazil*, I
(London, 1824), p. 105.

[6] Nash: Op. cit. A. Ferreira Moutinho had already touched on the subject
in his *Noticia Histórica e Descritiva da Provincia de Matto Grosso* (São
Paulo, 1869).

the verandahs of acquaintances or relatives the processions which Mawe noticed attracted so many people—whites, mestizos, Negroes, mulattoes.[7] Moreover, this English traveler saw in São Paulo, within the confines of the whitewashed country residences, many Negroes and mulattoes. His testimony hardly bears out the claim that the inhabitants of São Paulo in colonial times were free of all trace of African blood and were darkened only by that of the "noble savage," that is to say, the Indian. Even before the boom days of coffee in the second half of the nineteenth century, São Paulo had a considerable Negro and mulatto admixture, and not merely a dash of African blood.

Some of the country houses Saint-Hilaire saw in São Paulo looked out over, not only orange trees and *jaboticabas*, but coffee groves, too. Almost plantations. On one, which belonged to a brigadier general, half a league from the city, there were also many apple, pear, chestnut, peach trees, as well as a grape arbor; and pasture for the animals, as on the plantations of the interior. That of Joaquim Roberto de Carvalho was like the Big House of a plantation: a terrace on which to rest after dinner; an orchard; and one did not even have to go to church to hear mass, for the house had its own chapel.[8]

These country houses were also to be found in the outskirts of Rio de Janeiro and Recife. The newspaper advertisements are full of them. In Recife, during the last years of the colonial epoch and the early period of independence, the Big Houses of the suburbs were used less as year-around residences than as summer homes, where the rich went to spend their holidays and take the water cure, with river baths and cashew juice to purify the blood. With modifications, the custom continued until the end of the nineteenth century.

For the most part, the houses were single-storied, like the country residences of São Paulo, with a four-gabled roof like the plantation houses, and protected by low terraces or porches. The trees most common in these houses of the North were guavas, cashews, oranges, coconuts; later they came to include mangoes, jack fruit, and bread-fruit.

---

[7] John Mawe: *Travels in the Interior of Brazil* (Philadelphia, 1816), p. 91.
[8] A. de Saint-Hilaire: *Voyages dan l'Intérieur du Brésil*, I, p. 294.

*Mansion in Rio de Janeiro (1850). Residence of
the Baron of Itambi on the beach at Botafogo.*

On the terrace the men played cards; under the mangoes there were alfresco lunches, gay and at times with wine. When the parlors were lighted it was with candles in hurricane lamps, and the girls in their hoop skirts played games with young men wearing tight-fitting, narrow trousers, or danced the quadrilles they had been taught by French dancing masters. James Henderson [9] and Maria Graham saw something of the social life of the country residences around Recife: Poço da Panela, Monteiro, Ponte d'Uchoa. And Father Lopes Gama has also left us various sketches of these diversions. It is apparent that the suburban residences of Recife were not as gloomy as those of São Paulo; the illumination, even in colonial times, was more abundant, more cheerful, brighter, fish oil being employed rather than the cheaper castor oil, which the Paulistas preferred.

Curiously enough, however, it would seem that certain refinements, such as glass windows, first made their appearance in the city dwellings and even in the plantation houses of São Paulo and Minas.

[9] James Henderson: *A History of the Brazil* (London, 1821). For a description of the country houses of Pernambuco, see M. H. L. Seris: *A travers les Provinces du Brésil* (Paris, 1881), p. 109.

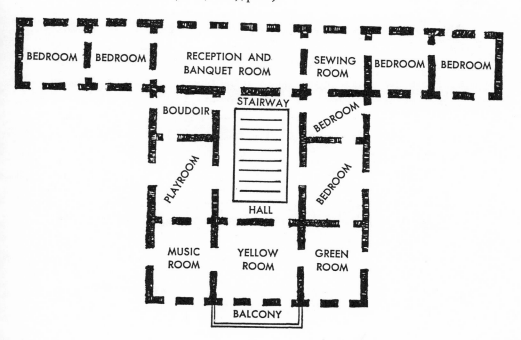

In the South, and not in the East, which was in closer contact with Europe. In Rio de Janeiro itself, the wooden-shuttered window predominated until the close of the colonial epoch. This may be explained, in part, by the severer climate of the provinces of São Paulo and Minas, where the days were darker, more overcast, and with frequent rain. Without glass windows, the inside of the houses was unbearably depressing on wet days.

Saint-Hilaire remarked that in the city of São Paulo the residence that did not have glass windows was the exception. And this luxury was rarely lacking in the residences of Minas Gerais. Not many years ago I saw near Barbacena an old plantation house (of the eighteenth century, to judge by its appearance) with a glass-enclosed terrace. A magnificent terrace, where one could spend the rainy days without having to light oil lamps or candles for the ladies to sew and the gentlemen to play cards. And this in spite of the fact that the transportation of glass to the interior of Minas must have been difficult and costly.

In São Paulo the city residence developed more slowly than in Recife. But from 1611 to 1617 Alcantara points out that the real-estate inventories listed buildings of this superior type. At times they were hybrid houses: part two-storied, part one. Some of them had only a bedroom on the second floor. Those having attics were rare; but they all had their hall, their hand-plastered walls, their living rooms, and bedrooms. The roof, which in the early days was of sapé grass or straw, was being replaced in the better houses from the end of the sixteenth century by tiles. By that time, tiles were being manufactured in São Paulo, but they were not cheap. Therefore, a tiled roof must have been a sign of affluence, "a thousand costing sixteen hundred or two thousand milreis, a staggering sum in that day," says Professor Alcantara Machado.[1]

The hybrid house—half one, two, and even three stories—sprang up especially in cities built on uneven ground or at different levels. In Ouro Preto and the capital of Bahía, for example, sometimes the front of the house was of one story, and the sides of several.

As has already been pointed out, it was in Recife that the most

---

[1] José de Alcantara Machado: *Vida e Morte do Bandeirante* (São Paulo, 1930), p. 21.

characteristically urban type of building first appeared. Thus, the residence which Kidder saw there in the early days of independence, six stories high, was, he wrote, "of a style unknown elsewhere in Brazil." This type of house was the typical residence of the wealthiest people of Recife: the sugar brokers, the business gentry. The warehouse and slave quarters were on the first floor; the business offices on the second; on the third and fourth, the drawing room and the bedrooms; on the fifth, the dining rooms; on the sixth, the kitchen. And even above this sixth floor there was a belvedere or turret, from which to look out over the city, enjoy the blue of the sea and the green of the papayas, the cool air.[2]

In Recife, too, the houses of decorated tiles reached their greatest splendor. Roy Nash states that the area where the painted tile was most employed in the building not only of churches, but of houses as well, was the eastern strip between Maceio and São Luis do Maranhão.[3] The very area where the Dutch influence was greatest, and which, given the Hollanders' traditional love of cleanliness, affected the hygiene of the bourgeois home of the northeast. But it is not to the Dutch that the predominance of the painted tile in the architecture of the fine houses and churches of Brazil should be ascribed. Tile was abundantly used in Portugal, and from there it was first transmitted to Brazil. A Moorish influence, via Portugal. The thing that most struck the commander of the French ship *La Venus* in the architecture in the cities of Brazil was the Moorish influence, which was noted also by another Frenchman who was in our country during the first half of the nineteenth century and who saw it from a professional point of view, the engineer Vauthier.[4] To the Moors can be attributed the love of fountains, so frequent in the gardens and courtyards of the city residences of Recife, of public fountains with their spouts around which the lower middle class of Salvador gathered at night to enjoy the cool, to bathe, and wash their feet. The plentiful use of water in the cities. The river bathing

[2] Daniel P. Kidder: *Sketches of Residence and Travels in Brazil*, II (Philadelphia, 1845), p. 115.

[3] Nash: Op. cit.

[4] L. L. Vauthier: "Casas de Residencia no Brazil" (tr., introduction, and notes by G. Freyre), *Revista do Serviço do Patrimonio Histórico e Artístico Nacional*, 7 (Rio de Janeiro, 1943), p. 128.

even beside the bridges. Especially in Pará, where Kidder and, years later, Warren saw so many naked people—men and women, old folks and children—delighting in their river bath within sight of the whole city.[5] There are those who attribute this to our Indian heritage; but it is also a Moorish trait.

We must never forget the influence of the Moors by way of the Portuguese, nor that of the Mohammedans by way of the Negro, on the cleanliness of body and house in the Brazilian cities. It was this that made up to a degree for the lack of public hygiene in cities so filthy that the cleaning of streets, yards, beaches, and roofs was left almost officially to the vultures or the tides. The vultures came with the regularity of municipal employees to devour the refuse and dead animals and even the bodies of the Negroes, which the Charity Hospital buried on the beach or in the cemeteries, in a shallow grave, often with a whole arm sticking out. With the same bureaucratic regularity, the tide came in and swept the beach clean; at times it flooded, as it still does, whole villages of shacks and huts.

Until the early years of the nineteenth century, the beach below the walls of the city residences of Rio de Janeiro, Salvador, and Recife was a place where one could not walk, let alone bathe. Here garbage was dumped; here the huge barrels of excrement, litter, and the refuse of houses and streets were brought and emptied; here dead animals and Negroes were thrown. Sea bathing is a recent habit of the gentry or bourgeoisie in Brazil, who, in colonial days and the early years of independence, preferred to bathe in the river. "Beach" in those days was synonymous with filth. The river was a noble place. Many of the large country residences, many a tiled house, indeed the whole fashionable section of the Madalena in Recife —which today turns its back on the river—were built facing the water. In the morning one bathed in the river and in the afternoon one rowed on it in canoe or boat, with sunshade unfurled. By the river route one moved from one house to another.

At night, when the moon was full, the students of Recife went out on the river in boats to serenade the girls in the houses of

---

[5] J. E. Warren: *Pará; or Scenes and Adventures on the Banks of the Amazon* (New York, 1851), p. 9. See also G. Freyre: *Interpretação do Brasil* (Rio de Janeiro, 1947), pp. 124–5.

Madalena and Ponte d'Uchoa. This custom has come down almost to our own days. The river troubadours were admired for their voices and their lyric gifts, and from among them came more than one famous poet.

Many country houses, and even city mansions, had their straw bathhouse beside the nearest river, where the better class of people undressed, and then slipped into the water. Some of the more modest ladies in their chemises. Nearly all of them first crossed themselves and commended their soul to the saints, like the grandmother of Lopes Gama. Rarely did the men forego a swig of rum to fortify themselves. The water attracted but, at the same time, aroused fear. It had a sinful flavor. Perhaps this was a lingering trace of medieval Christianity, which frowned upon water and regarded bathing almost as a sin. Little by little river bathing in Brazil acquired a sweetly Christian character, to the point where people bathed under the advocation of Our Lady of Health.

But the most typical manner of bathing in the city residences was in the house, in a wooden or rubber bathtub. The newspapers of the first half of the nineteenth century are full of advertisements of wooden tubs, which were gradually replaced by those of better type. For older people, it was always the warm bath, lying down, or the sitz bath. According to certain travelers in colonial days, Mawe was one of them, the ladies of the upper class overdid the warm bath, and this was one of the things that debilitated them. This, too, was the opinion of certain hygienists of the Empire.

Soap, which in the beginning was homemade, was one of the products most quickly industrialized in Brazil. Soap for washing clothes. Soap to lather the bodies of the gentry. Much expensive soap was imported from Europe. In the nineteenth century the wealthier Negroes began to import soap from Africa. The consumption of soap was so great that by the middle of the nineteenth century a large part of the factories of the Empire were manufacturing it.

Naturally, among the inhabitants of the shacks the taste for soap did not thrive. Nor among the denizens of the slave quarters. The "billy-goat smell," variously known as *budum, catinga, inhaca, cherio de bode*, of the Negroes, around which a whole branch of folklore sprang up in Brazil, was undoubtedly the exaggeration of their natural body odor because of the lack, not so much of bathing, as of soap among people who had to do the hardest work.

For neither the Negroes nor the mulattoes—not to mention the Indians and mestizos—were ever averse to bathing in Brazil. The tradition of the pleasure in the public fountain, in the delight of the bath or, at least, the footbath, was not confined to the North, but was equally true of the center and the South of the country. The Negro street urchin was famous for his love of river bathing. The newspapers of the first half, and even the second, of the nineteenth century were full of complaints about shameless youths, and even grown men, who in public places, or in view of the most aristocratic residences, stripped off their rags, and went bathing completely naked.

As for sanitation, the system which prevailed for many years in the cities was that of the "tiger"—a barrel which stood under the steps of the mansions, into which the contents of the chamber pots were emptied, and, when full, was carried away and dumped on the beach. It is plain how inferior, in this respect, the city houses were, compared with those on plantations, ranches, or the country houses.

Martius found the city houses in Salvador very pleasing, those large, square, well-built residences, with a front verandah. But he deplored the lack in nearly all of them of "a certain convenience, from whose absence the cleanliness of the streets does not benefit." [6] Luccock refers to the matter in terms which reveal his disgust, and, to cover up his repugnance, he displays his classical learning: "Cloacina has no altar erected to her in Rio and a sort of *Pot de Chambre* is substituted for her temple." [7] But these chamber pots, some very large and known as "captains," others of china, very pretty, pink with gold trim, on which the ladies—so the old women tell—used to sit in their bedroom, smoking and chatting, were for

---

[6] Just as Martius and other travelers of the early nineteenth century were appalled at the lack of sanitation in Salvador, others were equally shocked by the sanitary shortcomings of the two main seaboard cities, Rio de Janeiro and Recife, in the colonial epoch and the first decades of the Empire. In this connection, see P. Barbosa and C. Barbosa de Resende: *Os Serviços de Saúde Pública no Brasil, Especialmente na Cidade do Rio de Janeiro de 1808 a 1907*, I (Rio de Janeiro, 1909),

[7] John Luccock: *Notes on Rio de Janeiro and the Southern Parts of Brazil* (London, 1820), p. 112.

the gentry, the more aristocratic of the bourgeoisie. Even today, there are those who will not hear of any other way of relieving themselves. There died not long ago in Rio a distinguished doctor, of the older generation, who had grown up in strictly patriarchal surroundings and who, sitting on his huge chamber pot, read and studied every morning. Some of the more comfort-loving aristocrats of town or plantation house had in their bedroom an upholstered chair with a hole in the middle beneath which stood the chamber pot.[8]

Most of the residents of the city relieved their bowels in the woods, on the beach, in the back yard, beside the walls and even in the city squares. Such places were always covered with fresh excrement. As Luccock puts it: "thickly strewed with ever fresh abominations." It was the normal thing for men to urinate in the streets, usually against the walls of a house. In the *Diario do Rio de Janeiro* of March 3, 1825, there appeared this typical complaint: "For a long time, although the people living near the Church of St. George, alongside the Rua da Moeda, have been asked to refrain from throwing dirty water and offensive urine into the street at night, they continue to do so. Therefore, they are hereby requested to refrain from so doing, warning them that if this goes on, the matter will be brought before the judge empowered to act in such matters, for the heat of the season makes the foul odor even more unbearable and jeopardizes people's health."

The habit of defecating squatting, like the Indians, was so widespread, not only among the country people but among the poor of the cities, that even today there are Brazilians, of country or humble origins, who are incapable of sitting on a toilet; they can only relieve themselves by squatting on the seat, often leaving it soiled. That is why our public toilets are so rarely neat and clean. Even in some private homes, in cities with sanitary facilities, it does not occur to anyone that the toilet can be a clean place, completely different from its predecessor, the privies with a barrel, from which the bottom was removed, half buried in a hole. The use of such privies placed at a distance from the house became general in the suburban homes of the second half of the nineteenth century.

---

[8] Freyre was writing in 1936.

The Big House of city and suburb, the residence with door and verandah giving on the street, the country house, had, like the plantation, its detractors, as well as its lyrical or sentimental apologists. But to criticize the patriarchal city or country house, in the sense of distinguishing its qualities from its defects, we must consider its architectural design with regard not only to the climate but to the needs and social requirements of the culture, the family, and the economy of its day.

Not that the architectural design of the old city houses was a model of domestic hygiene for the tropics. It was difficult to combine hygienic conditions with the exigencies of the moral and economic climate of the times. The patriarchal system demanded that the womenfolk, especially the young ladies and the teen-age girls, should sleep in bedrooms of Moorish style: rooms without windows, in the rear of the house, inaccessible to even a glint from the eyes of Don Juans, much bolder fellows in the city than in the country. The women were permitted to peep out at the street through the shutters, the jalousies, the bars of the convent, but without being seen by any passer-by; only gradually did verandahs giving on the street make their appearance, and pergolas discreetly covered with vines. The entire household, especially the women and children, had to be protected from the sun, which was bad for one and brought on fever; from the evening dew; from the damp, from drafts; from wind, rain, street odors, mad dogs, runaway horses, drunken sailors, thieves, gypsies.

This explains the somewhat forbidding appearance of the mansions, as though the street and they were enemies, the shards of glass on top of the walls, the spear points of the gates and iron grilles (on which the Negro street boys, chased by the dogs while trying to steal mangoes or sapodilla plums, often left pieces of gouged-out flesh); the thickness of their walls; their dampness; their stale air; their darkness; the fierce statues of dragons, lions, or mastiffs at the entrance.

However, from the days of Dom João VI, the street began to stand up for its rights. The newspapers and even the municipal ordinances of the first half of the nineteenth century are full of edicts and decrees against the mansions and in favor of the street. Inhabitants of the Big Houses were forbidden to chop wood on the sidewalks, or to empty out their dirty water in the street during the day. "Nobody may throw water from his verandah during the daytime, and may do so only after nine at night, first clearly calling out three times: 'Watch out for the water,' under penalty of a fine of a thousand milreis and payment of damages caused to passers-by," reads an ordinance of the municipal countil of Pernambuco in 1831. And of Salvador in 1844: "The slops of the houses are to be taken to the sea at night in covered receptables; those found emptying such slops into the streets . . . will incur . . . a fine of two thousand milreis or twenty-four hours' imprisonment."

Fletcher did not find any of the old city residences he saw in Rio de Janeiro attractive. Ugly, gloomy dwellings, with the space badly distributed. Those of Fletcher's day no longer had the colonial window gratings, but still loomed forbidding and hostile from the street. Inside, they were equally unpleasant. On the ground floor the carriage house and stable, opening onto the street; on the first floor, kitchen and dining room. An inner courtyard on the ground floor as a rule separated the carriage house from the stable; on the first floor, the kitchen from the dining room. This courtyard inside the house or behind it, often U-shaped, recalling those of Andalusia, is still to be found in the old residences of Minas. And in a few plantation houses of the North, like that of Massangana, in Pernambuco. It was there, among the flowers of a small garden, that the ladies of the house, shut up indoors most of the time, would go for fresh air, chatting with the maids, playing with the parrots, with the monkeys, with the pickaninnies. Not all the city houses could afford the luxury of lavish gardens such as that which a nabob in Minas had laid out for his mulatto light-of-love. Nor those gardens at different levels, with terraced flower beds on the hills, almost hanging gardens, which Mawe admired in the rich houses of Ouro Preto.[9]

In Recife, as in Rio de Janeiro, it was a common sight in the fine city houses to see gardens that reflected Moorish influences, water falling all day from the mouth of a dragon, tiles gleaming amidst the plants and fountains. Rio de Janeiro had country houses that were famous for their gaily tiled gardens, with charming porcelain figurines and jardinières. There are nineteenth-century lithographs

[9] Mawe: Op. cit., p. 119.

of gardens of city and country residences, gay with cool fountains and filled with figures of bearded dwarfs, cupids, powerful, bronzed, respectful slaves setting an example to those of flesh and blood, beautiful women representing the four seasons and the twelve months of the year; some in solemn postures, holding aloft lighted torches, which in the nineteenth century became gaslights. The gardens were also full of pagodas or summer houses, hedges of Brazil cherry or passion flowers, walks lined with palms, elephant's-ears, ferns.

The Brazilian garden, as long as it kept to its Portuguese tradition, was one in which the human, practical quality predominated, reminiscent of the Chinese. In contrast to the formal French or Italian type, it was irregular, varied, full of surprises.

In the old Brazilian gardens, various plants such as rosemary and rue, were cultivated for purposes wholly unornamental: the protection of the house against the evil eye. With the same object, ox horns were stuck into the rose bushes. Other plants were grown mainly for their fragrance, for their "hygenic aroma"—no small virtue in those days of pestilential streets and stables practically inside the house: mignonette, jasmine, angelica, mint, Arabian jessamine, carnation. The leaves of the cinammon tree were strewn about the parlor when guests were expected. The bark was grated to be sprinkled over rice pudding. The whiff of cinnamon coming from a house meant either a wedding or a baptism, or that a son had just returned from Europe or the capital. The smell of lavender meant a new baby. The smell of incense, mass in the chapel or a death in the family.

Still other plants were grown in the garden and elsewhere in the grounds as household remedies, teas, sudorifics, purges, cooling drinks, sweets for special diets: oranges, lemons, lemon-verbena. Many were grown for the bright color of their flowers—the poppy, for example, which was also used to shine the boots and black shoes of the gentlemen. Others were for the domestic cult of the dead and the saints: scabiosa, immortelles, strawflower. Red flowers or very pale blue. They were always being cut to adorn the coffins of little angels bound for heaven and young ladies who had died of consumption. At times people came from the shacks to the mansions to ask for flowers to put on the pasteboard boxes or the small pine coffins in which the poor buried their angels. Some of the mansions which had large gardens sold flowers, as well as water, to the poor.

In the gardens of the country houses there was always a grape arbor supported by posts or iron columns. Shady nooks where one could eat on hot days. The tradition of lunch or tea in the open air lived on in the country houses of the nineteenth century.

A wall—sometimes topped with broken glass—always guarded the patriarchal garden from the sight of persons in the street. In the homes of the more sophisticated, iron fences began to appear as early as the first half of the nineteenth century,—in great measure due to the pressure of the advertisements of English importers. And atop the posts, over the entrance, and on top of the house, china figures representing Europe and Asia, Africa and America, vases and pineapples, busts of Camoëns and the Marquis of Pombal —as well as dragons, lions, and fierce mastiffs. From the early years of the nineteenth century, French gardeners were appearing in Rio de Janeiro, as is evidenced by an advertiesment in the *Diario do Rio de Janeiro* of January 12, 1830: "French gardener to look after vegetable and flower garden, familiar with all kinds of foreign plants . . ."

Along the inside of the wall some people had tile-covered stone benches built. And, in the less conservative homes, summer houses where even the daughters of the family could enjoy the afternoon cool and look out from a distance at the street and the passers-by. These were for the most part Negroes, an occasional Englishman on horseback, sometimes some important personage coming out from the city in his carriage. But, in those early years of the nineteenth century, it was almost always a closed carriage; once in a while the novelty from England—the "English carriages with windows" and "top that can be lowered"—that an advertisement in the *Diario do Rio de Janeiro* of December 6, 1821, speaks of.

If in the old city mansions with door and verandah facing the road or the street the gardens were nearly always small and narrow, resembling those of Andalusia, on the country estates and suburban dwellings they were huge, and forming part of the vast vegetable garden, joining the pasture fields, the fish pond, with jack fruit, guavas, cashews, papayas, genipaps, and other useful trees that supplied food and drink. Ouseley, who knew the Brazil of the first half of the nineteenth century, describes in detail the country place known as "Vila das Mangueiras," where he lived in Botafogo and which was later occupied by Prince Adalbert of Prussia. It seemed to him typical of the patriarchal country residences of Rio de Janeiro; it stood in a grove of orange trees of every variety, lemons, bananas, palm, as well as many fruits and plants imported from China and India.[1] In the French type of garden the flowers were separate from the kitchen garden or the orchard.

It was in the country houses that Mansfield saw the prettiest gardens of Recife—"gardens and vegetable gardens." [2] The outskirts of the city seemed to him "to comprise one big, somewhat neglected garden," that of one house adjoining that of its neighbor, all with their bananas, palms, coconut trees.

Architecturally, the country house for a long time resembled the plantation house more than that of the city, being more horizontal than vertical. Even though several stories high, its form was almost that of a cube. In this type of house, neither mansion nor humble dwelling, Allain found one of the most interesting features of domestic architecture in Brazil.[3] Pereira da Costa lists as the outstanding characteristic of the country place in the North its square lines, with the overhanging roof, such as the plantation houses generally had. Kidder mentions the predominance of such eaves in the country houses of Pará. And Araujo Vianna points out the same feature in the South, where the homes of the wealthy, outside the city, employed a barrack-like type of construction, with projecting roof of hollow tiles, supported by pillars or masonwork columns, forming a verandah.

As for the interior, the country houses resembled those of plantation and ranch in spaciousness, but not in ventilation. In the city house all the rooms, except for one or two large parlors facing the street, were nearly always closed and dark. This bad distribution of space in the city houses of Rio de Janeiro was attributed by De Freycinet to the fact that the family spent most of its time sleep-

---

[1] William G. Ouseley: *Description of Views in South America* (London, 1852), p. 40.

[2] Charles B. Mansfield: *Paraguay, Brazil, and the Plate* (Cambridge, 1856), p. 95.

[3] Emile Allain: *Quelques Données sur la Capitale et sur l'Administration du Brésil,* 2nd ed. (Paris, 1886), p. 111.

ing, without need of light, or looking out at the street through the shutters, receiving visitors only on rare occasions. All it needed was a parlor—which was brightly lighted on festive occasions, and dark bedrooms to sleep in. But this is exaggeration or malice on the Frenchman's part.[4]

What is indisputable, however, is that the interior of a patriarchal city home in the Brazil of the eighteenth century or the first half of the nineteenth was nearly always reminiscent of a church. The light entered only through the front room, and a little filtered through the courtyard or the back parlor, the cracks of the shutters, or the unceilinged roof of the bedrooms. The sun was eschewed. The air was feared.

The thick walls kept the inside of these houses cool, when inferior construction materials did not make them damp and sticky. They were walls, as Fletcher pointed out, almost like those of a fortress; even in the adobe houses,—some of them so well built that they lasted for centuries.

Naturally, in adapting itself to Brazil, the patriarchal architecture of the Portuguese had to solve the problem of excessive light and heat. They achieved this in part by utilizing the experience they had acquired in Asia and Africa, as has been pointed out by distinguished students of our civil architecture, Araujo Vianna and José Marianno Filho among others. Nor did this escape the eye of Vauthier in the first half of the nineteenth century, to whom we owe such intelligent observations on the patriarchal architecture of North Brazil.

The plantation house or suburban residence was protected from the sun by the thickness of its walls and the overhanging roof, by outer walls that surrounded it and guards on watch at night, while the city dwelling, with its fear of the sun, drafts, and thieves, became a damp, dark place, almost a prison. It is interesting to note how Europeans or North Americans, traveling in Brazil during the first half of the nineteenth century or the first decades of the second, reacted to the patriarchal type of urban house in cities such as Rio de Janeiro and Salvador.

Captain Vaillant remarked of the houses of Rio de Janeiro at the time of Pedro I that they were badly designed for the tropics. They

---

[4] Louis de Freycinet: *Voyage autour du Monde*, I (Paris, 1827), p. 179.

lacked the airiness which, in his opinion, should be the prime requisite of houses in a tropical climate.[5]

Rugendas found houses in Rio that were far too narrow, "the height and breadth in disagreeable contrast," and sad-looking.[6] This was Ida Pfeiffer's impression, too; she had hoped to find, in the seat of the new American Empire, not gloomy latticed windows, but gay terraces and verandahs. In Bahía she would have found them; as we have seen, Martius was full of enthusiasm for the houses of Salvador, with their verandahs wide-open to the sea; and later, Fletcher had the same opinion of the capital of Bahía. A city of well-spaced houses, with drawing rooms in which there were always lights and the sound of music.[7]

Rugendas found the houses of Rio not only unaligned, but poorly situated, squeezed in between the hills and the sea. But there were some built on top of the hills, with broad verandahs as spaciously set as those of Salvador, houses with a view of the sea and the bay, and fanned by the breeze from the forests. They were, for the most part, the houses of foreigners, chiefly English. But Brazilians, too, with country habits, who moved into the city without yielding to city demands. They, too, had their instinct about the best places to live. Fletcher was enchanted with the suburban houses he visited in Santa Teresa, Laranjeiras, Botafogo, Catumbi, Engenho Velho, Praia Grande, making special mention of the city mansion of Baron Andrai and the country place of a Mr. Ginty. Maria Graham had the same impression of the houses on the outskirts of Rio as of those she saw near Recife, toward Monteiro and Poço da Panela; Debret, of the patriarchal residences he visited in Rio; James Henderson, of the mansions of Bemfica, Madalena, and Poço in Pernambuco; Saint-Hilaire, of the country houses of São Paulo; Mawe, of the great houses of Ouro Preto. What better judges, if not of the comfort—which they might have preferred more along European lines—cer-

---

[5] Commandant Vaillant's remarks on Rio de Janeiro in the first half of the nineteenth century are summed up in C. de Mello Leitão: *Visitantes do Primeiro Imperio* (São Paulo, 1934).

[6] Maurice Rugendas: *Voyage pittoresque au Brésil* (Paris and Mulhouse, 1835).

[7] J. C. Fletcher and D. P. Kidder: *Brazil and the Brazilians* (Boston, 1879), p. 176.

tainly of the good or bad location of the suburban houses in the early years of the nineteenth century.

At first, when the predominant type of city house was the barred Moorish type of dwelling, the exaggerated desire for privacy of the patriarchal family protected it in Oriental fashion from contacts with the street. But after the arrival of the Prince Regent, the city house underwent a more rapid Europeanization, and not always for the better. That of the suburban house proceeded more slowly. "The houses of Rio de Janeiro," wrote Dr. Paula Candido in 1851, "seem designed for Lappland or Greenland rather than for latitude 23° south." [8]

The houses expressed the tastes of their owners, each "a self-styled architect"; "each makes his own blueprint." With the inevitable errors of construction. De Freycinet speaks especially of the stairs, nearly always so badly built that they were "veritable rib-breakers . . ." [9]

Almost half a century after De Freycinet, under the Second Empire, Dr. Luiz Correa de Azevedo, in an address to the Royal Academy of Medicine, said that the construction in Rio de Janeiro "was the worst in the world." And almost repeating the words of Dr. Paula Candido: "On examining the houses, one would imagine they were buildings for the Eskimo or Greenland; small, narrow windows, low, narrow doors, no facilities for ventilation, hot, close rooms, damp, dark, suffocating bedrooms, hallways through which one can barely pass, and always that open drain in the kitchen, that filth close to where the daily meals are prepared, beside a pestilential, evil-smelling place where the piled up refuse produces all sorts of miasmas." Miasmas were the obsession of the hygienists of the day.

On the other hand, there had been, since the end of the eighteenth century, in the more important or wealthier cities, houses built with comfort in mind and of excellent materials. The Portuguese nobles who came out with the Prince Regent established themselves in these mansions. The Count of Belmonte, for instance, lived ten years in a house that had just been built by a local patriarch, "the father

---

[8] Francisco de Paula Candido: *Relatorio sobre as Medidas da Salubridade Reclamadas pela Cidade do Rio de Janeiro* (Rio de Janeiro, 1851).

[9] Freycinet: Op. cit., p. 181.

of a very large family," says one historian; the noble parasite took possession even of the owner's slaves. And the principal residence of the royal family itself was an old country estate, the Quinta da Bõa Vista.[1]

The colonial city mansions, historians say, were generally painted oxblood red on the outside. Others were faced with tiles, especially those of Recife and São Luis do Maranhão. To judge by the newspaper advertisements of the first decades of the nineteenth century, many were painted red or yellow, some green or blue. A large number were whitewashed.

Inside the house, papered walls represented the height of fashion. Luccock saw some where the drawing rooms were partly whitewashed, partly painted in bright colors. The doors, as a rule, were painted yellow. Sometimes the ceiling of the drawing room was painted with flowers, as can still be seen in certain old residences of Santa Luzia in Minas Gerais. On the ceilings of the more devout homes there were little fat-cheeked angels holding garlands of roses. In a Big House on the outskirts of Rio, Maria Graham saw village scenes painted on the drawing-room walls. When she asked about them, she learned that the paintings were the work of a Negro artist.[2]

It was under the Empire that glass doors became fashionable, not only those giving on the street, but inside the house as well. And glass windows, and skylights and glass tiles which let in a little more light; and stuccoed ceilings in the drawing rooms. These reflected European influence, which, with the arrival of Dom João VI, triumphantly invaded many sectors of our way of life, even the more intimate; cuisine, furniture, amusements, domestic hygiene. There were others it could not displace. Spittoons in the drawing room and toothpick holders on the dining table, for example, held out for a long time against the new fashions.

Before table services of china and glass of English manufacture

---

[1] It is indicative of the prestige of patriarchalism in Brazil that, when the court of Portugal was transferred to Brazil, the sovereigns took up residence in the Big House of a private country estate.

[2] Maria Graham: *Journal of a Voyage to Brazil and Residence There During the Years 1821, 1822, 1823* (London, 1924).

had become generalized among the residents of the city mansions, the tableware was for the most part Dutch china and wide-mouthed Portuguese bowls; instead of mugs and cups, coconut shells and gourds cut in half, in the purest Indian style, were used. The rusticity of these coconuts and gourds was in contrast to the fine silver forks and spoons. Everyone had his own knife, used only to cut meat; for other purposes one used one's fingers.[3]

But it was not only china from Holland that Luccock saw in the houses of the South. Thanks to contacts with the Orient, one frequently saw in the china closets and sideboards of the rich houses, in Recife or Salvador at any rate, platters from India, soup bowls from Macao, porcelain from China. Rice pudding was sold in the street in dishes of Chinese porcelain. And on moonlit nights, says one historian, the more modest citizens of Recife often sat out on the sidewalk in front of their houses to eat their fish, their meat cooked in brown sauce, their crab fritters, on dishes from China or India whose blues and reds gleamed in the moonlight.

The table was patriarchal. The master of the house, seated at the head, sometimes served. When there were women guests, the husband and wife were always present. But this was after customs had become sophisticated through greater contacts with Europe. Earlier, it was rare for a woman to sit at the first table, at least when there was company. At family meals, the patriarch served himself first, and of the best; if there was only one pineapple, the imperial part, the crown, was for him; the rest for wife, children, and relatives.

The tables in the finer city houses were almost as large as those of plantation or ranch, even though the guests were fewer. There were not so many hangers-on. According to Luccock, the tables were too high for comfort, and in matters of domestic comfort we can accept the word of an Englishman. The tables, nearly always of rosewood, were heavy, solid, as though they had sunk roots into the floor. There were gentlemen who boasted that their table was always set. Owners of country places and city mansions, and not only plantations, like old José Antonio Gonçalves de Mello, whose

---

[3] Luccock: Op. cit., p. 125.

country house in Poço da Panela is still standing, with its almost conventual arcades. Or the Baron of Catas Altas, in Minas, who carried his extravagance to the point of insisting that his house was a hotel, with the table always set. His hospitality ruined him.

In the more frugal wealthy homes, dinner was generally served between two and four in the afternoon. It consisted, as a rule, of a hearty soup, roast or boiled meat, manioc mush with hot pepper sauce. The beverage was, for the most part, water, which was put to cool on the window sill in thick clay jugs. As for intoxicating liquors, a little Port wine with dessert, and a swallow of rum before the black beans. Indian tea, like other teas, was for a long time looked upon as a medicine, and sold in drugstores. Its use became fashionable among those Brazilians who were in closer contact with the English around the beginning of the nineteenth century. By the middle of the century advertisements like the following, in the *Jornal do Commercio* for October 25, 1848, were common: "For sale: female African slave who knows how to make men's shirts and the most difficult articles of women's attire, starch, wash, cook, make all kinds of preserves, dress and turn out a lady, prepare tea, and do all that is required of a perfect domestic . . ." By this time not only a perfect lady, but a perfect servant in the area of Rio de Janeiro, Pernambuco, and Bahía knew how to serve tea properly. The use of coffee did not become general until the middle of the nineteenth century.

Dessert consisted of rice pudding with cinnamon, fritters, hominy seasoned with sugar and butter, or jelly with cheese from Minas Gerais or molasses with cheese. Fruits such as pineapple, soursop, mango, Brazilian cherries, raw or in preserves or pudding. Black beans was a favorite dish, indispensable with fish, and in Pernambuco and Bahía it was prepared with coconut. The beans were cooked with pork loin, salt meat, bacon, pork head, sausage, and mixed with manioc meal to form a thick mush seasoned with pepper sauce. From shrimps, oysters, and other sea foods spicy dishes were prepared in the kitchen of the city mansions, more accustomed to the seasonings of the Orient and Africa than the plantation: "dishes characterized by the excess of strong seasonings, especially pepper, which was used abundantly in the midday and evening meal," says Dr. José Luciano Pereira Junior of the cuisine of the wealthy homes of Rio de Janeiro prior to 1808.[4] Fresh meat, he goes on to say, "was not sufficient to meet the demands, so a great deal of salt meat from the North was used, as well as pork loin provided in abundance by Minas." This is borne out by the reports of French travelers in Bahía: a great scarcity of meat, not only beef, but chicken and mutton too. In Rio, Luccock observed a strange religious prejudice against mutton: it was the flesh of the animal symbolic of Our Lord —"Lamb of God, who carries away the Sins of the World"— and not to be eaten by good Christians.[5]

Instead of bread, which was little used in Brazil until the beginning of the nineteenth century, a kind of tapioca fritter was eaten at lunch, and at dinner, a mush of manioc meal cooked in meat or fish broth. And rice, which was another substitute for bread on the patriarchal table. Rice became as important an article of diet in Brazil as in India. Introduced by the Marquis of Lavradio, who governed Brazil from 1769 to 1779, it became, in the opinion of the French, authorities in matters of food, better than the rice of India.[6] But due to the lack of proper protection on the part of the authorities, by the end of the Empire it was supplanted by the inferior product of the English possessions.

Butter was hardly to be found in the market. But by way of compensation, there was an abundance of cheese from Minas.

The most common article of diet in the seaboard or river cities, such as Salvador, Olinda, Recife, Rio de Janeiro, São Luis, Desterro, was probably fish and shrimp, for many country estates had their own fish pond, which supplied their needs and provided fish for sale, the rich selling the less esteemed varieties to the poor. Even today, the old scale of values is followed in classifying fish, and there are those which, though of good flavor, are considered fish for the poor, and are sold cheaper. There are fish of first, second, third, fourth, fifth, and sixth class, whose standing is even made official in certain cities by the Department of Markets.

[4] J. L. Pereira Junior: *Algumas Considerações sobre . . . o Regime das Classes Abastadas do Rio de Janeiro em seus Alimentos e Bebidas.* Thesis presented to the Faculty of Medicine of Rio de Janeiro (Rio de Janeiro, 1850), p. 32.
[5] Luccock: Op. cit., p. 125.
[6] Allain: Op. cit., p. 187.

It is worth pointing out, not merely as a picturesque detail, but as a habit which perhaps explains many ailments in patriarchal days, that the Brazilian ate quickly and without properly masticating his food. A number of foreigners observed this, among others Tollenare and Saint-Hilaire. The latter wrote that the people of Minas ate very fast, always leaving him behind.[7] Apparently those of Bahía were slower eaters than the rest of the Brazilians, and more given to conversation and gaiety. More courteous, more polished, more urbane, more of the city than of the backwoods, in this as in other respects. There were grounds for the song sung by the people of Salvador in the streets of their opulent city when the "Republicans" of Pernambuco disembarked there in 1817:

> *Bahía is a city,*
> *Pernambuco, a cave.*
> *Hurrah for the Count of Arcos,*
> *The patriots to the grave.*

The arrangement of the furniture in the city residences and the designs of furnishings were equally conditioned by the patriarchal order of things. Around the table there were chairs for the master of the house and the guests; for others there were, for the most part, taburets or stools; at times the meal was eaten on the floor, on rugs. It would seem that only in the most elegant houses did everyone sit on chairs; the master, at the head of the table, always had the largest, an armchair, like a kind of throne. Even today, the rosewood armchairs that are left from those days look like thrones, being higher than other chairs. And wide, as though to accommodate a substantial volume of flesh.

In the parlors of the city residences the furniture was arranged with rigid symmetry: the sofa in the center, an armchair on either side, flanked by several straight chairs. At times a table holding large candelabra. Luccock found the patriarchal sofa in the parlors of Rio de Janeiro "at once clumsy and fantastical in its pattern."[8] These armchairs and sofas were not, as might have been supposed,

---

[7] Saint-Hilaire: Op. cit., II, p. 210. He remarks: "The Mineiros are not given to talking while they eat. They swallow their food with such dispatch . . . that anyone observing them would say that they were more chary of their time than any other people in the world." (p. 213)

[8] Luccock: Op. cit., p. 109.

the color of the fine woods of which they were made, rosewood for the most part, but were painted after the Oriental fashion in red and white, with decorations of clusters of flowers. The English visitor was told that some of that stiff, heavy furniture was close to a hundred years old, dating from the beginning of the eighteenth century.

Saint-Hilaire, more tolerant than Luccock, admired some of the parlors he saw in Brazil, with the walls painted in bright colors. The older houses displayed figures and arabesques; the newer ones were painted to imitate wallpaper. Tables took the place of the mantle-pieces in European houses; on them were set the candelabra with glass chimneys, the girandole, the clock. Sometimes there were framed engravings: the four seasons, battle scenes, portraits of French and English heroes. The *Journal do Commercio* for October 25, 1848, advertised "candelabra for the table, to be attached to the wall, or hung from the ceiling, of all qualities and in the latest fashion." In the more fashionable houses chandeliers gleamed, like those advertised in the same newspaper for October 30 of the same year by the auctioneer Carlos, who announced an "extraordinary auction" carried out by order of the Baroness of Sorocaba at her mansion on Ladeira da Gloria.

The same stiff fashion of arranging chairs and sofas persisted throughout the entire nineteenth century, attracting Fletcher's attention when he visited us around 1850. What disappeared almost completely was the fashion of painting the rosewood furniture. In the churches one still occasionally found such furniture and even tiles painted white. The nineteenth century introduced the fashion of lace doilies on the back of the chairs, which was to persist until its close.

In the bedroom stood the almost sacred patriarchal double bed. "Well-built beds, but not at all modern," Luccock remarked, having to confess, however, that the linen was excellent. The mattresses and the bolsters were generally of vegetable floss. The house in which the sheets were dirty or grimy was rare; perhaps because there was no mistress of the house or careful chambermaid, like the one where Captain Manuel Thomé de Jezus lived when he became a widower and was old and practically bedridden. There the Englishman Mansfield said that he had to sleep in a filthy bed.

The beds, like most of the other furniture of the better houses, were of rosewood. Brazilwood, lignum vitae, and guaicum were also used in the furniture of the fine homes. The patriarchal system established categories even in the woods used in building and furniture. Only "noble" woods could be employed in the furniture of these houses, some of which was manufactured in Brazil, some in Europe, of Brazilian woods, by skilled cabinetmakers. The newspaper advertisements of the first half of the nineteenth century make mention of furniture imported from Portugal, such as "a rosewood cradle built in London," and "rosewood furniture of latest design polished in the French manner." Rosewood cut, finished, polished in Europe or by Europeans, but Brazilian rosewood, with which the mahogany or oak of Europe could not compare.

The mosquito net was widely used. Mosquitoes must have been terrible in those days, with so many marshes near the city. And not only mosquitoes, but flies too. And fleas and bedbugs. There were Negro houseboys and girls whose duty it was to fan away the flies from the faces of their white masters and mistresses while they ate, slept, or played cards.

Around the bed, a series of hampers and leather trunks, where the good clothes were kept, completed the furnishings of the patriarchal bedroom in typical residences of Rio de Janeiro, Salvador, or Recife. At times the clothes were hung on the walls or from the ceiling to protect them from roaches and rats. According to Luccock, one rarely saw anything resembling a closet or wardrobe.

Before retiring for the night, it was customary to wash the feet, and before and after meals, the hands. Saint-Hilaire says that in the interior of Minas Gerais, in the homes of the colored people, it was the master of the house himself who came to wash the visitor's feet, with the simplicity of the days of the apostles. In the Big Houses and the city mansions the water was brought in a large basin, sometimes of silver, by a houseboy. It was also the custom before lunch to offer the visitor a thin coat, of alpaca or some similar fabric, to take the place of the heavy frock coat. When the ladies went visiting, it was often to spend the day, and they, too, made themselves comfortable in a dressing sacque and house slippers without stockings.

Many customs and superstitions grew up around the complex of "house" or "city mansion" in patriarchal Brazil. Some were a legacy from Portugal. When a person clapped his hands together in the Oriental manner at the door of a city house and shouted: "Is anybody home?" from inside came the question "Who's there?" and a house-boy came to open the door. The caller was supposed to enter right foot first. An open parasol must not be brought into the house: it was bad luck. Nor a slipper worn on the wrong foot: the mother of the wearer would die. Nobody wanted to live in a corner house:

> *Corner house,*
> *Death or ruin.*
>
> *Corner house,*
> *Bad luck.*

In Recife, as in Rio de Janeiro, various corner residences were known to have been the scene of death or misfortune. In this one, a fire and looting; in that one, a murder at the foot of the stairs; in the other, the elopement by way of the verandah of a girl who later was very unhappy. It is understandable; a corner house is more exposed, not to vague mischance, but to attack, abductions, revenge. The same superstition sprang up in other Brazilian cities.

It is also curious to note that the superstitions of the city mansions applied to certain foods, endowing them with a religious significance and considering them wholly or in part taboo for the patriarchal board. The early chroniclers tell that old Thomé de Souza would not eat the head of fish, in memory of the head of St. John the Baptist. Pork was eaten by many, and they even boasted of it, but it may have been to show that they were not Jews. A superstition even existed about bananas. "No good Catholic in Brazil," says Luccock, "cuts a banana crosswise, for in the center there is the figure of a cross . . ."[9]

Nor should we forget the papers with salutary prayers, fastened to the doors and walls to protect the house against thieves, sickness, evildoers. Nor the fires lighted at the front door on midsummer night to frighten away the devil. Nor the thick black cloth with which the front of the house was hung when some member of the family died, nor the Indian counterpanes, the branches of orange,

---

[9] Ibid., p. 139.

the palm leaves, the cherry boughs, the flags, the paper lanterns with which it was bedecked on festive occasions.

There were always watchdogs on guard at the patriarchal residences. They were unchained at night and allowed the run of the yard. They barked fiercely at the least noise. At times they fell victim to balls of meat filled with ground glass or poison which professional thieves or exasperated neighbors threw them.

The city residence or country house kept its riding horses in the stable; some of the country places had dairy cows, goat, ram; hardly one did not have its dehorned ram with a ribbon around its neck. Well cared for, clean, pretty, this was for the children to ride on in the afternoon. There were always chickens and turkeys in the henhouse; sometimes ducks and guinea hens; a rabbit hutch; a pigsty; a cage of crabs being fattened—and all protected from thieves by the watchdogs. The cat was the indoor animal, the pet and favorite of the women. It had important duties, such as the protection of clothes and food against the mice, rats, roaches, always lurking about the trunks, the cupboards, to gnaw the clothing, the furniture, the books, which had other enemies to contend with: mildew, silverfish, termites. This explains why few books and manuscripts of the Big Houses and city dwellings were handed down from one generation to the others. This explains, also, the lack of esteem of the younger people for books, papers, even old pictures, which at times were burned in the back yard in little autos-da-fé. Moraes, the famous lexicographer, chose to throw his entire archives, which must have been one of the most valuable collection of documents on Brazilian civilization of the patriarchal epoch, into the river out of fear of the revolutionists of 1817.

The only remedy for ants was prayer. Hence written prayers were often pasted on the jars of molasses or compote dishes of preserves, commending them to the care of St. Blaise.

The more domestic saints were St. Anthony, St. John, St. Peter. St. Engracia and St. Longinus were also closely linked to family life during patriarchal days. Both of them were very helpful in finding lost objects. And after St. Anthony, the most miraculous. In the big city houses, in the plantation houses, where there was so much space, so many dark corners, badly lighted passageways, something was always getting lost, a thimble, a piece of needlework, a roll of lace, a gold coin, all of which kept the three saints busy. St. Longinus was regarded as the "noise-loving saint," and to find the lost object with his help or guidance it was customary to shout his name three times. In more than one residence of Salvador, St. Cosme and St. Damian were held in special devotion; among the gentry of Rio de Janeiro the favorite saint for a long time was St. George, in whom the nobles who rode out of their houses saw a kind of protector and not merely a representative of the privileges of their class against the pedestrians. I shall return to this in a later chapter.

With the passing of the years, there was hardly a city residence which did not get the reputation of being haunted. Rio de Janeiro, Salvador, São Paulo, Recife, Ouro Preto, Sabará, Olinda, São Cristovão, São Luis, Penedo—all these older cities to this day have their haunted houses. In one, a young man stabbed his sweetheart, and, ever since, the stairway has creaked or moaned all night long. In another, because of money buried in the ground or the wall, a lost soul appears. In a third, because of a master's cruel treatment of his slaves, there is the sound of weeping at night. And at times when one of these old houses collapses or is torn down or built over, human bones are turned up, buried treasure, gold coins of the days of King José or King João.

The city residence, which by the seventeenth century already predominated in the more thickly settled areas along the seaboard, giving it a European air, during its three centuries of tenure underwent a series of changes not only in structure but in contour. Up to a point, this was also true of the great mansions or country homes of the rich in the suburbs.

The shanties, the huts, or the cabins suffered little change. The differences between them are more of a regional nature, depending on the material employed—palm fronds, coconut fronds, cane stalks, reeds, sapé grass, tin, wood, withes or nails—rather than on the type of structure, in some places more pronouncedly African, in others more Indian. The early chroniclers found a resemblance between the cabin of the Indians, made of straw, and that of the North Portuguese peasants, some of which were of straw, others of wood or adobe.

Portugal did not transmit to us the tradition of the huge plantation house, as it developed here, but of the residence of the gentry.

These houses of the sixteenth century, city residences with balconies overhanging the street, were better-class homes rather than palaces or castles. A palace which was not the property of the king was rare. And only the convents were large and monumental.

With the introduction of sugar cane in Brazil and the establishment of the sugar industry (to which the political economy of the king accorded feudal privileges in the first century of its development), the population fell into the master-slave division, and the colonial dwelling into houses of stone or adobe and houses of sapé grass or straw; into "white man's house" and Negro or mestizo's house; into mansion or shanty.

As far as being in keeping with the tropical milieu, the shanty had advantages over the more elegant types of residence, or, certainly, over the middle-class variety, crowded close to one another, the bedrooms without window or skylight. It is not that we are trying to hold up the shanty as a model dwelling. Its shortcomings were many; like the huts, the unplastered adobe shacks, the caves of Minas Gerais, it was a breeding place of disease. But as far as the quality of its materials is concerned, and even the plan on which it is built, the shanty or the house of the poor is better adapted to the hot climate than many a rich dwelling, or the one-story house of the middle class. The materials and the design are not to blame, at least not directly, for the system of back-yard sanitation common to many shanties—with the outhouse often alongside the well—or for sleeping on the bare ground; nor for the fact that the adobe structure is left unplastered. What I am referring to is the plan in its pure, or ideal aspect, and the materials, which combine to give better ventilation and lighting than those to be found in the typically patriarchal dwellings—with their interior bedrooms, their halls, their clammy walls—and the middle-class houses.

"Lighting and ventilation," wrote Professor Aluizio Bezerra Coutinho, speaking of the thatched house of the interior of northeastern Brazil, a type of house which, in his opinion, is comparable to the huts of the natives of Oceania, praised by Gerbault, "were achieved by means of large openings in the front wall and were much more satisfactory than windows, however high." This system of ventilation is the same as that to be found in a certain type of shack in the eastern subregion of the northeast, in urban, suburban, and rural areas. It is manifestly superior to that of houses roofed with tile or zinc, materials "quickly heated by the sun and which, being good conductors of heat, warm the inside air." These observations coincide with conclusions arrived at in the Philippines prior to those of the Brazilian investigator and confirmed by recent studies such as those of Anatole A. Solow, J. W. Drysdale, Robert C. Jones, G. C. W. Ogilvie, John B. Drew, B. Maxwell Fry, J. Compredon.[1]

The ideal house for the tropical areas of Brazil would be one which did not eschew the materials used by the natives and the Africans, nor their building design, but which made better use of the native and African experience. Those who sincerely, or to lend glamour to their programs of oversimplified or dramatic Messianism, look upon the shanty or the hut as the greatest misfortune we have to contend with, and who in their solution to the problem of cheap housing in the North of Brazil rule out the use of thatch in the building of small houses, are presenting the problem in terms which are completely anti-Brazilian and anti-ecological. The shack made hygienic, with proper sanitary facilities and flooring, would seem to be the intelligent answer to this problem in the form in which it has confronted the authorities for many years, that is to say, demanding an immediate solution. Not only an intelligent answer from the point of view of our present economic resources, but from the point of view of setting, climate, and regional landscape. Due to climatic conditions, the problem is more difficult in the South of Brazil and calls for more expensive solutions, the employment of materials which afford better protection than thatch against cold and frost.

It is unfair to judge the thatched shanty by its disfigurations and its shortcomings. By the defects of its location—mudflats, mangrove

---

[1] A. Bezerra Coutinho: *O Problema da Habitação Hygienica nos Paises Quentes em face da Arquitetura Viva* (Rio de Janeiro, 1930). See also *The Architectural Use of Building Materials* (London, 1946); J. Compredon: *Le Bois, Matériaux de Construction Moderne* (Paris, 1946); John B. Drew and E. Maxwell Fry: *Village Housing in the Tropics* (London, 1946); Robert C. Jones: *Low Cost Housing in Latin America* (Washington, 1944); J. W. Drysdale: *Climate and House Design* (Canberra, 1947); Anatole A. Solow: "Housing in Tropical Areas," in *Housing and Town and Country Planning*, No. 2 (Lake Success, 1949).

swamps, beside a brook, where it is ordinarily built—and not by the advantages of its material and its design.

The shanties have preserved to our own time the primitivism of the early days of the colonization. They were the refuge of the mestizo, of the runaway slave, of the free Negro. Of the white man who had become socially integrated with the half-breeds. For many Negroes or mulattoes, eager for freedom, the shanty was preferable to the slave quarters of stone and mortar, close to the home of the plantation owner and forming part of the Big House of plantation, ranch, or country estate. And in more than one Big House of the patriarchal era, the thatched slave quarters were in contrast to the owner's home of stone or adobe, although in many others the slave quarters were built of the same material as the Big House.

José Rodriguez de Lima Duarte, in an essay on slave hygiene in Brazil, published in 1849, describes slave quarters which were in reality shanties, each cabin being about twelve feet square, and some smaller, covered with sapé grass or palm trunks, and windowless.[2] But the usual type of quarters was built of stouter materials to safeguard the slave and prevent his escape. They consisted of adjoining cubicles, each with door and window, forming a single building, easy to supervise and guard, like a jail or an orphanage.

The contrast between the quality of the building materials and, above all, the location of the house was sharp in the case of the Big House and the shanty of the free sharecropper, whose life was far more difficult than that of the slave. As it was between the city residence and the shanty in the city itself or in the suburbs.

Azevedo Pimentel speaks in one of his studies of "huts of straw standing in swamps" in Valongo. There the Negroes arriving from Africa, often suffering "from scurvy, scabies, buboes, dysentery," [3] were housed from the time of the Marquis of Lavradio. These huts were probably the first slums in Brazil erected on mudflats or man-

---

[2] J. R. Lima Duarte: *Ensaio sobre a Hygiene da Escravatura no Brasil.* Thesis, Rio de Janeiro, 1849.

[3] Azevedo Pimentel studied the diseases brought to Brazil by African slaves, who, before being assigned to plantation, ranches, or factories, were crowded into temporary quarters near the city residences of Rio de Janeiro, Recife, and Salvador, thus exposing these areas to infection.

grove swamps, land that was good for nothing and undesirable for living purposes.

In other thatched shanties, built on other swamps, the poorest sector of the free inhabitants of the city of Rio de Janeiro took refuge, that which would later build its miserable "favelas" on the hills. The more indomitable, the less submissive Negroes, gathered in the shanty settlements of Palmares, or in Mato Grosso, in the remote backlands, in Amazonia. And not merely on the outskirts of the cities.[4]

---

[4] In Rio de Janeiro, Valongo, the section set aside for the Negroes, who were not always passive or submissive, grew so large that frightened whites began to speak of the city as "besieged" by this African subcity. See H. J. do Carmo Netto: *O Intendente Aragão* (Rio de Janeiro, 1913), p. 27.

CHAPTER VI

FURTHER CONSIDERATIONS ON
MANSIONS AND SHANTIES

UNDER THE still vivid impression of Brazil's independence, Francisco de Sierra y Mariscal, in his "Ideas Geraes sobre a Revolução do Brazil e suas Consequencias" (General Ideas Concerning the Revolution of Brazil and its Consequences), went so far as to say: "Here trade may be said to be the only aristocratic calling. The privileges of the planters serve only to discredit them, for they are authorized, up to a point, not to pay anybody . . ." And combating the general idea that the planters form a single class, rich and well fed, he remarks: "Anybody can be a plantation owner and there are many kinds of plantation . . ." And he adds: ". . . Most of them have reached the point where, so they can eat beef twice a week and keep a horse in the stable, two hundred people have to die of hunger, these being the slaves, who are allowed to work for themselves only on Saturdays, and support themselves with what they earn that day, working for their masters the rest of the week." [1]

This explains why at the beginning of the nineteenth century the majority of the plantation owners constituted an element of unrest,

---

[1] *Anais da Biblioteca Nacional do Rio de Janeiro*, XLIII–IV (1920–21), p. 62.

rather than of defense of the existing order. Said Sierra y Mariscal: "This class does not constitute an order," that is to say, a conservative aristocratic order. On the contrary, to a large extent they belonged to the democratic order of those who had "nothing to lose . . ." "The plantation owners favor this order because it is the party of the revolution by means of which they hope to free themselves from their creditors." For the same reason, "the majority of the clergy" was in the same situation, and also "the government employees, who hope to get their hands on the remains of the fortunes of the Europeans." All of them in a precarious situation, for even the seemingly rich gave little thought to conserving or increasing their patrimony.

The result was that many who were born rich found themselves as poor as church mice in their old age. But always contemptuous of manual occupations, which were for Europeans or slaves. Hence the marked contrast between the Europeans, who arrived poor and died rich, and the Brazilians, who were born rich and died poor.

Sierra y Mariscal pointed out the difference between the son of the rich Brazilian, who fell into bad habits because "the father in his affection gave him free rein," and the son of the Portuguese, who emigrated to Brazil "with nothing but his own two hands"; and if he had no relative or acquaintance there, "his first bed and home was the arcades of a church"; when "he secured work as a clerk or apprentice there was nothing he would not do"; and with "his work and savings" he amassed a fortune, and once he was rich, he was esteemed. To be sure, the Brazilians looked down upon him because he had begun poor and lowly; but once he was wealthy, it was he who looked down on the Brazilians as "good-for-nothing, immoral, lazy, and poor." And as in his days as a poor youth he had taken up with "poor women"—often, Sierra y Mariscal might have added, colored, or the half-breed daughter of his wealthy employer who was also Portuguese—"this, too, gave grounds for mutual recriminations." Moreover, as the Portuguese who emigrated here at the age of ten or twelve had had no opportunities for education, he rarely knew how to bring up his children properly.

Yet withal, in the opinion of observers like Sierra y Mariscal, "trade constituted the only aristocratic calling," because of its followers' more stable position and their interest in preserving the state along the lines laid down by the patriarchalism of the period, a patriarchalism more urban than rural in its dominant tendencies. In this patriarchalism, the State was the head of the heads of the family, especially the wealthier, those most in accord with the *status quo*, the more law-abiding, those seeking progress only within the framework of order. These friends first of order, and only secondarily of progress, in the eighteenth century were no longer—allowing for a few exceptions—the planters, landholders, ranchers, but the important figures in trade, industry, and manufacture. They leaned toward conservatism rather than toward innovations stemming from French influences. They were the new knights-commander, new barons, new viscounts, in whose champagne there could still be detected a tang of salt cod, as some wag of the nineteenth century said of a rich wholesaler of Recife. They constituted a stronger factor in the national economy than the country gentry, for all the aroma of cane syrup about their lands, their mills, their houses, their very persons, once almost sacrosanct.

The planter or rancher in this phase of the transfer of power from the Big House of the interior to the mansions of the cities was not the passive or hapless victim of the new ruling class. He contributed to his own downfall.

If, as a journalist of the mid-nineteenth century pointed out, the "misgovernment" of the Empire had been bringing about the ruin of agriculture by the excessive taxes laid on it for the benefit of the Court and the cities, "the cultivators of our lands are even more at fault and deserve the severest censure for the negligence and senseless poverty under which they work." To the problems of slave labor there were added plagues such as "ants, weevils, locusts," and all this "compounded by the haughty sloth in which most of our landowners live, answering everything with hollow boastfulness," looking upon themselves "as the nobility of the provinces," "the rural magnates," the "protectors of trade," when "the way they are going they are the imposters of the provinces, the rural poor, the leeches of trade"; "the taxes they pay the nation do not equal their swindles, allowing for a few exceptions, which are as rare as a sunny day in the rainy season." He goes on to say, with special reference to the province of Bahía: "It lacks machinery, it lacks tools." But instead of the planters seeking solutions for the problem of substituting slaves and animals by machinery, talk and estimates of machinery and tools make them dizzy, and they go on using Negroes and oxen, but without looking after them as the old planters did. The first thing they should do is "to take proper care of the slaves and oxen, which are their main working equipment or implements . . ." But instead, what does one see "in this heartless region"? Negroes whose diet is "a miserable ration of rotten dried meat," who are cruelly flogged, "and whose apothecary and doctor are Epsom salts and Leroy's emetic, these remedies applied, hit-or-miss, by a Negro woman called a nurse who, being too stupid to work on the plantation, is made hospital director; the oxen plod along struggling against the yoke and tormented by the goad; when the day's work is done, they are turned out in the fields, left to the rain, the sun, the cold; and if the animal is new on the place and does not know where the watering place is, it dies bellowing of thirst. And yet they complain of the loss of their slaves and oxen!" And he continues, cruel and sarcastic, on the plantations of Bahía "the objects of iron and wood are looked after," but not the ox. "The ox that dies neglected in the fields should be skinned and his hide put on the plantation owner, who should go about on four feet, the laughing stock of other animals."

This was the opinion of the disillusioned critic of the sorry state of agriculture in the province of Bahía.[2] The article also criticized the "agriculture of the country places," referring to the clearings around the suburban estates of Salvador, clearings in which, for the most part, "all that was grown was grass, which caused a bad impression on outsiders . . ." Meanwhile, there swarmed around these houses and through the streets "lazy, superfluous slaves," "a million African or Creole women selling papaya preserves and sticky coconut candy, the profit from which does not pay for their cost." This without counting the idle Negro urchins—grandma's darlings—who spend their days stoning the roofs, or the "fat Negro women . . . known as seamstresses, lacemakers, embroiderers," of which at the time there were "a quarter of a hundred in every house" in Salvador.[3] In these middle-class, yet patriarchal residences, luxury reached heights

---

[2] *A Marmota Pernambucana*, July 30, 1850.
[3] Ibid.

rarely attained by the Big Houses of the plantations. From the first half of the nineteenth century some of the wealthiest planters of Rio de Janeiro, Bahía, Pernambuco used these as country places, converting their city homes into veritable mansions, where they spent more time than on their lands. "In proportion to our circumstances, I doubt that there is a city in the world where luxury has reached such a point as in our own Pernambuco," wrote the author of *O Carapuceiro*.[4] The plantation owners, living most of the year in their town residences, and the big businessmen, their agents and brokers, masters of equally sumptuous homes, competed in extravagance.

The prejudice against "those engaged in trade" was no longer so strongly felt by Brazilians. The critic of the newspaper *O Conciliador*,[5] who voiced the opinion or sentiments of many who did not agree that the Portuguese who settled here and "married our daughters"—some of them half-breeds and mulattoes, for whom their predilection was notorious—were "just as good," put forward the argument that Brazil had not opened its doors to foreigners to have them remain in the cities and marry "our daughters," but to work our land, "For Brazil is an agricultural country that offers great advantages to anyone who comes here in search of bread; but our cities cannot and should not admit these foreigners," who "bring with them nothing but hunger, onions, and stupidity." Let the Portuguese and other foreigners come to till the land. Let Portuguese women "from twelve to twenty years old" come to "perform the household duties and take the place of the Negro women, who are so prejudicial to the proper upbringing of our families." But not those Portuguese who monopolize our small storekeeping and coastwise shipping, reducing the Brazilians to the "condition of slaves." Nor those who, looking upon themselves as adopted sons, meddle in our politics, some of them "giving money to combat Brazilians in the elections" and "all of them flattering those in power, provided they let them continue to enjoy this fountain of gold. . . ." The language of the editors of newspapers like *O Conciliador*, was

---

[4] M. do S. Lopes Gama: "O Luxo no Nosso Pernambuco," *Diario de Pernambuco*, October 31, 1843.

[5] Recife, June 25, 1850.

highly reminiscent of that of the pamphleteers of the bloody and unforgotten days of the Praia Revolt. The same language of those other chauvinists who in Rio de Janeiro in *O Homem do Povo Fluminense* of December 24, 1840, had called the Portuguese "that race of Jews," supported in their anti-Portuguese tirades by *O Pavilhão Nacional* (1850), *O Sino dos Barbadinhos* (1840), *A Sineta da Misericordia* (1849). The attitude of many Brazilians now was that trade—a calling once considered utterly base—should be for them, the native sons, not the "adoptive," the foreigners who were acquiring a power greater than that of the owners of lands worked by slaves, who were becoming increasingly more dependent on the city merchants.

One of the points stressed by *A Revolução de Novembro* of Recife in its editorial of September 29, 1850, was precisely this: that "the agricultural class" was being reduced to a "class that faces ruin because of the huge debts it owes the Portuguese." The editorial touched upon another point that is of particular interest to this study of ours: that "the children of the Portuguese" were considered by their fathers as enemies "and that they were being replaced in their homes, their rights, their inheritances by other Portuguese through marriage with their daughters . . ." The Brazilian or half-breed sons were becoming "the outcasts of fortune," that is to say, of the fortunes accumulated by Portuguese fathers who, through a perversion, economically or sociologically explicable, of the sense (not to say "instinct," as Veblen does) of the patriarchal transfer of power, favored their daughters in the person of the sons-in-law who had come out from Portugal as clerks, who offered little likelihood that they would throw away "the family fortune," turning into poets, politicians, lawyers, or Brazilian intellectuals of one sort or another.

In spite of their weakness for half-breed or mulatto women, the Portuguese distrusted the romantic Bohemianism of the half-breeds or mulattoes—even their own sons—who, contemptuous of trade and inclined toward the liberal professions, toward literature, toward actresses, toward opera singers, might dissipate the wealth often amassed by heroic efforts, prosaic though they were.

The fierce rivalry between students and clerks during the nineteenth century in those cities which were both commercial and intellectual centers, like Rio de Janeiro and São Paulo in the South

and Salvador and Recife in the North, at times involved the white or
half-breed sons of Portuguese merchants, students in the faculties of
law or medicine, where they found themselves aligned with the sons
of plantation or ranch owners, army officers, and high government
officials; and the future brothers-in-law of these young men, that is
to say, clerks of store or warehouses, bookkeepers in the sugar mills,
who almost always were the successors of their fathers-in-law. It
was a rivalry that at times took on amusing features, as, for example, the attempted monopoly by the students of the use of frock
coat, top hat, cane, and black shoes. Only on Sundays did the students
lay aside their heavy clothing—at times to the point of nudity—in
their "republics," which were, as a rule, on the second or third floor
of the city houses. On that day the clerks came down from their
"castles," generally installed in the attic or top floor of the warehouses or stores, where they were provided all week, if their employer was generous, with good, satisfying food (far better than that
of the students, who, when their allowances ran low, economized on
their meals) strolled out in the streets and squares, went to the
cafés and beer gardens, which on weekdays were full of students,
professional men, and army officers. Only on Sundays were the
clerks well-dressed, perfumed, and, on occasion, bathed, some of
them even displaying diamond rings, cuff-links, and gold- or silver-
headed canes as though they were students or members of the
learned professions. And it was at cane point that the rivalries between the two groups over actresses or chorus girls were threshed
out.

It is understandable, up to a point, that the Portuguese businessman should have preferred as head clerk his Portuguese son-in-law
to his own son, half-breed, or Brazilian-born, in view of the severe
discipline which the young Portuguese apprentice underwent in the
warehouse or store, where his life was not too different from that of
a slave. A white slave, who received his training in the despotic,
monosexual warehouse. He grew up under a discipline which the
Brazilian-born son of the Portuguese lacked, spoiled by his mother,
and even at times by his father, so he would seem the son of a landowner or planter and not of a tradesman or tavern keeper. It was
not the son of the plantation-owning gentry that the business needed

if it was to continue prosperous and strong, but these white semi-slaves, who emigrated from their village in Portugal at the tender age of eight or nine. In its issue of September 6, 1849, the *Revista Universal Lisbonnense* commented that "Portuguese emigration to Brazil was made up, almost in its totality, until a few years back," of persons who were little more than infants." Those in greatest demand as clerks and even to work in factories were boys from ten to fourteen. "Wanted: several boys between the age of twelve and fourteen, preferably Portuguese, for a cigar factory," runs an advertisement in the *Diario de Pernambuco* for December 4, 1841. In the Situations Wanted section of the same paper for October 21, 1841: "Portuguese boy for work in sugar warehouse or bill-collecting." "Portuguese boy, recently arrived, seeks work of any sort." And on February 11, 1842: "Portuguese boy who can cipher and write reasonably well seeks employment in a store. 14 years old."

At times the clerks ran away, like the slaves. This was the case of one José Manoel Arantes, who ran away from the house of the shop-keeper Joaquim Guimarães, according to an advertisement the latter had published in the *Diario de Pernambuco* for February 15, 1843; the wording was similar to that of the advertisements for runaway slaves. Advertisements of this sort were frequent. Yet, even with this risk, the tradesmen preferred the Portuguese boys.

On March 11, 1852, the *Revista Universal Lisbonnense* began the publication of a significant series of articles "In Defense of the Portuguese in Brazil." The first was reproduced in a Brazilian newspaper: "The Brazilian farmer sends his produce from the interior to the Portuguese merchant . . . but when he seeks employment for his son he receives a sharp, gruff refusal—Brazilians are no good at trade, they don't adjust . . ." The Portuguese merchant prefers to the sons of Brazilian farmers, whom "he knows to be dissipated, loose, and irresponsible," the young Portuguese who reach him in a virgin state from their country villages, "brought up at the handle of a plow, a mattock, obliged to earn their bread from the day they can walk . . . accustomed to privations from birth." These lads or children could not take up farming or herding in the backlands of Brazil. All they had was their persons. Where could they find the means to set up a farm or a ranch? "For this, land and manpower are needed, but they lack the means to secure the one or the other. Therefore, they must follow the calling most suited to their circumstances, which is trade, where they can start out as clerks."

The third article in the series is of interest here because of the successful rebuttal by the champion of the Portuguese of the charge made by *O Argos Maranhense* of discrimination on the part of Portuguese merchants and craftsmen in Brazil against colored people engaged in the same trade or work: "Let the editors of the *Argos* visit the shop of the blacksmith, the shoemaker, the tailor, the carpenter, the cabinetmaker, or any other, and they will find there many Portuguese working side by side with colored people, whereas the white Brazilians they find will be few, if any. Let them walk through the market stalls, and they will find there plenty of Portuguese, who, for the most part, live only with the former class. And, if the *Argos* makes a careful investigation, it will find not a few Portuguese surrounded in their homes by children, even legitimate ones, who are of African race on the maternal side."

On the other hand, there were many poor white Brazilians who would not serve in the ranks of the National Guard, except as officers, so as not to rub shoulders with colored people. In this respect—the willingness to fraternize with colored people—of all Europeans the poor Portuguese was the quickest to integrate and leave colored descendants. His predilection for making his Portuguese son-in-law his successor in the management of his warehouse or store was motivated by economic reasons, not by race solidarity or concern for purity of blood. What he feared in the Brazilian, even his own son, was his dislike for business routine, and for the hard, monotonous, and, at that time, manual work of store, counter, warehouse.

More than one Portuguese in Brazil was murdered by his own son. "The other day an adoptive Brazilian was murdered in his own home by one of his sons," wrote the author of "In Defense . . ." These were rare, very rare cases, which would never justify the generalization that at any time the Brazilian sons of Portuguese merchants had been systematic parricides. The fact, however, that such crimes did occur would seem to indicate that a resentment existed in many Brazilian sons of Portuguese immigrants, even though they only exceptionally went to such lengths, against the preference shown for brothers-in-law born in Portugal. There were numerous cases of Brazilian professional men and intellectuals, sons of Portuguese, who were characterized by their hatred for Portugal: a sublimation of or compensation for their parricidal fury. The case of the poet Casimiro de Abreu is typical of many young Brazilians who under the influence of a "romantic passion," for the most part of literary origin—and this literary origin French, English, or German—rebelled against the patriarchal system, now no longer rural or, in its own fashion, feudal, but urban and commercial. Unable to adapt themselves to the prospect of being clerks, or irritated and frightened at the thought of turning into prosaic, dull, fat businessmen, they went to the other extreme, leading a Bohemian existence, given over to drinking, women, gambling, proud of the tuberculosis they developed, the "occupational disease" of romantics, poets, Bohemians.

Nor should we lose sight of the fact that there were clerks—and not merely merchants, industrialists, and artisans—who, since the end of the eighteenth century, had become growingly aware of the dignity of their calling through the closer contacts between the Brazilian cities and a Europe already industralized, commercialized, middle-class, even proletarian, and of the possibility that their economic power might become political and ennobling. As ennobling as the honors conferred on individuals and even whole families because of their vast landholdings and many slaves.

If from the beginning of the eighteenth century the monarchs of Portugal had been conferring prestige on the "peddlers" to counteract the excess of economic and political power acquired by the feudal landholders of Brazil, at the beginning of the nineteenth century it was the Brazilian press itself that began to glorify the figures of the merchant, the industrialist, the artisan, attributing to them a major role in the national life.

In 1821 there were already persons in Rio de Janeiro who desired "ardently that the National Industry of the United Kingdom should be further stimulated," and, to this end, that there should be started in Rio de Janeiro, with His Majesty's permission, "an annual subscription for the purchase of Machines or Models." Machines or models with which to encourage our industry, crafts, trade, liberating us from the tyranny of the foreign manufacturer. This pioneer of the industrialization of Brazil, an industrialization identified with its dignity, was Ignacio Alvarez Pinto de Almeida, from whose pen came this significant manifesto in the *Diario de Rio de Janeiro* for September 12, 1821.

Of like intent—favoring the Brazilian manufacturer or artisan—is the "Address to the Ladies," published in the same newspaper for September 18, 1821. It deplored "the depraved habit into which we have fallen of attiring ourselves only in articles manufactured by foreign hands, giving them the support we deny the national workman, sending off to remote lands the currency which, if it circulated within the nation, would liberate it from the abyss of poverty into which it is sunk." To counteract this, the ladies could do their part by "foregoing many things which flatter the appetites and which are not yet made here, or are of poor quality . . ."

These documents are indicative of the movement on the part of those Brazilians attempting to stimulate the development of the country through trade, commerce, manufacture, industry, so long economically negligible and socially disdained to the almost exclusive glorification of the great landowner. Indicative also of the appraisal of business figures in a society in transition from a patriarchal regime to that of "shopkeepers" was the conferring of titles of nobility by the king on industrialists and businessmen, who, for the most part, had begun their commercial career as mere clerks.

Many a clerk found in the living quarters of the warehouse or shop where he worked sweetheart and wife: the daughter, niece, or goddaughter of his rich employer. The Brazilian business system became a kind of urban version of the agrarian system, that is to say, patriarchal and even endogamic after its own fashion.

The patriarchalism, the family sense, the personal relationship characteristic of big business in Rio de Janeiro—and, in fact, of all the cities during the Empire, large or small—surprised the shrewd European, Ladislas Paridant, who wrote a book that is little known but very suggestive, *Du Système Commercial à Rio de Janeiro*, which was published in Liége in 1856. "The commerce of Rio de Janeiro is governed by a series of unjust and outmoded usages and customs which the Portuguese, in their state of decadence, have not known how to revise, and which the other foreign merchants in Brazil, less numerous than they, have not yet been able to change."

The outmoded customs which this Northern European found

were characterized by "a unique quality of familiarity, a marked
fondness for long and noisy conversations." Nor was this all: the
customer was served cakes and wines, just as were salesmen and even
peddlers in the patriarchal homes, to whom the more generous plantation owners even sent Negro or mulatto girls at night to keep them
company. In the warehouses and big business firms of Rio de
Janeiro in the middle of the nineteenth century, alongside the sales-
room there was, according to Paridant, "a table covered with cakes
and wines, among which the sparkling are the most abundant." Nor
should it be forgotten that there was a patriarchal table on the top
floor of the warehouses, where owners, clerks, customers from the
interior, foreign customers ate abundantly.

We can draw the following generalizations: the tendency in Brazil, once trades and handicrafts and, especially, business and industry
came to be recognized as activities essential to the good of the country and compensatory of the efforts of those engaged in them, or
who knew how to organize and manage them, was for these practitioners or directors to assume the manners, gestures, and customs of
the rural patriarchs. In this sense, Minas Gerais took precedence over
the rest of Brazil. The Count of Assumar wrote—at any rate, the
remark is credited to him—in the early eighteenth century that the
Mineiros, though of humble origins, once they had made their fortune, trapped themselves out in titles such as "colonel," "field marshal," "brigadier," thus imitating the rural as well as the military
nobility of the older regions of the country.

In the Brazil of the nineteenth century, successful wooden-shoe
clerks in time became barons, viscounts, grandees of the Empire.
Tradesmen, manufacturers, and even highly skilled craftsmen came
to be outwardly as noble as the landholders, and more so than many
of them, owners of sumptuous mansions, fine carriages, table services
stamped with their coat-of-arms, resplendent uniforms, glittering
decorations. That same mobility which made possible the rise of half-
breeds, mestizos, colored persons to the sociological position of
whites, also favored the rise to the status of nobility of tradesmen,
manufacturers, artisans, of low origin and difficult beginnings.

Andrew Grant in the early nineteenth century observed that the
attitude of persons of standing toward commercial enterprises had
undergone a change in "the last few years." Even the "inveterate

prejudices" against trade on the part of the nobles "were becoming modified" under the "growing liberality"—or liberalism—of the epoch. A number of these nobles were connected with manufacturing enterprises in Rio de Janeiro. A "gentleman of high rank" had set up a rice-processing establishment which employed almost a hundred slaves.[6]

It seemed a pity to the English observer that at the same time that industry, trade, and commerce were developing, Brazil should continue to import Negroes as though they were livestock. The result was that the white master, even those residing in sumptuous mansions, was more debased and unfortunate than the slave.

What happened was that the more intellectually advanced members of the rural gentry accepted industry, crafts, even trade, without giving up the system of slave labor, in spite of their basically bourgeois French and English influences. In this situation of contrasts, Minas Gerais was again the forerunner, and, up to a point, Pernambuco in the eighteenth and even as early as the seventeenth century. But where the contrast was most striking was in Maranhão, at one and the same time so hidebound and so progressive, at the beginning of the nineteenth century.

"There are no farm implements aside from the hoe, and no machinery aside from the wretched slave . . . Transportation is for the most part by river, and when overland, by oxcarts, even poorer than those of Portugal . . ." Yet in that region of colonial Brazil, in spite of the edict of January 5, 1785, forbidding factories or industries in Brazil, there were "rice-hulling factories, cotton gins, sugar mills, distilleries, and cotton mills." Factories operated by slaves and not machines: ". . . The motive power is supplied exclusively by slave arms, and these factories look more like an African dungeon than a pleasant and interesting industrial establishment." [7]

It can be seen from such testimony that the region of Maranhão, (which from the early nineteenth century had rivaled Bahía and Pernambuco in the magnificence of its city residences, was in advance of coffee-growing São Paulo in this respect, and went hand in hand

---

[6] Andrew Grant: *History of Brazil* (London, 1809), p. 151.

[7] Antonio Pereira do Lago: *Estatistica Historica-Geographica da Provincia do Maranhão Offerecida ao Soberano Congresso das Cortes Gerães* (Lisbon, 1822), pp. 56, 64.

with Minas Gerais), was an area of precocious or premature industrialization, but not mechanization, of its economy, which continued
to be based upon slave labor as much, or perhaps more, than the
purely agrarian regions. However, with that early development, its
social organization lost some of the pleasanter features of paternalism
or benevolent patriarchalism. This explains why these three areas
were characterized, in the precocious phases of the industrialization
of their economy, by the severing of the links between master and
slave, or by the exploitation of the worker—reduced to the state of
substitute for the machine—by the employer.

As was natural, this relationship was reflected in the diet of the
slaves, which in the industrialized areas nearly always changed for
the worse. For the objective of these early industrialists was to utilize
to the fullest the youthful energy of the slave (the substitute not
only of horsepower but of machine power) rather than to prolong
the life of a useful servitor through an adequate, if coarse diet, and
adequate housing in slave quarters, even though they had the air of
a prison.

These were the slaves who comprised the major part of the slave
population of the colonial epoch and the early decades of the Empire. In the opinion of various keen-sighted and objective foreign observers—Tollenare, Pfeiffer, and Hamlet Clark—they were better
fed and housed than the free European workers and peasants of the
same period.

On the basis of what we can gather from other sources about the
diet of those slaves who were typical of our patriarchal system, we
may say, broadly speaking, that the slaves of the rich plantation or
wealthy town home were the best nourished of all the sectors of society in patriarchal Brazil. Their diet consisted of beans and bacon,
corn, manioc porridge, yams, rice. According to the German geographer A. W. Sellin, in certain regions rice was "the basic diet of the
slaves," and not only of the masters.[8]

Okra, coconut oil, taro, and other greens or "yarbs," cheap and
easy to cultivate, which the white folks disdained, also entered into
the diet of the typical slave. Greens for whose introduction into

---

[8] A. W. Sellin: *Geografia Geral do Brasil,* 2nd ed. (Rio de Janeiro, 1889),
p. 146.

the Brazilian cuisine, indifferent, as a rule, or hostile to vegetables, the African can be thanked. As cook or confectioner, he contributed —principally through the so-called "cuisine of Bahía"—to the enriching of the Brazilian diet through the greater use of cooking oil, vegetables, "leafy greens." And even of milk and honey. The African, while a slave, was by and large better nourished than the free Negro or mulatto and the poor white of shanty or hut of the interior or the cities, whose diet was normally limited to dried beef or salt cod with manioc meal. Better nourished than the plantation owner or the rancher or the mine owner of average or modest means— and these were the majority—whose diet, too, was characterized by the excessive use of dried beef and salt cod purchased in the cities, and hardtack, dried fish, and manioc meal. As for the rancher's table, where fresh meat was plentiful, there was always a scarcity of vegetables and, for a long time, of rice, which was lacking on the table of the northern backwoodsman, where the staples were cheese and jerked meat, and which was as poor in vegetables as the other patriarchal boards.

As for the diet of the wealthy plantation owners and the richer city dweller, we must remember that it suffered from the excessive use of products imported from Europe under far from satisfactory shipping conditions. The result was that the gentry who disdained the fresh vegetables and greens eaten by the Negroes or slaves consumed many food articles which were rancid and even spoiled.

These are facts which must be borne in mind to offset the generalization, based, for the most part, on anti-slavery sentimentalism or the doctrinaire zeal of those who try to fit the history of patriarchal societies into this or that "ism," that in such societies the slave was always and from every point of view a "martyr," a "victim," "undernourished." The truth of the matter is that there were societies, like that of Brazil, in which, by and large, the slave of the authentically patriarchal regions was better nourished, better treated, led a better life than in those already industrialized or commercialized, which were characterized by the disappearance of the personal relation between master and slave, with the latter reduced to the condition of not even an animal, but a machine. Even at the risk of being repetitious, this is the point I wish to stress here.

It is interesting to note that these regions were not the most rustic nor the most "Oriental," in the sense of being the most distant socially and culturally from Europe. On the contrary, they were the most European from the cultural point of view, like Minas Gerais and Maranhão. Maranhão is known to have been characterized during its early industrial phase by its harsh treatment of the slave, his poor diet, his short life expectancy, and yet it was one of the regions in closest contact with the triumphantly bourgeois and industrial Europe of the nineteenth century, which was England. Pereira do Lago speaks of ladies there who were educated in England, something which at the time did not happen anywhere else, only the sons of the richest and most liberal families being sent there or to other of the more advanced countries of Europe. At the same time, according to this qualified observer, the colored women of Maranhão were outstanding in their degradation: "Nearly all of them are deformed, stupid, uncouth, unkempt, always barefoot, revealing at every moment signs of indecency, without a trace of modesty, walking about the house and the streets in a shift of homespun or cotton, without a blouse or a kerchief . . ." [9] Very different, indeed, from the mulatto and Negro women of Pernambuco, Rio de Janeiro, and, above all, Bahía, famous for their fine dresses, their expensive jewelry, their kerchiefs, shawls, their dainty footgear. This type of Negro or mulatto woman was rare in Maranhão because of the gulf between masters and slaves, the result of a system no longer patriarchal but perverted by a rapid—not gradual as was the case in Bahía, Pernambuco, and Rio de Janeiro—imitation of bourgeois, commercial industrialism.

Before this substitution took place among us, which characterized a complete transitional cycle in areas such as Maranhão, the slave as a rule enjoyed protection of his body and his health and tolerance for his rites, customs, and habits, which it was in the interests of the master of plantation and city mansion to grant to those who were his feet and his hands.

One noteworthy fact stands out: the soldiers of His Majesty in colonial Brazil would seem to have received rations that were markedly inferior to those of the slaves on the majority of the plantations, ranches, and city estates of the period. If we can believe the

---

[9] Ibid. p. 82.

testimony of Lindley, confirmed by Andrew Grant, the artillery troops in the colonial barracks of the opulent city of Salvador—for the most part youths or adolescents who needed an abundant diet, and not grown men who could afford the luxury of abstemiousness —were fed almost exclusively on "bananas and manioc meal," with an occasional ration of fish: "one or two little fish," according to the Englishman.[1] And according to the same source, in Bahía, that is to say, in the suburban residence area, "the more opulent part of the inhabitants possess each a country house . . . generally situated on the banks of a river . . . They are well stored with poultry and domestic cattle, but from total deficiency in the art of cookery, their tables are not much better supplied here than in the city; and indeed they may be said, in a great measure, to exist in poverty and want in the midst of abundance." An observation borne out several decades later by another Englishman, James Wetherell,[2] who more than once makes mention of the insipidness and lack of variety of the food served at the master's table compared with the delicious dishes prepared in the slave quarters, such as the okra and fish stew.

The market of Salvador, whose African population was more numerous and certainly more influential than that of Rio, would seem to have been better supplied with vegetables than that of any other large city of Brazil at the beginning of the nineteenth century. At least, this is what one would conclude from the emphasis Andrew Grant lays on the abundance of yams, manioc, string beans, cucumbers to be found there.[3]

On the basis of Grant's observations one could go on to say that land around Rio de Janeiro was devoted to the cultivation of unspecified vegetables "for the whites," and "rice, manioc, corn, etc.," for the Negroes.[4]

However, from the reports of other observers, one gathers that the outskirts of such cities as Rio de Janeiro, Recife, and Salvador itself were, in the first half of the nineteenth century, being turned into fields of hay or forage for the increasing number of animals at the service of the cities' rich; and of easily grown vegetables and

---

[1] Grant: Op. cit., p. 224.
[2] James Wetherell: *Stray Notes from Bahía* (Liverpool, 1860).
[3] Grant: Op. cit., p. 240.
[4] Ibid., p. 154.

fruits more used by the slaves than the masters, by the blacks than the whites—yams, okra, squash, plantains—eliminating those more highly prized European vegetables whose cultivation was more difficult and costly in a tropical climate.

Grant observed that it was generally believed in Brazil that the hot climate made the production of butter difficult, which he countered with the fact that in India, a country of even hotter climate, "excellent butter" was to be found. What the Brazilian wanted to avoid was the trouble of churning it.

To be sure, the climate was more favorable to the cultivation of tropical food plants than those of Europe. But it is evident, too, that the slave, who was of tropical origin, and was also the worker, cultivated the plants that were to his liking with more enthusiasm than the European varieties which the masters preferred.

Referring to the diet of the slaves on plantations which he considered typical of Brazil at the beginning of the nineteenth century, Rugendas wrote in his famous book:[5] "On every plantation there is a patch of land assigned to the slaves, varying in size according to the number of slaves, each of which cultivates it as he wishes or can. In this way, the slave not only assures himself a healthy and abundant diet, but often sells the surplus at a good price." He then goes on to say: "The situation of the slaves also depends to a large extent on the principal type of cultivation of the plantation to which he belongs; thus it is much worse on new fields and plantations that are being cleared than on those that have already been built up, especially when the new establishments are far from habitated areas, for then the slaves are exposed to all the inclemencies of the weather and bad living conditions as, for example, when their quarters are in the swamps . . ." And he adds: "The slaves are also better treated on the small plantations than on the large, for working together, eating the same food, enjoying the same diversions tends to eliminate nearly all the difference between slaves and masters."

"The young slave is almost always sure of receiving his freedom from his godfather," Rugendas goes on to say, referring to the Negro child who was the godchild of a wealthy master. A master who felt

---

[5] Maurice Rugendas: *Voyage pittoresque au Brésil* (Paris, and Mulhouse, 1835).

himself obliged to act almost as a father, which was a way of affirm-
ing his patriarchal power as well as a display of his economic standing. This latter aspect was denied the poor master, whose patriarchal
responsibility, according to oral tradition, at times took the form
of true fatherly tenderness, allowing the slave godchild to grow up
almost like his own children, with the same food, the same playthings,
the same clothing. Hardly a slave until he reached a certain age.

There were numerous cases of slaves who, under the patriarchal
system, as godchildren of rich plantation owners and city magnates,
enjoyed a special status as a result of which they benefited in their
health and their education. However, such cases should not be considered typical. The typical ones were those who enjoyed no protection beyond that which the system felt to be in its own interests.

"The diet furnished by the masters to the slaves on ranches and
plantations consists of manioc meal, beans, dried meat, fat pork,
and plantains," Rugendas observed. This diet would be meager if the
Negroes had not had the possibility of supplementing it "with fruit,
wild vegetables, and even game." As for the diet of the slaves of the
wealthy city homes, Rugendas did not hesitate to classify it as
"good"; the domestic servants did little work, and those whom their
masters hired out to work in the street in general "enjoyed considerable freedom." [6]

"Considerable freedom" became the portion of the emancipated
Negroes and mulattoes, but not that good diet regularly provided
by the plantation owners and city magnates; nor that same care
which, curiously enough, in certain aspects was more pronounced in
the cities on the part of the wealthy burghers who still retained a
patriarchal attitude. The statement published in the *Idade d'Ouro do
Brazil* for September 25, 1818, by the sugar-mill owners, that is to
say, the wealthy residents of Salvador, is significant. Salvador's economy had not become industrialized, nor its industries mechanized as
swiftly as those of São Luis do Maranhão, and the document in question reveals a sense of patriarchal responsibility joined to the concern
of the employers for their fortunes endangered by the possibility of
accidents to the free workmen. "The owners of the sugar mills of this
city and its environs," the statement reads, "hereby notify the plan-

---

[6] Ibid., p. 179.

tation owners and cane producers that they are not to use crates weighing beyond forty to fifty arrobas, as the law provides, because of the great strain this puts upon the cranes, thus endangering the lives of the sailors and other persons loading and unloading the ships bringing them to this city. In the event that they exceed the aforesaid weight, if any accident should occur, their owners will be held responsible for any damages."

Here we have the first glimmer of accident insurance for workers, and it is of urban rather than rural origin. But it is the protection of the workers by the employer in the interest of the protection of the latter's property rather than the demand for his rights on the part of the worker, threatened in life or limb, and not merely menaced or repressed in his religion, his rites, and other native cultural values, as was the African slave, by the patriarchal system, of which, moreover, he came to form a part. A repression which was perhaps stronger in the proximity of the city mansion than the Big House, although it should be pointed out that in both places the African was able, thanks to his diplomacy, astuteness, and passive resistance (whereby the oppressed in general defends himself with feminine subtlety against the oppressor), to communicate to his Brazilian master the taste for many of his values, including those having to do with diet.

Professor Thales de Azevedo has pointed out in a recent study the advantages for the colonial settlers of Brazil to have been able "to eat, in their pastries, their sweets, stews, and other dishes, not only cashews or peanuts, with their high protein content, but also wild spinach, which of all Brazilian vegetables is the richest in calcium, our varieties of pepper with their abundance of vitamin C, and especially coconut milk and palm oil, that amazingly rich source of one of the carotin series which is transformed in the body into vitamin A, which is indispensable to the protection of the cutaneous and mucous membranes and which, at the same time, plays an important part in the formation of visual purple." [7]

And after recalling the statement of Professor Josué de Castro [8]

---

[7] Thales de Azevedo: *Povoamento da Cidade do Salvador* (Salvador, 1949), p. 307.

[8] Josué de Castro: *Geografia da Fome* (Rio de Janeiro, 1946), p. 279.

to the effect that the sauces of palm oil and pepper are "a concentrated infusion of vitamins A and C," he goes on to say: "The strong teeth of the Negro, considered a hereditary trait, depending on glandular conditions peculiar to the constitutionally tall, athletic type, which is more frequent among the African Negro, may well be related to the consumption of palm oil in their continent of origin."

Moreover, the investigator of Bahía points out, the consumption by the colonial Brazilian of foods such as the different varieties of yam, "rich in elements of Group B vitamins, which as has been proved, greatly contribute to keeping up physical energy, resistance to muscular fatigue, and if we accept the conclusions of investigations which have not yet been completed, to initiative, alertness, good humor," supplemented the lack of proteins in the diet of the poor as a result of their relatively slight consumption of fresh meat . . ." [9]

The use of such articles of food—yams and similar tubers—"by the slaves and the poor," Professor Thales de Azevedo adds, bearing out theories I have already set forth in *The Masters and the Slaves* and other essays, "would seem to explain why, aside from factors of a social and economic nature, that stratum of society was the most energetic and hard-working, whereas the whites surprised foreigners by their laziness, their habit of staying indoors, men and women of the upper classes always sitting or lolling on sofas, rugs, hammocks, or cots . . ." [1]

He thus recognizes the superiority of the diet of the inhabitants of the slave quarters and of the Africanoid population of the shanties—who remained faithful, whenever possible, to the eating habits of the Africans, which were respected, in the majority of the slave quarters, city or country, by the masters because this was economically to their advantage—over the diet of the upper classes, which the whites or mestizos of the humbler homes endeavored to follow or imitate.

Another advantage the slave of Brazil had over the whites or near-whites of plantation or town residence was the fact that he worked almost naked. In the opinion of the doctor of Bahía, "a possible explanation of the low incidence of tooth decay among the Negroes is

---

[9] Azevedo: Op. cit., p. 311.
[1] Ibid., p. 312.

that their habit of going undressed and their prolonged exposure to the sun, together with their habitual consumption of fats, such as palm oil, have been factors which have contributed to making that resistence hereditary." [2]

In contrast to the slaves' taste for going naked, which the majority of the owners encouraged for economic reasons, and their prolonged exposure to the sun, was the social repugnance toward nudity and sun—a form of vanity of race and class—of the whites, whether plantation owner, city resident, rich or poor. They took exaggerated care to avoid both. The parasol became not only a mark of social standing, but also a means of protecting the white or pale or faintly colored skin from the tropical sun which might darken it. The black or brown African had no need of such protection, although, once he was free and had a little money, one of his chief concerns was to use a parasol, put on shoes, and, if possible, attire himself in a silk frock coat or a uniform trimmed with gold braid.

As a rule, the free Negro or mulatto believed that it was to his advantage to dress and even eat like the wealthy whites, to whom he felt linked by his freedom. To leave off rum for wine, greens for pork. To exchange bare feet or sandals for shoes, even though they hurt his feet; the thatched house for that of stone. In much of which he was mistaken.

However, what he was really seeking was to free himself from the complex of slave and African; to resemble the white gentry in attire, gestures, even diet. Nothing made a former slave or son of a slave so happy as to put on the frock coat of a doctor or the uniform of the National Guard or the army—even though this seemed ridiculous to the whites or even the colored street urchins. In his private diary, Francisco José do Nascimento—a Negro of Ceará who became famous as an Abolitionist—tells how much he suffered when he was mocked in the streets of Fortaleza one day while wearing the uniform of an officer of the National Guard. "I never thought I would suffer such shame as I did today," he wrote. "Wearing the uniform of an officer of the glorious National Guard, as I crossed Ferreira Square, a group of gentlemen made fun of me." [3]

---

[2] Ibid., p. 311.

[3] See Edmar Morel: *Dragão do Mar, o Jangadeiro da Abolicão* (Rio de Janeiro, 1949).

Negro women who put on French hats instead of turbans were a laughing stock. Although by copying the usages and habits of their "betters" these free Negroes enjoyed certain advantages over the Negro slaves clinging to their African habits and customs, in other aspects they destroyed their ecological adjustment to the tropical climate of Brazil, which resembled that of Africa.

The villages of shacks, huts, or shanties that grew up in the cities under the Empire evidently represented the desire on the part of free Negroes or runaway slaves to revive African styles of living and association. Some of these villages took on aspects of the organization of the African family, with "fathers," "uncles," and foster-brothers" living in shanties which made up supra-family communities or "republics." But many of the slaves had absorbed, in the shadow of the patriarchal homes of Brazil, European and Christian family sentiments, which were grafted on their basically or traditionally African patterns. This may explain, in part, the desire of a number of free Negroes or mulattoes living in the cities to imitate the whites or Europeans, since, like them, they were free, and living in houses, not slave quarters.

The traditional phrase among the free Negroes of Sergipe when they moved from the slave quarters to the area of the shanties—a phrase recalled by Felte Becerra—is meaningful: "Now I am going to have a window and a back door." [4] This was the complete negation of the typical slave quarters which had neither front window nor back door, being in effect a prison, or a "dovecote," as Joaquim Nabuco called them.

And it is worth mentioning that more than one shanty of free mulatto or Negro went so far as to boast a front porch, where the owner could make a display of his indolence, stretched out like a gentleman in his hammock; and his wife could enjoy the luxury of having her daughter delouse her hair, like the mistress of the Big House or the lady of the city mansion.

There were also shanty mansions, with a basement or first floor, an even more daring imitation of patriarchal and European architecture on the part of the free mulattoes or Negroes than the front or side porch. But perhaps the porch—which influenced even the architec-

---

[4] Felte Bezerra: *Etnias Sergipanas. Contribução a seu Estudo* (Aracajú, 1950), p. 160.

ture of chapels or churches of the interior, giving them a domestic, a lay, a Brazilian quality—was the most ostensible element in the transformation of the shanties into patriarchal dwellings.

The porch of the shanties, in imitation of that of the Big House, was an advantage which the city homes with window and front door lacked. "Narrow, deep houses, without ventilation, and teeming with inhabitants" is the way Miguel Antonio Heredia de Sa describes the houses of Rio de Janeiro in a thesis presented to the Faculty of Medicine of Rio de Janeiro and published there in 1845.[5] And he goes on to say: ". . . In this city, public hygiene is something to which nobody gives the least thought, or rather, it is completely alien and unknown."

In surroundings of this sort, living conditions were such that "bodies ten and twelve years old lodged aged souls." There was a lack of "public hygiene," domestic hygiene, "alimentary hygiene," exercise. To all these shortcomings was added the "damp, hot climate, the polluted air, reeking with nauseous vapors, miasmas, etc.," and "the sedentary life, syphilis, onanism, sodomy," which explained why the man of the city of Rio de Janeiro was predisposed toward tuberculosis—and the woman too.

For in Rio de Janeiro "the destruction of our fair sex" was "shocking." She was the principal victim of "luxury and its terrible effects" and of the "despotic tyrant known as fashion." For "we Brazilians, always imitators, always ready to accept the bad, always monkeys, as foreigners rightly call us, give little heed to whether the prevailing fashions have any relation to our physical environment. The result is that in Rio de Janeiro, where the hot, humid climate is conducive to ailments of the digestive tract and lungs, the ladies lace their corsets and stays so tightly that not a few of them suffer fainting spells; they spend whole nights at dances and parties, where they dance swift waltzes, suited only to cold climates, then cool off with frozen sherbets, etc. . . ."

This as far as the young ladies or mistresses of the patriarchal mansion were concerned. There were, however, in residences on the business streets such as Alfandega, Sabão, and part of São Pedro,

---

[5] Miguel A. Heredia de Sa: *Algumas Reflexões sobre a Copula, Onanismo e Prostitução* (Rio de Janeiro, 1845).

other variants of the "fair sex": prostitutes who not only suffered from many of the same ailments as the decent women, but communicated to the masculine population terrible diseases, the worst of which was syphilis. "No police measures prevent them having sexual intercourse when they are infected with syphilis," exclaims the doctor, eager to see "public hygiene" implanted in the capital of what was still for the most part a huge "plantation colony."

Prostitution took on such increment in Rio de Janeiro after the arrival of Dom João VI that in 1845 there were in the Brazilian capital, in great numbers, the three classes of prostitutes mentioned in an earlier chapter: the "aristocratic," living in residences and even mansions; those of the small houses and "shutters"; and the trash, scattered about in shacks, huts, shanties. The clients of those of the first class were "gentlemen of standing"; those of the second, "neither rich nor poor"; those of the third class, "men unspeakably low."

The gay amusement spots of fashionable harlotry in Rio de Janeiro around the middle of the nineteenth century were once aristocratic dwellings which had become public places, such as the Hotel Pharoux, the Chico Caroço, a dance hall, the Caçador, with dancing and gambling tables. In the latter in 1865 a man was killed and his body was thrown out of the window.

These aspects of the matter are dealt with by Ferraz de Macedo, who broadens Lassance Cunha's classification into a "classifying map," in which prostitution is divided into *public* and *clandestine*. The first, in turn, is subdivided into the *difficult* (which includes, in its first bracket, flower sellers, cigar sellers, chorus girls, and bit-part actresses, etc., and in its second, the "unemployed," living in fine houses, or even expensive hotels); the *easy* (those living at home, in lodgings, or brothels); and the *very easy* ("the overage or worn-out," tenement dwellers, living with some man).

Clandestine prostitution was subdivided into women "of good class" (widows, married, unmarried or divorced women), women of "low class" (free, manumitted, slave), and sexually aberrant persons, male or female.

It was around the middle of the nineteenth century that the prostitute de luxe, in the guise of actress or soubrette, Italian, French, or Spanish, for the most part, became a feature of the Brazilian scene. Some of them residing in houses in which they had been set up, others in expensive hotels, they could be seen driving about the city in style, in barouches with the top lowered, and with coachman and footman, displaying dresses, hats, and shoes of the latest fashion. They came to influence in this way the styles of dress of decent but worldly women, who observed them from the windows of their homes. However, this influence, although it had its beginnings in the mid-nineteenth century, became noticeable only toward the close of the century. For a long time the separation between the "decent" woman and the "kept woman" was so rigid that this would seem to be the chief reason why the ladies of Brazil were so slow in adopting the use of hats. Hats were for "kept women." The mantilla was the only headgear used by the really proper lady.

Newspaper advertisements seem to have contributed to the general use of products which, until the beginning of the nineteenth century, were definitely designed for this or that class, this group or the other of our society: not just for women, but for *women* and *ladies;* not just for men, regardless of the class to which they belonged. Advertisements of North American patent medicines would seem to have played an especially important part. They purported to cure numerous and varied ailments from which anyone might be suffering, not the "gentleman" or "well-born" on the one hand or "the slave" on the other. And also lamps for wall or hall arriving in Rio de Janeiro in 1850 and advertised in the *Jornal do Commercio* for January 22 of that year: "Lamps manufactured along the same lines, and for this reason the cheap ones give as good light as the more expensive." Such products, patent medicines, lamps, children's toys, could not fail to help wipe out the lines of demarcation between classes and subclasses, divisions and subdivisions of Brazilian society, between ladies and "kept women." Dr. Sherman's Tablets "for the treatment of certain obstructions peculiar to the sex," which at first were used only by a certain class of women, would seem to have come into general use by the middle of the nineteenth century, at least in Rio de Janeiro.

It is in the matter of perfumes that the scale of values characteristic of patriarchal society has come down almost to our own days. Certain perfumes were used only by actresses or "entertainers," never by a lady; others exclusively by colored women, never by a white woman of distinction. Whether because of Oriental influence

or some other still to be discovered, men were almost as much given
to the use of perfume as women. Nevertheless, women outdid them.
Francisco Bonifacio de Abreu, referring principally to the first half
of the nineteenth century, points out that ladies left their boudoirs
to attend a dance reeking of perfumes or scents. This excessive use
of perfume brought on "palpitations, giddiness, nausea, vomiting,
etc." [6] Nor could he understand how ladies went to dances even
when they were indisposed, nor that girls should get up from a
sick bed to go to a ball, first kneeling before the image of St.
Anthony or St. Gonzalo to implore the saint to protect them from
drafts or the night air. The result was that many of these delicate
creatures became consumptive. And not only girls but boys. In
Abreu's opinion, the excessive use of ice among the better classes
contributed to this. And also "the vice of Onan."

But it was not only the excessive use of ice, nor the so-called "vice
of Onan." We have already seen that overindulgence in tea and warm
baths was characteristic of patriarchal city society, especially in Rio
de Janeiro. The excessive use of coffee was pointed out by Mello
Franco as a cause of nervousness and tremors of the hands, in which
idea he was supported by Joaquim Pedro de Mello. [7]

These were novelties for the Brazilians of the first half of the nineteenth century: tea, coffee, ice cream, as well as the use of white
bread and beer, which for a long time was so insignificant in our
country as to be sociologically or culturally negligible. Being novelties, it was natural that they should have been used to excess, and
fashion made them so popular that drinks and refreshments more
appropriate to the climate or the milieu were looked down upon.

As for the substitution of sea bathing for the warm bath in the
home, which was another campaign carried on by the Brazilian doctors of the nineteenth century, this was difficult to accomplish. In
1846 Joaquim Pedro de Mello had to admit, in his book already
referred to, that: "sea bathing is difficult for the city dwellers, for the
nearby beaches are filthy and are a garbage dump where the populace throws whatever it likes."

---

[6] Francisco Bonifacio de Abreu: Thesis presented to the Faculty of Medicine of Rio de Janeiro (Rio de Janeiro, 1845).

[7] Joaquim Pedro de Mello: *Generalidades acerca da Educação Physica dos
Meninos* (Rio de Janeiro, 1846).

Even so, it was an advantage for an inhabitant of mid-nineteenth century Rio de Janeiro, which was already becoming crowded with houses, large and small, to live on a hilltop or beside the sea: "the latter an invaluable adjunct to any property in this city, where there is no sewer," as *O Boticario* for May 26, 1852, puts it.

Since 1825 José Maria Bomtempo had been fighting for a Rio de Janeiro more open to the breezes from the sea, or "better ventilation" to offset the dangers of the miasmas from ditches, churches, cemeteries, the ill effects of the dampness of the soil. He even went so far as to hope for the demolition of the hills of San Antonio and Castelo; and to consider it "his duty as a doctor" to say and to write that "the desirable dwelling was a house of various stories well off the ground," and that "single-storied houses should be avoided," although he recognized the fact that "unavoidable circumstances made them necessary." [8]

Many Brazilians of the first half of the nineteenth century were of the opinion that nice people, families brought up along good patriarchal lines, should live, if their home was in the city, in a house several stories high, leaving to others of lower social standing the one-story houses. Some of the apologists for this type of house as the residence of nice people based their conclusions on hygienic considerations, not unmixed with class, racial, and status biases; in the case of others, their concern was frankly and outspokenly social. Among the latter was Antonio Luiz de Brito Aragão e Vasconcellos, who early in the nineteenth century, in his "Memoirs on the Establishment of the Empire of Brazil," said it was the duty of the State in a country like the Brazil of his day "to make the married state seem more desirable, less burdensome, and more advantageous than that of the bachelor." And, in keeping with the patriarchal concept which prevailed among us at the time, "a monarch should be the civil father of his vassals," and, in the opinion of Aragão e Vasconcellos, the sovereign should assign public posts to aid "those persons most in need who are the fathers of families," to whom, in preference to the unmarried, "tracts of land should be given to cultivate . . ."

His preference for married men is understandable in view of his

---

[8] José Maria Bomtempo: *Estudos Medicos Offerecidos a Magestade do Senhor D. Pedro I* (Rio de Janeiro, 1825), p. 10.

desire to see Brazil develop along the lines of "good polity," which was inseparable from stable marriages and also from stable, well-built homes, laid out in the cities in straight lines, and wherever possible, several stories high. He even goes so far as to say: "It would be in the public interest if any householder possessed of a single-story dwelling, and not in a position to build one of several stories, were compelled to sell it to another who could and would build such a house, receiving just compensation therefor; this would prevent the best streets, where the finest buildings should be, from being occupied by one-story, insignificant dwellings."

This attitude, that the house of several stories represented the peak of Brazilian civilization, would seem to have been general among the enlightened figures of the close of the eighteenth and beginning of the nineteenth century. And not only among Brazilians, but among northern Europeans as well, nearly all of them completely imbued with bourgeois ideals. In *Voyage dans les Deux Amériques publié sous la direction de M. Alcide d'Orbigny*, Ouro Preto, far from being held up as an outstanding example of city architecture, is described as being of "mean appearance." [9] São Luis do Maranhão fares better: "The houses, two or three stories high, are, for the most part, built of gray, dressed stone, with well-laid-out interiors." These houses reflected the contact between the residents of that capital and the highest European civilization of the epoch, which was no longer the case of Minas, whose society was now in a state of industrial decline and was reverting in various aspects to the rural ways of life from which the discovery of gold had deflected it.

One of the marks of elegance or modernity in the life of the capital of Maranhão—modernity as understood by a city Frenchman or Englishman—was the role of women in this small urban area of northern Brazil: "They have established the custom in this city of domestic ascendancy over the men, who find this easier to accept than to combat." Some of these women had been educated in Europe, and nearly all of them sent their children to school in France or England. This explains the European atmosphere of São Luis de Maranhão in the first half of the nineteenth century, at the time that

---

[9] Alcide d'Orbigny: *Voyage Pittoresque dans les Deux Amériques* (Paris, 1836), p. 169.

this Europeanization was succumbing to the customs of the country in Ouro Preto. These rustic influences were still, on the whole, the strongest in Brazil in spite of all the re-Europeanization that was taking place with regard to certain fashions and habits.

We should bear in mind in this connection that the bourgeois dwelling, though still patriarchal, was always an index of this process, though it varied from one area to another. This re-Europeanization, in the form of urbanization, had first manifested itself in the northeast in the seventeenth century, in the Minas Gerais area in the eighteenth century, and in the first half of the nineteenth century mainly in Rio de Janeiro, Salvador, São Luis, São Paulo, and then once more in Recife.

In Vila Rica, Rugendas observed a curious aspect of the predominance of the non-Portuguese European influence over the Portuguese or Luso-Brazilian: the roofs of the houses were "pointed like those of the north of Europe, which is more understandable in Vila Rica, because of its climate and altitude, than in the ports of Brazil, where they are, nevertheless, common." [1]

This pointed roof was to be found in the old part of Rio de Janeiro, with its houses three or four stories high, narrow, with only three front windows, in contrast to "the lower houses" of the "more modern section of the city," and with the tall houses of Salvador with their flat roofs.[2] The pointed roof was to be found in Recife mainly "on old buildings constructed wholly along European lines, tall, narrow, and with pointed roof," even more reminiscent of northern Europe than those of Vila Rica.

At the beginning of the nineteenth century, Andrew Grant said of the houses of Salvador that most of them were built in the style of the seventeenth century, enormous, for the most part, but lacking in taste and comfort. "In recent years" there had been going up in the outskirts of the city "fine dwellings belonging to the better classes." The "lower classes lived in low tiled huts or cabins." [3] The better houses were of stone, though some were of adobe; those of the poor were of thatch.

---

[1] Rugendas: *Voyage Pittoresque au Brésil* (Paris e Mulhouse, 1835).
[2] Ibid., p. 18.
[3] Grant: Op. cit., p. 206.

James Wetherell, who lived in Bahía for fifteen years in the early nineteenth century, has left us in his *Stray Notes from Bahía* a careful description of a shanty or city hut: "built of stakes of bamboo, etc., interwoven with pliant twigs. These net-like walls are built double, and the interstices are filled up with mud and clay. The roof is thatched with palm leaves, and this is frequently finished previous to the walls being commenced, so as to preserve the earthen walls from destruction by rain during the process of building . . . The floor is the natural earth . . ." [4]

---

[4] Ibid., p. 51.

CHAPTER VII

BRAZILIANS AND EUROPEANS

Iᴛ ɪꜱ ᴛᴏʟᴅ of Dom João VI that when he arrived in Bahía in 1808 he immediately ordered the city lighted up, "to show the English." Others say that the famous phrase originated at the time the slave trade was forbidden, when laws were passed in Brazil to satisfy British demands rather than to be obeyed. This was the version Emile Allain picked up in Rio de Janeiro, and he interprets it as being the equivalent of the French "to throw dust in the eyes."[1] Whatever its origin, the phrase remained. And it is highly characteristic of that attitude of simulation or pretense the Brazilian assumes, as does the Portuguese, before foreigners. Especially the Englishman, who by 1808 was no longer the heretic nor the "animal" who had to be sprinkled with holy water before being received in one's home, but, on the contrary, a person looked upon as superior in many respects.

Under the gaze of this superior being, the Brazilian of the nineteenth century forsook many of his traditional customs—like dancing in the church on St. Gonzalo's day, for instance—to adopt the manners, the customs, the way of life of the new wave of Europeans who were settling in our cities. From false teeth to the use of bread and beer, which had been very slight before the coming of the English.

---

[1] Emile Allain: *Rio de Janeiro. Quelques Données sur la Capitale et sur l'Administration du Brésil*, 2nd ed. (Rio de Janeiro, Paris, 1886), p. 147.

During three centuries of relative isolation of Brazil from non-Iberian Europe, and, in certain regions, of a highly specialized economy and intense endogamy—as in São Paulo, Bahía, Pernambuco—a Brazilian type of man and woman had developed, or, at least, the outline had emerged. A type of master, another of slave. But there was a midpoint between the two: the mulatto, who little by little was budding out into university graduate, priest, doctor, with his academic diploma or his appointment as captain of the militia serving him as a certificate of whiteness. This middle race comprised our middle class, which was so weak under our patriarchal system.

In the social landscape many Asiatic, Moorish, African characteristics could be discerned, the native elements transformed in a clearly Oriental and not purely Portuguese sense. The house, with the eaves of the red roof in the shape of a pigeon's wing, recalled those of Asia and Asia Minor, with their projecting balconies and the windows divided into small lozenges; the means of travel of the wealthy —palanquins and litters—were those of Asia; the ideal woman, plump and pretty, with big breasts and hips, was that of the Moors; the feminine habit of sitting cross-legged on mats and carpets, at home and even in church, again was that of the Moorish women, as was the habit of covering the face, leaving only the eyes exposed, when setting out from home for church. Moorish was the fondness for painted tiles on the front of the houses, the dado of the halls; the fountains, the wells. The table china came from India and Macao; the bed hangings of the rich were also from the Orient; many of the food seasonings were Asiatic and African, many plants and dishes, and many of the fruit trees about the houses—the Indian palm, the mango, the breadfruit, the dende palm, the fig. One might almost say that whole, living segments, and not merely fashions or vestiges, of these extra-European civilizations had been transplanted here, the native element acting as a kind of human glue to bind all these imports from Africa and Asia, and not merely Europe, to the earth. The Portuguese colony of America had taken on qualities and conditions of life that were so exotic, from the European point of view, that the nineteenth century, during which Brazil's contacts with Europe were renewed—a different Europe now, industrial, commercial, mechanized, representing the triumph of the middle class—was in the nature of a re-Europeanization. A reconquest or a renaissance, like that which took place in medieval Europe with regard to Graeco-Roman culture.

This came about at the close of the eighteenth century and the beginning of the nineteenth, as a result of assimilation on the part of the minority, imitation on the part of the majority (in the sociological sense, first noted by Tarde). It was also the result of coaction or coercion, as in the case of the treaty of Methuen in 1703, which made Brazil almost a colony of England, with Portugal ruling it only politically; and later, in the time of the Empire, of a series of moral attitudes and patterns of living which, of their own accord, the Brazilians would not have adopted. At least not with the rapidity with which they were followed by the minorities, which take the lead in such social transformations.

The reconquest, however, had to take its precautions, for there was opposition, partly of a natural order, partly of a cultural. The climate, for example, was hostile to the Nordic. And under cover of the climate, malaria and yellow fever harassed the Europeans. As did the bubonic plague, syphilis, liver ailments, chigoes, given the lamentable lack of hygiene. These operated in the sense of slowing down the re-Europeanization of Brazil and of preserving, in so far as was possible, the extra-European traits and hues which had become intensified during centuries of isolation.

There were nativists who even rejoiced over the violently anti-European action of yellow fever, a terrible scourge which, sparing the native, was remorseless toward the foreigner—especially the blond, blue-eyed, freckled people.

But the fair foreigner dug himself into the hostile land with a heroism which has not yet been duly honored. Only today, visiting some of the old Protestant cemeteries—those of Recife or Salvador or Rio de Janeiro—which date from the beginning of the nineteenth century, and seeing the number of victims buried in those damp grounds, overgrown by rubber plants, shaded by huge palms, can one form an idea of the hardihood with which the English, to conquer the Brazilian market and establish a new zone of influence for their imperialism, risked death from the yellow fever which was so virulent in this part of the tropics. The inscriptions follow one another with melancholy monotony: "James Adcock, architect and civil engineer who after nearly three years of residence died here of yellow fever in the 39th year of his age." "In memory of Robert Short, fifth son of William Short of Harrogate, died of yellow fever, aged 19 years." "In loving memory of my beloved husband Ernest Renge Williams who died of yellow fever, aged 26 . . ."

Once the reconquest of Brazil by Europe began, it did not stop. Even today it overwhelms us, with the European of Europe now being substituted by the quasi-European of the United States. The blond martyrs have triumphed in part, at least, in the battle joined in Brazil between the Nordics and the tropics. It was yellow fever that was vanquished. And this reconquest brought about a change in the Brazilian scene in all its aspects.

The re-Europeanization began by dimming the African, Asiatic, or indigenous elements in our life, whose bright colorfulness was typical of our landscape, attire, and habits. The color of the houses, the palanquins, the women's shawls, and the men's ponchos. The colors of the interior of the churches, the reds, the golds, the scarlets. The color of the furniture, which, even when of rosewood, was painted red or white.

All this, which gave such an Oriental tone to our daily living, began to fade as it came into contact with the new Europe; it turned drab, and became the exception—the color for feast days, processions, carnival, military parades. The New Europe imposed upon a still rustic Brazil, which cooked and worked with wood, the black, the brown, the gray, the navy blue of its carboniferous civilization.

Black frock coats, black boots, black top hats, black carriages sombred our existence almost overnight, made of our attire, in the cities during the Empire, almost heavy mourning. This period of the re-Europeanization of our landscape by the introduction of blacks and grays—civilized, urban, middle-class colors, in contrast to the rustic, Oriental, African, plebeian—began with Dom João VI, but became even more pronounced under Dom Pedro II. The second Emperor of Brazil, when but a stripling of fifteen, already dressed and thought like an old man; at the age of twenty-odd he was "the saddest monarch in the world," according to a European traveler. He seemed to feel comfortable only in his Prince Albert and black silk hat; and uncomfortable, ridiculous, out of character, in his royal robes and crown. He felt comfortable only in European attire and in accord with the new civilization of Europe, the indus-

trial, the gray, the English, the French, which finally, through one
of its victims, the poet Verlaine, begged for "no color, merely the
nuance." With the Gothic, military civilization, the Catholic and ecclesiastical, Dom Pedro's links were very tenuous. He did not even
like to ride horseback; he was the typical city European.

This frock-coated Emperor, who was one of the first persons in
the world to talk by telephone, in his high-pitched, almost effeminate
voice, became the model of the younger generations of Brazil, the
propagandist of the latest fashions of Europe in a country which had
been isolated from developments there for three centuries as a result
of its contacts with the Orient and Africa, its rural, somewhat backwoods patriarchalism, and by the growth of a way of life adapted
to its climate, and perhaps to the physical and psychological characteristics of its inhabitants, dark-skinned and even Negroid. In the
matter of color preference, there are those who are of the opinion
that dark-skinned persons have a preference for red, due to the
greater pigmentation of the retina; and that fair-skinned persons are
more inclined to the blues and grays.

It is not merely a figure of speech to say that the blackness of
clothing, carriages, machines gave Brazil the air of being in deep
mourning. Everything would seem to indicate that the mortality
among us rose with these first manifestations of the re-Europeanization of our life and customs. In 1849 a doctor raised his voice in
alarm at the increment of tuberculosis under the Empire. In enumer-
ating the causes for this dismaying increase, Dr. Joaquim de Aquino
Fonseca pointed out as one of the more important, the closer relations between the Empire and Europe. These relations had had a
great impact on our dietary habits, "introducing a variety of abuses,"
and also on the dress of the city dwellers. Habits which had changed
in the sense of a slavish imitation of attire suited to a cold climate,
garments of thick, heavy cloth totally unfit for the tropics, but which
European industrialism, seeking a market for its products, had made
fashionable. Imperialist colonialism, to use the Marxist phraseology.

"Formerly," says Dr. Aquino, who, incidentally, had studied
medicine in France, "clothing was lightweight and loose, and completely in keeping with the warm climate of the city, facilitating the
respiratory movements and, consequently, the oxygenation of the
blood, and preventing perspiring, thus avoiding the ill effects of

drafts, so frequent here. But the French fashions, which make lacing necessary to correct certain bodily defects, hamper the respiratory movements of ribs and diaphragm, thus interfering with the oxygenation of the blood; and the woolen fabrics turn garments into veritable stoves, predisposing their wearers to affections of the respiratory system . . ." [2]

In the eighteenth century, which was perhaps, as far as customs were concerned, the most autonomous, the most rustic, the most Brazilian in our social history, Vilhena rebutted the criticism on the part of certain European travelers of the loose clothing worn by Brazilians in the intimacy of their homes. He pointed out that this laxity, which was so distasteful to those who came from colder regions, was in keeping with the tropical climate of the colony.[3] Luccock, such a severe critic of our manners in the last years of our authentically colonial existence, associated the fact that children went about in the house almost naked—"nothing but linen under garment"—with the hot climate, which made heavy clothing unbearable.[4]

But with the re-Europeanization of our country, even the children became martyrs to European fashions. Perhaps the greatest of all were the little girls. The fashion plates of the nineteenth century are full of models of dresses for girls of five, seven, nine, which were practically strait jackets of silk, taffeta, grosgrain. Little five-year-old girls obliged to wear two or three petticoats over their pantalettes. And not only this excess of petticoats. A cap of black velvet trimmed with pheasant feathers; high black kid shoes.

The doctors raised their voices in vain, saying that the clothing of the Brazilian child should be just enough to protect his body from changes of temperature; that children in a tropical country could not and should not be raised like English, German, or Russian. Brazilian parents, especially those of the city, wanted no part of the injunctions of finicky doctors. They dressed their children in true European style. Never mind if the poor things suffered rashes, chafing. What mattered was for them to seem English or French.

---

[2] Joaquim de Fonseca quoted by Octavio de Freitas in *A Tuberculose em Pernambuco* (Recife, 1896).

[3] Luiz dos Santos Vilhena: *Cartas*, etc., p. 89.

[4] John Luccock: *Notes on Rio de Janeiro and the Southern Parts of Brazil* (London, 1820), p. 127.

Nor was it only children's clothing; their entire upbringing was re-Europeanized as the colony, and later the Empire, came into closer contact with the ideas and fashions of England and France. And here we observe a contrast; whereas the contact with English and French fashions had the effect of making life more artificial, of stifling our senses and depriving our eyes of the taste for pure and natural things, the contact with ideas, on the contrary, brought us more precise notions of the world and of tropical nature itself. A spontaneity which Portuguese and clerical education had caused to dry up in the Brazilians.

The system of monoculture, which had laid waste the physical landscape about the houses, the teaching in the Jesuit schools, which laid waste the intellectual landscape, allowing only orthodox Catholic ideas to flourish (which, as far as the Jesuits were concerned, were only the Jesuitical), destroyed in the Brazilians, principally in the educated classes, not only the relations between man and nature —a rupture whose effects can be felt even today in our ignorance of the names of the plants and animals which surround us and in our indifference toward their habits or peculiarities—but also the curiosity for learning, the desire and the pleasure of knowing, the joy in the adventures of the mind, the senses, and the scientific exploration of nature. This curiosity, this pleasure, this joy were transmitted to us toward the end of the eighteenth century and throughout the nineteenth by the Encyclopedists and the French and Anglo-American revolutionaries. And during the nineteenth century by French and English teachers who opened schools here, to the great indignation of the priests.

These teachers and those Encyclopedists did the Brazilian a certain amount of harm, instilling in him a fictitious liberalism; but they did him good, too. They opened up to him new zones of sensibility and culture, restoring to a degree his intellectual spontaneity, which had been stifled in so many aspects, not so much by the Inquisition as by the uniform teaching, which was useful, highly useful from the point of view of the social integration of Brazil, but which held back and almost dealt a death blow to the intelligence, the powers of discriminating, criticizing, creating.

There is nothing more enervating to the mind than the exclusive or almost exclusive teaching of Latin or any dead language. This was the type of teaching that grew up among us under the influence of the religious schools.

In proportion as the teaching of the Jesuits was creating in the colonial cities small elites of scholars, for the most part unctuous Latinists (among whom, notwithstanding, certain rustic temperaments stood out, as in the case of Gregorio de Mattos [5]) the reading of Latin became the only reading that was considered worthwhile—Virgil, Livy, Horace, Ovid. Anyone who read a story or novel in the vernacular felt the mistrustful eye of the Inquisition or the Jesuits upon him. The only intellectual pleasure of the Bachelors or Masters of Arts educated by the Jesuits was to read and learn by heart the old Latin poets.

In the academies established in Rio at the begining of the eighteenth century, and in that of Mariana and Olinda—institutions whose pedagogical orientation differed from and was even antagonistic to the system of the Jesuits—high priority was still given to the study of Latin, although in that of Olinda science and living languages were included in the curriculum. Beginning with Father Pereira's grammar, *The New Method*, and Phaedrus's *Fables*, the teaching of Latin proceeded through Ovid and Horace. It was a stern discipline and would have been excellent if it had not been exclusive. The student went through the most difficult phase of declinations and conjugations with the aid of quince switch and ferule. But in the end he could not write even a brief note except in solemn, lifeless terms, avoiding living words even in his conversation.

Rhetoric was studied in Latin authors, reading Quintilian, reciting Horace, learning the orations of Cicero by heart. Cicero's speeches continued to be the main source for logic. Philosophy was that of the orators and the priests. Many of the terms, and always the tone, were that of the *Apologetics*, which undermines the dignity of analysis and compromises the honesty of criticism. Hence the oratorical tendency characteristic of the Brazilian, impeding his ability to think clearly as well as to analyze things, facts, people. Even when dealing with matters which call for the greatest verbal restraint, precision, a conversational rather than oratorical tone, all possible objectivity, the

---

[5] Colonial poet of Brazil, known for his social criticism.

Brazilian unconsciously raises his voice and rounds out his phrase as though he were taking an examination in rhetoric.

The teaching of Greek, which might have given a different rhythm to the style of our writers and a different perspective to our early intellectuals, never acquired the same importance as that of Latin. The Franciscan friars, who in 1772 established in Rio de Janeiro, with a royal charter, the first institution with university aspirations, included Greek and Hebrew in the curriculum. But this attempt had neither the vigor nor the efficacy that might have been expected. The Franciscans in Brazil were the "Bohemians" of religious activities as compared with the Jesuits, whose efforts were always so well concerted. However, the official study of French and English dates from the establishment of this program of advanced studies set up by the Franciscans.

For a long time the study of these languages carried with it a taint of religious or political deviation, a hint of intellectual waywardness. Nevertheless, they were revolutionizing the life of the Brazilian elite, which, up to then, had been isolated from the new intellectual trends as a result of the almost exclusive study of Latin. With the study of French there began that contact with those new ideas which later on, acquired at first hand in France by Brazilian students of medicine and philosophy, supported the Revolution of Minas Gerais,[6] directed by intellectuals under the influence of French or Anglo-American thought, and that of Pernambuco of 1817,[7] sparked by priests who were no longer content to read only Latin, but read French also and could even get the sense of English. Luccock observed that in Rio de Janeiro at the beginning of the nineteenth century French books were in demand; those in English were still avoided, perhaps, he suggested, because it was regarded as the language of heretics who were even more dangerous than the French.[8] The same aversion seems to have been felt for the language of the Flemings when they occupied the North of Brazil, as well as for

---

[6] An uprising against Portuguese domination.

[7] A movement in favor of a republican form of government.

[8] Luccock: Op. cit., p. 129. See also G. Freyre: *Ingleses no Brasil* (Rio de Janeiro, 1948).

Two-story chalet superimposed on original colonial dwelling: a result of the re-Europeanization characteristic of the middle of the nineteenth century.

French and English, both of which were also spoken in that region of Brazil during the Dutch domination.

Seventeenth-century Recife for thirty years heard many different tongues spoken in its streets and many of its homes. Even though the Dutch language seems to have left few, if any traces, in the Portuguese of the North, the records of their occupation make it clear that Dutch was taught in the schools for the Indians directed by Calvinist pastors and missionaries. The catechisms and religious tracts would seem to have been written not only in Dutch but in Portuguese and Tupi, and the missionaries were required to know the language of the Indians or Portuguese. It should also be pointed out that even the names of the Dutch who remained in Brazil and married Portuguese women took on a Portuguese form or disappeared. Nevertheless, the Dutch influence brought about, in that part of Brazil where it predominated during the seventeenth century, the Europeanization of Brazil in a non-Portuguese sense. As the result of a series of contacts with Northern European culture, the northeast became slightly different, and for all time, from the rest of the colony.

Various features of this Europeanization persisted in the landscape and the spirit of the people even after the North had been reconquered by the Catholic Portuguese. I use the term "Catholic Portuguese" because during the Dutch domination, under Hebrew names translated into Portuguese—Isaac, Jacob, Abraham—and family names undistinguishable from the Portuguese—Campos, Cardoso, Castro, Delgado, Pinto, Fonseca—a strong current of Sephardic culture, that of the Portuguese Jews who had come out from Amsterdam, was at work among the inhabitants of the Brazilian northeast, in the sense of social and intellectual differentiation. Moreover, it seems that even earlier there were, mainly in Bahía, a number of New Christians, some engaged in the practice of medicine, others in trade, and even in the sugar industry.

If Bahía became the first center of medicine in Brazil, in the city of Salvador, as early as the seventeenth century, there were already Jewish converts skilled in the treatment of the sick and who prescribed pork so that no informer might throw suspicion on them. Medicine was always one of the specialties of the Sephardim; it was their way of competing with the confessors and chaplains in influencing the great families in Christian countries and the important figures in the government. There is no doubt that it was they who brought it to Brazil in its more advanced forms, and developed it in Bahía and Recife. Velozino, one of the greatest Jewish physicians of the seventeenth century, was from Recife.[9]

Dutch-Jewish Recife became the greatest center of intellectual differentiation in the colony, which the Catholic efforts toward integration attempted to isolate against the new learning and the new languages. Under Count Maurice of Nassau, in a grove of cashew trees, the first observatory of America was built; in what had been mangrove swamps, a botanical and a zoological garden. Piso and Marcgraf made their appearance, the first to study from a scientific approach the natives, the trees, the animals of Brazil; Calvinist ministers preaching new forms of Christianity; the artists Franz Post and Zacarias Wagner painting plantation houses, Indians' huts, Negro cabins, cashew trees along the riverbanks, colored washerwomen with bundles of clothes on their heads, Indians, half-breed, Negroes; Peter Post drawing up the plans of a large city of tall houses and

---

[9] Dutch Recife attracted Jewish scholars from Europe as well as doctors and technicians. See M. Keyserling: "The Earliest Rabbis and Jewish Writers of America," *Publications of the American Jewish Historical Society*, No. 3 (New York, 1895).

City mansion in Recife, in the second half of the nineteenth century. It already shows the new European influence.

deep canals on which one could travel by canoe as in Holland. A wealth of intellectual, artistic, scientific, religious differentiation. The Portuguese and Catholic monopoly had been broken in Pernambuco, the monopoly on architecture, religion, ways of life; and, for a time, even the monopoly on language.

In that Recife, so different from the other colonial cities by reason of its way of life and its multifarious population of Dutch, French, Germans, Jews, Negroes, half-breeds, Catholics, Protestants, during a period of thirty years not only were nearly all the languages of Europe and several of Africa spoken, but in the synagogues a Hebrew that differed from the corrupt, garbled version of the Ashkenazim was studied and written, the old and aristocratic Hebrew maintained in all its purity by the black-bearded, sad-eyed rabbis whom the Congregation of Amsterdam sent out to Pernambuco. In the kitchens of many a home, with the liberty that the Jews enjoyed under the Count of Nassau, favorite Israeli dishes were undoubtedly prepared, and it is possible that the custom of cooking beans overnight, that is to say, food prepared on the eve of the Sabbath, may be a Jewish legacy. On country estates, lambs were raised and chickens fattened to be slaughtered according to the Mosaic law, and eaten during the Passover with unleavened bread and bitter herbs. And in the rear of the shops, and even in public, the God of Israel was worshiped, Judaism was practiced. Perhaps even the Kabbala, which accorded so well with the lively imagination of the Sephardim.

The male children were circumcised. The mournful *piyyutim* were recited, not always fearfully and under the breath. Perhaps at the very hour that in the Papist churches and even in the street, in processions authorized by the Count, praises were being intoned to the Virgin Mary and the Infant Jesus, and the French, Dutch, or English faithful were singing hymns glorifying another God, that of St. Paul and Calvin. And meanwhile, from the nearby woods, from the shanties in the mangroves, there reached the stone churches and synagogues the shouts of Indian medicine men or the howls of bands of Negroes singing the praises, of Xangó or Saint Barbara, imploring a bountiful harvest of corn to fill their cooking gourds, commending one of their dead to the deities' care, and the bolder ones calling upon Exú.

Deep in the mangroves, in strange, deserted places, perhaps in the stretch of isthmus connecting Olinda with Recife, where later a student was murdered, a soldier was shot, and a Negro woman disappeared one dark night—some say swallowed up by the mud, others, carried off by Exú; amidst the mangrove swamps and the secluded spots, along the shore where the heathen Negroes were buried, the more barbarous forms of religion flourished. And it seems that on Sundays the hurly-burly reached its height. Bold groups came to sing and dance under the walls of churches and fine residences. More than once the Reformed Assembly of Recife lodged a complaint against the excesses of the Negroes, the Papists, and the Jews. The Reformed Church wanted no voice but its own raised in praise of the Lord on Sunday. The scandalous way in which the Papists and others practiced their rites was a profanation of the Lord's Day. The songs and cavorting of the Negroes would arouse the divine wrath. All that hubbub in the street disturbed the services in the churches of the true God (the Dutch Reformed).

However, it can be sensed, amidst the fruitless complaints of the cantankerous members of the religious assemblies, that the Dutch government, at least in the time of the Count of Nassau, turned a deaf ear on these incitements to religious hatred, permitting Papists, Jews, even Negroes to abuse the freedom that had been allowed them. It was in abuse of this freedom that the native midwives took to baptizing the children of Protestants according to the Catholic

*Mansion in Rio de Janeiro in the middle of the
nineteenth century. (Drawing by M. Bandeira after
an etching of the period)*

rites; the Jews, to assembling openly in the market place, and even
trying to make converts of the Christians, the bolder going so far as
to circumcise the sons of Christians. In Serinhaem, certain Protestants who refused to kneel before the images of saints being carried
in a procession were not only insulted by the Papists, but even beaten.
And nearly all the Dutch owners of sugar mills not only fell into the
Portuguese habit of starting to grind their cane on Sundays, but some
even requested the priest's blessing on the mill, while in the cities
many a Calvinist adopted the habit of crossing himself at the sound of
the church bell.[1]

Christianity in its more lyric form, that more poetically associated
with the life and labors of man, was getting the upper hand of the
prosaic puritanism of the Reformed Church.

Thus, the Dutch domination was an epoch of transculturation
with the conquerors coming to terms with the conquered. In the latter the experience of the "times of the Flemings" affected their lives
in the sense of universalizing them. Their adjustment to Portuguese
rule in America would never again be complete, nor their social re-
integration to the Portuguese pattern absolute.

---

[1] See in Jean Crespin: *A Tragedia de Guanabara* (Tr., Rio de Janeiro,
1917) the appendix: "The Reformed Christian Religion in Brazil in the Seventeenth Century."

In the sense of differentiation, the influence of the Sephardic culture and Jewish trade, so cosmopolitan in the relations it engenders and establishes, was particularly strong in the North of Brazil. This same cosmopolitan trade would later exert its influence on a zone as landlocked as that of Minas Gerais, which in the eighteenth century and the beginning of the nineteenth suddenly appeared on the scene with a multiplicity of relations with Europe.

What the mere fact of being coastal did *not* do for areas where the European influence would have seemed more natural (certain eastern regions of the colony quickly developed the characteristics of isolation or social stagnation usually associated with inland areas), the variety of cultural contacts created by the development of the diamond trade did for Minas Gerais. In contrast to the trade in gold, that in diamonds and other precious stones, by its very nature, refused to allow itself to be limited by the controls of the mother country. It went out to seek its own markets, which were principally those of Holland, under the control of Jewish techniques and finance. This explains the commercial relations of Minas with non-Iberian Europe,[2] which came to include intellectual and political relations of liberal trend, as well as practical, one of whose expressions was the greater use of window glass in its wealthy homes. This luxury consumption was not limited to window glass, but included a multitude of articles imported from Europe at great expense for the homes of the rich Mineiros. The canopied beds, the clothing of men and even women, the ideas and the reading of the educated persons reveal how that society, so separated from Europe by miles and mountains, surpassed the coastal areas lying closer to Europe in the quality and manner of its way of life.

Nor does wealth alone explain all this brilliance of life and ideas in eighteenth-century Minas. We have already mentioned those rich planters of Goitacases whom Prince Maximilian found at the beginning of the nineteenth century living in miserable mud dwellings, not much better than shanties, lacking all stimulus of an intellectual or psychological nature to complement the economic. A fine house with luxurious fittings, horse and carriage, fashionable attire in Brazil did

---

[2] See Manoel Cardozo: "The Brazilian Gold Rush," *The Americas*, III, 2 (Washington, October 1946), p. 140.

not always mirror the economic standing of their owner. The regions where the European influence was strongest were not always the richest. Economic determinism alone is not valid in the interpretation of a long series of social processes; nor geographic determinism when it attempts to account for such complex and dynamic facts as those having to do with human beings. What is apparent in the social history of the Brazilian family, so varied from the sixteenth century on in the types of beings it produced and its cultural achievements, so uneven in its modes of dwelling, dress, and transportation—an aristocracy imbued with European ways living cheek by jowl with settlements of Indians, eighteenth-century Portugal side by side with nineteenth-century France or England—is the great variety of cultural contacts with Europe, which was bourgeois from the seventeenth century. This variety was nearly always the result of the stimulus—rarely of the imposition or determination—of economic conditions or geographic facilities. At times, as in the case of Minas Gerais, the cultural factor outweighed geographic difficulties. Or, as in the case of the wealthy planters of Goitacases, social isolation—whose causes have not yet been explained; psychological, perhaps—created a type of life which, on the basis of economics alone, should have been diflerent.[3]

Social isolation sterilizes the individual or the human group and gives rise to a lag in living habits, as the students of isolated cultures have repeatedly pointed out. In the case of Brazil, it must not be assumed that the degeneration of the backward culture, which took place here when it came into contact with the more advanced, rules out the phenomenon of cross-fertilization. The only thing to be borne in mind is that the reciprocity between cultures, not radically different but unequal in their technical and military resources, is never accomplished with complete success. The conquered are not always able to prevent the loss of prestige of elements seemingly external or ornamental, but which are in reality fundamental to their life and economy. Elements affected by the science—medicine, for the most part—religion, and ethics of imperialism seeking, for economic reasons, not regional diversity but standardization; avid of expanding markets for its industries. The nakedness of primitive peo-

---

[3] Alberto Ribeiro Lamego: *O Homem e o Brejo* (Rio de Janeiro, 1945).

ples or the differences of dress and footwear among the civilized—
like the bound feet or the pigtails of the Chinese, for example—are
differences which are morally repugnant to imperialist Europeans.
But over and above this moral repugnance there is nearly always the
indirect stimulus of the economic desire for markets for their stand-
ardized products.

A case in point is the straw house of the natives of the tropics, the
Afro-Brazilian shanty. The repugnance of the European imperialists
for the shanty was not always for moral or hygienic reasons alone;
the economic factor may well have entered into it.

Prince Maximilian felt real contempt for the homes of the landholders of Goitacases, who, despite their wealth, lived in such anti-
European fashion. But in the Prince's contempt there may have been
a sense of economic superiority, which European imperialism had
created even in its scholars and scientists. Perhaps, through Maximilian, European imperialism was speaking—indirectly, of course—lamenting the fact that those rich were living in so favored a land without the comforts European industry could supply.

Saint-Hilaire's reaction seems to have been the same in Rio Grande
do Sul, when he pointed out the extreme simplicity of the homes of
the wealthiest ranchers. Mere shelters. The physical comforts of the
master practically the same as those of the workers. Straw-thatched
houses, squat, built of logs chinked with mud. The living rooms without windows, and instead of doors—glass doors were unheard of—
separating one room from another, curtains, of coarse cloth for the
most part, made by some slave. The furnishings—two or three rustic
chairs of leather. The beds with a bottom of cowhide. A board dais
where the lady of the house worked and a plank table where the
owners ate the same barbecued meat and drank the same bitter maté
tea as the inhabitants of slightly more rustic homes, their hands.[4]

But even in the slavocrat regions, where the differences in the type
of life between master and worker were more marked, Saint-Hilaire,[5]
and before him Dampier, in the early seventeenth century, had observed a certain contempt on the part of the rich for domestic com-

[4] A. Saint-Hilaire: *Voyages dans les Provinces de Saint-Paul et de Sainte-
Catherine* (Paris, 1851). See also Arsène Isabelle: *Viagem ao Rio da Prata e ao
Rio Grande do Sul* (Tr., Rio de Janeiro, 1949).
[5] Saint-Hilaire: Op. cit.

forts; the luxury they prized was, in the city, fine clothing; in the country, the silver-trimmed fittings of their horses. And, above all, the number of their slaves and the extent of their holdings. In Rio Grande do Sul, the size of their herds and the quality of their horses were for many the greatest mark of social distinction.

The exceptions were part of the northeast, where colonization had begun in the sixteenth century with large, well-built houses and chapels; and later on, in the eighteenth century, the region of Minas Gerais, where Mawe, at the beginning of the nineteenth, still found in the rich houses traces of comfort and even of luxury in the European manner, which reflected not only the economic advantages and the fertility of the soil the colonists had found and developed, but also their closer contact with Europe.

The diamond trade, which attracted to Minas European interests, and, above all, the intervention of Jewish technique and finance, overcame the physical gap which separated that region from Europe, and gave rise to a series of special relations between the wealthy middle class of Ouro Preto, Sabará, Santa Lucia and the urban, industrial civilization of Northern Europe. Stimulated by the greater variety of foreign contacts, the forces of social differentiation became accentuated, bringing about a violent break with those of integration. Hence the revolution of Minas Gerais, which was a clear manifestation of the cultural, and not merely the economic, differentiation which had taken place in that area. Of the same nature were the Pernambucan revolts of 1710, 1717, 1724.[6] In all of them, economic reasons played a part, but not the only one. Together with other influences, they conditioned cultural attitudes, including the inclination toward liberal forms of government, which developed in these two regions, so different topographically, the one landlocked, the other coastal.

Through these two regions, differing in their geographical situation and in the moral make-up of their settlers, Brazil became one of the countries of America which profited most from the best the Jew had to offer in cultural values and in stimuli to our own intellectual development.

---

[6] Independence movements; the two nineteenth-century ones aimed at a republican form of government.

Through the doctors and teachers which the congregation of Amsterdam sent out to Recife and Salvador, Brazil received from the old Sephardic culture many valuable contributions of a scientific, intellectual, technical nature. Moreover, the Sephardic Jew who came to Brazil from Holland was not wholly alien to the predominant culture of Brazil, that is to say, the Iberian or Hispanic. The hymns he sang were inspired by Spanish and Portuguese poets. And instead of the niggardliness, the avarice, the rapaciousness of the Ashkenazim, his habits revealed a magnificence which was very Spanish and Portuguese: the pleasure he took in rich clothes of silk and velvet for festive occasions, an abundant table, his love of learning, his intellectual bent.

These traits, which even today, after the lapse of centuries, are still to be found, though somewhat dimmed, among the Jews of Spanish origin dispersed in Constantinople, Smyrna, and Salonica, the Sephardim brought to Brazil in their full flower. Their brief exile in Holland had not withered their profound Spanishness. Therefore, this apparently exotic colonization of the Sephardim in Brazil—people whose Portuguese names persisted, though at times in garbled form, even in New Amsterdam—was in reality a colonization by people of the same family, so to speak. A colonization which did not basically disturb the process of social integration of the new Portuguese colony, but rather tended to balance differentiation with integration.

The principal element of differentiation which the Jews brought to Brazil was their aptitude for international trade, which enriched us with a variety of contacts which would have been impossible had we been exclusively Portuguese. And also their scientific and literary inclination, which was stimulated in them by their multiplicity of contacts, in contrast to the rustic, Old Christian Portuguese. This inclination had been stimulated in them not only during exile, but in the Iberian peninsula itself when, barred from politics and a military career, they found compensation for their repressed desires of glory and triumph, personal or of family or race, in an intellectual or scientific career: medicine, teaching, literature, and, up to a point, mathematics and philosophy. Fathers merchants, sons doctors—this was the process of their social ascent in Portugal.

Scattered through the north of Europe, the Italian republics, the Near East, Africa, wherever the Sephardim, whom the Inquisition had driven out of Spain, settled, they established business relations with one another, and thus developed a vast international network of trade. Brazil came to share in the benefits of this in the seventeenth and in the eighteenth centuries, developing contacts through the Jews with Holland and England, with the Near East and the Italian republics.

This explains, in large part, the cultural upsurge in Pernambuco during that first century when the differentiating influence of the Jews joined forces with that of the Dutch, or, more strictly speaking, that of Maurice of Nassau; as well as in the cities of Minas Gerais of the eighteenth century, where the Jewish infiltration was less apparent and probably more commercial than social or intellectual. There are those who are of the opinion that Bento Texeira Pinta of Pernambuco, the first poet to sing the beauties of Brazil and the glory of Portugal in the sixteenth century, was himself a Jew.[7] And Jewish literature on the American continent began in Pernambuco with a poem written by Aboab da Fonseca in the seventeenth century.

In the South, for the most part in Minas Gerais, the fact that certain of the best old families have typically Semitic features would justify the conclusion that there was a strong admixture of Jewish blood in the old diamond region. Historical records bear out the fact that not a few persons, and even whole families, in the captaincy of Minas, especially in Vila Rica, Serro Frio, and Paracatú, were condemned by the Inquisition for persisting in the practice of Judaism.

The trade in diamonds and precious stones, which certain investigators of the Jewish expansion in America believe to have been controlled in the eighteenth century by the Jews, brought about rela-

---

[7] This possibility was first suggested by the author of this book in the preface to the edition of the poem by C. Pereira da Costa (Recife, 1927), and also by Joaquim Ribeiro, on the basis of internal evidence. It was later accepted by the well-known authority on Brazilian colonial history, Rodolfo Garcia, in his introduction to *Primeira Visitação do Santo Ofício* (São Paulo, 1929). João Peretti, of the Institute of Archaeology, History, and Geography of Pernambuco, reached the conclusion that the Bento Texeira who wrote *Prosopopeia* was not the same man who was accused by the Inquisition (*Barleu e Outros Ensaios Criticos*, Recife, 1941). But another member of the same Institute, the best contemporary Brazilian authority on Dutch Brazil, Gonsalves de Mello, has found evidence that the Texeira who wrote the poem was the one accused by the Inquisition.

tions of a very special sort between the cities of Minas Gerais and the north of Europe, leading to that area's greater Europeanization. Mawe was highly enthusiastic about the European style of living he found in Vila Rica: "The homes of persons of the upper class in Vila Rica are much more comfortable and better furnished than those of Rio de Janeiro and São Paulo."

The European style of dress in Olinda, Recife, Salvador, and even São Luís do Maranhão, which was so pronounced in the sixteenth and seventeenth centuries, paled there in the eighteenth century, to surpass itself in the mountains of Minas Gerais. These might have been thought a barrier against European influence; but the region became flooded with new influences, both in fashion and ideas, brought in by returning students, peddlers, and even Englishmen. It was in Minas that those ways of living and patterns of creature comforts developed which so delighted Europeans like Mawe and Saint-Hilaire. "I have never seen such magnificent beds as those of the wealthy inhabitants of this captaincy, including those of Europe," wrote Mawe, referring to the beds in which the mansion dwellers of Ouro Preto slept.

In contrast to these rich city dwellers, so European in their ways, the wealthy planters, masters of many acres and slaves, slept in a hammock or a cot. Saint-Hilaire, comparing them with the residents of Minas, says: "In the homes of the planters no furniture such as we are accustomed to is to be found; clothes are kept in trunks, or hung up on ropes to protect them against damp and insects. Chairs are rare, and people sit on wooden benches or stools . . ."[8]

As for dress, Mawe observed in Vila Rica at the beginning of the nineteenth century that the ladies preferred to follow the English fashions. And Saint-Hilaire, attending a ball given by the governor, Dom Manuel de Castro Portugal, for the elite of Minas, did not find the gulf he expected between the attire of the ladies and European fashions. The only thing that surprised him was that, in an intermission between the European quadrilles, a mulatto girl danced a fandango with much whirling of skirt and shaking of hips. The French scientist was somewhat shocked. It was as though the hot breath of

---

[8] Saint-Hilaire: *Voyages dans le District des Diamants et sur le Littoral du Brésil*, I (Paris, 1833), p. 253.

Africa had blown through that pleasantly tempered European, mid-dle-class atmosphere.

It was in the churches that the ladies clung to the bonnets, capes, shawls, mantillas, covering part of their face. These capes, formerly much used in Portugal and Spain, survived for a long time in Brazil, pointing to the resistance of the Moorish fashion to the penetration of that of Europe, but Europe triumphed in the ballroom and theater.

In the minutiae of decorum, in concepts of modesty, the Brazilian women, with their Moorish heritage, held out longest against English or French influences. Moreover, the foreigner was always looked upon in our colonial society, and even for a long time under the Em-pire, as a potential Don Juan, and the inside of the home, city or country, was barred to him. We have already seen how Tollenare was offended by this excessive reserve on the part of the upper-class ladies of Recife. He avenged himself by catching a glimpse of the daughters of a gentleman of Pernambuco, "shy as Mooresses," naked in their bath, their backsides plainly visible.[9] Saint-Hilaire observed the same shyness on the part of the young ladies of Minas.[1] In front of a foreigner the women were overcome with embarrassment. And not only the rustic daughters of the plantation, but the young city ladies as well, whom he had seen at formal dances in their French dresses, and so at ease that between dances they played and sang. Their timid-ity was reserved for home consumption.

It is curious to observe in our portraits of Empire days, in the old photographs which yellow in the bottom of drawers or in the family albums, how much more Europeanized the men were, not only in dress but in their social physiognomy, so to speak. The wives beside their husbands, the daughters beside their father or brothers, at times look like Malay or Chinese women alongside English missionaries with mustaches or North American doctors with beards. Two races —in appearance, at any rate—created by the profound social differ-entiation between the sexes. The man more European in attire, bear-ing, urban aspect; the woman, even when pure or almost pure white, more Oriental, more Asiatic, more rural, if not because of her less

[9] Tollenare: "Notas Dominicais Tomadas durante um Viagem em Portugal e no Brasil em 1816, 1817 e 1818," in *Revista do Instituto da Arqueologia, Historia, e Geographia*, XI, 61 (Pernambuco).

[1] Saint-Hilaire: *Voyages dans l'Intérieur du Brésil*, I (Paris, 1830), p. 208.

European dress, because of her melancholy expression, as though downtrodden or segregated, which gave her a resemblance to the women of the Orient.

The Europeanization of her attire did not always signify in Brazil the liberation of the woman from man's excessive domination. Nor did even the liberation from man bring about liberation from prejudices and traditions which, as far as she was concerned, created a deep intellectual separation from Nordic, bourgeois, industrial Europe. The habit does not always make the monk.

In 1872 Correa de Azevedo, deploring the use which had become so generalized among men of "the heavy frock coat of London or Paris" and the substitution of the straw hat "by that black, graceless, hot, heavy stovepipe" of a top hat, pointed out the adoption of French manners by the ladies of the court and the large cities, which "only the word coquetry" could describe.[2] It consisted of greeting in the French manner, dressing in the French fashion, speaking a few words of French and English, strumming sentimental waltzes on the piano. French or Italian music instead of the *fado*, with its Moorish plaintiveness, and the tender *modinha*, half-African, so in vogue during the eighteenth century sung to the accompaniment of guitar or harp. The newspaper advertisements bear abundant witness to these changes during the revolutionary first half of the nineteenth century, which were estranging Brazilians from their typical Portuguese-Brazilian customs and instilling in them French, English, Italian, German, Slavic tastes, as well as North American, which, about this time, began to compete with European. This was the case of beer brewed in the United States and imported into Brazil as early as 1848, according to an advertisement in the *Jornal do Commercio* for December 11: a beer "which has taken the place of English beer in nearly all tropical climates, where it is much preferred." And dances, too; in the same paper for September 18, 1848, one Mme Degremonte, "pupil of the Conservatory of Paris," advertised herself as a teacher "of all types of social dancing, as well as the polka, the mazurka, the cracovienne, the tarantella, the bolero," all exotic dances.

With the decline of the slave-based economy, increased impor-

---

[2] Luiz Correa de Azevedo: *Annaes Brasilenses de Medicina*, XXIII, 11 (Rio de Janeiro, April 1872), p. 432.

tance was attached to all foreigners coming to our shores, not merely as merchants, like the English since the Treaty of Methuen, nor as dressmakers, dentists, doctor, midwife, dancing master, teacher, governess, but as workmen: builder, mason, cabinetmaker, carpenter, small farmer, farm worker. As artisan or workman to take the place of the Negro and the home industries, and, at the same time, satisfy the growing desire of the more progressive middle class to modernize their homes, furniture, cuisine, means of transportation.

It was then that the Germans, Irish, Italians, and Swiss came to settle in the country, preferably in areas of higher altitude and better climate, some starting factories for the manufacture of butter and cheese, others, small farms, some going to work in the coffee plantations of São Paulo and even on the sugar plantations of Bahía, like a group of Irish there who became degraded by their excessive indulgence in rum. The bolder or more adventurous went to settle in the forests of the north, like that group which set out romantically for Catucá, the almost virgin jungle of Pernambuco, where they planned to make charcoal. Unfortunately for them, the jungle was full of runaway slaves, who one day killed a considerable number of the blond invaders.

Still other Europeans set up in the cities as workmen and artisans, like the group that came to Recife in 1839 with August Koersting at the invitation of the president of the province, the Baron of Bôa Vista. Machinists, stonemasons, carpenters, bricklayers. The chalets, the houses built in Gothic or Tuscan fashion, which came to substitute the old, square colonial homes that fitted in with the landscape, date from this period. Also of the early nineteenth century are the stuccoed houses with molded cornices and stone fences. The Europeanization of our architecture, both plans and technique, began in the cities with public buildings, and finished up on the plantations, where many an orientally spacious house was replaced by a narrow, two-story chalet. To this period belong the houses which have the air of public buildings or theaters; showy, conspicuous, without the modesty of the old homes, which hid behind hedges of thorn, high walls, convent grilles.

In Rio de Janeiro the Europeanization of the public buildings and the residences of some of the wealthiest residents of the Court began under the French architects who came out to Brazil in the time of Dom João VI.

It was Grandjean de Montigny [3] who drew up the plans for palaces and schools in the French style, as well as the blue prints or sketches for various plantation houses. The French taste, not only in architecture, but in desserts, wines, the finish of furniture, and dress, dominated in upper-class, wealthy circles. And, coinciding with the more advanced tendencies toward separatism and independence, went the taste for the ideas of French and English political writers. Montesquieu was the inspiration and guiding spirit of Frei Caneca, who had already shaken off the Portuguese intellectual tradition. A reaction had set in against Portuguese values. Everything that was Portuguese was "in bad taste"; everything French or English or Italian or German was considered "in good taste."

As was natural, a strong rivalry developed between the native workman or artisan, for the most part free Negroes or mulattoes— for the slave could not indulge in the luxury of being anyone's rival —and his foreign counterpart, who enjoyed great publicity, thanks to the newspapers, and the protection of the government. This bad feeling existed, too, between the minor public servants, the Brazilian petit bourgeois, the mulatto or mestizo proletariat, and the Portuguese grocer, the "sea crab" turned keeper of store or market stall. The Portuguese who was looked upon as dirty and miserly, who took up with some Negro woman, who slaved for him and whom he often abandoned after having got all he could from her. It was this grocer who sold salt cod and dried beef to the gentry come down in the world, the "native sons," who on their miserable salaries as public servants could not afford fresh meat.

In an article published in the journal *O Progresso* in 1846 on the problem of the colonization of Brazil, the author asked why "instead of learning the trade of tailor, stonemason, carpenter," which were falling more and more into the hands of foreign workmen, "the sons of poorer families continue to seek public employment," those of the country flocking to the cities. He recognized the difficulties that con-

---

[3] A French architect who came to Rio de Janeiro in the early nineteenth century and designed a number of public and private buildings.

fronted the son of a poor family who wanted to live by his own efforts, cultivating a patch of land or selling salt cod or dried meat. In agriculture, the latifundium was squeezing out the small, independent farmer. In trade, unless a law was passed returning the retail trade to the hands of nationals, the native-born Brazilian was helpless.

As a matter of fact, the rivalry between the native-born Brazilian and the European merchant or workman became so envenomed that it led to the outbreak of a social drama which was bloodily repressed, and which even today is regarded by superficial observers as a mere political revolt: the so-called Praia Revolt of Recife in 1848.[4] In Rio de Janeiro and Bahía the rivalry between the two elements often took the form of bloody clashes between "sailors," that is to say, Portuguese or Europeans, and *capoeiras*, or street ruffians.

The resentment over the foreign workman or artisan who was displacing the mulatto, the Portuguese shopkeeper crowding the poor Brazilian out of the retail trade, kept growing in the cities to the point at times of chauvinistic outbreaks against Europeans, as happened in Rio de Janeiro, Recife, Belem.

However, the Europeanization of work and of trade, up to a point, came to prevail with the decline of the rigidly patriarchal economy and the industrialization of Brazil. With the new rhythm of life, which called for clocks, so rare in the days when time was hardly counted by hours, and much less by minutes, but by the rising sun, the noonday sun, the setting sun. With the new ways of living, of comfort, of architecture created by the opening of the doors to European trade, and which the free mulatto, the native workman, were not able to satisfy. Only foreigners of the sort the Baron of Bõa Vista invited to settle in the province of Pernambuco, and who gave his government its glory at the same time that it gave his name its unpopularity.

Snuff, vinegar, candles, cloth, brooms, brushes, bedspreads, charcoal, cashew wine, soap, sandals, shoes, all of which in the Big House had been the work or trade of the Negro, the mulatto—with, at

---

[4] The uprising of Pernambuco, known as the Praia Revolt, was a protest of the Liberals against the return of the Conservatives to power. The leader of the movement was the congressman Nunez Machado. The rebels attacked Recife on February 2, 1849, and suffered defeat; Nunez Machado lost his life on the field.

most, a Portuguese foreman—were no longer manufactured at home but in the cities, and on a big scale, with new procedures. The economic landscape of the Empire became enriched with factories making ice, soap, macaroni, gin, pasteboard boxes, pianos, organs, umbrellas, glass, chocolate, saws, shredding tobacco. With trains, sanitation in the cities, gaslighting—nearly all the work of English engineers—the European workman, the white artisan, the foreign technician became as necessary as the air for breathing. Nativists howled about the competition of the fair foreigner, at whose hands the "native sons" were suffering.

But the European technician won the day; until the mulatto learned from him how to run the trains, the lathes, the machines, to manufacture glass and macaroni and vermicelli. The North American scholar, John Casper Branner, traveling through the interior of Brazil at the end of the nineteenth century, was amazed at the rapidity with which a simple mulatto of Minas Gerais repaired a huge locomotive that had broken down in the middle of the trip. It marked the assimilation of European or Anglo-Saxon techniques by the "native mulatto," and a new phase in the relations between Europeans and Brazilians. As well as a new phase in the Brazilian economy and way of life, with the evaluation of the descendants of slaves, thanks to their technical skill, and the devaluation of the descendant of the plantation owner, the city magnate, the heir to the cane fields, because of his lack of skill.

CHAPTER VIII

RACE, CLASS, REGION

I N A patriarchal society, such as Brazil was during almost the whole period of slavery, with divisions or zones sociologically equivalent to those of so-called feudal societies, it was not citizens or even subjects who constituted the basic or decisive elements of our population, but families and classes. And these families and classes were separated, up to a point, by the races which entered into the ethnological composition of the Brazilians, with their differences of physical characteristics, cultural background, and, principally, their initial or decisive status.

With time, these races took on regional coloring in keeping with the physical conditions of region, landscape, or climate, and not merely the cultural conditions of the social medium. The ruling class was made up of the white or European invaders and their pure descendants or those with an insignificant admixture of color; those ruled and utilized as instruments of production, transport, and labor were the natives. In view, however, of their numerical shortage or their limitations, cultural rather than physical, for such tasks, Africans and their pure-blooded descendants, or mixed with the Indians, or even with the blood of the ruling class in their veins, took their place.

As for families grouped about their natural and social fathers—or

merely social—their standing varied more according to their economic position and the regional conditions of the area where they
lived than to their social or ethnic origins. The classes were made up
of rulers and ruled; the masters at one extreme, the slaves at the other.
And somewhere between the two were the products of the miscegenation which had been going on between rulers and ruled since the
beginning, and which often brought about the shifting of individuals
and even whole families from one class to another, from one race to
another, regardless of biological or even cultural characteristics. The
large-scale amalgamation which took place, the social and ethnic
fluctuations within the organization, give rise to certain doubts as to
the dominantly feudal character attributed to the patriarchal organization of the economy and society of Brazil during slavery days.
How is it possible to admit the existence of a Brazilian feudalism
when, as is well known, one of the main characteristics of the feudal
system was its rigidity?

To repeat the interpretation already suggested in the first pages of
this study, the fluctuations were of content and substance, not of
form. In forms, the Brazilian organization was for centuries predominantly feudal, even though with capitalist overtones from the beginning. Sociologically it was characterized by patriarchalism, even
though the economic and geographic content varied, and the ethnic
and cultural preponderances which gave it regional coloring.

The sociological study of Brazil reveals a process of integration,
flowering, and decay of the patriarchal or tutelary form of family
organization, economy, and culture. This integration, flowering, and
decay—phenomena arrived at in different periods in different areas—
never took place independently of another equally typical process:
the amalgamation of races and cultures which acted as the principal
solvent of all that was rigid in the more or less feudal system of relations between men in situations created less by race than by class,
group, or individual.

Among Brazilians the two processes permeated one another.
Rarely did they collide or come into violent conflict, even though
such conflicts did occur. From the beginning of the colonization, the
tendency was in the direction of the interpenetration of these two
processes. Until the most recalcitrantly aristocratic aspects of the
patriarchal structure of family, economy, and culture had become

tinged by the democratic, democratizing, even anarchic elements always present in the amalgamation of races and culture.

This brought about what may be considered, from the sociological point of view, the beginning of the decline of the patriarchal system, first the rural, which was the most rigid and probably the most typical; then the semi-rural, semi-urban. And along with this decline there took place—or is taking place—the development of forms which some call particularist, or individualistic, of family, economic, social organization. There began to emerge more clearly the *subjects* and then the *citizens*, formerly almost nonexistent among us, so great was the loyalty of the individual to his natural or social father, who was the patriarch, the guardian, the godfather, the head of the family; and so complete was the relationship of each of these natural or social fathers to the political father of all, His Majesty the King, later replaced by the Emperor. He was the political father not only of the patriarchs but of the sons of the patriarchs, not only of the whites but of the colored, not only of the rich but of the poor, not only of the men of the coast but of the men of the backlands. A substitution which was in a way a transmutation—a transfer of the prerogatives of the patriarch to the King—which explains why one João Pinto Ribeiro could write in Lisbon in 1646: "For the King is the father of his vassals, relatives and nonrelatives, friends and nonfriends, the equal father of all his children. For in the house of the King his vassals are his children." [1] An idea repeated by the Marquis of Peñalva when he wrote that the "true" models of a king were, as a rule, "the patriarchs of the Old Testament," "the family heads," [2] who, moreover, in Brazil would seem to have followed in the footsteps of the ancient lords who were the absolute masters of wives, children, and slaves, carrying to extreme lengths the use, and abuse, of the *potestas patrem*.

When the assumption of this power by the King or Emperor began in Brazil, there had already taken place among us on a large scale the extension of paternal authority which the Portuguese of Portugal had experienced only in slight measure in their dealings with Moors and Africans: that of a white patriarch who was the father not only of

---

[1] João Pinto Ribeiro: *A Santidade do Monarcha Ecclesiastico Innocencio X* (Lisbon, 1646), p. 32.

[2] Marques de Penalva: *Dissertação a favor da Monarchia* (Lisbon, 1799), p. 17.

whites but of colored persons; not only of persons of his own economic status but of those whose status was not so much inferior as servile. Before, however, the kings of Portugal took under their protection all their subjects, various patriarchs and fathers of families established in Brazil, like Jeronymo de Albuquerque in the sixteenth century, had already extended to their natural colored children their paternal protection. Perhaps it was from them that the kings, or political fathers, took their inspiration for adopting similar attitudes with regard to their poor or colored subjects, in contrast to those natural or social fathers—among the latter certain of the Jesuits in the seventeenth century—less understanding in their sense of paternal responsibility than Jeronymo de Albuquerque. Be that as it may, such sentiments or ideas on the part of certain patriarchs can be credited with considerable influence on the interpenetration of races and classes which had been operating since the beginning of the colonization and bringing about the transfer of colored persons from the class to which they would seem to have been condemned by their maternal race and, up to a point, by their status of "ruled," if not to the status of rulers, at least to that of marginal beings or intermediaries between the rulers and the ruled.

The transfer of individuals and even of whole groups by these and other means from one social level to another became, from the close of the eighteenth, but above all during the nineteenth century, one of the strongest stimuli to the development of so-called individual forms, which were, at the same time, ethnically and culturally mixed, of family, economy, and culture, alongside those patriarchal families of Portuguese descent, each day less powerful and ethnically and culturally less pure.

This explains families such as those Prince Maximilian encountered among Brazilians of the rural areas at the beginning of the nineteenth century, families of *caboclos*, that is, descendants of Amerindians or mestizos of Amerindians and Europeans, who lived in villages, around a Catholic church and a Portuguese priest, persons whose dress and language were, like their religious worship, Portuguese. From the American Indian, however, they had kept, in addition to the methods of building their dwellings, the use of hammocks for sleeping and of clay cooking utensils, as well as two-string bows, in whose use they were expert from boyhood. And, of course, their main dishes, utilizing manioc meal, which, in the form of porridge, the Portuguese adopted as the diet of convalescents, children, and old people.

Their greatest ambition, the Prince observed, was to be looked upon as Portuguese, adopting the latters' given and family names. Hence—from this desire to be considered Portuguese—the contempt with which they spoke of their savage brethren, whom they called *tapuias*.[3]

They had a captain-major of their own race whose functions were similar to those of the captain-majors of predominantly white or mestizo settlements, that is to say, the functions of a super-patriarch. But evidently settlements like the one described by Prince Maximilian—São Pedro dos Indios—and that visited by Maria Graham during the same period [4] were made up of groups of families whose manners of living, economy, and culture (revealing traces of the excessive paternalism of the Jesuits, who were almost always the founders or organizers of such villages), departed from the orthodox patriarchal norms of the plantation and city houses and contributed to the decay of the strictly patriarchal system. In the eyes of such people and their descendants, the patriarchs of town and country were not the almighty figures they were to the people raised within the rigidly patriarchal framework. This perhaps explains the greater tendency on their part to rebel and even take up arms against the great landowners, the *balaiadas*, *tapuiadas*, and *cabanadas* [5] so frequent in the beginning of the nineteenth century. And it also explains the tendency of the descendants of these *caboclos*, more or less civilized, to enlist as soldiers in the service of the King, whose power was greater than that of the plantation owners, even though this superiority was at times purely theoretical.

These settlements of *caboclos* and descendants of American Indians who had been domesticated or civilized were less under the aegis of the plantation owner or city magnate than of the equally paternalistic Jesuits, Franciscans, or civil authorities. They resembled those

---

[3] Prince Maximilan von Neuwied: *Travels in Brazil in 1815, 1816 and 1817* (Tr., London, 1820), p. 32.

[4] Maria Graham: *Journal of a Voyage to Brazil* (London, 1824), pp. 284–5.

[5] Social and political movements indicative of the resentment the people of the interior felt toward more advanced regions and institutions.

villages of peasant soldiers in Portugal no longer under the protection of some semi-feudal castle but centered about convent or church. As the historian Alberto Sampaio has pointed out, when the old relation between the rustics and the castle came to an end, the church gave these peasants the cohesion needed to convert their villages into small communities.[6]

To what class did these rustics belong? They were not to be confused either with slaves, nor with the tenant farmers of the country estates under the illusion that they were freemen. The paternalism of the missionaries had not, to be sure, prepared them for a free life as subjects of the King. But, on the other hand, neither had it predisposed them toward subjection to great landholding masters. Theirs was a special social status: almost that of free men, who lacked only the initiative to make this condition a state of fact, or the techniques of economic independence to give stability to their desire to live like free men, materially independent of other men. Their submission to vicar or priest, the successors at times of the Jesuit missionaries but not their complete substitute in the harsh and dominant paternalism they exercised over the American Indians, was spiritual and political rather than economic and material.

In other instances, the substitutes of the missionaries were those civil directors created by Pombal's reform,[7] of whom what is definitely known is that they were the exploiters rather than the guardians, which the oversimplified anti-Jesuit law of the reform had hoped to make of them, of the Amerindian villages of huts and cabins, no longer the collective and somewhat promiscuous communities of their ancestors. Cabins or huts, or "houses of *caboclos*," which represented the consecration of a monogamous union as against free love, that of the family constituted on Catholic instead of native norms, although there were cases of Amerindians or their descendants in such villages who reverted to their former sexual freedom.

In other cases, the villagers, instead of being dominated by the complex of "seeming Portuguese" like those of the settlement Maximilian speaks of, reacted against the religious indoctrination which

---

[6] Alberto Sampaio: *As "Vilas" do Norte de Portugal* (Oporto, 1903), p. 117.

[7] A secular reform directed primarily against the Jesuits.

uprooted them from the backlands to settle them in the proximity of the larger European type of village. They returned to the backlands, reincorporating themselves to their savage cultures.[8] The Crown attempted to prevent this by giving greater protection and freedom to the Amerindians and making their incorporation into the culturally Portuguese and Christian society easier. This is revealed by the measures contained in the law of June 6, 1755, apropos of the fact that almost no progress had been made in the religious training of the Indians of Grão-Pará and Maranhão, who, it was pointed out, having come from the wilderness into the villages, "instead of multiplying and prospering in them so that their comforts and advantages would act as a stimulus to those scattered through the forests to come and seek in the settlements through temporal happiness the greater end of eternal bliss, becoming members of the society of the Holy Mother Church, it has been seen that on many occasions, although thousands of Indians have come down, they have died out until now the number of settlements and their inhabitants is very small, and even these few live in great poverty, which, instead of inviting and encouraging the other wild Indians to imitate them, serves them as a warning to withdraw to their wooded homes, with lamentable harm to the salvation of their souls and great damage to the State, its inhabitants lacking those to serve them and help them to cultivate the many and precious fruits in which the lands abound . . ."

In view of this situation, on which "all opinions are in agreement that the cause of such pernicious results was due, and still is, to not having maintained the aforesaid Indians in the freedom decreed for them by Their Holinesses and Their Majesties, my predecessors . . . always being twisted [the laws passed by them] to the benefit of private interests . . ." [9] By edict of the King, the Indians were completely free, in keeping with the law of April 1, 1680; they could serve anyone they wished, in keeping with the law of November 10, 1647; their civil status was the same as that of the other subjects of the King; they were equally qualified for all honors, privileges, liberties; by the terms of the law of September 10, 1611, no Indian could

---

[8] Graham: Op. cit., p. 284.

[9] *Coleção de Leis*, quoted by Perdigão Malheiro in *A Escriavidão no Brasil*, Part 2 (Rio de Janeiro, 1866–7), pp. 98–102.

be held as a slave, the sole exception being the offspring of an Indian and a Negro slave, who, until further measures were taken, would continue in the possession of their masters; when employed in agriculture or industry the Indians were to receive salaries in keeping with the usual wages in the state or area, payable at the end of each week in money, cloth, tools, or other goods, as the workers prefer; the Indians were to be restored to the full use of their property; the lands adjoining their settlements were to be divided among them, and the Indians upheld in the control and possession of their lands for themselves and their heirs; they were to be settled in the backlands according to their wishes, building churches there, and inviting missionaries to instruct them in the faith and to care for their lay instruction as well.

This law is socially significant in the clarity and scope of its endeavor to substitute for the paternalism of the missionaries that of the King; and also because of the way in which it attempted to put into effect the forgotten charter of April 1, 1680, defending the Amerindians against the prevailing economic system, latifundarian, monocultural, and slavocrat, and protecting the liberty of the Indians and their free use of possessions and lands against the inroads of the encroaching whites: ". . . Nor are they [the Indians] obliged to pay rent or tribute of any sort for the aforesaid lands, even if they have been given in grant to private persons, for in such concessions there is always a clause against hardship worked against any third party, and much more in the case of prejudice or harm to the Indians, their first and natural owners . . ." [1]

The substitution of the paternalism of the priests by that of the King was emphasized in the decree of July 7, 1735, abolishing the temporal power of the missionaries and declaring it incompatible with their religious duties. But how to substitute those missionaries, so many of whom were accused of taking advantage of their material power over the natives? The King endeavored to solve the problem by the decision that, for posts of administration and justice in the Amerindian settlements, "the Indians living there" were to be preferred, and the government of the villages should be left in the hands of the headmen whom "the sergeant-majors, captains, lieutenants,

---

[1] Ibid., p. 70.

and bailiffs of the tribes" named as their subalterns. This was the elevation of the Amerindians to the rank of subjects, responsible to the King for the government of their communities, and protected by the King himself from other social fathers who might attempt to dominate and exploit them; priests or patriarchs. Their status was not that of slaves possessing nothing and unqualified to aspire to honors and posts; it was that of small landowners, with the same rights as the whites to honors and posts. Race was not a disqualification. The decree of 1755 in this respect was absolutely clear, stating that there was no stigma attached to the marriage of Portuguese or whites to Indian women, but, on the contrary, benefits for the state, and for this reason, through the voice of the King, it officially sanctioned such marriages as being of great expediency for "the development of the state," conferring special protection on the offspring of such unions, giving them preference for any employment, honor, or dignity, and forbidding their being insulted by the name of *caboclo* or any similar epithet.[2] All that was required of the Amerindians, to achieve the status of subjects, was that they become Christians.

If laws such as these of 1755 were at first limited to the region where the contact between the white settlers and the Indians was greatest—the extreme north of Brazil rather than São Paulo or Rio Grande do Sul—it was not long before they became effective for the whole country. The edict of August 17, 1758, made them all-embracing and, at the same time, put into effect laws which at first were in the nature of an experiment.

It is surprising that statesmen returning to the problem of incorporating the native of Brazil into the society founded here by the Portuguese should have thought that they had hit upon the precise methods of bringing this about by suddenly conferring on the Amerindian race the same rights, responsibilities, and class consciousness as the Europeans, when the first experiments would seem to have failed. The natives recently brought into the Portuguese society and the Christian culture lacked the capacity for self-government expected of them by certain statesmen of Portugal. As for those accustomed to the paternal tutelage of the Jesuits and other friars, they were simply grown children as unprepared to govern themselves as were those

---

[2] Ibid., p. 105.

who had grown up in the shadow of the Big Houses, which utilized the Indians almost as though they were slaves, less for routine agricultural work, at which they had early been replaced in the richer zones by Africans, than "to hunt and fish for us," as the Crown attorney of the state of Maranhão, Manoel Guedes Aranha, specified in the seventeenth century.[3] The native settlements which developed into towns or judicial districts, such as the one Prince Maximilian saw, almost without other supervision than that of the priest, or other authority than that of their own captain-major, were the exception.

Moreover, we should bear in mind the fact that in Brazil there was not one race of Amerindians, but many, with regional differences of culture, subrace, and even class differences, pointed out by Mendes de Almeida in one of his most thoughtful pages: " . . . The Indians have their aristocrats, the *moacára*, and a body of nobility, *moacaráeta*." [4] And the always perspicacious Father Vieira had already taken note of the native hierarchy when he informed the Provincial Francisco Gonçalvez, in a letter of October 5, 1653, that among the Indians there was a ceremony which was the equivalent of arming a knight among the Europeans, and that they also distinguished those who by birth or occupation were like the nobles among the whites. From this nobility the rulers were chosen.[5]

Everything indicates, however, that for the majority of the colonizers the Amerindians were one: the Amerindian or Indian. The necessary attention was not given to their differences of culture, class, subrace. This may explain in part the failures of the attempts to leave in native hands the government of their settlements, without taking into account the class differences between them, but instead arbitrarily substituting them by others.

By and large, it was the stark reality of the problem that obliged the Portuguese administrators of Brazil to modify the idea of having these villages or settlements governed by the natives themselves, and this modification turned into the most deplorable distortion of the original generous and democratic plan. It was decided that, until the

---

[3] Manoel Guedes Aranha: "Papel Político Sobre o Estado do Maranhão . . . (1655)," *Revista do Instituto Historico*, etc., XLVI, p. 1.

[4] João Mendes de Almeida: *Algumas Notas Genealógicas. Livro de Familia* (São Paulo, 1886), p. 318.

[5] Ibid., p. 318.

Indians were capable of governing themselves, there would be a white or Portuguese administrator appointed by the governor of the captaincy.[6] Even though this decision was hedged about with a thousand and one precautions to safeguard the dignity of the natives and assure their incorporation into the Portuguese society and the Christian culture as free men, equipped to hold any post or honor conferred upon free, white, Christians—one of the provisoes was that the Indians were not to be called "Negroes, because of the offense and affront this implied, putting them on the same footing as Africans, as though they were meant to be slaves of the whites"—the truth of the matter is that the administrators, in the majority of cases, soon became the oppressors and exploiters of the natives. The intention of the kings of Portugal, to do them justice, was nearly always to give official sanction to the tendency of the majority of the Portuguese to look upon the natives of Brazil as they had formerly looked upon the Moors, as being white for all social effects, including marriage. This idea, which was also that of certain popes, met resistance, however, on the part of individuals who, during that first century of colonization, were interested in equating the Indians with the Negroes. Not content with ignoring the differences among the Africans, and looking upon them all as Negroes or blacks, differing only in the language the various tribes spoke, the tendency of the first Europeans in Brazil was to lump all the Amerindians together under the arbitrary figure of "the Indian," which did not exist. And economic considerations led them to enslave them all, reducing Africans and Indians to the equally arbitrary figure of "Negro."

This was undoubtedly the reason for the Amerindians' repudiation of agricultural work as fit only for real Negroes. (The truth is that this type of work had been repugnant from the start to the nomadism of the natives of this part of America, incapable, as they were, of settling down to prolonged, sedentary tasks.) Hence, probably, the aspiration of the *caboclos*—especially the "nobles"—to become *cavaleiros*, that is to say, to ride horseback, at which many came to rival the whites, the *caboclos* or descendants of the Indians being the best mounted herders, a skill which, within the European patterns of culture, was eminently aristocratic. Prince Maximilian observed in Bra-

---

[6] Perdigão Malheiro: Op. cit., Part 2, p. 106.

zil that the Portuguese were good riders, who liked a horse with a pacing gait, and to train them to this they tied pieces of wood to their hoofs. In addition, they used huge spurs, which the more elegant *caboclos* and mulattoes imitated when they could, like those Maximilian saw in São Bento: sword at side and spurs tied to their bare feet. A display of the insignia of the ruling class on the part of men still too linked to their own culture to renounce their habit of going barefoot.

Still another upper-class habit adopted by the recently civilized *caboclos*, as though in testimony to the fact that they were free men, was that of always being accompanied by hunting dogs, like those which were used by the whites to hunt runaway slaves, and not merely wild animals. For hunting, like the use of firearms, was the prerogative of free men and not the occupation of slaves or Negroes, who, as a rule, accompanied their masters in their great hunts in a purely servile capacity, and not like the Indians, as guides or companions of the Europeans or the sons of Europeans. To their dexterity with bow and arrow, the *caboclos* added their skill in the use of firearms, which they were given in order to assist the whites in their hunting of animals and at times even of men who were considered dangerous. Not only wild animals but wild men, that is to say, those who had rebelled against the order established by the Europeans and their descendants.

The Indians could also indulge in the luxury of competing with the white gentlemen in the aristocratic abuse of tobacco, a habit native to the Amerindians and forbidden the majority of slaves during the long working hours. Just because the "Negro smoke" was the disdained marihuana, many slaves preferred tobacco in the form of snuff or even pipe to the African plant.

According to tradition, the civilized *caboclos*, men and women, smoked like chimneys, some of them with a pipe in their mouth all day long. This vice, originally theirs, in its more refined forms, such as the handmade cigar, the briar, not the clay pipe, perfumed snuff in a box often imported from the Orient and sometimes even made of gold, became the pleasure or privilege of the upper class.

If, in many instances, the Christianization or Europeanization of the Amerindians and Africans and their descendants was only superficial, only outwardly altered their habits of "inferior races" converted into servile classes, in other cases it resulted in the transformation of descendants of savages or primitive beings into near fanatics of the orthodoxy—political, moral, and religious—of the first Europeans, only partially assimilated by them. Perhaps more out of loyalty or attachment to a region better suited to people of primitive culture and a rustic rather than urban economy than for reasons of "race" or class, certain groups of them held out stubbornly against the deviations from such orthodoxy of the whites of the seaboard themselves. Hence their often illogical participation in the civil struggles of Brazil. Instead of attacking the order established by the whites, on more than one occasion the position taken by the *caboclos* and colored people was the defense of orthodox European or traditional values, which they felt were threatened by innovation or change.

That is the only explanation of the war to the death of the *cabanos* and the *papa-mels* of the North—many of them backcountrymen of Indian descent, who were joined by Negroes and mulattoes of the plantation in the hope of achieving their freedom—against the liberals, progressives, and the promulgators of new ideas of the cities and seaboard. "The Liberals are against inequality, when from the time Christ assumed human form there has been inequality," said the *papa-mels* of Alagoas in reply to the proclamation of September 11, 1832. In this way, these men of lower class gave proof of their fidelity to royal absolutism and their stern, class-conscious patriarchalism. And they added: "What the Liberals want is for sons no longer to obey their fathers, nephews their uncles, godchildren their godfather; what they want is, if she takes their fancy, to carry off another's daughter, or some pretty woman . . . proceeding in all against the law of Our Lord Jesus Christ. And, finally, they do not wish to obey the King, when God himself has said to the King that when his subjects fail to obey him he should destroy them with pestilence, hunger, and war." [7]

In this movement, which was both patriarchal and monarchical, of country people against the liberals and progressives of the city, small farmers and cattle raisers, many of whom were the descendants of *caboclos*, participated, and not only Negroes and mulattoes

[7] M. Lopes Machado: "O 14 de abril de 1832 em Pernambuco," *Rev. do Inst. Arch., Hist., Geog. Pernambuco*, XXXIII, p. 32. Cf. also Astolfo Sera: *A Balaiada* (Rio de Janeiro, 1946); and E. Cruz: *Nos Bastidores da Cabanagem* (Belem, 1942).

who were the slaves of the plantations of that area—a region of small plantations. Recently civilized Amerindians, like those of Jacuipe, with their captain-major,[8] took part in the struggle, the struggle of Absolutists against Constitutionalists, of the supporters of the restoration of Dom Pedro I against the nationalist supporters of Pedro II.[9] This was perhaps out of a sense of regional solidarity—backlanders against the seaboard; perhaps out of a vague sense of loyalty to the monarchy, inasmuch as in Brazil the kings of Portugal had left the well-established tradition that the Crown was the protector of the Indians in particular and of colored people in general. And it is true that on more than one occasion the Crown defended them from the abuses of wealthy individuals or exploitation by powerful members of the clergy. Even from discrimination on the part of the Jesuits against those of colored blood.

As for the outbreak in Pedra Bonita,[1] where backlanders of Pajeu das Flores in the province of Pernambuco, for the most part *caboclos*, under the leadership of a mystic who was a kind of bloody foreshadowing of the fanatic of Canudos, went to the lengths of human sacrifice,[2] it was the expression of a longing or desire for the return to absolute monarchy, and, at the same time, the repudiation of the dominant form of vast landholdings—the plantations—which did not fit in with the ideas of property of the *caboclos*, who owned nothing but a few milk goats. Before the organization in Brazil of a "black guard" to defend the paternalist or maternalist monarchy of the Braganzas, made up, for the most part, of Africans and their descendants, which greatly hampered the anti-monarchic activities of white

---

[8] Ibid., p. 63.

[9] This was the revolt in Pernambuco known as the Cabanada (1832–5), which had as its object the restoration of Pedro I to the throne.

[1] There, a group of fanatics formed a half-religious, half-political sect, in the hope that a political messiah would appear in Brazil.

[2] The superstition existed in Pedra Bonita that the sacrifice of a number of innocents would disenchant a kingdom "where the proletariat . . . would become noble, rich, and powerful," as Tristão de Alencar Araripe recalls in his preface to A. A. de Souza Leite's *Fanatismo Religioso. Memoria sobre o Reino Encantado no Comarca de Vila Bela* (2nd, ed., 1898, p. 8). In addition to human sacrifice, "there was the sacrifice of dogs . . . which on the day of the great event would be resurrected as invincible dragons to devour the landowners." (p. 9)

men like Silva Jardim, or the advocates of a republic, such as the mestizos Saldanha Marinho and Glicerio, there were numerous groups of *caboclos* and their descendants who aligned themselves with the oldest institutions brought to Brazil from Europe against all innovations, even the egalitarian, by which they stood to benefit. What happened was that, being conquered races, they felt less in need of abstract freedoms than of the effective protection which kings and popes seemed better able to give them against white masters and Catholic priests. The truth is that on many occasions the natives of Brazil, and even the Negroes brought in from Africa, received positive protection from kings and popes against the abuses of individuals and even of the clergy. It was natural that this protection should have created among the Amerindians and Negroes, and their descendants, class sentiments which were stronger than those of race. Yellows, blacks, browns were as much the sons of God and the Virgin Mary as any white, as much the subjects of the King as any Portuguese. As we have already pointed out, this was the basic principle of the Portuguese colonization of Brazil: the fundamental importance not of race, but of religious status; of political status, not of color.

This quickly gave rise to the transfer of values and sentiments which in other areas are tied in almost exclusively with race and class. The civilized, Christian colored man could be socially as Portuguese as any Portuguese, as Christian as any Christian. The priesthood itself had long been open to Amerindians and, in exceptional cases, to the descendants of Africans, as in the case of the great Antonio Vieira. The military profession had long been open to these two non-European elements because of the defense needs of the colony, permitting them to occupy high posts with the approval of the King, as in the case of Camarão [3] and Henrique Diaz,[4] among others.

This being the trend in our country from early times, it was natural that the Indians and the Africans should have behaved less like two races oppressed by the white man than, variously and diversely, according to the status of each individual or each family in society (class) and in his physical-social or physical-cultural space (region).

---

[3] Antonio Filipe Camarão, a leader of the Indians during the Peddlers' War.
[4] Military leader in the era of the struggle against the Dutch, who commanded Negro troops.

For we must not lose sight of the force with which the regional situation of the individual or family, independently of color, race, class, and the condition of being naturalized or native-born, led to his integration with cultures, or regional expressions of culture, such as that of the backlands, the backwoods, the gaucho. In proof of which, in addition to the examples already cited, there is that of Canudos, where, around the figure of Antonio Conselheiro, individuals and families of the most diverse ethnic origins and position gathered. Their "conscience of the species" was for the most part that of backlanders clinging to a pastoral and patriarchal mode of existence which paralleled a remote phase of the transition from primitive cultures to the European and Catholic. In proof of which, too, is the situation of the Amerindian and even the Negro on the rustic ranches of Rio Grande do Sul, where, according to a distinguished modern historian of the region, "the Negro was more of a companion than a slave." [5] This situation was accentuated when the Negro, in an eminently military region such as Rio Grande do Sul, found in soldierly activities the road to social ascent. The same road as in the northeast in the seventeenth century in the days of a war in which Portuguese and Brazilians of all classes, races, and regions fraternized, joined against the common enemy, the Dutch invader. [6]

Professor Dante de Laytano has already brought out the fact that, contrary to the general opinion, Rio Grande do Sul came to have a numerous population of African origin. The map of Cordova (1780) indicates that in Cachoeira, Triunfo, and Anjos da Aldeia the Negro element was more numerous than the white, and in Rio Pardo, Mostardas, and Viamão, almost equal; this preeminence disappeared with the fusion, dispersion (including flight to the Plate River), and the lack of newcomers. [7] The fusion of the African with the Amerindian would seem to have been considerable in that region; in this connection, Professor Laytano quotes the interesting report of Saint-Hilaire: "The Indian women say they give themselves to men of their own race out of a sense of duty, to white men for gain, and to Negroes for pleasure." This would seem to indicate that in a pastoral

---

[5] Dante de Laytano: *O Negro no Rio Grande do Sul* (Porto Alegre, 1941), p. 8.

[6] Manuel Diegues Junior: *O Bangue nas Alagoas* (Rio de Janeiro, 1949).

[7] Laytano: Op. cit., p. 10.

area, such as Rio Grande do Sul, characterized for two centuries by wars, skirmishes, feats of horsemanship, the Negro managed to attract the attention, and even the admiration, of the native women, thanks to his superior gifts. Among them, his aptitude for fighting; according to Saint-Hilaire, "the Negro is braver than the Indian," that is to say, the Indian of Rio Grande do Sul. In this way, the Negro came to outstrip the Indian, and also because of his acceptance as a comrade by the whites on the ranches. This situation, lifting him above the status of bondsman, gave rise, in that remote area of Brazil, to the employment of the African or his descendants in herding or military service.

Thus, the regional situation modified that of race and class which, in other areas—the richer plantation regions—made the Negro a contemptible being in the eyes not only of the whites but of the natives, making it necessary—to cite an extreme example—for the Africans and their descendants who had fortified themselves in Palmares to take the native women by force. This is not to say that the social formation of Rio Grande do Sul came about without distinction between ranchers and hands, like that which on the great plantations divided men into masters—white or near-white—and slaves—Negroes and half-breeds. We must not confuse the large ranches with the small ones, which were the equivalent of the poor plantations of the North; the Big Houses of the authentic ranches were the counterpart of the plantation mansions. These ranch houses were often richly furnished, "with elegant furniture, pianos, and in some, orchestras, as in that of Colonel Macedo."[8] If on the numerous small ranches there was little social difference between the ranchers and the hands, or between the whites and their colored servants, on the large ones the gulf was apparent, as on the plantations, in dress, food habits, behavior, dances. The fandango, for example, was in the beginning a "ballroom dance of the upper classes," and it was not until the second half of the nineteenth century that it "descended to the hands' quarters," and was replaced by dances which were not only genteel but completely European, such as the gavotte, the

---

[8] João Cesimbra Jacques: *Ensaio sobre os Costumes do Rio Grande do Sul* (Porto Alegre, 1883).

waltz, the polka, among others. The factor more persistently active in the gaucho region than in the other areas of Brazil in narrowing the gulf between classes and races, and creating an aristocracy based on bravery independent of color or rank, was the frequent state of war, including civil war, in which the inhabitants lived for many years.

To be a plantation owner was, by and large, to occupy an honorable and ennobling position in the patriarchal society of Brazil. But this position invariably suffered restrictions imposed by the regional situation of the owner or his holdings. It was not the same to own a plantation that made brown sugar in Piauí, or a manioc plantation in Santa Catarina, as to own a sugar plantation in Pernambuco or Reconcavo da Bahía. And the Bahían city dweller, that is to say, of Salvador, utilized the fact of that city's being the capital of Brazil as a motive of supervaluation of his origin or regional situation. It was as though Salvador were the only civilized, urban, polite region of Brazil; all the rest was backwoods.

To this attitude the gaucho reacted in his own fashion, with contempt for any Brazilian of the North who could not ride a horse with the skill of those of the far South, and associating this limitation with the fact of being a Bahían. To be a Bahían was to ignore the manly art of riding. It was to be overcivilized, almost effeminate. Therefore, the term "Bahían" became one of both praise and disdain, depending on regional circumstances of origin and social formation. And the same thing was true of "gaucho."

Captain-General Caetano Pinto de Miranda Montenegro wrote from Pernambuco, in a letter of January 13, 1806, to Viscount Anadia, that: "All those who live outside of Recife and Olinda are called *matutos* (backwoodsmen) here; they are the yokels of Portugal; and even though the name does not fall pleasantly on the ear, I have not heard the same complaints from those to whom it is applied as when *carioca* is used for the inhabitants of Rio de Janeiro." [9] Montenegro knew Rio de Janeiro at first hand; he had grounds for stating that the appellation *carioca* did not please its native sons, although today it is free of any pejorative implication. The Recifans

---

[9] Ms. in the Archives of Pernambuco.

for some time were contemptuously called "peddlers" by the people of Olinda, many of whom, nevertheless, moved from their old homes in Olinda to mansions in Recife.

Thus, from the regional criterion set forth here as being essential to the understanding of the individual or special group within the totality of Brazilian society, one must separate the political, administrative, or geographic idea of state, province, or captaincy. I am employing a sociological criterion. And in keeping with this criterion, the resemblances between the backwoodsmen of different provinces and captaincies, or between men of the interior, that is to say, men of the small cities of interior Brazil, such as Father Feijó [1] of Itu and Father Ibiapina [2] of Ceará, were greater than between Feijó and the Andradas [3] of Santos; or between Ibiapina and the more cosmopolitan Maciel Monteiro [4] of Recife.

This does not imply that in the characterization of the Brazilian, individual or group, by status, I consider preponderant, or invariably definitive, his regional cultural situation and the political power that went with it. What does seem definitive was the social-cultural class situation—especially the economic—which for a long time in Brazil was that of the slave opposed to the master, but at the same time symbiotic with that of the master within a family constellation made up of the patriarch and his wife, children, poor relatives, tenants, slaves—the patriarchal household.

One must, however, bear in mind the fact that, from the early days when Brazilian society was taking shape as a family system of organization, there existed subgroups whose class situation, fitting into neither of these two categories, gave them functions similar to those of intermediary groups or classes in more complex societies. Subgroups of artisans who had come out from Portugal or Europe were joined by mestizos who had a trade, were skilled in calligraphy and other bureaucratic abilities which they had learned from the

---

[1] See Note 2, Chapter IV.

[2] A Catholic priest who became famous as a missionary and educator in the interior.

[3] Three brothers, José Bonifacio, Antonio Carlos, Martim Francisco, who achieved prominence as leaders of Brazil's political independence under a monarchical form of government.

[4] A Brazilian poet and diplomat of the nineteenth century.

whites. Since the earliest colonial days they had begun to emerge from the shadow of the plantation houses and city mansions and, above all in those early days, from the religious schools. From there they spread through the freer social zones or areas, competing at times with the artisans who had come out from Portugal or Europe.

Referring to these artisans and also, in a general, somewhat vague way, to the "exiles, Jews and foreigners," Edmundo Zenha points out in a recent essay that they were not systematically kept from holding municipal office as in Portugal, where the institution of "good men" became a closed corporation.[5] It was natural that this institution should have undergone the same modification as others in Brazil, including styles of living and architecture brought in from Europe.

Zenha says, as does Affonso de E. Taunay,[6] that, although "by legal disposition" and "custom of the mother country" they might not "hold office in the council" nor "form part of the good men," they appear more than once among the elect.

Taunay recalls that, when in August 1637 Manuel Fernandez Gigante was appointed attorney of the City Council of São Paulo, "he was suspected of working-class origins"; however, he denied this and stated that if he were "he would immediately renounce his post," for which reason, the historian goes on to say, after quoting the expressive words of the former artisan whom his appointment had ennobled, "he was accepted." This, like other cases, reflects the fact that, once the artisan or small tradesman had achieved a degree of economic stability, he could turn his back on his trade or shop and be elected to the council or made mayor. On occasion, such repudiation was verbal rather than real.

Did the same thing happen in other urban centers of the epoch? In Olinda, for example, or Salvador, Rio de Janeiro, or São Luis? As a matter of fact, with reference to São Luis, the historian of São Paulo quotes the remark of the Englishman Southey to the effect that in 1685 there were in the city "more than a thousand Portuguese." "Many of them were hidalgos," Southey states, and adds: "It would seem that anyone serving in any official post, even if only

[5] Edmundo Zenha: *O Municipio no Brasil* (*1532–1700*) (São Paulo, n.d.).
[6] Affonso de E. Taunay: *Na Era das Bandeiras* (São Paulo, 1922), p. 59.

for three months, acquires nobility, enjoying not only distinction over the mass of the population, but also certain privileges which render the increase of the class a handicap to the State." And in Tapuitapera, "across the bay . . . the nobles have multiplied to such an extent as a result of holding public office that the Brotherhood of Mercy, made up of mechanics and persons of low class, ceased to exist because all its members had been ennobled." [7]

The war against the Dutch, which in the cities of the North raised even Negroes to the ranks of nobility, facilitated the ennobling of the humble in reward for their military service and even acts of bravery. It also seems to have moved rightful members of the artisans' brotherhoods into those of the nobility. We shall return to this matter of the brotherhoods playing as important a part in early urban Brazil as a royal appointment or a municipal post in conferring nobility on their members, instead of receiving it from them, as in theory or by tradition should have been the case. If in Pernambuco the conflict between the leading class of Recife, made up of men engaged in trade who had recently come out from Portugal, and that of Olinda, made up of planters long established in Brazil (some even of Amerindian ancestry, on which, moreover, they prided themselves), was in the nature of a civil war, this would seem to have been due to the greater vitality of the agrarian nobility of the Pernambuco area, which had been colonized by Portuguese who belonged to the petty provincial nobility of the kingdom, and were probably of better quality than the first settlers of other areas. Keeping themselves reasonably pure by inbreeding, and being numerous enough to occupy all the seats on the municipal council, this group was more obdurate in its refusal to accept tradesmen and mechanics than other regions. For this reason, the inhabitants of Olinda rebelled against the political and economic power of the so-called "peddlers," as though this were a betrayal of their sacred privileges, they the born owners of lands, as well as of slaves, holders of political posts and not merely military commissions.

Perhaps in no other area of older Portuguese colonization were

---

[7] Robert Southey: *Historia do Brasil*, IV, p. 390, quoted by Zenha: Op. cit., p. 95.

the distinctions of color and class as clearly marked as in Pernambuco, the New Lusitania. These distinctions were reflected in the objectives and statutes of the brotherhoods, sodalities, and guilds which there and, in a measure, in nearby areas—principally, Bahía— seem to have flourished more vigorously than in São Paulo. The silversmiths, for example, had in Pernambuco, as in Bahía, not only their guild magistrate, whose induction into office was carried out before the municipal council, but also a sodality, that of St. Eloy, Bishop, to whom a statue was erected in the eighteenth century in the Church of the Hospital of Paradise of Recife. The shoemakers were also organized into a brotherhood, that of St. Crispin and St. Crispinian; carpenters and masons comprised the Brotherhood of St. Joseph. Annually, the various guilds elected their magistrates in the presence of the council, without, however, being represented on it. They comprised the totality of the Trade Corporation, which, according to Pereira da Costa, "exercised over their members . . . a certain authority and enjoyed a number of privileges such as taking part in the formulation of trade regulations or price-fixing for their respective occupations." This same historian discovered in the Municipal Archive of Olinda a record of *Requisites for the Trade of Carpenter*, dated June 15, 1793, which would indicate that the carpenters of Olinda still formed a guild almost until the nineteenth century. It is known that until 1770 it was legally forbidden for anyone to exercise any trade "without a certificate of examination in his trade . . . duly approved by the local senate." This assured the trades their dignity as well as their technical standards.

There are also on record instances of vigorous resistance by the guild magistrates, in defense of that dignity, to the demands of former mechanics who had become slaveowners and endeavored to have their Negro or mulatto slaves, to whom they had taught their manual skills, examined so they would not have to practice with their own hands trades that were considered base, and who saw the opportunity of rising from the artisan to the bourgeois and even noble class by exploiting slave labor. When Koster was in Pernambuco at the beginning of the nineteenth century, he observed that mulattoes were, for the most part, the best artisans; but he also observed that there were colored men among the wealthy planters, and the rich inhabitants of Recife,[8] and, therefore, among the so-called "rich men" or "good men"[9] who could belong to the municipal councils and the brotherhoods of the wealthy and noble. However, there were limits to such changes of status; they never occurred in the case of black men, only light or near-white mulattoes.

Such transfers would seem to explain why the old guild brotherhoods had nearly all disappeared by the end of the eighteenth century, to be replaced by brotherhoods of the type of the Blessed Sacrament, which demanded that candidates for membership be not only white but able to contribute generously to the treasury of the brotherhood. These were brotherhoods which suited the former mechanics or artisans, white or near white, whose success at their trade made possible their transformation into slaveowners and even councilmen. And, once in this office, it is understandable that they would lend an attentive ear to the colored artisans who, on their own initiative or through their masters, petitioned the aldermen to give them the test denied them by the magistrates of the guilds.

Undoubtedly, there were among the old Christians of the colony, whites or near whites, those who were too set in their habits of masters and Christians to feel at ease rubbing shoulders with the new members of the aristocratic brotherhoods whose hands were still calloused from their base callings, or who were still tainted by the practice of Israelite rites, which were also considered debasing. Hence the existence of brotherhoods which were very strict not only in the matter of candidates' racial purity but also of their length of tenure as Catholics and gentlemen. It was this length of tenure which consecrated the true aristocrats or nobles—not merely "good men" or "rich men"—distinguishing them clearly from the outwardly seeming or the jumped-up by reason of their wealth. Such was the Brotherhood of Our Lady of Refuge in Olinda, established "by young unmarried men" in the sixteenth century, and reorganized under a new charter in 1783, which required that its

---

[8] Henry Koster: *Travels in Brazil* (London, 1816), pp. 393, 398.

[9] On "rich men" and "good men" see, in Edmundo Zenha: Op. cit., passage from Antonio Luiz Seabra: *A Propiedade. Comentario a Leis dos Forais* (Coimbra, 1850), p. 91.

candidates be not only "young and unmarried" but free of all taint of Negro, Jew, or mulatto "for three generations back"; that they follow no "base trade"; nor be "public, notorious sinners." The last three demands may be considered typical of the qualifications for admission to the colonial sodalities of the most aristocratic cut. Others, such as the Blessed Sacrament, also aristocratic, or, rather, plutocratic, limited themselves to demanding of their candidates, in addition to decent habits and being white, the ability to make generous donations. And they admitted not only unmarried but married men, and women as well.

Naturally, the qualifications for membership in the aristocratic sodalities changed with regional variations in the ethnic composition and social formation, including the economic, of the population. In Sousa, a Brotherhood of the Blessed Sacrament could not be as exacting with regard to the unimpeachable whiteness of a candidate as in Olinda or Salvador or Recife, where the investigation went back three generations, thus safeguarding the brotherhood from the presence of persons having Negro, mulatto, or Jewish blood, and also, in certain cases, Moorish.

A careful study of the social, and in so far as possible, the ethnic make-up of our brotherhoods, throws great light upon the factors of race, class, and region, which, in their totality, characterize the formation of Brazil. Without taking into consideration the above-mentioned factors, which are nearly always intermingled among us, the student of our formation would be in danger of arriving at erroneous generalizations concerning the individual or group which he considers representative. Generalizations which hold good for countries of greater ethnic purity or more clearly defined class structure lose their validity or force in Brazil. Thus, the position cannot be taken that our formation has been essentially aristocratic in the sense of a single race, class, or region. It was characterized by an aristocratic form with varying substance or content, at times proclaiming itself noble or white (and allowing the natives to adopt old Portuguese given or family names), at times native (with Indian names coming to substitute the European in certain epochs); at times glorifying the plantation owner, at times the city gentry; at times converting the coastal dweller into the hero of our national formation, at times assigning this role to the Paulista, the backlander, the mountaineer; at times making of sugar the prime article of the national economy, at times transferring this majestic role to coffee.

I have already indicated the double connotation of the word "Bahían," to some the maximum expression of aristocratic urbanity and manners, to others, of the incapacity for manly, military action, looked upon as the true mark of breeding and birth. We have also seen that at one time the word *carioca* carried a denigrative sense, as did *mascate* when applied by those of Olinda to those of Recife.

In Brazilian social ecology, the constant during colonial days and the first half of the nineteenth century was the position of the slave of the slave quarters, later replaced by the pariah of shack or shanty, the performer of menial duties, from whom the other elements of society always wanted to distinguish themselves, endeavoring in all possible ways to establish themselves as members, or imitations of the gentry, or merely as free men. As gentry in general, for though the rural gentry, white or near white, was for us the predominant figure of the gentleman as opposed to the servile Negro, it was not, nor is today, the only noble or gentlemanly one envisaged by the Brazilian imagination.

Our social formation reveals varying predominances, depending on the complex of region, class, or race, or one of these conditions, in a decisive moment of superiority or prestige: the white in relation to individuals of colored races and subraces; the owner of great plantations or ranches in relation to the poverty-stricken tenants of such holdings or the slaves needed for their cultivation or for herding or mining; the Old Christian in relation to the New Christian and the non-Catholics; the native-born Brazilian in relation to the Portuguese or naturalized Brazilian; the inhabitants of the more Europeanized seaboard in relation to the more rustic interior. But none of these predominances was and, much less is today, absolute, there being many instances of inversion or confusion of superiority: a distinguished personage with the dark skin of a race generally looked upon as servile or inferior; backlanders superior to those of the coast in economic power and political prestige; landowners so dependent on city agents as to be their economic vassals.

In spite of such inversions and confusion, there can be distinguished in the totality of Brazilian values, habits, styles of life, and culture elements which have preserved characteristics or peculiarities of class, race, or region such as types of dwelling, bed, or grave, methods of transportation, domestic and wild animals, food, medicines, clothing, shoes, headgear, worship, vices, amusements, children's toys, garden plants. Thus, it is known that from the earliest days in Brazil St. Benedict was the "saint of the Negroes," and St. Onofre the "saint of the poor." The samba was for a long time a dance of slaves or blacks in which whites or gentry never took part. There are a number of Negro remedies, as well as those used by the *caboclos*, the backwoodsmen, the backlanders, which were disdained by the "civilized" as unfit for the well-born. In those areas where European influence was strongest, the "civilized" took great care to use, and even abuse, food, drink, and expensive medicines imported from Europe, which were in the nature of the hallmark of the superior race and class, beings to whom the food, drink, or remedies of the rustic sector of society might do more harm than the ailments themselves. The newspapers of the first half of the nineteenth century are full of advertisements of remedies recommended as suitable for "delicate persons," "the genteel or well-born," such as "Guilhie's Elixir to Prevent Cholera," or "Le Roy's Tonic for Ladies and Gentlemen," some of which came to be disdained by "Ladies" and "Gentlemen" and sold by the jugful "for backwoodsmen and Negroes."[1]

As articles of food suitable for "nobles" the advertisements of the same epoch recommended ham, raisins, and green peas, in contrast to the dried beef, salt cod, squash looked upon as common, coarse, or rustic fare. Even today, fish is divided into classes according to social status, with a veritable hierarchy which becomes especially marked during Holy Week. Catfish, definitely looked upon as inferior, was known during colonial days as "old mulatto."[2]

The disdain of the "progressive" Brazilian for the straw-thatched hut or shanty, which, from many points of view, is a type of dwelling admirably suited to the tropics, would seem to be due, in large measure, to the fact that it was associated for centuries with a class,

---

[1] J. F. Sigaud: "A Moda dos Remedios e os Remedios da Moda," *Diario de Saúde ou Ephemerides das Sciencias Medicas e Naturaes do Brazil*, I, 81 (Rio de Janeiro, April 18, 1835).

[2] John Mawe: *Travels in the Interior of Brazil* (Philadelphia, 1812).

race, and region looked upon as inferior, and which often had been the birthplace of these "progressives" or "reformers" anxious to remove the stigma of such origin. The children of the backlanders, and, in the cities, of the poor or lower middle class, were raised on goat's milk, while those of the upper class in the cities and the more prosperous agrarian regions were raised on cow's milk or by a wet nurse. The distinction between goat, animal, and goat, human, both for the rearing of infants, is frequent in the advertisements of the newspapers of the first half of the nineteenth century.[3]

Sleeping in a bed was, for a long time, a mark of social distinction in a medium where the use of the hammock for sleeping, and not merely resting, was general. It was also employed as an aristocratic means of transportation, principally for ladies, to take them from one house to another, or even from city to city, or from city to plantation or ranch.

The prisons, too, reflected the distinctions of class and race. It was unthinkable among us that persons of different race and class should be sent to the same prison for the same crime. In 1729 the Bishop of Pernambuco, Dom Fray José Fialho, arose like a wounded lion in defense of those priests who were lodged in the prisons of Olinda and Recife, "It being a great outrage and offense against the sacerdotal habit that these priests should find themselves in the company of common malefactors, most of them mulattoes or Negroes . . ."[4] And for years Brazilians anxiously sought the title of captain or sergeant of the militia and, later, of the National Guard because of the right or privilege it conferred upon the bearer of such title to be put in a special prison when accused of a crime, with military honors. The holder of an academic title was also entitled to special treatment.

The same thing happened with the first hospitals established in Brazil. They set themselves up in old patriarchal suburban houses, adapting them to their new functions. Like that of Santo Amaro, installed in one of those mansions in the city of Recife around the middle of the nineteenth century, they were divided to accommodate

---

[3] At times these advertisements are somewhat ambiguous: "For sale . . . a nanny goat with no bad habits; knows how to cook and look after a house, wash, iron, and sew; refined manners. . . ." (*Diario de Pernambuco*, November 8, 1830.)

[4] Ms. in Mss. Section of National Library, I, 3,3,20.

persons of different categories. Categories which corresponded as much to the region of origin of the patient—backlanders, plantation dwellers, foreigners employed in trade and offices, sailors—as to his class or race—poor, free, slave, white, black, mulatto.

The English, since the beginning of the nineteenth century, had been setting up in the leading commercial cities of Brazil their own chapels and cemeteries, hospitals or rest homes for the exclusive use of their sailors, unmarried businessmen, technicians, and foundry workers. The rest homes and hospitals differed not only on the basis of race, class, or region of origin of the patients, but also in the techniques and medicines used by the doctors and the religious rites administered to the dying in an epoch when the divergence between Catholics and Protestants was great, as was that between the therapeutics of English and Latin Europe.

Great, too, were the differences between the English and Luso-Brazilians with regard to the type of footwear used by the middle classes and proletariat of the two countries, and also their personal habits, habits very difficult to reconcile among the inmates of the hospitals. The horror of the British is well known, not only for excessive expectoration, spittoons, toothpicks, but also for the wooden shoes of rural Portuguese origin which in Brazil became the accepted type of footwear in the cities among small and even middle-class and great Portuguese and Brazilian businessmen, and among workmen, stevedores, free Negroes, and mulattoes of market place and street. The trade in wooden shoes became one of the most important in Brazilian cities in the middle of the nineteenth century; and tradition has it that even brothers of the Blessed Sacrament wore them in their processions. Businessmen, and not just clerks of Rio de Janeiro, Salvador, and Recife, went to mass in wooden shoes. Former merchants transformed into plantation owners—like Gabriel Antonio in Serinhaem—wore wooden shoes when riding horseback, in contrast to those members of the rural gentry who had fallen on evil days but who, even indoors and naked from the waist up, wore riding boots.

These wooden shoes, clacking over the paving stones of Recife, Salvador, Rio de Janeiro, must have sorely wounded the delicate

ears of the English employed in the warehouses and offices of these
cities, and possibly their reaction, given their almost fanatical love of
silence, to this kind of noise explains the spread of rubber-soled shoes
among us—believed to be an English invention, though it was really
only a perfection of a Brazilian technique—which for some time
were manufactured principally by the Scotch of the Clark Factory.
The rubber-soled shoe was the antithesis of the wooden shoe, which,
on the feet of patients and servants of hospitals, must have made the
best of them veritable infernos for English sick or convalescents, and
possibly for the backlanders, as well, accustomed to soft sandals.

Wetherell, in his *Stray Notes from Bahía*, speaks of the use in
Bahía during the first half of the nineteenth century of sandals "by
many priests" and "the majority of the backwoodsmen," whereas
wooden shoes or clogs were widely used in the city.

The exclusively English hospitals, and the division of hospitals
such as that of Drs. Ramos and Seve into "categories," would seem to
have been based not only on race and color prejudices on the part of
the British, and on the part of certain classes toward others within
Brazilian society itself, but also on differences of regional and national cultural forms and ways of life between the two nations and
between the various classes or subclasses. It is even more difficult
than consorting in hotels, restaurants, and churches for beings differing widely in cultural forms and ways of life to have to coexist in
hospitals and rest homes, where the heightened sensibility of the
sick or convalescent makes mutual tolerance almost impossible.

The way of dressing in the principal cities of Brazil during the
first half of the last century, an epoch which, in what were then the
most important areas of Brazil, clearly marked the beginning of the
decay of the rural patriarchy, with no sharp differentiation, as before,
between generations, between the old men and the young, revealed
more clearly and picturesquely than other aspects of culture the
differences of class, race, and region among Brazilians. With the
decline of the rural patriarchy as the greatest economic, and not
merely moral, force among us, there came a tendency for the different regional and racial styles of dress to coexist with those of the
cities, that is to say, with those of Western Europe, of which Brazil,
detaching itself from half-Moorish Portugal, became not only an
economic but, in many aspects, a cultural colony as well. This ac-

counts for the fact that the wealthier plantation owners did not appear in the city except in bourgeois attire of frock coat, silk hat, and high shoes. The first soft hats were a bold innovation. Leather or coarse straw hats, heavy country shoes, were seen in the city on the backwoodsman, the herder of the backlands, the small plantation owner, men who were gentlemen after their own fashion, but backward, archaic. The cities had to force their way of dressing upon them.

The first half of the nineteenth century abounded in city ordinances having to do with the manner of dress and designed to do away with the more rural or rustic styles of attire. They clearly evidenced the victory of urban over country fashions, and must have coincided with the revolt of the rural population against the tyranny of the seaboard cities.

In 1831 the City Council of Recife rejected as an insult to the city's dignity the habit of the backwoodsmen and plainsmen of going about in shirt and drawers: "Nobody may appear in the streets of this city and its suburbs in shirt and drawers; trousers must be worn . . ." These same persons were forbidden to enter the city riding or mounted on pack animals; they were to lead their animals "by the halter or tie rope." [5]

And at a walk. No backwoodsman was to come into the city trotting or galloping, as though the streets were highways and they, the backwoodsmen, were cavalry among the infantry. Those who galloped within the city limits would, if they were freemen, be fined thirty milreis, and if slaves, receive three dozen lashes. These ordinances were carried out by mounted orderlies and officers and soldiers and, it is fair to assume on the basis of what we know of the epoch, by men wearing riding boots and silver spurs, for these made up the officer corps of the militias or the National Guard, and trotting or galloping, for these honorary officers enjoyed rights which even made whites of those who held high-ranking posts. Nearly all the important planters of the period were honorary officers of the militia or National Guard. Nearly all of them had their title and enjoyed the privileges that went with it. Nearly all of them made of their riding boots and silver spurs the shining insignia of their

---

[5] "Posturas da Camara," *Diario de Pernambuco*, December 13, 1813.

standing as gentlemen or rural gentry. So between them and the backwoodsmen, the plainsmen, the yokels, shod in sandals or cowhide shoes, who did not know how to manage a horse with their spurs, the social and cultural difference was naturally great, even though, as far as whiteness was concerned, the backlanders, many of them fair and blue-eyed, were often pure white, whereas the racial purity of plantation and ranch owners might be questioned.

More important than race as the basis or prerequisite of prestige was class and even the region of origin or residence. We must not forget that in Pernambuco the owner of large acreages of cane in the so-called jungle zone was the equivalent of a great planter in the Bahía area of the Reconcavo or a great rancher in Rio Grande do Sul: a privileged being by reason of his region and the extent of his holdings. An advantage which, linked to that of being of the white race, the upper class, and the so-called stronger sex, placed him in the ranks of the well-born and socially prominent.

Let us return, however, to the municipal ordinances of the Brazilian city councils in the first half of the nineteenth century, which, like those of Recife of 1831, and of Salvador of 1844, refer to people's race, class, and regional situation. We shall discover, through their definitions of status and their restrictions on individual freedom, the power of the whites over the blacks, of the masters over the slaves, and, as evidence of the shift from the rural patriarchy to the urban, that of the city population—or its elite—over that of the country. Naturally, exception must be made of the more powerful or wealthy planters, men ennobled not only with the title of baron or viscount, conferred by the Emperor of Portugal, but with that of captain of the militia or National Guard, which comprised an auxiliary of the constitutional army rather than an autonomous force. And the constitutional or royal army, even though its ranks had included colored men from the early days of the Empire, became an affirmation of the power, culture, and predominantly European interests of the Court and provincial capitals, which had triumphed over the scattered, semi-anarchic, rustic population of the interior.

Among the ordinances of the City Council of Recife—a city repeatedly referred to in this chapter because it was, during the period under consideration, the most typical of all Brazilian capitals, with the possible exception of Rio de Janeiro (which in certain aspects was atypical), in the process of re-Europeanization of Brazilian landscape, life, and culture—those are particularly significant which have to do with Negroes, whose behavior or dress was considered unsuited to their servile state. Thus it was forbidden in the city of Recife, as of December 10, 1831, "to shout, scream, or cry out in the streets," a restriction directed against the Africans and their outbursts of a religious or festive nature. Negro porters were also forbidden to go about the streets singing "between nightfall and sunup." [6] This was a severe restriction, given the African habit of lightening work with song. In Salvador, by ordinances of 1844, "dancing and singing, shouts and shrieks" were forbidden "in the hours of silence." [7]

Moreover, no black slave could go about the city of Recife "by day or night, with a cudgel, or any arm, visible or hidden, under penalty of suffering from fifty to a hundred and fifty lashes in prison, depending on the type of arm, after which he will be turned over to his master. . . ." Only the bearers of "hammocks or litters" may carry "the necessary crotches, for their rest, and the haulers of wood, small sticks to help with the load."

From early colonial days, the governing officials in our country had seen fit to forbid slaves and blacks not only the use of jewels, but also arms, considering that both should be regarded as the insignia of the ruling race and class. Arms were not only looked upon as insignia, but as aids in the event of a conflict between masters and slaves. Hence probably, there arose among the free Negroes and mulattoes of the cities—especially in Rio de Janeiro and Recife—the art of *capoeiragem*, by means of which a person without arms could fight advantageously with police or persons bearing arms.

Also in Recife, by decision of the councilmen in 1831, "those games" were forbidden "in streets, squares, on beaches or stairs, which Negroes and vagabonds are in the habit of playing, under penalty of two to six days' imprisonment, if they are free, or twelve to thirty-six stripes in prison, after which they will be handed over to their masters . . ." An interesting detail is that of the graduation

---

[6] "Posturas da Camara," 1844. Ms. Arquivo da Prefeitura do Municipio do Salvador.

[7] "Posturas da Camara," *Diario de Pernambuco,* December 13, 1831.

of the punishment in proportion to the age of the offender. The punishment varied not only with the free or slave status of the offender, but also with his age.

Moreover, the great concern of the City Council of Recife of 1831 was to give the city's life all possible European semblance. Anyone found "naked on the shore" or "taking a bath uncovered, without due decency," would be punished by imprisonment or the lash. An exception was made in the case of persons "belonging to a military order," who would be turned over "to their respective commanding officers, who would apply the adequate penalty . . ."

In spite of the severity of these measures, unofficial documents of the period indicate that until the second half of the century it remained the custom of the poor of Recife to bathe nude, at times close to the main bridges of the city and in sight of the ladies of the most aristocratic residences. And in the city of Belem do Pará, the North American Warren, when he came there in 1850, saw men, women, and children of the lower classes bathing naked with the greatest nonchalance.[8] Moreover, almost until our own days it was the custom in the North for the gentry themselves to take their river baths nude, near their suburban or inland homes. They merely undressed modestly in straw bathhouses on the riverbank or in the water. The ladies and children went to the river at one hour; the gentlemen at another. Thus, the bath had all the advantages of outdoor bathing without being hampered by the heavy dark flannel bathing suits worn by the people of the upper classes in Brazil when sea bathing began in Rio de Janeiro in the first half of the nineteenth century, though it did not become generalized until the second.

The populace of the cities, however, who had no bathhouse in which to undress for their baths of pleasure or cleanliness, was obliged to undress in the woods and walk naked to the river or sea, scandalizing the inhabitants of the city mansions, who could not bear to have the view from their verandahs sullied by the brown, black, yellow, blotches of plebeian nakedness. Moreover, there was "harm to the health of the inhabitants" who drank the water of the rivers polluted by the bathing of this rabble. And so the city councils

---

[8] John Warren: *Pará; or Scenes and Adventures on the Banks of the Amazon* (New York, 1851), p. 9.

joined forces with the justices of the peace in persecuting the poor people and the colored who, with their bathing, polluted the waters of the rivers and "comported themselves in a manner contrary to public morality," thus incurring the penalties established by the Criminal Code in Section 7, Article 12, and not merely those provided by the municipal ordinances.

What a number of these injunctions and prohibitions, favoring a single group or, at most, a single minority and regional class, race, or culture, would indicate is that, parallel with the process of Europeanization or re-Europeanization of Brazil, there came an intensification of the old system of oppression not only of slaves and servants by the masters, of the poor by the rich, but of Africans and natives by those who considered themselves the surrogates of European culture, that is to say, the leading city residents. The residents or owners of the fine mansions. Such oppression could not fail to provoke uprisings and insurrections, like the many that have been mentioned.

It was impossible for these groups not to react with irritation, resentment, and rebellion when they were forbidden in this highhanded fashion their expressions of religious fervor, their recreation in keeping with the old traditions and customs of their maternal culture: work songs, regional attire, jewels, ornaments, amulets. Persons who were apparently free men, like the backlanders, the backwoodsmen, the small farmers, who were ordered in humiliating fashion not to enter the cities seated on their pack animals, but alongside or in front of them, and humbly, at a walk, through dirt and mud, like peons unfit to appear before the eyes of the residents of the city mansions aping the manners of gentlemen.

The right to gallop or canter through the streets of the cities was the prerogative of officers and militiamen, the prerogative of men dressed and shod in European style. The water of the rivers became polluted when it was the colored urchin, the poor man, the slave who bathed in it. The air of the cities resounded with an abominable din when it was Africans who were singing their work songs, or their voodoo or carnival chants, so different from the litanies sung in the Catholic processions, the festivals in the churchyard, the rosaries before the saints' niches.

What was taking place was a vast attempt at the oppression of non-

European cultures by European, of rural values by urban, of religious manifestations and amusements of the slave population repugnant to the gentry, who controlled the municipal councils and the justices of the peace and the chiefs of police. How could the first half of our nineteenth century have been different than it was in those socially or culturally decisive areas? It was an epoch of such frequent social and cultural conflicts among groups of the population —conflicts which were complex under their deceptively simple political exterior—that its characteristic note was one of unrest and alarm.

During preceding centuries there may have been greater forbearance, wisdom, more of a sense of compromise on the part of the civil authorities (probably on that of the ecclesiastic, too) and of the more important landowners toward cultures and peoples they considered inferior, represented by elements which, when not enslaved, were oppressed, disdained, or simply looked down upon by the whites, by the Old Christians, and by the residents of urban areas or those dominated by the Big Houses. Disdained or scoffed at because of idiosyncrasies of race or class, of culture or region distasteful to the dominant groups of the population.

At the close of the eighteenth century, in an audience with the Minister of State, Martinho de Mello e Castro, to discuss the matter of the dances of the Negroes in Brazil, the Count of Pevolide, a former governor of a captaincy, was of the opinion that such dances should not be considered more indecent than "the fandangos of Castile and the *fofas* of Portugal and the *lunduns* of the whites and mulattoes of that country." The Negroes dance "in tribal groups and with the instruments typical of each," "whirling like harlequins" and "with diverse movements of the body." From these acceptable dances those should be separated which are deserving of complete reprobation like those danced by the Senegalese Negroes "in the secrecy of their homes or in clearings, with a black mistress of ceremonies, an altar to idols, adoring live buck goats and other fetishes of clay, anointing their bodies with oils and cocks' blood, eating cakes of cornmeal after pronouncing heathen blessings on them, making the countryfolk believe that those cakes so blessed bring good luck, working love spells on men and women, and the credulity of certain persons is so great, even those one would not think so ignorant, such as friars and priests, who have been taken prisoner in the ring I threw around such houses, and to unmask whom I had to make confess their deception in the presence of the blacks of the house, and then turn them over to their authorities so they could be punished as they deserved, and I had the Negroes severely flogged and ordered their masters to sell them far away." [9]

In the opinion of the Count, the Inquisition ought not confuse certain dances with others. And apparently guided by the opinion of a man so versed in Brazilian affairs, Minister Mello e Castro wrote to the governor of Pernambuco that the dances of the Negroes, "even though not entirely innocent, should be tolerated for the sake of avoiding, through this lesser evil, greater ones, and always employing all the gentle measures which your good judgment suggests to gradually do away with amusements so contrary to decent customs." When later a complaint came from Goiana against the *batuques* of the Negroes, Governor Dom Thomaz José de Mello replied to the complainants in an official communication of November 10, 1796: "As for the *batuques* which the Negroes of the plantations and this city are in the custom of celebrating on holy days . . . they should not be deprived of this entertainment, for it is the greatest pleasure they have in all their days of slavery." [1]

This reflected a wise compromise or an intelligent tolerance of differences of race, class, and cultural behavior which those municipal councils lacked in Imperial Brazil, and those justices of the peace, those provincial presidents, those chiefs of police, those priests who spent their time harassing the *batuques*, the *candombles*, the *maracatús* of slaves and Africans as though they were waging a crusade. In Salvador, in keeping with ordinances issued by the City Council in 1844, "*batuques*, dances, and gatherings of slaves in any place and at all times" were forbidden.

This policy of coercion and violent repression met with the approval of the leading organs of opinion of the period. In 1856 the

---

[9] Ms. in Mss. Section (Coleção Pereira da Costa), State Library, Pernambuco.

[1] Ibid.

local police, applauded by a newspaper as enlightened as the *Diario de Pernambuco*, dispersed a group of Negroes of Rosario dancing in Recife at carnival time, not "because," as the newspaper points out, "it believed that such innocent diversion disturbed the public order, but because from dancing they went on to drinking, and then came the disturbances . . ." Therefore, according to this same source of information, "the police had acted very wisely."

This is not surprising. From the same newspaper came support for far more violent measures taken by the police against Negroes and slaves. Two Negroes ingenuously went to complain to the sub-commissioner of Bõa Vista that their masters had punished them with whippings which they considered unjust, whereupon he ordered that "each be given a double dose." The *Diario de Pernambuco* applauded this abuse, saying "this is an excellent way to handle such complaints." A Negro had no right to complain to the police about punishments inflicted by a white master. A slave had no right to ask redress for punishment at the hands of his master. And nothing shocked the moralists of that upright journal more than for the police to tolerate what was known as "the raising of flags," with "groups of little girls singing in the manner of Guinea." Such a custom made us "seem like savages in the eyes of foreigners." [2]

These were the eyes which probably worried us more than the eyes of God around the middle of the nineteenth century. The eyes of the English, of the French, of the Europeans.

It was from these eyes that it was most important that we hide African customs and celebrations, Guinea dances in the street, back-landers wearing their regional costumes in the large cities. This explains the favorable report in a newspaper of November 26, 1856, of a "gathering of Negroes" in Ponte Velha do Recife, in which they "completely imitated the etiquette of the drawing room, dancing, playing, conversing, eating, and drinking in the most orderly manner." [3] This was as it should be. It was a sight fit for English and French eyes, the African Negroes of Brazil amusing themselves in keeping with the canons of white drawing rooms. No dances of Guinea, or *batuques*, or voodoo rites. Just like a gathering

---

[2] *Diario de Pernambuco*, November 12, 1856.
[3] Ibid.

in a bourgeois patriarchal home. Dances copied from the whites, music copied from the whites. European refreshments. Food cooked according to European recipes.

Out of consideration or fear of "foreign eyes," and in response to the pressure of interests (and not merely cultural values) represented by these eyes, critical or contemptuous of all that departed from the prevailing customs and fashions of Western, carboniferous, bourgeois Europe, we did away, during the first half, or, to be more exact, the whole nineteenth century, with certain rustic or Orientally patriarchal survivals, with certain of the most picturesque expressions of cultural, racial, class and regional differences. These had coexisted among us under the tolerant primacy of the European element, the Portuguese Catholics. This equilibrium was destroyed in the interests of emphasizing, by the harsh elimination of differences, the supremacy or superiority of the European, upper-class, urban element.

Typical of the epoch was the wane in prestige of expressions of a culture that was now Brazilian and no longer merely patriarchal. This was the case with the *modinha* sung to the accompaniment of the guitar in family gatherings and street serenades; the taking of snuff prepared in Rio de Janeiro or Bahía, or imported from Lisbon or even London, a habit which had become general among the plantation and city gentry; the mestizo dishes or sweets, rejected as being "African" or "coarse"; the saints of cashew wood carved by rustic sculptors employing a technique half-European and half-Asiatic or African, reminiscent of the statues of O Aleijadinho; the hammocks of cotton fiber and feathers made by the Indians; the furniture made of native woods by mulattoes who took delight in rounding the legs of tables and chairs and in softening the European style of the patriarchal and conventual furniture, giving it forms they had learned from Portuguese workmen steeped in influences of the Far East and Africa itself; the art of lacemaking of the countrywomen of the interior; and of pottery pitchers, jugs, to keep water cool; basket weaving; silver buckles and jewelry wrought by mestizo hands, with details and variations as typically Brazilian or regional as those which gave dishes or sweetmeats which had originated in Portugal new flavor due to the addition of tropical ingredients, like rice pudding made with coconut milk, couscous made with manioc meal, fritters eaten with molasses.

The newspaper advertisements of the epoch reveal the rapid replacement in the better homes of the guitar by the English piano; the *modinha* by Italian or French arias; the snuff of Bahía and Rio de Janeiro by the cigar of Manila and, later, of Havana; the homemade sweets or tidbits by those imported from Europe and bought at the confectioner's or the grocery store; homemade remedies by those from Europe and purchased at the apothecary's; the hammock by the sofa, the settee, the rocking chair; the wooden saints of local manufacture by European models; furniture made to order by the cabinetmaker by that manufactured in Portugal, Hamburg, England, France, and even the United States; the native laces by those imported from Europe; clay cooking utensils by those of iron; jewelry of heavy gold or silver made in Brazil by that imported from Europe and exchanged here for the local product by Alsatian Jews who specialized in this trade.

Many years were to elapse before a readjustment came about in Brazilian national, mestizo habits, crafts, and techniques which, during the first half of the nineteenth century, were sharply divided into values or habits characteristic of "superior" and "inferior" race, class, and region, after having achieved an almost pan-Brazilian status as a result of miscegenation and the fusion of national and regional cultures.

Such differences came to accentuate others which were inseparable from the slaveholding organization of society. Differences in manner of speaking, gestures, insignia of rank, which were sharply marked in rulers and ruled. The voice of authority—and several foreign observers remarked on the habit of Brazilian ladies in slavery days of talking in a shrill, unpleasant voice,[4] the result of giving orders to slaves or servants—and that of the slaves: "meek," gentle, tactful, sweet, and even "poetic," as a newspaper advertisement puts it.[5] The master had one manner of walking, the slave another, although the latter's tendency, when employed as page, maid, or valet, was to imitate the gestures of the family of which he was, sociologi-

---

[4] A. Saint-Hilaire: *Voyages dans l'Intérieur du Brésil*, II (Paris, 1830), p. 284.

[5] *Diario de Pernambuco*, May 27, 1830.

cally, a member. The grown-ups had a code of behavior very different from that of the children or young persons, who in the presence of their elders did not raise their voices, laugh, or smoke. The gestures of men were very different from those of women, which were supposed to be characterized by their charm, delicacy, sweetness, submission to fathers and husbands, the spirit of sacrifice where their children were concerned.

Ailments were different, too. Even though, logically, those brought on by a sedentary life should have been typical of the upper race and class, and those caused by overwork should have been typical of the serving race and class, it should be pointed out that the chief affliction of the masters was "gentleman's ailment," that is to say, sciatica brought on by long journeys on mule or horseback, as a result of the heat transmitted from the body of the animal—especially the mule—to the rider's legs.[6] At the same time, ailments associated with a sedentary life were common among the Negroes in the slave quarters, such as that which was attributed to the chill of the floor or the earth, where many of them slept, and which especially affected the field hands, turning them gray, pale, and killing them. The disease was known at the time as "intertropical hypoemia," or "hookworm," which a doctor of Bahía, Dr. Wucherer, linked to the ancyclostoma duodenal, already associated in Egypt with the anemia of the slaves who went barefoot. Another doctor of the mid-nineteenth century, Lima Santos, in a study entitled "Consideracões sobre o Brasil, seu Clima, suas Enfermidades Especiais" (Reflections on Brazil, its climate, and special diseases), published in the *Diario de Pernambuco* for August 9, 1855, held this to be due not only to the climate but to social causes. "Children," he wrote, "are, as a rule, the most affected, and Negro slaves, especially those of the country. The ignorant look upon one of the symptoms of the ailment as a bad habit, known as 'the habit of eating dirt.' But this error is harmful because of the resulting neglect of the illness and because of the atrocious treatment of those suffering from it. Oppilation being a disease which induces a disorder of the blood, and the impoverishment of its content, it is evident that it must be

---

[6] Mawe: *Travels in the Interior of Brazil*, 2nd. ed. (London, 1821), p. 481.

combated by scientific methods, and never by severity, and strenuous exercise, as is the custom. The development of oppilation may be attributed to climatic reasons, and the lack of hygiene among those living in damp places, such as poor children and the slaves of unfeeling masters. I have observed that in places where the heat is intense, and the humidity great, as from Rio de Janeiro to the Amazon River, this ailment is prevalent. But apart from the climatic conditions, it is our belief that the principal cause lies in the nature of the soil and in the diet . . ." For "the part of the population which suffers most is that which is undernourished, like the poor and the slaves," that is to say, the slaves of "unfeeling masters" and the poor who live in places exposed to the inclemencies of the weather. The devastating oppilation in patriarchal Brazil was a disease of race, the African; of class, the servile; and of region, the agrarian and latifundarian. Mainly of the coffee subregion. In the opinion of a Brazilian doctor of Rio de Janeiro who had made a careful study of the problem from the middle of the nineteenth century, although conceding that the combined action of heat and dampness of certain regions intensified the malady, he found it to be more widespread where the slaves were overworked and more exposed to the rain and the sun, as was the case in the coffee-growing areas, and where living conditions were worse. One of the contributing causes, in the opinion of Dr. Peçanha da Silva, was the clothing of the field hands —"going almost naked" or "wearing heavy dark blue flannelette garments"—and their diet: in the South, manioc meal and black beans, "with an occasional morsel of fat pork," or cornmeal, sweet potatoes, squash, with a protein deficiency." On plantations where the vegetable diet of the slaves was supplemented by meat, as on that of the Marchioness of Paraná, oppilation was unknown.[7]

The habit of eating dirt, clay, ashes, coffee grounds, or chewing tobacco, or smoking marihuana, or drinking rum were "vices" almost exclusively associated among us with persons of "inferior" race, class, and region. These were vices of slaves, Negroes, country

---

[7] "Relatorio sobre a Nota ou Memoria do Dr. Julio Rodrigues de Moura pelo Dr. Peçanha da Silva," *Annaes Brasilienses de Medicina*, I, Vol. XIX (Rio de Janeiro, 1861).

louts. And the ailments to which they gave rise were despicable. Not so the veneral diseases of which the lads of well-born white landholding families boasted, looking upon them as proof not only of virility but of superiority of race and class, the class and race which had women from an early age. Snuff taking, the passion for cock and finch fighting, horse trading became established as habits of the upper class and white race, which in time were picked up by the lower and colored classes. From these, by way of compensation, certain dishes, diversions, religious cults, and even bodily adornment and prophylaxis, made their way up to the Big Houses and city mansions. This explains the acceptance of okra, of manioc meal and meat stew, of shrimp cooked with green peppers and dende oil, of the samba, of amulets, of silver jewelry of the type worn by the Negroes, of salves and teas made of African or native herbs, of the pointed knife as a defense weapon aristocratized, with time, into the silver-handled dagger of gentlemen and gentry. It also explains the transformation of the habit of delousing, which was common among slaves and poor, into the voluptuous custom of *cafuné*—head-rubbing—among the ladies and even the gentlemen of the rural gentry.

At the same time the Negroes, slaves and descendants of slaves, were graciously allowed to have ailments, and not merely vices, which were considered the exclusive privilege of whites or masters. The right to have anemia. To suffer from rheumatism. To die of a heart attack and even of yellow fever. And the use of appurtenances which had for a time been the insignia of the dominant race, class, and region, as well as of the stronger sex, such as cane, riding boots, silver-handled quirt, pistol, top hat, high shoes, frock coat, gloves, rings. These were concessions reluctantly made by masters to slaves in Brazil, by the whites to the blacks, signifying the recognition of Negroes and slaves, and their descendants, as beings capable or worthy of sharing, in the case of exceptional individuals, the power or authority exercised, or the leisure enjoyed, by the white gentry by right of birth.

The decline of the cane and the parasol as insignia of the dominant class and race, and the generalization of their use, regardless of the social position of their user, dates from the twentieth century. Our folklore bears witness to certain aspects of the generalization of these insignia of the upper class. As for instance:

> *Negro with gloves,*
> *Sign of rain.*

The first colored women to dress like the whites were hooted by the street loafers, by those of their own race who protested at seeing them "get out of their color." The same thing happened with colored men using high hat, frock coat, gloves, and cane.

Certain racial and class characteristics which have been more resistant to the disappearance of the rigid frontiers between class, race, and region in Brazilian society are worth mentioning here, but merely mentioned in passing, for they deserve a separate study. As, for instance, the gestures, manner of walking, talking, laughing, singing typical not of slaves or servants, but of the *capoeiras* or *capadocios* of the cities, the "bad men" of the interior, the street loafers of Rio de Janeiro, of Bahía. It should also be pointed out that many Negroes who grew up on rich plantations acquired from their masters gestures, ways of speaking, walking, laughing typical of the upper class and the "superior" race, to the point of becoming, culturally and sociologically, members of the same family, their manners contrasting with those of the majority of their race and class.

In such cases, typical race and class characteristics became fused with the traits and habits of the dominant family, anxious to show its social and cultural superiority not only in its children, but in its servants as well. Godchildren, servants, natural children were often permitted to take from their fathers, godfathers, or white masters aristocratic European family names, another form of the intermingling of plebians with gentry which has contributed to the democratization of Brazilian society thanks to the patriarchal system itself, which among us was contradictory in various of its social effects.

CHAPTER IX

ORIENT AND OCCIDENT

THERE ARE those who think I have overstressed the importance of the Orient in the formation of the society that developed in Brazil under the patriarchal regime. The fact of the matter is that the Orient gave content, and not merely certain decorative touches, to the culture that came into being here and to the setting created by the predominantly patriarchal conditions of coexistence, in general, and the exploitation of the land and of men of one race by those of another, in particular. And not only cultural content and color. The Orient contributed to stimulating the noble and the servile forms of this coexistence among us, the hierarchal forms of family and social life. Ways of living, dressing, transportation which could not fail to affect ways of thinking.

Only the vigor of British capitalism in its quest for markets for its suddenly explosive production of glass, iron, wool, earthenware, cutlery, and coal—a production served by a truly revolutionary system of transportation—managed to blunt, in a relatively short space of time, the Oriental influence on the life, landscape, and culture of Brazil. For it would seem that, at the close of the eighteenth century and the beginning of the nineteenth, nowhere else in America had the palanquin, the rush mat, the market stall, the public fountain, fireworks, concave tiles, the litter, latticed windows, women's shawls and turbans, the whitewashed or brightly painted house in the form of a pagoda, with the corners of the eaves upturned like the horns of the moon, the painted tile, the Indian coconut palm and the mango tree, couscous, taffy, sugar paste, sweet rice and milk with cinnamon, the cloves of Molucca, the cinnamon of Ceylon, the pepper of Cochin China, the tea of China, the camphor of Borneo, the nutmeg of Banda, the fabrics and porcelain of China and India, the perfumes of the East, acclimated themselves so well as in Brazil. In conjunction with native values, and those of European and other origins, they formed that symbiosis of nature and culture which developed in our country. And as though our relationship with the Orient were ecologically closer than with the Occident, with its mystique of ethnocentric purity or its systematic intolerance of the exotic, the latter was to be found here only in certain French and English styles and cultural manifestations generalized along the seaboard after the coming of Dom João VI. Or through an occasional outcropping of some strictly Western manifestation on the part of the Portuguese, in contrast with their instinct or policy of expansion, which was always aimed at reconciling Oriental and Occidental values.

Until the transfer of the Court of Portugal to Rio de Janeiro, as far as Brazil was concerned, the seat of European culture was Portugal, with the exception of the short-lived control of the French in Rio de Janeiro and Maranhão, of the Dutch in the northeast, of the English in Amazonia. And this Iberian source of culture was never, in Brazil, exclusively European, but to a large degree impregnated with Moorish, Arabic, Israelite, Mohammedan influences. Oriental influences conmingled with those of the Occident, Oriental survivals which had not been completely absorbed in the Western predominance over Portugal or Iberia.

In 1809 a fervent apologist of the Westernization of Brazil, referring to customs—many of Oriental origin—which had developed here into typically Brazilian ways, called them "awkward, superannuated usages which could barely be tolerated when this part of America was known as a Portuguese colony," being, as they were, customs "which for a long time have been rejected by cultivated and perfectly civilized nations . . ."[1] The "perfect civilization"

---

[1] Luis Gonçalvez dos Sanctos: *Memorias para Servir a Historia do Reino do Brasil*, I (Lisbon, 1825), p. 136.

being the Western, the Christian, the European, it was toward this state of human perfection that Brazil should direct its steps, shaking off the Asiatic and African vestiges in its culture, its life, the gestures of its people, in its very landscape. During the first half of the nineteenth century, and, to a certain extent, throughout the entire century, there was a veritable zeal on the part of many leaders of Brazil and persons of standing to bring European trees and plants into our country, in contrast to the Portuguese policy of the colonial period, which was, for the most part, that of enriching Lusitanian America with trees, plants, and animals, for practical or decorative purposes, proceeding from Asia, Africa, and the islands of the South Atlantic rather than from Europe. From regions climatically closer to tropical America. Debret could still observe in the early years of the Empire that the Brazilian "does not borrow his innovations only from Europe; he goes in search of them to Asia as well . . ." [2]

Among those "awkward usages," unworthy of "a perfect civilization," it was natural that that eloquent apologist for the West, Father Gonçalvez dos Sanctos, should have included—referring principally to Rio de Janeiro—the use of latticed windows or shutters, which "detract from the beauty of the city's view, and make it less brilliant," in addition to being "uncomfortable, bad for the health, cutting off the free circulation of air, revealing the lack of civilization on the part of its inhabitants . . ." Therefore, the residents of Rio de Janeiro should "throw aside the proof of their former state of colony," represented by the shutters or Oriental blinds, and thus contribute to the "ennobling," that is to say, the Westernizing or Europeanizing of the Court, "and make it more noteworthy and splendid in the eyes of foreigners, who are beginning to flock to it in large numbers . . ."

This confirms the fact we have already pointed out that the Brazilian of the seaboard or the city lived, during the nineteenth century, obsessed by the idea of "the eyes of foreigners." In the same fear of these eyes as formerly of the eyes of the Jesuits or the Inquisition. And the "eyes of foreigners" were the eyes of Europe, the eyes of the bourgeois, industrial West, whose patterns of culture,

---

[2] J. B. Debret: *Aquarelas relativas ao Brasil publicadas por R. Heymann* (Paris, 1939).

ways of life, designs of landscape were in conflict with ours, strongly tinged, as they were, with Oriental influences. Invaded or deflowered by Portugal, it was as though the Orient had taken revenge on the bold semi-Occidental conqueror, fanning the embers of dulled Oriental heritages in his culture and even blood, and adding to old African and Asiatic traits a number of new ones. Many of these were transmitted to Brazil from earliest colonial days, and here they took on a development of their own as a result of the policy of segregation from Europe adopted by the Portuguese with regard to their American colony after the discovery there of emeralds and diamonds, in addition to the gold of Minas Gerais.

In Portugal itself, up to the nineteenth century, the Oriental characteristics were more evident than perhaps anywhere else in Europe, with the exception of Turkey and Asiatic Russia. They were in sharp contrast to those of typically Western Europe, to which the Prince Regent and his policymakers did everything in their power to approximate Brazil, even detaching it from Portugal. And the Regent's advisers, and he himself, acted less in the interests of a policy in keeping with the established Portuguese or Iberian procedure than of following the English policy of dominating extra-European peoples and cultures to provide their industries with markets. The "eyes of foreigners," or, to be more exact, of the English, came to govern Brazil less through their consuls and salesmen than through those Anglophile Portuguese and Brazilians such as Count Linhares [3] and the economist Silva Lisboa, to whom the salvation of Portugal or Brazil lay in sloughing off, as quickly as possible, all that was Oriental in their culture and acquiring the forms, colors, gestures which prevailed in the perfectly civilized West, represented by France and England—above all, the latter. This explains the sociological implication of the phrase which had become general in Brazil from the beginning of the nineteenth century: "To show the English."

The "eyes of the foreigners," under which Brazil was to achieve the category of a civilized kingdom or nation, were, as we have said, for the most part those of the English. The Anglophile already referred to in connection with the significant proposal of the removal

---

[3] A Portuguese administrator during the colonial epoch.

of the shutters from the residences of Rio de Janeiro tried to justify police intervention against the owners of the houses in question, invoking "many reasons of a moral and political nature." Among those of a political nature there were probably those of economic policy as well: the desire of the English to see the lattices or wooden shutters replaced in the mansions—only the mansions—of the principal cities by glass windows and iron balconies.

The fact that the measure affected only the mansions would seem to indicate that shutters were considered "awkward" only in this fine type of building. The "reasons of a moral and political nature" ceased to exist when the shutters were on the poorer type of urban dwelling, the house of one story, halfway between the fine residence of the rich and the shanty of the poor or indigent. By the police order which put an end to shutters in the city of Rio de Janeiro, they were to disappear from "the windows of mansions . . . in a period of eight days." On the balconies of those houses which as yet lacked "iron grilles," a "period of six months" was granted so that during this brief interval the wood could be substituted by iron, as well as the Moorish lattice by English glass. An exception was made in the case of the shutters of "single-story houses, which do not affect the beauty of the view . . ." [4]

That the single-story houses did not affect the beauty of the "view" or aspect of the city is questionable. However, what does seem to be a fact is that the inhabitants or owners of such houses were unable to replace in days or months the shutters of their homes with glass windows.

According to Father Sanctos, this change produced "general satisfaction." General satisfaction, it would seem, on the part of the Westernizers, who were the reformers or modernists of the period, in revolt against "the prejudices with which our grandparents brought us up."

For the Westernizers, it was as though the disappearance of this Oriental feature of domestic architecture marked the decisive victory of the West over the East in the struggle between cultures or civilizations of which Brazil had been the battlefield for years. Their goal was the complete triumph of Occident over Orient in Brazilian life,

---

[4] Sanctos: Op. cit., I, p. 137.

so the country would become a Western or sub-European cultural area.

When the Westernizers were also, as in the case of the English and French, the manufacturers of household equipment, clothing, toys, food, vehicles, or their Brazilian importers, sentiment was backed up by self-interest. Whence the need to arouse the new generations against the "prejudices of our grandfathers"—old fogies clinging to shutters, rush mats, and palanquins; silks, porcelains, perfumes, and fans of China; and the habit, not only of children but of adults too, of amusing themselves with fireworks and kites after the fashion of the Chinese.

What Brazil needed was what one of these Westernizers, rejoicing over the enforced removal of shutters from the big houses of Rio de Janeiro in 1809, called "unshadowing." Unshadowing by means of English glass in homes and carriages still Orientally covered with lattices and curtains. Unshadowing of the cities, by means of wide streets to replace the Orientally narrow alleys of Rio de Janeiro, Salvador, Recife, São Luis do Maranhão, São Paulo, Olinda. Unshadowing of the churches by the substitution on the part of women of capes, mantles, mantillas, or shawls by transparent French veils which did not hide the charms of face and bosom of the young ladies. Unshadowing of men's faces by the use of English scissors and razors, on sale in the Brazilian shops of the nineteenth century, on the heavy beards known as "Moorish," "Turkish," or "Nazarene." Unshadowing by means of Western systems of illumination, replacing whale oil, the tallow candle, the Oriental paper lantern, by the kerosene lamp, the English or Belgian chandelier (which also burned kerosene), by gas. Unshadowing customs, manners, habits, gestures in the relations between men and women, between fathers and sons.

We shall see further on how, with this "unshadowing" under the influence of Western techniques of production, transportation, urbanization, illumination, street paving, architecture, the preservation and preparation of food products, the sanitation of streets and houses, Brazil entered upon a new phase of moral and material existence. But this does not mean that this new phase represented nothing but advantages for our people and our culture still in the formative stage. In many aspects, what we had imitated, assimilated, or adopted from the East represented a deep-rooted, often healthy adaptation of man to the tropics, which that "unshadowing" broke off or brusquely interrupted.

For the tropics cannot be vanquished without shading them in some way or other, as the Arabs or Orientals do. Nor without narrow streets, shawls, broad parasols to protect one from the sun's rays. Nor the shade of spreading Asiatic and African trees, such as the mango, the breadfruit, the *gameleira*, around the houses, the squares, and along the road. Nor hollow roof tiles, verandahs, curtains, shutters or blinds, mats on the floor. Nor cooling drinks of tamarind, lemon, coconut water, for the hot hours. Nor oil, cloves, pepper, saffron to color the food and spice it, to stimulate the palate made languid by the heat. Brazil had assimilated these Oriental contributions through the Portuguese, the Moors, the Jews, the Negroes, and converted them into its own patrimony. They became a link between man and his home and tropical America. Nor could they fail to affect his mentality and his spirit.

It was not only ecologically that Brazil, officially colonized by Europeans, was so closely linked to the Orient. Through the experience and cultural instruments acquired from the East, it adapted itself to the tropics to the point of becoming, in various aspects of its organization and landscape, an area poised between East and West. A kind of vast Portuguese Goa. The meeting of East and West produced a mixed type of culture much like that encountered in Portuguese India by North Europeans, who came away amazed at the new combinations of color and human beings and ways of life.[5]

Economically, too, Brazil and the Orient had been brought so close together that the regular and irregular commerce between them during the colonial era constituted one of the firmest bases of the Brazilian agrarian and patriarchal system. For certain Oriental textile centers, such as Malabar, Brazil was a valuable customer. "Asiatic trade, principally that of the coast of Malabar, is seriously

---

[5] Alberto C. Germano da Silva Correia: *La Vieille Goa* (*Aperçu Historique, Recueils de Voyageurs, Saint François Xavier, etc.*) (Bombay, 1931), Chap. III. Also *Os "Lusos descendentes" da India Portuguesa. Estudo Historico, Demografico, Antropometrico e Aclimativo* (Lisbon, 1925).

affected by the stagnation of the vast and varied textile trade with Brazil," wrote Domingos Alves Branco Moniz Barreto in 1837.[6] Before the English took over or absorbed the Brazilian market, Brazil received from Asia large supplies of cheap fabrics for the use of slaves and the poor, and not merely high-grade materials for the wealthy. And Portuguese America bought many notions and knicknacks of Asiatic and African manufacture in the Orient before the French monopolized this trade: glass beads, imitation pearls, coral. And tin plates, wooden-handled knives, lead solder, powder, bullets, pistols, swords, daggers.

Moreover, all this trade developed along with the trade in slaves from Africa and depended upon the stability of the agrarian, patriarchal, slaveholding system for its maintenance. By attacking this system, English industrialism killed another bird with the same stone: Oriental manufactures, to which the Brazilian economy was linked by a series of reciprocal advantages, such as the exportation by Brazil to Africa of a considerable amount of tobacco and rum.

It was not unusual to find Brazilians of the epoch who came to consider the affinities between Brazil and the Orient, which were the result of the similarity of the patriarchal system which prevailed in both, the basis or climate for an economic reciprocity that could survive the abolishment of the slave trade. One of these was the aforementioned Moniz Barreto, who favored the importation into Brazil of "free men" of Africa, who should "engage in agriculture" or "learn, through apprenticeship, trades and crafts."[7] In his opinion, "the great inequality in the distribution of wealth"—typical of a country semi-feudal in its economy, like Brazil—aroused such an aversion in the European laborer, farmer, or craftsman, that we could not count upon this type of free man. Whereas the African of humble origin, even if he were free, would not be surprised by such conditions. On the contrary, he would adjust to them almost effortlessly. This argument was to be employed some years later by the advocates of the importation of Asiatic laborers to Brazil, where the "great inequality in the distribution of wealth" would not produce

---

[6] Domingos Alves Branco Moniz Barreto: *Memoria sobre a Abolição do Commercio de Escravatura* (Rio de Janeiro, 1837), p. 26.

[7] Ibid., p. 45.

the same disagreeable effect on an Asiatic peasant as on a European workman of England or France, a peasant of Germany or Switzerland, or even of Spain or Portugal.

What mattered to these advocates of the importation of "free men" from the Orient to Brazil was to satisfy the English demand for the abolition of the slave trade. They were not ignorant of the fact that in Brazil "free" Africans and Chinese would be virtually slaves under a patriarchal system which resembled that of the country of origin of such workers. They would not protest, like the Northern Europeans or even the Southern, against their serf status, to which they had been accustomed for ages. On the contrary, what they would miss most would be a patriarchal master who would give them protection in return for the slave or semi-slave labor they performed for him. On this point, the Orient and Brazil could have come to an understanding to their mutual advantage, if, to the purely social and economic aspects of their relations, there had not been added the cultural and the ethnic. Inasmuch as with the transfer of the Court to Brazil—a Court dominated by the English—Europe had taken on new prestige in Brazilian eyes as the model of "perfect civilization," this attitude, radiating from the cities or the more cultivated areas, of necessity went hand in hand with the devaluation of non-European ethnic and cultural values.

This explains what amounted to real campaigns at this time on the part of Europeanized doctors and other Europeanized men of science in Brazil branding the "yellows," and not only the "blacks," as undesirable elements in the ethnic and cultural composition or re-composition of the country's population. According to them, the population of Brazil should endeavor to approximate that of Europe, culturally and ethnically. It would be utter folly to add, to the already large number of Africans brought into Brazil as slaves, more "free" Africans or Asiatics. The "Aryanists" felt that the presence of Asia and Africa lowered us in European eyes. We should completely rid ourselves of this handicap instead of encouraging or augmenting it by the introduction of new Africans and Asiatics, who would accentuate the black, mulatto, yellow hue of our people and preserve in our culture and landscape the loud reds and yellows which no longer met with the approval of European taste.

The "Aryanists" did not want the traffic in African slaves to be followed by that in ostensibly free Asiatics,[8] though as enslaved as the Africans and, like them—or even more—an alien element in the development of a white population of European culture in Brazil. And this development should be, they held, something sacred to every patriotic, enlightened Brazilian. The government must not be allowed to increase the number of Asiatic immigrants on the grounds of introducing the cultivation of tea or the silkworm.

This opinion had been growing since the first decades of the Empire. It became so strong, after the middle of the century, that in 1879 Dr. Costa Ferraz felt it incumbent on him, as a doctor and scientist, to sound this frightening tocsin: "Mongolism is threatening Brazil." "The fatherland" was already suffering many ills, due "in great measure to the lack of foresight and the disdain for science's repeated warnings . . ." And to these there was now added Mongolism: "Brazil, whose discoverers have made it suffer the terrible canker of slavery, one of the main reasons for its backwardness, is now threatened, after half a century of independence, with the worst of all scourges, Mongolism." [9]

The uncompromising enemy of Oriental immigration perhaps forgot that from the hygienic point of view such colonization, as represented by the Chinese, was far from justifying the fury it aroused in doctors, particularly concerned with the sanitary aspects of the matter. For the fact is that in an experiment in colonization carried out around the middle of the nineteenth century in Mucurí with foreigners of different origins, the Chinese surpassed the Germans themselves in cleanliness. At a distance of three hundred feet from a German house "the stench was overpowering." [1] The blond colonists' feet were alive with chigoes "because their dirty bodies attract the harmful insects . . ." It was useless to tell them that the parasite could be removed with a scissors or needle, and that the best remedy was to bathe in the river daily and keep the body clean. "They tried

---

[8] L. P. de Lacerda Werneck: *Ideias sobre Colonização Precedidas de Uma Sucinta Exposição dos Principios Gerais que Regem a População* (Rio de Janeiro, 1855).

[9] "O Mongolismo Ameaça o Brasil!" in *Annaes Brasilienses de Medicina*, XXXI, 2 (Rio de Janeiro, 1879), p. 11.

[1] Theophilo B. Ottoni: *A Colonização do Mucurí* (Rio de Janeiro, 1859), p. 34.

to cure themselves with salves and poultices, and it was impossible to convince many of them that the Brazilian habit of washing, at least the feet, every night was a necessity for the poor man, and not, as the European proletariat believes, a whim or luxury of aristocrats and sybarites." [2]

While this was happening with the German settlers, the Chinese, "as they have no aversion to water, were never troubled by chigoes in Mucurí. I have yet to see one of them limping for that reason. Of the eighty-nine who went to Mucurí three years ago, only two have died." [3]

Moreover, the Chinese were not the only Asiatics brought into Brazil to compete with the African slaves in agricultural and domestic work. There were those of other origins, as can be seen from newspaper advertisements of the first half of the nineteenth century, in which they are interspersed among Negroes or runaway slaves. As in the case of a cook of "Asiatic or Kaffir race" who, according to an advertisement in the *Diario de Rio de Janeiro* for May 30, 1822, disappeared from a house at 364 Rua do Sabão. He was a man between twenty-eight and thirty, almost black in color, small, thin, with kinky hair, who walked like a sailor. It could be seen at first glance "that he was a foreigner by his features, which are not those of a Negro." He spoke Portuguese badly, a little English badly, the same as French, "even though he tried to pass himself off as French."

The reasons "of a physical nature" adduced by the Brazilian doctors, who were also patriots, against "the Asiatic invasion of Brazil," that is to say, the admission of Asiatics in larger numbers than those who came in during the colonial period as cooks, peddlers, tea growers, were undoubtedly eugenic rather than hygienic or cultural. The experience of Mucurí, which was looked upon by foreign observers as a splendid laboratory for the study of groups of different races and their reaction to a tropical medium, was, from the hygienic point of view, eminently favorable to the Asiatic colony in Brazil.

In the course of normal trade, Oriental merchandise reached colonial Brazil in Portuguese ships arriving from Lisbon and Oporto not only with cargoes of wine, wheat, flour, salt cod, and cheese from

---

[2] Ibid., p. 35. [3] Ibid., p. 35.

Portugal that is to say, Europe, but also with goods from the Orient to be exchanged here for cotton, sugar, rum, coffee, tobacco, lumber, medicinal roots. The balance of trade in this exchange was favorable to Lisbon, as an English observer pointed out at the beginning of the nineteenth century, in spite of the fact that the slave traders also brought from the African markets wax, gold dust, and other goods, which they traded for inferior grade cotton, rum, and tobacco.[4]

It was natural that, in view of the fact that all other foreign trade was forbidden Brazilians and foreigners because of the policy of segregation and monopoly Portugal followed toward its American colony, the more venturesome members of the colony, on the one hand, and the bolder or shrewder foreigners navigating the waters of the South Atlantic, on the other, should have developed the taste for, the techniques, and the methods of smuggling. The *sub rosa* trade with the Orient was very tempting. Its products were in great demand not only by a population characterized by Oriental influences from the early days of its formation, and which persisted in certain traits and habits, but by the many Portuguese officials, army personnel, priests transferred from the Orient to Brazil, as well as by the steady importation of slaves, who were steeped in the same influences.

The restraints on trade in colonial Brazil were so numerous that they stimulated smuggling, as Lindley pointed out. And he may be considered an authority on the subject, for he knew from close observation the irregular activities of the English who acted as intermediaries between Brazil and the Orient, not only in the epoch when these activities were taken pretty much as a matter of course by the Portuguese authorities in America, but also in the days when they were severely attacked. Such attacks seem to have contributed to the hostility of the English toward Brazil's trade with the Orient. This illegal and semi-clandestine trade seems to have been carried on also at the end of the eighteenth century and the beginning of the nineteenth by the rivals of the English in maritime shipping, the North Americans. This must have been a contributing factor to the British policy of the nineteenth century of dominating or cornering the Brazilian market, which Great Britain flooded with its products

---

[4] Thomas Lindley: *Narrative of a Voyage to Brazil* (London, 1805), p. 259.

in those very fields which had been the specialty of Africa or Asia: fine textiles and porcelain. And also with certain products of the Orient, naturally at much higher prices than those of English manufacture, and carried in English bottoms.

English ships bound for the East Indies, China, and other parts of the Orient nearly always had to put in at ports en route, due to the long voyage, to take on supplies of water and fresh food, and to repair damages they might have suffered. It so happened that Pernambuco, Bahía, and Rio de Janeiro were good ports of call for such purposes. These visits of the English ships were frequent, and, with the excuse of putting in, they stayed on, trading with the inhabitants. Thus, before the official opening of Brazilian ports to foreign trade, Brazil was already welcoming, in addition to ships from India, which always alleged the need to "reprovision" or "make repairs," English ships, and at times Anglo-American, which entered the three main ports of the colony on the same pretext.

In this way, for many years Brazil maintained contact with the forbidden lands of Europe and the Orient, but principally the Orient. Even when Portugal decided, at the beginning of the nineteenth century, to obstruct and hamper all European trade with Brazil other than the official or authorized, via Lisbon or Oporto, foreign ships, or Portuguese vessels bound for Lisbon from the Orient, continued to put in at Brazilian ports: ". . . Scarcely a ship arrives without making some contraband sales, as the very persons appointed to prevent this are themselves smugglers," Lindley wrote.[5]

In Andrew Grant's opinion, nowhere in the world, except China or Japan, were so many obstacles put in the way of foreign ships entering as in Brazil.[6] Yet, for all this, trade between the Orient and Brazil was of considerable volume throughout the eighteenth century and the early years of the nineteenth.

These illegal entries on one pretext or another which facilitated direct trade between Brazil and the Orient and Europe were of long standing. The metropolitan authorities put restrictions on this trade for reasons that were mainly economic, just as for motives that were mainly political they restricted the contacts of colonial Brazil

---

[5] Ibid., p. 285.
[6] Andrew Grant: *History of Brazil* (London, 1809), p. 122.

with the English and French, who were not only heretics in religion but liberal in politics. But a number of Portuguese officials in the colony would seem to have found it worth their while to tolerate this interchange, not only for personal reasons, but for the general good of the colony. The obstacles were, in large measure, if not "to show the English," for the English to overcome. And their triumph was achieved thanks to the gold which the smugglers distributed among authorities and officials.

In a study published in 1922 in Salvador da Bahía, "Alfândega da Bahía—Sua Historia Documentada Com a Copia de Manus critos Existentes no Arquivo Público do Estado" (The Customhouse of Bahía—Its History Based on Manuscripts in the State Archives) various interesting documents have been transcribed. One of these is the royal edict of February 8, 1711: "I the King make known to all to whom this my edict in the form of law is communicated, that, having been informed that four warships from East India, all of them English, had put in, some at Bahía de Todos os Santos, and others at Rio de Janeiro, and were introducing merchandise from Europe and India, and taking on much gold and tobacco from Brazil, I determined that to avoid this great harm the governors of our territories be ordered not to allow in their ports any English vessels or those of any other foreign nation, unless they formed a part of the fleet of this kingdom and were traveling with it as agreed in the treaties; if, due to storm or shortage of provisions, they were obliged to put in, in such cases they should be aided in what they need and ordered to depart without allowing them to carry on any trade. And inasmuch as such trade cannot be carried on unless the governors consent to or tolerate it, and a rapid and effective remedy must be applied because of the consequences that may follow from the toleration or concealment of such trade . . . it is my will that persons who trade with them, or consent to such trade, or who, knowing of it, do not impede it, if it be the Governor of any of my overseas conquests, he shall suffer the penalty of paying to my exchequer three times the emolument he received or was to have received for his services as Governor, and his property shall be forfeit to the Crown, and he shall be disqualified from holding further office . . ." And another edict reproduced in this same study, dated January 27 of the same year, ordered the arrest of any captain setting out under orders for one port and unloading his cargo in another.[7]

When Brazil had made itself independent of Portugal, and had become a zone of British influence or control, it did not at once break off its ties with the Orient, despite the obstacles the English put in the way of direct trade between Brazil and the ports of the East traditionally linked to our economy and our culture. As late as 1827, Indian china was still being shipped directly from Macao, and sold at Rua dos Pescadores, Number 2, in Rio de Janeiro. Dinner sets, soup tureens, bowls from Nanking and Canton were on sale there, blue or enameled. Also blue porcelain from Nanking, "of finest quality." [8]

In 1828 "good fireworks" for church festivals were still being imported from China. The shop on Rua do Sabão, Number 100, in Rio de Janeiro, evidently specialized in articles from the Orient, for there "uxim tea" and "shells of mother of pearl" were available.

The list of articles imported for wholesale trade published in the *Jornal do Commercio* of Rio de Janeiro for December 20, 1828, reveals the fact that Brazil was still receiving from the Orient large quantities of Indian cloves, yellow wax, tea, Indian china, Canton porcelain, ivory, "tortoise shell from Mozambique." In addition to these importations in bulk, there was also that of special and delicate articles such as trays, porcelain, jewel boxes, furniture, including "sewing tables from China."

Although they are not listed in the advertisements of the newspapers I have examined, it is known that, during colonial days and the early years of the Empire, back-scratchers of ivory were imported from the Orient for the use of the refined. And we should not forget that, as the result of Oriental influence, there grew up in colonial Brazil the fashion among persons of the upper class of wearing the fingernails long, which lasted until the end of the Empire. Also the use of diamond, emerald, ruby rings, some of them imported from India, calling attention to the genteel and aristocratic status of their wearers, who were not obliged to work with their

---

[7] *Diario Oficial*, Salvador, July 2, 1922.
[8] *Jornal do Commercio*, November 10, 1827.

hands or employ plebeian instruments or tools. Lindley wrote: "The singular custom of permitting the nail of the thumb or fore-finger (sometimes both) to grow to a hideous length and then paring it to a sharp point, is common to both sexes." [9] And he added that this strange excrescence, in addition to indicating that its wearers were persons of leisure, had its practical applications: it was useful for cutting and dividing tobacco leaves for the cheroots gentlemen liked to smoke, took the place of toothpicks after meals, and aided in the playing of the guitar, which at that time was an aristocratic instrument, although it was being displaced by English pianos, or the early music boxes.

The same thing was true of the sedan chair, as common to the large cities of Brazil until the beginning of the nineteenth century as the litters, likewise of Oriental origin, in the sugar-growing regions. In Salvador da Bahía, for many years the wealthiest city of Portuguese America, and also the hilliest, with the most winding streets, the most richly ornamented sedan chairs were to be found. They were trimmed with gold and silver, and hung with heavy curtains, sometimes of silk, and adorned with figures of Cupids, angels, dragons. And the palanquins or sedan chairs of the most aristocratic or wealthiest persons were carried by Negroes in colored livery— frock coats, breeches, blue and red kilts,[1] even though they went barefoot, like those Koster encountered in Recife.[2] There was no type of footwear that could withstand the roughness and filth of the streets, in addition to the fact that the sumptuary laws did not permit slaves to go shod. Only exceptionally were these waived in favor of maids or pages who were like members of the families, maids who went to parties with the excess jewelry their mistresses could not put on shining in their ears or around their necks.

The idiosyncrasies of Salvador's geography and social situation enabled the palanquin to hold out there against the carriage, the horse-drawn wagon—the new western methods of transportation —longer than in other cities. When Brazil had become independent, Kidder was surprised on his travels through the North of the Em-

---

[9] Lindley: Op. cit., p. 273.
[1] Ibid., p. 250.
[2] Henry Koster: *Travels in Brazil* (London, 1816), p. 274.

pire at the number of palanquins in Salvador, where he did not see a single omnibus, cabriolet, or chaise, which by that time were numerous in Rio de Janeiro and even in Recife. Only palanquins and sedan chairs, whose colored porters eagerly offered them to white gentlemen passing by: "Chair, sir, chair?" They were still curtain-hung, typical of the old Oriental and patriarchal love of privacy, which the growing use of window glass was doing away with, exposing to the public gaze the interior of houses, palanquins, shops.

Kidder pointed out the fact that the richness of curtains and ornamentation, as well as the livery of the bearers of the palanquins, was an index of the economic status, the social standing, and way of life of their owners.[3] Lindley had made the same observation almost half a century earlier, scandalized by the excessive ornamentation of the palanquins of Bahía. Where the palanquin was rare, as in the extreme South of Brazil, the men of the gentry exhibited their rank or wealth by the silver trimming of their horses' gear. Exactly like the Portuguese or their descendants in India.

Moreover, the triumph of the West over the East in Brazil was more difficult and slower, in certain environments, or in relation to certain ways of life, than would appear at first glance. Not only did the palanquin hold out in certain areas against the carriage or horse-drawn conveyance, but the porcelain of China against the European, Indian fabrics against those of English and French manufacture, the shawl or Oriental cloak against the European veil for attending mass, and the English or French lady's hat for lay festivals. Even the victory of window glass in house and carriage over shutter, blind, silk curtain, or bamboo hanging, was slow in much of Brazil. Only in the wealthy mansions of Rio de Janeiro would it seem to have come overnight.

The generalization of the use of individual knives and forks among the Brazilian middle class marks one of the decisive victories of the West over the East. The influx of cutlery during the early years of the nineteenth century would warrant a separate study. The newspapers were filled with advertisements of table knives and forks, kitchen knives, butcher knives, scissors, razors, garden shears. And

---

[3] D. P. Kidder: *Sketches of Residence and Travels in Brazil,* II (Philadelphia, 1845), p. 21.

also scalpels and other surgical instruments. Articles of steel and iron with silver, German silver, tin, horn, wood, handles, and even combined with Oriental materials, such as ivory and tortoise shell.

English kitchen utensils made their appearance. Iron stoves, European candlesticks of brass and tin. And leather articles, such as harness for horses, saddles for men, and even for ladies, whose use spelled the doom of palanquins, sedan chairs, litters, the end of trips on which ladies and children rested on soft quilts and mats from the Orient. Even oxcarts were spread with these quilts and mats to make the travel of the gentry more comfortable.

Naturally, the importers of Western manufactures did all they could to overcome the attachment of the Brazilians to their Oriental quilts and mats by playing up the great bodily comfort to be found in the new articles of Western origin. Hence the startling advertisement of Affonço St. Martin, who, according to the *Diario de Pernambuco* for May 22, 1840, offered for sale in his "French shop" on Rua do Cabuga in Recife "a large assortment of saddles for ladies, children, and men, including those stuffed with rubber, known as rump comforters."

Recife, less conservative than the capital of Bahía and, in certain aspects, more exposed to transoceanic influences than Rio de Janeiro itself, was not, however, immediately lured by the siren voices of the West. Only little by little did it break some of its closest ties with the Orient. Including the fondness for painted furniture, imitating lacquer. If on its level streets the triumph of the Western carriage over the Oriental palanquin was swift, inside its houses many things were still done in Oriental fashion and with articles from China or India. In 1840, "lacquer tea caddies with gilded feet," "lacquer work baskets for ladies," "fans of lacquer and paper," imported from India, were still preferred by some to their Western substitutes, to judge by an advertisement in the *Diario de Pernambuco* for June 30.

In that year the same newspaper advertised the arrival of a great variety of Oriental goods from Manila and Batavia aboard a Spanish ship bound for Santander, which would seem to have employed the same technique—almost routine—of earlier ships from India putting in at Brazilian ports. If it did so, it was because there was still a ready market and eager demand in that area for such products eighteen years after our independence. The importance attached to the arrival of that ship by the advertisements of the commission agent Oliveira is significant. And the number and variety of articles offered for sale by this agent indicate that the monopoly of Brazilian markets by the West suffered not wholly negligible interruptions, during which our culture received fresh touches of Oriental color.

The cargo of the ship contained articles such as embroidered and printed Tonkin scarfs, Chinese shawls, silk handkerchiefs of many colors, silk for dresses, mosquito nets for beds, sewing boxes, tea caddies and snuff boxes of tortoise shell and ivory, bottleholders, dishes, trays, glasses, lacquer washbasins, poker chips of mother of pearl, chessmen, fans ranging from those of finest quality "to less expensive," some of them even made of silver, tortoise-shell and ivory combs, books with exquisite illustrations, Canton cloth, which was especially desirable for shirts and handkerchiefs, figurines of mandarins dressed in silk, lacquer tables, cigar cases, clothes hampers.[4]

Around the middle of the nineteenth century there came an increase in the variety of silks, fabrics, china, furniture, glass, iron, steel articles which European ships had been bringing to Brazil since 1808 from England, Hamburg, and France, at lower prices than their Oriental counterparts. The Western imitations of ivory, tortoise shell, silk, cashmere, cambric were bringing within reach of Brazilians articles which, when authentic and handmade, had been accessible only to the gentry, the wealthy. The triumph of the industrialized West over the artisan East had a definitely democratizing effect. The use of combs, fans, perfumes, once limited to a favored few, became general.

The Orient began to disappear from stores, newspaper advertisements, house interiors, attire, and personal habits as the result, up to a point, of this democratization of articles which the factories of the West could mass produce, even though at the sacrifice of quality or authenticity. And the West gradually took possession of Brazil as a semi-colony, took possession of the very landscape, which for long years had been stamped by forms and colors of the Orient. By the coconut tree, for example. And, from the end of the eighteenth and beginning of the nineteenth century, by the mango, the jack fruit,

---

[4] *Diario de Pernambuco,* May 20, 1840.

the breadfruit; as well as the cinnamon tree, the Indian pepper, the clove, camphor, the castor bean.[5] Trees and plants brought directly from the Orient or introduced after the conquest of Cayenne, where a number of these Oriental varieties were already acclimated.

A reaction against the Oriental influence on the landscape, the gardens, the trees that lined the streets of Brazil likewise dates from the first half of the nineteenth century. Anglicized and Gallicized Brazilians joined forces with Englishmen and Frenchmen in experiments of adaptation of trees and plants of Europe to Brazilian soil. Hence the fashion of walnut trees, of strawberries for dessert.[6] And, since 1799, the English had sent us the paper mulberry, together with the cedar of Lebanon, pine seedlings.[7] Apple and pear trees began to make their appearance in those areas which prided themselves on their "European climate."

Nevertheless, in this field the East held its own against the efforts of the West to supplant it. Its trees continued to rival the native ones in luxuriance and productivity. There are parts of Brazil today where the old indigenous trees, such as the brazilwood and the trumpet tree, today seem exotic because of their rarity, whereas the mangoes, the jack fruit, the cinnamon, the coconut, the tamarind spread as though the land had always been theirs. The same is true of the zebu (*bos indicus*), which was introduced long ago and crossed here with cattle of European stock, producing that crossbreed which C. A. Taunay, a specialist in rural matters, in 1839 considered a "sturdy and beautiful race, with smooth, even markings and glossy coat," which various stockbreeders told him they preferred to the ordinary race because of "the good service they gave . . ." [8]

It is curious that the nativist tendency which glorified rum and cashew wine and rejected Port wine, and sang the praises of manioc over wheat flour, should not have championed Brazilian na-

---

[5] C. A. Taunay: *Manual do Agricultor Brazileiro* (Rio de Janeiro, 1839), p. 101.

[6] Ibid., p. 78.

[7] F. Borges de Barros: "Novos Documentos para a Historia Colonial," *Anais do Arquivo Publico e da Inspetoria dos Monumentos do Estado da Bahía*, XX (Salvador, 1931), p. 158.

[8] Taunay: Op. cit., p. 101.

tive trees and plants. Neither those introduced from Asia or Africa nor those of European origin seem to have been rejected under the guise of a patriotic or nativist cult of the indigenous. Only an occasional voice was raised in praise of typically Brazilian trees and ornamental plants, which were rarely employed by the mayors or councilmen in the days of the Empire for the beautifying of squares, streets, or roads. To be sure, in the first half of the nineteenth century, in the more patriotic cities, the Brazil-nut tree enjoyed a certain vogue; and in Belem, Andrea planted mango trees along one street which later aroused the admiration of foreigners. The Negro slaves stopped to rest in the shade of the *gameleira* trees from their heavy work on the quays and in the streets of the city, the back-breaking tasks of carrying bales of cotton, sacks of sugar and coffee, grand pianos, sofas and beds of rosewood, barrels of night soil, for their white masters. It was a tree which for many of these Africans was sacred, and possibly, in part for this reason, aroused aversion among the more European-minded whites. Possibly it was a *gameleira*, which became famous in Salvador as the "suicide tree" of those Negroes or slaves unable to endure the *banzo*—the blues or homesickness for Africa—or the humiliation of their slave labor. Baron Forth-Rouens, who visited Bahía in 1847, learned that the tree had been chopped down, after having been the scene of many acts of desperation on the part of Negroes or slaves.[9]

Among other tendencies during the second half of the nineteenth century deserving of study because they show how hard city Brazilians tried to seem European was the contempt for Asiatic and African trees, plants, and fruits already acclimated. The more refined Brazilians were ashamed of the breadfruit, the mango, the oil palm, the coconut itself, which was eaten on the sly, or in the intimacy of the river bath, like the cashew, the hog plum, the medlar, and not at the tables or at sweet shops. For this reason, the efforts of those doctors who endeavored to establish in Rio de Janeiro "a pharmaceutical garden . . . especially for the cultivation of native

[9] "Bahía en 1847," *Deux Lettres de M. Forth-Rouens, Envoyé et Chargé d'Affaires en Chine*, published by M. Henri Cordier in *Journal de la Société des Américanistes de Paris* (new series), IV, 1, p. 6.

medicinal plants which comprise the *materia medica* of Brazil" were fruitless. One doctor of the period, J. F. Sigaud, wrote: "The north wind is blowing across our confines: will not ice, that agent of energy, perhaps come to change suddenly the order of remedies held and boasted of as infallible?" And he asked prophetically, in view of the decline in prestige of old medicinal compounds based on plants or herbs of the Orient or the tropics, displaced by those of cold Western Europe: "Who can tell whether British grog, and water with rock sugar, will not have to be relentlessly sacrificed to the ice of the United States? What a revolution water, condensed or liquid, hot or cold, in monstrous blocks or in delicious sherbets, will produce on the world, on men!" [1]

The old-fashioned vegetable and flower gardens of native plants, combined with those of the Orient, were being replaced by numerous varieties of flowers—roses, dahlias—and fruit trees, "from Portugal, France, and Hamburg," which were recommended not only for city gardens but also "for the interior of the province and those of North and South." [2] It was the north wind bringing us its seeds. It was the beginning of the systematic Westernizing of the most rustically patriarchal landscape of the interior, where roses and dahlias, as well as apple trees, were arriving with the prestige of their novelty, and bringing into contempt flowers, plants, and trees of the tropics, native or imported from the Orient. It was not long before whites whose olfactory sense or palate had been more contaminated by Western culture discovered that the smell of certain native jasmines resembled that of the sweat of Negro women slaves, and that the taste of dende oil was so coarse and barbarous that only coarse and barbarous persons could endure it.

Infiltrations more subtle than those of taste, smell, gesture, attire, forms of architecture, morals, even aesthetics from the Orient were slower in being dislodged by their European equivalents or opposites. Or, for many years, the substitution was more apparent than real.

---

[1] *Diario de Saúde ou Ephemerides das Sciencias Medicas e Naturaes do Brazil*, I, 1 (May 9, 1835).
[2] *Diario de Pernambuco*, July 6, 1857.

In colonial Brazil and that of early Empire days the custom of sitting crosslegged on rugs, mats, or the floor—men and women alike —was not the only Oriental legacy. There was that of clapping hands at the door of a house to announce oneself, which is still a typically Brazilian custom. There was the fondness for the parasol, not only to protect the person of rank from the sun, but to indicate his social status. There was the habit of wearing long nails, another display of social standing or superior category. There was the habit of betrothing girls while still children to men sometimes older than their own fathers. Of ladies not appearing before strange men. Of wearing mantillas or shawls. Of dressing the hair in elaborate coiffures in preference to the European custom of hats, of the maids wearing turbans. The liking for bright colors, strong perfumes, highly spiced dishes.

The custom of bowing, on solemn occasions, with characteristic kowtowing on the part of the governed before the rulers, was also Oriental; and when not to the rulers in person, before the portraits of monarchs or princes. Oriental, too, was the custom of kneeling in the street when the queen or any member of the royal family passed after the Court was transferred from Lisbon to Rio de Janeiro, or of slaves or members of the lower classes displaying obsequious respect in the presence of the gentry.

"Many Portuguese are like Negroes in this custom," observed the Frenchman Arago,[3] referring to the habit of kneeling in the street as the queen or princes went by. In his opinion, only a person of inferior race or servile station was capable of getting down on his knees before princes. The fact is that almost throughout the entire Orient, including the most civilized areas, the person of the prince was almost divine to his subjects, and the Portuguese became so imbued with the custom that only little by little did the "Great Revolution" and "the Enlightenment" change their semi-Oriental manner of revering princes, parents, grandparents. "Nor is there a country where children show greater respect for their parents," the same writer goes on to say of Brazil. "After meals they always kiss their hand and never sit down in their presence unless authorized to do so

[3] J. Arago: *Promenade Autour du Monde*, I (Paris, n.d.), p. 115.

by a gesture or a glance." Naturally, Arago was referring to the Western countries which he knew; in the Orient he would have found even greater displays of children's respect for parents—and not merely subjects' for monarchs—than those he had observed in Brazil in the reign of Dom João.

Another Orientalism in our country shocked Arago: the fact that there were castrati, or eunuchs, who sang in the churches. "They are all singers in the royal chapel, and receive good salaries. One can hear them in all the churches but never in the theater." The strange thing was that these castrati were Europeans—Italians—and not, as might have been expected, Orientals from Christianized areas, such as Goa. Nor recruited among the Africans who had already been converted to Christianity, whose masters were in the habit of having them taught to sing and play for religious festivals. In a patriarchal and slaveholding country like Brazil, it in no wise suited the interest of slaveowners to have their young Negroes castrated to dulcify their voices for the singing of litanies and hymns, thus losing them for the purpose of procreating other slaves.

Nor should we forget the gypsies, another touch of Oriental color, even though of remote origin. These nomads adapted themselves only marginally to our patriarchal system, in the capacity of small, and at times sadistic, slave traders in the cities and horse sellers or tinsmiths in the interior. Possibly this was the origin of the name *gringo* applied to them in certain areas,[4] as later to Englishmen and other foreigners of unfamiliar aspect engaged in trade or mechanical occupations.

Kidder still found in Bahía a quarter known as the Mouraria, which had been set aside for the gypsies.[5] In 1718 the King of Portugal banished to Brazil various families of gypsies, forbidding them the use of their language so it would disappear, and with it their custom of living apart and at times as parasites. Thirty years later, it was clear that they were as undesirable in Brazil as in Portugal.

The greatest harm they did was stealing horses and mules from the miners, in spite of all the precautions taken against these sly

---

[4] F. A. Pereira da Costa: "Ciganos." Ms. in Mss. Section of Pernambuco State Library.

[5] Kidder: Op. cit., II, p. 43.

thieves. It is also possible that they were responsible for the mysterious disappearance of colored children, whom they sold as slaves.

The ghetto was an Orientalism which does not seem to have existed, properly speaking, in any city of Portuguese Brazil. Dutch Recife seems to have had a kind of ghetto, with its Street of the Jews, its synagogues, its illustrious rabbis. Among us, the Jews for the most part concealed their origin, secretly practicing their rites, observing their customs, their dietary laws, and enjoying their gold, silver, and precious stones, thus avoiding the severe penalties of the Inquisition. However, not on this account should the Jews be dismissed as more or less secret agents of Orientalism, stressing only their internationalism.

The Brazilian of patriarchal days, rural as well as urban, always felt a vague hostility toward "Jews" and "Moors," probably a Portuguese legacy of the struggle between Christians and infidels in the peninsula and the Orient. Struggles recalled in the form of folk spectacles, such as the combats between Moors and Christians, which was once an important feature of Brazilian festivals, and the street celebrations on Easter Saturday.[6] The Christians were always victorious and the Moors routed and punished. And Easter Saturday ended or began with the effigy of Judas being carried through the streets and burned by the urchins in what was evidently a popular expression of religious hatred of the Catholic for the Jew and of social hatred of the oppressed for the oppressor: of the poor ne'er-do-well for the rich businessman, not always Jewish, but nearly always so considered.

The Orient continued to make itself strongly felt until the early days of the reign of Pedro II. In 1828, Walsh informs us, there were still houses in Rio which specialized in the importation of Oriental merchandise.

Under the pressure of new English and French fashions, a number of customs mainly of Oriental origin were lumped together with European survivals of the prebourgeois and preindustrial epoch of Europe, as "archaic," "shameful," "unworthy" of a nation like Brazil, no longer a mere plantation colony of Portugal, but a kingdom

---

[6] Robert Walsh: *Notices of Brazil in 1828 and 1829*, I (London-Boston, 1830–1), p. 187.

and even an empire. Outmoded customs came under attack, some repressed by the police, others ridiculed by Western-minded progressives in newspapers and satirical comedies.

One of the customs inveighed against was that of the mantillas, shawls, or capes in which the ladies swathed themselves. This vestige, so intimately linked to the mystique of the patriarchal family organization, was one of those which held out most stubbornly against the attempts of the reformers.

Mawe observed that the women of São Paulo, "famed throughout Brazil for their charms," were to be seen at mass or in the street, at the beginning of the nineteenth century, dressed in black silk, with a long veil, also of silk and edged with lace, over their heads. Veil and shawl were being replaced in part by a long cloak of wool trimmed with velvet, lace, gold, depending on the lady's social position. With this cloak some wore a round hat, like a man's, or a lady's riding hat. At dances the ladies of São Paulo appeared with gold chains looped many times about their neck, and with their hair full of combs, often of gold, like the women of the Orient.

In Minas Gerais, Mawe saw ladies dressed in English fabrics and "wearing a number of gold chains about their neck, which they always put on when they go visiting or receive visits." A good Oriental fashion combined with the use of Western clothing. He also observed that the use of hats was still rare among the women of Minas, except for the elderly, among whom the use of bonnets, usually black, was an insignia of age and gentility. As for the poor, or those of servile class or race, they used shawls, bright cotton or flannel scarfs. At the time that Mawe was in Brazil the ladies, even when dressed in European fashion, went without hats and were amazed to learn that English ladies used hats.[7]

Even though I have found few references in newspaper advertisements, or in wills or inventories, to furniture of Oriental manufacture or design, there was a considerable amount of it among us, made of sandalwood or ebony and inlaid with ivory or mother-of-pearl. Not all of it had been imported directly from the Orient. It may have been the work of Indian cabinetmakers established in Lis-

---

[7] John Mawe: Op. cit., p. 393.

bon, to whom Ramalho Ortigão refers.[8] However, Ramalho also speaks of workshops set up in India by Portuguese workmen; and we have already seen that the regular and illegal trade between colonial Brazil and the Orient was greater than has generally been supposed. It seems probable that in early days we received, in addition to vases, embroideries, and paintings from China, like those Maria Graham saw in the drawing room of a Salvador mansion,[9] furniture from India as well as China.

As for our colonial churches, it is known that more than one was embellished with objects from the Orient, some of which may be seen in museums like that of Sacred Art in Salvador. Schaeffer, when he was in Brazil in 1849, was amazed to see in a monastery of Rio, built, according to him, in 1671, "a large China figure of our Saviour on the Cross" in a chapel ablaze with Oriental colors: "the walls adorned with procelain and China squares, relieved by gilt and scarlet lines."[1] One of the churches in Sabará in Minas Gerais which I visited in 1936 is decorated in a manner that gives the inside of the Catholic temple the coloring of a pagoda. Possibly the conversion or indoctrination of the natives by means of "decorative painting" in the churches[2] was accompanied on more than one occasion by the use of Oriental adornments or decorations. Buddha and Mohammed seem to have had a hand in leading the natives of Brazil to Christ or Rome.

The great resemblance between colonial Brazil and Portuguese India during the seventeenth and eighteenth centuries is not surprising. We have already seen how strong and steady the trade between the two areas was when Brazil was a colony or a vice-royalty. When the Portuguese Court moved from Lisbon to Rio de Janeiro, one of the effects of this transfer of the political seat of the Lusitanian Empire was to shift a great part of the Indian trade to Brazil,

---

[8] Ramalho Ortigão: *O Culto da Arte em Portugal* (Lisbon, 1896).

[9] Maria Graham: *Journal of a Voyage to Brazil and Residence There During the Years 1821, 1822, 1823* (London, 1824).

[1] L. M. Schaeffer: *Sketches of Travel in South America, Mexico, and California* (New York, 1860), pp. 14–15.

[2] Luis Jardim: "A Pintura Decorativa em Algumas Igrejas de Minas," *Revista do Serviço do Patrimonio Historico e Artistico Nacional* (Rio de Janeiro, 1939).

thus intensifying the relations of Portuguese America with the Orient. Luccock, a shrewd businessman, saw with his English eyes the threat to Great Britain if she did not make haste to block them, as, in fact, she did through the Treaty of 1810[3] and the privileges she obtained for her own trade over that of Portugal itself. He considered the matter deserving of "the most particular attention," as he wrote in his book on Brazil, where he lived from 1808 to 1818.[4]

Portuguese ships of the Oriental line brought to Brazil from India mainly cotton cloth of various qualities, part of which was transshipped to Portugal, to the Portuguese colonies of the African coast, and to American ports south of the equator. These materials, which were in great demand, offered serious competition to those of Ireland, and created a graver problem for Great Britain than the earlier importation of Oriental manufactures to Portuguese America in ships that were neither English nor part of the Lisbon convoys. It was aggravated by the fact that, in addition to Indian textiles, the Portuguese ships brought tea, Nanking textiles, copper, silk, and various other products from China.[5] Mawe wrote that at the beginning of the nineteenth century there was a great abundance of such articles in Brazil.[6] He could have added from India, too. In a word, from the Orient.

Moreover, Luccock insinuates that there would be an advantage for Brazil if the Portuguese ships of the Brazilian-Orient line were replaced by English bottoms.[7] This was just what happened, thanks to the privileges the English obtained for their trade over that of Portugal, which proved harmful to Brazilian interests and immensely advantageous for the English. Imperial Britain profited by the reduction to a minimum not only of the trade, which for a time was very intense between Brazil and Portuguese Asia, but also of the relations between Portuguese America and the Orient.

---

[3] A commercial treaty between Portugal and Great Britain establishing economic privileges for Britain in Brazil, then a colony of Portugal and also the seat of Portuguese monarchy.

[4] John Luccock: *Notes on Rio de Janeiro and the Southern Parts of Brazil, taken during a residence of ten years in that country from 1808 to 1818* (London, 1820), pp. 594–5.

[5] Ibid., p. 596.

[6] Mawe: Op. cit., p. 318.

[7] Luccock: Op. cit., p. 507.

Koster, another British businessman who lived in Brazil in the early nineteenth century and who, like Mawe and Luccock, was a shrewd observer, wrote, commenting on the Treaty of 1810, that Article 21, referring to the prohibitive duties that might be levied on English products of the East and West Indies in Portugal, was by way of compensation for the preceding article, which laid prohibitive duties in Great Britain on certain Brazilian products competing with similar ones produced in the British colonies.[8] He must have been looking at the matter exclusively from the English point of view. For it could not be in Brazil's interest to exclude the importation of products of the East Indies—even those areas controlled by British trade—whereas it was to Great Britain's interest to favor the sugar and coffee of her tropical colonies over that of Portuguese America. The situations were completely different. Normally, it would have been to Brazil's interest to continue for many years the trade and numerous relations which for centuries had kept it in contact with an area of the world to which it had become ecologically and sociologically akin. But the intensive re-Europeanization of Brazilian society at the beginning of the nineteenth century, which coincided with the decline of the patriarchal system in its traditional rural areas, made the Orient remote and vague to our society and culture, still in its formative stage. So remote and vague that Oriental values, once current among us, became almost as rare—museum pieces, archaisms, curiosities—as in those countries of America whose civilization was the most unequivocally Western.

---

[8] Koster: Op. cit., p. 469.

CHAPTER X

SLAVE, ANIMAL, AND MACHINE

THE CULT OF St. George in Brazil has, among other sociological connotations, that of having been the cult of the rider, the noble, the warrior, the strong man, the slayer of dragons. This cult was the equivalent, in the upper social strata of the whites and in the culturally more enlightened zone of the Negroes, of the cult of the ox, the companion or helper of the passive slave and of the Negro who accepted his serf status and, at the same time, of the more culturally backward Brazilian of the grazing regions, characterized, too, by his affection for the nanny goat, "the mother goat" of the poor backlanders.

The *bumba-meu-boi*—the folk pageant in which the ox takes a leading part—and the cult of St. George, in its Christian aspect or in the veiled form of the cult of Ogun, came into being in Brazil as opposites or rivals and, at the same time, as dramatic expression of the same sentiment of man's identification with the animals most closely linked to his own status or to his endeavor to transcend it. Horse and ox, goat and mule were animals which, in our social development, contributed to lightening the burden of work for both slave and poor free man, and kept the master from having to depend exclusively on the work, the energy, the milk of slaves.

To be sure, slave or forced labor was little lightened among us by the increased use of these animals on plantations, ranches, for the transportation of persons and freight, the feeding of children and the nourishment of the sick, the convalescent, and even well persons in the form of fresh milk, curds, and cheese. The work of the slaves would be superseded only with the development of the machine, a kind of sublimation, effected among us mainly by the English, of animal energy into steam-powered energy. Especially horsepower, consecrated by the initials H.P. as the symbol or measure of motor power or traction. With the generalization of the use of the machine, the Negro's liberation from slavery and serfdom began, and the higher valuation of the animal, so long treated with a cruelty that made a deplorable impression on the more tender-hearted foreigners who visited us.

The development of the machine did not eliminate, as something contemptible or unimportant, the moral factor or the sentimental aspect, despite the theory of the historic materialists most unswerving in their economic interpretation of history. It is not without significance that the English, from whom, incidentally, we took over the cult of St. George-on-Horseback, should have outdone other nations in their affection for the noble animal of war and peace, of recreation and utility, to the point of having developed the "English trot," which, according to a well-known authority on the subject, is the gait which more than any other prevents the horse from being galled or bruised by the rider.[1] So the historian with the eye of a psychologist, and not merely of an economist, might discern in the "English trot" the first sign of a moral or sentimental impulse—without, of course, discounting the action of other stimuli—toward the invention of machines designed to substitute or supersede the horse, and along with the horse, the donkey, the mule, the ox, the camel as beasts of burden, as well as of warfare, and as the driving force of mills. These animals were cruelly worked and even mistreated not only in slaveholding civilizations, such as the Arab in bygone times, and the Brazilian in modern days, but also in those where human slavery no longer existed, but at the cost of the greater exploitation or utilization of animal power. As was the case of English civilization before the machine horse, the steam H.P., had replaced the animal horse.

---

[1] Lefebvre des Noëttes: *L'Attelage, le Cheval de selle à travers les Ages. Contribution a l'Histoire de L'Esclavage*, I (Paris, 1931), p. 257.

It was upon hearing the noise of the powerful motors "made in England" that Livio de Castro, in the final years of the Empire, rejoiced at the arrival of the "steam horse": "the steam horse appears on all four corners of the horizon like a frightening inundation . . ." [2] An inundation capable of reducing the patriarchal system of Brazil, which had been based on human labor rather than animal, to the state of shipwreck. The new systems of family and society would have to be based on machines, on coal, on the steam horse.

It is claimed here that the English contributed through the development of the techniques of production and transport—developments as much of a technical as of a moral nature—to the abolition of slavery. This does not mean that in their struggle, somewhat vague at first, later systematic, against slavery in Brazil, frank economic rivalry did not play its part. Machine production was still more expensive than that of slave labor, given the situation of the slave in tropical areas as compared with that of the worker in cool climates, where living is more expensive.

Among those early developments—those bearing upon transportation, which were closely connected with those of production by animal power or energy and with those of interregional trade—we have already mentioned the English trot. Another, which made its appearance in the eighteenth century, was the English saddle. By that time English horses were already divided into two classes or breeds: riding horses and work horses. The riding horses were bred for military, political purposes—including the rapid delivery of urgent correspondence of the ruling class—and for aristocratic diversion, for agility, speed, and elegance of form, bearing, and gait. The work horses, for faster haulage than by oxteam and for the safe transport of large loads or heavy cargo. This same differentiation of horses by "class" or "race," according to their use, soon appeared in Portugal, where, however, the large ones were used for hauling and the small and medium were preferred for war or as fashionable mounts. The saddle horse was supposed to be "sixteen and a half hands high, to make mounting and dismounting easier . . . and as a rule we have seen that these are fleeter than large horses, which are less spirited." The

---

[2] Livio de Castro: *A Mulher e a Sociologia* (Rio de Janeiro, n.d.), p. 350.

blooded horse should be "bay or dark chestnut, not white, roan, or light sorrel, because these are visible from a distance."[3] The large horse, considered less spirited than the medium-sized or small, and, at the same time, stronger, gradually became a work horse in certain countries. And, as such, the substitute of the human slave in a number of activities. In Brazil, however, as we shall see further on, it was the mule which, in the capacity of beast of burden, proved to be man's best slave. The best, and together with the ox, the most ruthlessly exploited.

Never were the same eloquent voices raised on its behalf as on that of the horse—"that noble animal"—which many considered to be as unfit by nature for a servile existence as "the noble savage" or the "proud Indian."

In his memorable essay, Lefebvre des Noëttes pointed out that every effort of a purely moral nature was futile or vain against the slavery demanded by old civilizations. Slave labor, "indispensable to these civilizations,"[4] could be displaced only by man's progress in the employment of horse or ox for transportation and agricultural and industrial tasks. Does this mean the absolute dependence of moral progress on material progress, as narrowly sectarian "historic materialists" claim, pointing out the importance of the confirmation of their philosophy contained in Des Noëttes's study? In the opinion of Jerome Carcopino, the author of the preface to this outstanding French work, such confirmation would "be too startling and sweeping to be unquestioningly accepted."[5] And he cites the example of the United States, where slavery continued to exist after the development of the techniques of traction, contrary to the "determinist" or "historic-materialist" aspect of Des Noëttes's thesis.

What would seem to be the case is that, without moral questioning or emotional disturbance, and merely as the result of material or technical advance, so-called moral progress is not effected. It was not effected in the United States; and in Brazil the Asiatic palanquin, carried by African slaves or their descendants, held out for a long time against the European carriage, English or French, drawn by horse

---

[3] José de Barros Paiva: *Manejo Real, Escola Moderna da Cavallaria da Brida, etc.* (1762), p. 10.

[4] Noëttes: Op. cit., p. 186.

[5] Ibid., p. iv.

or mule. Until moral indignation at its use—as at that of hammock or litter for carrying persons or goods in the interior—became general; until there became associated with this use the shame or embarrassment of its representing an Oriental survival in a civilization with claims to being regarded as European, the palanquin resisted the advent of the horse-drawn vehicle in the cities, as in the interior the hammock or litter held out against the oxcart, and the mill powered by mule or ox against the steam engine. To be sure, to a large extent because of inertia; because of difficulties of a physical nature, such as those encountered by animal traction on the slopes of Salvador, Olinda, Rio de Janeiro, so unsuited to horse and carriage; because of the lack of roads in the interior. But also because of the lack, or near lack, of feelings of pity for the slave and domestic animal abused by their masters. Feelings which, having become widespread at the beginning of the nineteenth century, contributed to the rapid substitution of human energy by animal, and of animal energy by machine and steam.

The patriarchal master of Brazil reserved such sentiments for slaves or servants whom he looked upon as members of the household; colored nurses, house servants, slaves with whom he had grown up. Toward others, his indifference often verged upon cruelty, upon the "complete lack of the idea or sentiment of conscience" [6] which Prince Maximilian had observed in the first half of the nineteenth century. He attributed this "lack of conscience" to several factors, including the inconstancy of everything in Brazil, but the principal culprit in the unstable moral organization of our country seemed to him to be nature, climate, the easy life, which did not encourage man's responsibility, including the system of slave labor.

Kidder, when traveling in Brazil around 1840, observed that in the capital of Bahía not a single wagon, chaise, oxcart was to be seen for carrying merchandise, persons, bundles: "no omnibus or cab, or even *sège* . . ." Everything was carried on the head or shoulders of slaves. He pointed out that the normal thing in Bahía was for them to carry sugar or cotton on the back and not on the head, as in the case of coffee in Rio de Janeiro. They were tall, powerful

---

[6] Prince Maximilian von Neuwied: *Souvenirs de Ma Vie* (Paris, 1868), pp. 193–4.

Negroes, those employed in Bahía for such work. And like the bearers of coffee in Rio de Janeiro, of sugar in Recife, of sugar and cotton in Salvador, they sang as they walked, as though to lighten their loads. The rhythm of the latter was that of a funeral march, in contrast to the gay tempo of their companions of Rio: "rather than the double-quick step of their Fluminensian colleagues." [7]

This absence of animal traction was the thing that most shocked Kidder in a city of the importance of Salvador and in an epoch when "iron horses" were already commonplace in Europe and the United States. Or, to use his own words: "The almost entire absence of horses and mules in the streets did not cease to appear singular. An unusual number of goats and pigs was hardly sufficient to supply the lack of the aforementioned animals."

At a time when in Western Europe and the United States the use of horse, mule, and ox as draught animals was already declining, and they were being substituted by steam power, in the old capital of Brazil, a city of maximum commercial, and not merely political, importance, not only had human traction not yet been superseded by animal, but it continued to be almost the only one.

This is not to be wondered at. Even in Rio de Janeiro there were still palanquins, such as that Colton saw carried by two slaves and followed by several servants. "A Brazilian lady of rank in her palanquin," he noted in his diary. He remarked that it was, nevertheless, considered "a quiet indication of rank," as he puts it, for every fine home to have a two- or four-wheeled carriage in its stable, even though many of them had no horses to draw it. As it was still easier to have a Negro than a horse or even a mule, the less wealthy ladies went about in a palanquin while the carriage stood in the stables. [8]

In Alagoas, Kidder had observed another interesting fact bearing on the history of transportation or traction in Brazil: that the mule had not been brought in originally as a beast of burden, a capacity in which it revealed itself as more useful than the horse. The fact of the matter is, however, that at that time sugar was hauled to

[7] Daniel Kidder: *Sketches of Residence and Travels in Brazil* (Philadelphia, 1845), p. 21.
[8] Walter Colton: *Deck and Port* (New York, 1850), pp. 62, 48.

Maceió, still an unpretentious city, for the most part of single-story adobe houses, in rustic wooden wagons drawn by six or eight oxen.[9] These were the oxcarts which in the agricultural or stock-raising hinterland of Brazil proved themselves capable of transporting sugar and other products over the primitive roads given the name of highways.

The patriarchal families, sufficient unto themselves in their great plantation or ranch houses, and visiting one another only on the infrequent occasion of some anniversary, christening, marriage, did not feel the need for good roads or rapid conveyances. They were satisfied with the poor roads and with slow and infrequent trips in hammock or litter, borne by slaves, or by oxcart carpeted with rugs and canopied with branches or counterpane.[1] In the sugar region, an occasional Amazon accompanied her husband on horseback trips, a custom more frequent in São Paulo and Rio Grande do Sul, more rustic and less aristocratic than the northern regions. The majority of the plantation and city ladies of the North preferred to admire, almost always through Moorish blinds, rarely at festivals or races, the skill and elegance of the gentlemen riders. In this art the aristocrats of the sugar area of Brazil astonished the Dutch, the English, and the French by their dexterity and fancy riding. None of these surpassed them in feats of horsemanship.

In this connection, the tournament staged by Maurice of Nassau, with other celebrations, in the days of his rule in Dutch Brazil is worth recalling. A tournament in which Europeans of the North and Portuguese or Brazilian gentlemen of the region met in friendly rivalry. It deserves mention not merely as a picturesque historical footnote, but because of the light it throws on the differences and contrasts between two cultures: one still patriarchal and even Oriental or Moorish in its monosexual character; the other more bourgeois than patriarchal and bisexual rather than monosexual in its structure, to the point where the women ate and drank with the men after attending the riding show. Differences which were reflected even in the gait of the horses ridden by the Nordics and the "Portuguese of Brazil."

---

[9] Kidder: Op. cit., p. 97.

[1] Antonio Egidio Martins: *São Paulo Antigo* (*1554–1910*), I (Rio de Janeiro–São Paulo–Belo Horizonte, 1911), p. 68.

The foreign ladies were greatly impressed by the feats of the horsemen of Brazil. Fray Manuel do Salvador states that there were "Englishwomen and Frenchwomen" who removed their rings and sent them to the riders of the Portuguese team, led by Pedro Marinho of Pernambuco, "just to see them gallop." The next day, there was a banquet for the riders, and dinners lasting until dawn, attended by Dutch, French, and English ladies, where the ladies "were better drinkers than the men," getting almost drunk, as "was the custom in their countries." [2] It may well be that, out of sight of Fray Manuel's wearied eyes, there were amorous encounters and a certain "sportiveness" between the Catholic Portuguese of Pernambuco and their admirers, the non-Catholic ladies of the North. But it is better not to pursue such hypotheses or suppositions.

In these festivities arranged by the Count of Nassau in Recife in April of 1641, the contrasts stood out in clear relief. First, that between horses trained and ridden by men belonging to a culture that was still feudal in certain aspects, and those trained and ridden by men of a culture that had become bourgeois. Second, the contrast between the women of the former culture, not only semi-feudal, and not only Catholic, but with Moorish traits, and the women of the Protestant or non-Catholic cultures of Northern Europe. Their religious bias, however, did not keep the Protestant ladies from admiring the Catholic participants in the tournament; it was the latter who avoided marriage with the women of the northern countries, less perhaps because of strictly doctrinaire or religious prejudices than for moral or social reasons. They were men accustomed to gentle and passive women, and it would seem that the free and easy ways of the ladies of the North attracted them for purposes of dalliance, rather than for marriage or connubial love. However, this was not the case with Brazilian women as regards Protestant men. A number of them married heretics. These women would seem to have discovered or glimpsed in those less brilliant practitioners of the equestrian art—perhaps because they were more considerate of their horses, looking upon them less as adjuncts of war than as instruments

---

[2] Fray Manuel do Salvador: *Valeroso Lucideno e o Triumpho da Liberdade* (Lisbon, 1648). Edition of 1942 published by the State of Pernambuco, I, p. 232.

of trade—men who were less tyrannical than the Portuguese or Brazilians in their dealings with the fair sex, whom the men of the
bourgeois culture of Protestant Northern Europe looked upon as
practically their equals.

It should be remarked in passing that the horses of the regions or
cities of Brazil which were sloughing off their rural and patriarchal
characteristics contrasted in agility and spirit with those heavy animals of Northern Europe utilized for hauling persons and loads
through the streets and highways. With the development of trade
under the stimulus of industrialization, these were becoming less
rough than the old roads, some of them even soft under the horses'
hoofs. And the animals were being treated like good and useful
giants, enjoying the same care the better masters in Brazil showed
their slaves. A marked improvement in roads came about at the end
of the eighteenth and the beginning of the nineteenth century, especially at the beginning of the nineteenth, with that revolutionist in
the technique of road-building, McAdam. An Englishman to whom
horses owe a new phase in their existence as man's servants.

At the beginning of the nineteenth century, Maria Graham saw
in Rio de Janeiro horses that were pretty but thin, fed on a diet of
corn and Guinea grass, which had recently been introduced into Brazil, where it grew prodigiously. The rank and file of horses did not
bring anything like the prices the beautiful animals of Buenos Aires
commanded. For carriage use, it was the custom to employ mules instead of horses, as they were stronger and could better stand the
heat of summer in cities like Rio de Janeiro.[3] Thus, in addition to
its duties as a rural beast of burden, in which it rivaled the ox, the
mule in early nineteenth-century Brazil had laid upon it the equally
harsh duties of urban transport. In the second half of that century, in
1865, Codman, watching the entrance of a mule train in Santos, observed that when the herders removed the harness many of the animals had bone-deep galls, the result of long trips over bad roads and
lack of care on the part of the drivers.[4] They suffered much the
same martyrdom in the cities, carrying over rough roads full of pot-

---

[3] Graham: Op. cit., p. 161.
[4] John Codman: *Ten Months in Brazil* (London, 1870), p. 60.

holes, in calashes or outmoded carriages, fat priests, voluminous baronesses accompanied by similarly obese Negro women, gentlemen bloated from lack of exercise and vast quantities of manioc porridge or monstrously swollen with elephantiasis.

In colonial Rio, as well as in the early days of the Empire—even after McAdam's successful process of paving, or macadamizing the roads—the streets were "detestably paved," and "as the drains are in the middle, toward which the badly laid, uneven stones slope, walking is difficult, and they are always full of puddles because of the rains . . ." [5] Only the hoofs of the sure-footed mules and the plodding oxen could compete with the bare feet of the equally strong Negro palanquin bearers and porters over the "detestably paved," muddy, dirty streets of Rio de Janeiro, Recife, or São Paulo. It was also Negroes or slaves who brought the water for drinking, cooking, and bathing to the houses from springs or public fountains, for in Rio, as in the other principal cities of Brazil, the abundance of Negroes to supply the bourgeois or patriarchal mansions with water and to carry away the night soil delayed the installation of conduits and drains. It was a source of wonder to Schaeffer, when he visited Brazil around the middle of the nineteenth century, to find that "hydrants and pipes" were "unknown to the Brazilians." [6]

For the transportation of persons or parcels there were Negroes "for hire," great strapping blacks, always provided with a pad for their head, and often wearing nothing but a loincloth, ready to answer the call of anyone desiring their services. Like the porters of coffee sacks, they carried "incredible loads." They resembled "messengers of Asiatic Turkey . . . bowed . . . under the tremendous loads they carried." [7] It could be said of them without exaggeration that they worked harder than beasts of burden, obliged, as they were, to bring their employer, at the end of the day, a certain sum; when they failed to do this they were punished, "as I witnessed more than once," wrote the Dutchman Van Boelen, who lived in Rio during

---

[5] H. J. do Carmo Netto: *O Intendente Aragão.* Reprint of *Boletim Policial,* XI (Rio de Janeiro, 1913), p. 6.

[6] L. M. Schaeffer: *Sketches of Travels in South America, Mexico, and California* (New York, 1860), p. 15.

[7] Carmo Netto: Op. cit., p. 7.

the early years of the empire.[8] Wilkes, who was in Brazil in 1838, wrote that the porters of Rio ran through the streets behind the leader of each group, who, to the sound of a gourd rattle, paced the others in a kind of trot. They all sang. And, as a rule, each of them carried a load of about two hundred pounds.[9] Ten years after Wilkes, Schaeffer was horrified to learn of "these poor degraded blacks"— the bearers of sacks of coffee, crates—"that about seven years finishes them entirely."[1]

A large part of the wealth of Rio de Janeiro, Salvador, Recife, or São Luis de Maranhão, until the substitution of transport by beasts of burden, came from these slaves, who were hired out by their masters as though they were horses or mules.

"This is one great reason that prevents the adoption of machinery in abridging manual labor, as so many persons have an interest in its being performed by the slaves alone," observed Walsh [2] apropos of the many Negroes who took the place of beasts of burden and transportation in the streets of the Brazilian cities. In the interior, they worked alongside the mules and oxen; at times even taking the place of the wind or the water which could run the sugar mills by means of belts or wooden wheels. The master of the slaves, who every evening came home with the money they had earned in the street, was not interested in the replacement of these remunerative humans by horses, and still less by expensive, complicated machinery whose uproar could be controlled only by foreign mechanics or pretentious mulattoes who had to be handled with kid gloves.

I have not been able to find information on which to base a reliable estimate of the number of slaves employed in colonial Brazil and during the early decades of the Empire in the transportation of persons and goods. It must have been very large. And the mortality among them very high. As high as among mules. It is known for certain that 260,000 mules were in use in Minas Gerais in 1837, of which

---

[8] Jacobus Van Boelen: *Viagems nas Costas Oriental e Occidental da America do Sul (1826)*, I, pp. 77–84. Carmo Netto: Op. cit., p. 7.

[9] Charles Wilkes: *Narrative of the United States Exploring Expedition During the Years 1838, 1839, 1840, 1841, 1842* (London, 1852), p. 21.

[1] Schaeffer: Op. cit., p. 15.

[2] Robert Walsh: *Notices of Brazil in 1828 and 1829* (London–Boston, 1830–1), p. 199.

no fewer than 18,000 to 20,000 died each year. To maintain the required number, some 60,000 mules were brought in annually from Sorocaba.

As for horses, their number was more or less limited to the needs of gentlemen, nobles, officials, heads of the troops of militia, or soldiers. For work on plantations and in the cities, the transportation of merchandise, for taking the womenfolk to church and to visit relatives, for the children's amusement, the patriarchal Brazilian of plantation or city found oxen, mules, donkeys, rams, and, above all, the Negro slaves, sufficient for his needs. This explains the resistance of many Brazilians of the upper class to steam horses when these began to make their appearance in the form of English machines and as the substitute, less for animals like the horse, which was looked upon as almost sacred and was relatively protected by its master, than for oxen, mules, and field hands or slaves. What was the need for an expensive, delicate, complicated machine to grind this, to do that, when there was cheap, simple, easy slave labor at hand? And why this widespread use of the horse, more difficult to feed, to care for, and to preserve than the Negro or the ox, the slave or the mule, when the horse should be an animal only for military use or travel, or for the pleasure of the master, the gentry, the officer? This must have been in the minds of many Brazilians of the ruling class, for whom St. George was the patron saint.

As for the gentlemen Brackenridge saw on horseback in the streets of Rio de Janeiro in 1817—riding small animals whose tails dragged on the ground [3]—many of them were probably devotees of St. George and wore the same decorations as those displayed by the "priests and nobles" whom that observer, with shocked Republican and Puritan eyes, saw or glimpsed riding in palanquins.

A news item in the *Diario do Rio de Janeiro* for June 11, 1822, reveals the fact that the Brotherhood of St. George, in its role as a sodality of gentlemen or nobles and, at the same time, of blacksmiths and metalworkers, was under the supervision of the Municipal Council itself. As that year the image of St. George had not appeared in the procession of Corpus Christi, the sodality was publicly cen-

---

[3] H. M. Brackenridge: *Voyage to Buenos Ayres Performed in the Years 1817 and 1818 by Order of the American Government* (London, 1820), p. 20.

sured by the governing board of the Council, which called its attention to Section V of the bylaws: "It is the duty of this sodality to
prepare the image of St. George each year to be borne in the procession of Corpus Christi, which will be carried out with due care, the
Blessed Image mounted upon a well-accoutered horse preceded by
a squire with sword and dagger and followed by a page dressed in
red, both on horseback; the trumpeter and drummer will also be
mounted, and the players of other instruments on foot . . . In addition, four Brothers will be chosen by the Board to accompany the
image of the Saint, two beside the stirrups and two holding the
bridle of the horse . . . The Master and Notary of the blacksmiths'
and metalworkers' Guild will accompany the Saint's entourage . . ." For the expenses of this cult of the horse, and not merely
the Holy Horseman, "any and all artisans working for a salary in the
trades listed in Section II, in any district of this city," will contribute
"320 reis annually, and the same holds true for emancipated Negroes
having establishments for such trades off the premises of their masters, who will pay for the slaves in question . . ."

The City Council of Rio de Janeiro went on to state that it was
the habit of the aforesaid sodality "to request from the Royal Stables
the white horse which St. George was to ride, and the Council
would request from the same stables the retinue to accompany the
Saint." The sodality, however, had neglected to provide, in that
year of 1822, "the saddle for the Saint's horse." "A shocking over-
sight," which deserved reprobation, in the case of a cult which was
plainly not that of the Saint on Horseback alone, but of the Horse,
the animal which guarantees man superior standing over other men
and even over dragons.

Those Negroes who resented their servile status and their social
inferiority and aspired to enter the ruling class—or at least to rule
over slaves and former slaves—made of St. George, alias Ogun,[4]
their saint or their patron, especially in Rio de Janeiro. Even if they
appeared in his procession only as the white men's pages, and not
mounted on horses from which to dominate with their glance the

---

[4] The identification of St. George with Ogun took place mainly in Rio de
Janeiro. Cf. studies of Arthur Ramos; also Edson Carneiro: *Candomblés*
(Bahía, 1948).

pedestrians, on workdays they had at their command strength and energy equivalent to that of the horse, and capable of endangering the established order. Strength which lay in the powerful muscles of strong men, of youths, of adolescents capable of rising against the whites, of assassinating them, of making them waste away by witchcraft. Thus, in Brazil St. George became the object of two contradictory cults: that of the ruling class, the whites and near whites, and of the ruled, the colored men who only outwardly accepted their domination by whites at times their inferiors in education, intelligence, technical skill, physical strength, and beauty. They reacted against this domination by what a Marxist would call "class struggle," and others, "the conflict of races" or "cultures," but the truth is that this struggle was the expression of a combination of antagonisms and never just one.

As pointed out by H. J. do Carmo Netto, in an interesting contribution to the history of the police in Rio de Janeiro, in the "fetishism" of the Negroes in colonial Brazil, Ogun was a kind of God of War or of Vengeance, whose emblem was a sword or an iron harpoon and whose altar was "a stone set at a crossroad, where his worshippers went to lay offerings such as a knife stained with blood or some other instrument of crime, after having committed a homicide or in preparation for one." [5] Thus, it can be understood how the Church of St. George in Rio de Janeiro became the shrine of the Africans' devotion to Ogun. And throughout most of Brazil, the image of the warrior saint—replaced in some places by that of St. Anthony—became for the Negroes the symbol of Ogun, about whom there grew up what Carmo Netto found to have been a "vast fraternity whose emblem was an iron bracelet," whose typical color was yellow, and whose insignia, at their shrines, was "a square, ornamented tambourine, symbolizing war." [6]

This same investigator relates to the cult of Ogun, or of St. George on horseback, the incident told by Van Boelen of a Negro in Rio de Janeiro in the early years of the Empire whom "superstitious ideas had kept from breaking his promise to carry out a criminal undertaking, even though the person under whose orders he was acting had repented and wanted to prevent the crime at all costs; only his

---

[5] Carmo Netto: Op. cit., p. 9.   [6] Ibid., p. 9.

parents, by means of exorcisms and cabbalistic rites performed over a stone set up on the corner of a street, succeeded in making him break the oath he had taken." The Dutch traveler knew this Negro, and it seems that he was one of those hired out or used as a porter. With regard to such hired Negroes, he reached this generalization: ". . . one should always be on guard against them, for as they have to turn over to their masters a fixed amount of money each day, they always try to come by it in some way; and cases are known of canoes paddled by them which late in the day or during the night capsized in the bay, after they had robbed the passengers and then drowned them. They let themselves be bought for almost nothing to put an end to some enemy of the person hiring them; and once they had given their word to do such a thing, they carried it out so faithfully that even the one who had arranged for the crime could not make them desist from it, for this was forbidden by their religion." [7]

From this, as from other testimony concerning Negro criminals in the leading cities of colonial Brazil and the early days of the Empire, the fact emerges that for many of them the crime was less that of the individual than of an enslaved race or an oppressed class or culture to whom the cult of St. George gave hope or encouragement that they could throw off the yoke of the whites. Meanwhile, they collaborated with the powerful armed saint, killing with dagger, club, poison, or witchcraft their own small dragon. For we must remember that witchcraft, sorcery, or poisons unknown to the whites were among the instruments of defense or aggression used by slaves against masters, by blacks against whites, in patriarchal Brazil.[8]

The antagonism between doctors of European training and, for the most part, whites, if not Europeans—during the first half of the nineteenth century there were a number of English and French physicians in Brazil—and the native or African witch doctors at times assumed the clear quality of class, race, or cultural struggle. A typical case is that of "Black Manoel," which in Pernambuco around the middle of the nineteenth century turned into a dramatic conflict,

---

[7] Ibid., p. 8.

[8] See Vigneron Jousselandière: *Novo Manual Prático de Agricultura Tropical . . . Fruto de 37 anos de Existencia* (Rio de Janeiro, 1860), p. 175.

outwardly between whites and blacks but, in reality, between survivals of African culture represented by the witch doctors and new therapeutic methods introduced by European-trained doctors. Manoel, an African healer, was allowed to treat victims of cholera in the Hospital de Marinha of Recife. Inasmuch, however, as various patients under his care died, he was "notified by the police that he was to give up his treatments." He refused to obey the order, and the police put him under arrest. This is contained in the report of the director of the Public Health Commission and confirmed, in part, by another doctor of the epoch who had studied in France: "A Negro of Africa made his appearance at the Guararapes plantation and claimed he could cure cholera. Persons ignorant of medicine, and without stopping to ask if this disease was known in Guinea, hearing that there was a Negro who could cure it, here in Bahía, a center of West Coast Africans, began to praise the therapeutic benefits of the herbs he employed for rubbing and internal use . . . Persons of social prominence took him under their wing; there was one who even hoped for a popular uprising which he could lead and shoot down doctors . . . and finally this Negro not only offered his remedy for sale at high price, but even to be peddled from house to house." [9]

The Public Health Commission attempted to control the situation. But "the enthusiasm of the Negro's protectors grew and they proclaimed his abilities in shops and on street corners; the populace rejoiced, and the Negroes grew insolent; the brawlers gathered in groups and rioted through the streets for two nights, shouting maledictions against the doctors; there was even a priest who, from the pulpit, spoke in favor of this Negro and attacked the doctors and apothecaries, claiming that they wanted to kill him because he cured the mulattoes and blacks . . ." Mobs gathered "to stone the apothecary shops and attack the doctors . . ." [1]

For some time there was not a doctor, not only in the interior of the province of Pernambuco—one of the most cultivated of the country—but even in its capital city of Recife who could compete in prestige with the Negro Manoel. It was not only blacks and mu-

---

[9] "Manifesto do Dr. Joaquim d'Aquino Fonseca sobre a sua Retirada da Commissão de Hygiene Publica," *Diario de Pernambuco*, February 29, 1856.
[1] Ibid.

lattoes who came from their shanties and slave quarters to consult him, but also the rich whites. He became a kind of dark St. George, complete with horse. He was offered "a cart so he could travel more quickly," Dr. Cosme de Sa Pereira tells in a curious account of the Negro's activities.[2] In those days a horse-drawn vehicle was the prerogative of whites of the upper class. In a report to one of the ministers, the president of the province had to admit that, amidst the epidemic that was running like wildfire through the whole country, there had appeared in Pernambuco the Negro Manoel, "with an extraordinary aura of prestige," brought from the interior of the province, "like the hope of redemption," by "outstanding persons such as Commanders Manoel José da Costa, Manoel Gonzalves da Silva, and the chief of staff, Sebastião Lopes Guimarães," all of whom state that the Negro has effected "instantaneous cures and that the people cheer him." This in contrast to their "lack of faith in doctors," which the ravages of cholera in the Big Houses and especially in the slave quarters, and of yellow fever in the city residences, had strengthened. The president of the province stressed the fact that if the Negro Manoel had been permitted to attend the black patients in the Hospital de Marinha it has been "to render him useless without risk of public disturbance, which would surely follow if other measures were employed; for the populace was already saying that the authorities wanted to put the Negro away so the doctors would be free to kill off the colored people, who were those whom the epidemic attacked most virulently."[3]

It is clear from this episode, which shocked the city of Recife and almost led to bloodshed, that various of the conflicts that arose in the patriarchal society of Brazil, which today are oversimplified by students of our development, some labeling them "class struggles," others, "racial struggles," were neither exclusively the one nor the other, but both, confused or contradictory, and, above all, a conflict

---

[2] "Analyse dos Motivos Apresentados no Manifesto do Dr. J. A. Fonseca Pelo Dr. C. S. Pereira," *Diario de Pernambuco*, Document 6 of the *Relatorio do Estado Sanitario da Provincia de Pernambuco no anno de 1856* (Pernambuco, 1857), p. 118.

[3] Documents 7 and 8 of *Relatorio do Estado Sanitario da Provincia de Pernambuco*, p. 225.

of cultures. European-trained doctors utilizing instruments and apparatus designed for the treatment of patients or the diagnois of ailments in cold climates or a European milieu had to fight a bitter battle with African or native healers, who knew the properties of tropical herbs and plants, and were at times, as in the case of the Negro Manoel, protected by the masters of patriarchal plantation or town mansion. These looked askance at the invasion of their rural or semirural domains by doctors not always disposed to be "surgeons of slaves" or even "family doctors." They were people close to the soil, who had more confidence in the herbs of slaves and Indians than in the French and English drugs the apothecaries dispensed; who preferred to conserve their traditional culture, mainly of Iberian origin, rather than to substitute it or modify it. Thus these whites joined forces with their slaves and the free blacks and mulattoes, likewise refractory, out of inertia or a sense of cultural self-sufficiency, to European therapeutic innovations, against the more Europeanized whites of the cities, for whom the medicine of Europe (English or French) was the only one which could really cure and check diseases.

The devastation of the African population of the slave quarters or shanties by the Asiatic cholera brought great discredit on this Europeanized element. Where was the power of European techniques? What good were the instruments, machines, the pretensions of these European-trained doctors when the Negroes and mulattoes were dying like flies? This gave rise to an ethnocentric interpretation of the phenomenon: the whites were allowing the doctors, nearly all of whom were white, to kill off the colored people. Economically, as the Negroes and mulattoes and the wilier slaves knew, it was all to the white master's interest not only not to have his slaves die, but to keep them healthy. But, inasmuch as the immigration of Europeans, such as the Irish, who were called "white slaves" by the populace of Rio de Janeiro, had begun during the early nineteenth century, it was natural that the Negroes and mulattoes should have suspected that the powerful or wealthy whites preferred to see the Negroes and mulattoes replaced by white workers. This explains the transformation of figures like the healer Manoel into St. Georges capable of slaying the dragon of Asiatic cholera. To the black sufferers such figures became redeemers, who could do more with their healing herbs than the European drugs, which were almost useless in combating the scourge from Asia.

While this was taking place with the more rebellious or dissatisfied Negroes, to their white masters the cult of St. George on horseback represented exactly the opposite: the maintenance of social order. Maintenance by military force, by riding down the rabble, by the use of firearms against dagger or knife, by strategy learned in military academies against the fighting methods of street ruffians and thugs.

Surprised at seeing the procession of St. George on horseback set out from the royal palace itself in Rio de Janeiro, Arago revealed his failure to understand the social importance of this highly important and contradictory cult in old Brazil.[4] So many Negroes desirous of their freedom, on the one hand (as the result of their social advancement as fighters and soldiers, as well as in their capacity of artisans, metalworkers, mechanics, bone-setters, machinists); so many whites bent on conserving their political power and their social superiority, on the other. This made it a cult, at the same time, and for opposite reasons, of the royal palace and the slave cabin, of mansion and shanty, of church and heathen altar, of members of a Catholic brotherhood and members of an African secret society, of plantation owner and city proprietor and the proletariat needed for the building of houses, furniture, carriages and the operation of machines, saws, lathes, forges.

For we must not lose sight of the fact that even though divided by hatred or rivalries of caste, language, region, and cult into Mozambiques and Congolese, Minas and Coromatins, Portuguese-speaking Negroes of the Gold Coast, the Africans and their descendants in Brazil underwent influences which lent them cohesion. The first of these was the slave condition of the greater part of them, even though this varied from that of house servant to field hand, or hired-out Negro; or from that of the slave on a big sugar plantation in the area of Pernambuco or Rio de Janeiro to that on a manioc farm in Santa Catarina or a clearing in Piauí. The second, that of being Africans or descendants of Africans, although this, too, was a varia-

---

[4] J. Arago: *Promenade Autor du Monde,* I, p. 59.

ble condition, given the diversity of color, features, or ethnic characteristics among them.

Other influences brought about among Africans differing in color, bodily characteristics, and slave status that "kind of relationship" observed by Koster,[5] which led them to treat one another as comrades, *malungos,* "a name held in high esteem among them." Among these other influences, there was that of having formed part of the same lot on the slave ship bound for Brazil, that of membership in the same Catholic brotherhood—that of St. Benedict, as a rule—or of the same gang of thugs or ruffians of the city. And, above all, that which derived from the fact of being devotees or initiates of a religious cult transformed into a secret movement of social rebellion such as that of St. George on horseback—or its equivalent, St. Anthony, soldier—behind which the Negroes and slaves disguised the cult of Ogun.

In the capital of Pernambuco, the Negro porters of the sugar warehouses, who formed a guild of their own, with their own director, as can be seen from an edict of September 13, 1776, passed by Governor José Cesar de Menezes, were under the protection of the King himself. They seem to have comprised the most important group of Negroes in the city, after those of the National Guard or militia. These were looked upon by many as dangerous, as is apparent from a letter of José Venancio de Seixas, director of the mint of Bahía, to Dom Rodrigo de Souza Coutinho in 1788, which reveals his concern over the formation of corps of militia made up of colored people. People "easily swayed" and capable under the "spirit of the age"—the age of the French Revolution—"of committing every form of excess." [6] It was the fear that Negro St. Georges, armed to defend order, might rise up against the whites, employing arms which only the whites should have the right to use and bear.

Forbidden the use of firearms, swords, walking sticks with concealed rapiers, the arms of the gentry and the masters, the slaves—principally those hired out as porters, who together with blacksmiths, metalworkers, machinists, seem to have comprised, in Rio de Janeiro as in Recife, the fighting aristocracy of the slave population

---

[5] Henry Koster: *Travels in Brazil* (London, 1816), p. 357.
[6] Ms. in Archives of Colonial History, Lisbon.

—became experts, like the ruffians and street loafers, in the use of daggers and knives, but, above all, in head-butting, tripping, kicking the feet out from under the adversary, which characterized the type of fighting known as *capoeiragem*. (Others made use of spells, witchcraft, mysterious poisons which crippled and killed whites.) The art of *capoeiragem* enabled them to compensate for the lack of firearms with their agility, with movements of the body which were almost those of the dance. The "dancers" of *capoeiragem*, with their small, swift, delicate feet, almost those of a girl, and shod, like the women of Bahía, in slippers with Oriental trimming, could confront armed soldiers, powerful northerners, English sailors, Portuguese "he-men," and wreak havoc on them and, to a certain degree, demoralize them. Challenging their technical superiority as soldiers or men armed with pistols, swords, daggers and their social superiority as whites, gentlemen. Perhaps these clashes account for the antipathy of the Portuguese for the Brazilian mestizos, with their small, agile feet, to whom the former gave the name of "goat feet"; and that of the mestizos for the Portuguese, who as a rule had big feet, often broad and clumsy, known in our folklore as "lead feet."

With the cult of small, delicate, and pretty feet, not only in women but in men as well, and of the slipper or shoe to set off these attributes, it was natural that this cult should pass from the social plane to that of sexual fetichism. Doctor Alberto da Cunha cites the case of a man who could achieve intercourse only "when he had covered the shoe of the woman he desired with kisses."[7] To this could be added others of Brazilians obsessed by the foot or shoe of their inamorata, some of whom have left famous sonnets in testimony to their obsession. There would seem to have been—and continue to be—instances of Brazilians of patriarchal background in whom the sexual desire or voluptuousness was aroused by merely rubbing one foot against the other. In such men the feet seem to have become areas of special sensibility, possibly as the result of the removal of chigoes from their feet when they were children by colored maids or nurses having soft, agile fingers.

The cult of the small and pretty foot, and elegant footwear to protect this genteel foot, impresses anyone who has studied the inti-

---

[7] Alberto da Cunha: *Obsessões* (Rio de Janeiro, 1898), p. 15.

mate history of our people as one of the most expressive factors in the development of personality according to the status or the social situation of the individual: the personality of the aristocrat of the plantation house and, principally, of the city residence as opposed to the tavern keeper with his big, clog-shod feet, or the Negro field hand who, like the shanty dweller, was obliged by the nature of his work to go barefoot, or at most, wearing sandals, and exposed to parasites, mud, filth. In view of this cult of the foot, this care, this desire of the gentry to protect the feet as well as the hands from exertion or rough work, befitting only slaves or animals, it is easy to understand why the Brazilian aristocrat was, in the colonial epoch and the beginning of the Empire, a highly skilled horseman and, at the same time, had a voluptuous fondness, like the Oriental nabob or potentate, for being carried about in palanquins or sedan chairs in the city, in litters in the country, by handsome, strong slaves and animals.

With the coming of the machine age, the taste developed among us for the carriage drawn by fine horses and driven by good-looking coachmen, the complex of machine, slave, and animal at the service of the gentry, who could not scuff their shoes or soil their feet walking over the rough roads or through the dirty streets. And it must also be borne in mind that to the cult of the small, well-turned foot of the rich aristocrat of palanquin or carriage there was conjoined, from colonial days, that of the foot, not only small and well-turned, but agile as well, like that of the thugs and ruffians, with their slippers and swaggering gait. These colored aristocrats could boast that they had no need of working with either feet or hands to live an easy life in the large cities of Brazil. The chief enemy of the ruffian was not so much the gentleman of the fine residence as the "lead-feet" or "ox-feet" Portuguese of grocery store, tavern, shop, warehouse, the carter, who became rich from his hard, monotonous, almost animal work, and on more than one occasion, thanks to his better economic status, took away from the Bohemian mulatto or the romantic highwayman—guitar player, ballad singer, samba dancer—his colored girl.

It was rarely possible for the "lead feet" to win a victory over the sandal- or bare-footed "goat feet" in a hand-to-hand combat. It was as though the black and mulatto ruffians were mounted on invisible

horses of Ogun or St. George when they fought the white shopkeepers, armed with pistols but on foot. Only the cavalry, with real
horses, could rout these devilish ruffians. The intimidating effects of
the cry "there comes the cavalry" has lasted almost to our own times,
scattering rioters or rebels on foot.

Elysio de Araujo tells how, in Rio de Janeiro at the beginning of
the nineteenth century, the talk of the town was the so-called
"shrimp dinners": the severe cudgeling by the grenadiers of the
Royal Police Guard of "vagabonds" or "idlers," who were rounded
up in the "dances which were at the time frequent in the outskirts of
the city." [8] At least some of these supposed Negro or mulatto "vagabonds" or "idlers" may be presumed to have been devotees of
Ogun ready to honor their saint or patron with a bravery more befitting fighters than criminal delinquents: military action, fighting,
war dances, the physical and even artistic expression of youthful, virile vigor. This vigor was deployed in the affirmation or defense of
their position as "sons of Ogun" or "St. George" as well as "sons" of
His Majesty, our King, or of the Emperor, our Father, or of the
Virgin Mary, when Our Lady was treated without due respect by
heretics of any sort, or the King or Emperor by foreigners. So true
was this that after their severe trouncing by the grenadiers of the
notorious Major Vidigal, who, with his gentle air and sweet voice,
was often the evil spirit of the Royal Police Guard, and their imprisonment for some time in the guardhouse, the "able-bodied" on
their release "joined the Army." [9]

It is a pity that the army officers lacked the imagination, the intelligence, the spark needed to grasp how useful the fighting art of these
ruffians would have been for the national defense. Those fugitive
slaves, unwilling to suffer their slave condition, or those descendants
of slaves, unadaptable to routine labors, would have made excellent
soldier-ruffians. For the historians of the epoch themselves, who
depended for their information exclusively on the police records, like
Araujo, point out that the crimes of the Negro or mulatto "idlers,"
the "thugs," the "ruffians" at their dances, "in taverns in the lowest
quarters of the city," or "in vacant lots" consisted in practicing "feats

---

[8] Elysio de Araujo: *Estudo Historico sobre a Policia da Capital Federal de
1808 a 1831* (Rio de Janeiro, 1898), p. 55.

[9] Ibid., p. 56.

of bodily skill and dexterity, to the vast delight of sailors and seamen, who, between puffs of smoke reeking of alcohol, applauded this entertainment." [1]

To protect themselves from harassment by the police, these idlers organized themselves, as was natural—and this was really the reason why the art of *capoieragem* among us ceased to be a typically Afro-Brazilian diversion to sink into crime and sexual aberrations—into gangs armed with daggers or razors, which "in endless forays sow terror and panic among the peaceable, bourgeois inhabitants of this old, backward city." [2]

In his study, Araujo points out that beginning in 1814 "the measures ordered taken against anyone found in possession of a razor or accused of having used such an arm for the purpose of attack grew steadily more severe." This would seem to indicate that only after the brutal attacks carried out by the police against them after 1808, just as against Moorish blinds, Oriental-style roofs, African merrymakings and remedies—and always with the same excuse or for the same reason: the offense of such Orientalisms or Africanisms to eyes, ears, and palate, not to mention the interests, of "perfectly civilized" Europeans—did the street rowdies resort to razor and dagger as weapons of defense against the police and even intolerant whites. Such accusations warrant careful study, for, as Araujo says, "they throw light upon the aggregate of exercises which constitute the game of *capoeiragem*," among which the most important was probably "butting."

On April 22, 1812, the soldier Felicio Novaes of the Second Regiment was charged with "having butted the Englishman William Lodgat," and he would seem to have left the "Mister" knocked out. He played the game by the orthodox rules, using neither razor nor dagger, only head, feet, and hands. The greatest of all would seem to have been the militia lieutenant, João Moreira, nicknamed the "Mutinous," in the days of the Marquis of Lavradio in the eighteenth century, who, though he handled sword, dagger, and cudgel perfectly, preferred using his head or his feet. Apparently certain of the colonial militias in the second half of the eighteenth century followed

---

[1] Ibid., p. 57.
[2] Ibid., p. 58. See also Carmo Netto: *O Intendente Aragão*, p. 14.

a more enlightened policy with regard to the practices of *capoeira-gem* than the captains-general with regard to the dances and festivities of the Negroes: not merely tolerating them but utilizing their values and techniques in the public interest.

If it was the English and French who complained to the police of the Prince Regent about the annoying dances of these ruffians, they probably regretted it. For the systematic persecution of the police turned these champions of kicking and butting into even more annoying dancers: dancers armed with razors and daggers. Dancers who, smiling, mincing, treading lightly, took to killing whites—mostly Europeans—slitting their bellies, whereas formerly they had only left them stretched out on the ground with their terrible butting, roughed up, it is true, and *hors de combat*, but alive. Just as in English prize fights.

By 1821 the situation in Rio de Janeiro gave cause for concern. The woundings and killings were becoming numerous, and many were the work of Negro and mulatto slaves. Hence the petition addressed to the Minister of War on February 26 of that year by an army commission asking that the police be allowed to take more vigorous action against slaves and impudent Negroes "in view of the fact that because of the absence of punishment by flogging, the only one which cows and frightens them, stabbings and killings are being perpetrated, like those in recent days, when there have been six deaths at the hand of these ruffians, and many knifings . . ." It seemed to the army commission that the chief of police was not taking adequate measures. Either this or he was not well aware "of the dangerous consequences that may be expected if individuals of this caliber are dealt with mildly . . ." Therefore, the commission recommended to His Royal Highness, through his Minister of War, that instead of arresting the unruly slaves—as though a prison sentence mattered to them, not to mention the hardship worked on their masters, who "had to pay the expenses of their imprisonment"—the police should subject all Negroes guilty of disorderly conduct or apprehended with "a knife" or "any suspicious weapon" to punishment by flogging, which might contribute to their "mending their ways." [3]

---

[3] Ibid., p. 61. See also E. Allain: *Quelques Données sur la Capitale et sur l'Administration du Brésil* (Paris–Rio de Janeiro, 1886).

An edict of December 8, 1823, issued by Clemente Ferreira Franca,[4] ordered the brigadier chief of police of the capital to strengthen the patrols in the outlying districts and slaughterhouse area to prevent the assembling of Negro ruffians. And by an order of November 26, 1821, he decreed, for the same reason, that slaughterhouses and taverns must be closed by ten at night.[5] Another ordinance, of 1825, this one issued by the chief of police of the Court of Brazil, Francisco Alberto Teixeira do Aragão, stated that slaves could be searched at any hour of the day or night for arms, inasmuch as they were forbidden, under penalty of flogging, "not only the use of any weapon of defense, but to carry clubs." Slaves were also forbidden, and not only slaves but any Negro or colored person, to stand on the street corners "without good reason" and even "to whistle or give any other signal."[6] This affected the street idler in two of his most cherished and characteristic freedoms.

However, it was these Negroes, these slaves, these ruffians, these idlers, held down and repressed in their youthful virile manifestations as though their games, their dance steps, their songs in praise of Ogun, their whistles, were a crime or indignity against the colony or the Empire, who put down the uprising of Irish and German mercenaries, the favorite troops of Pedro I when they revolted in 1828. It began on the morning of June 9 when the Germans quartered in São Cristovão, after setting fire to the barracks, rushed through the streets like blond devils, sacking taverns and mistreating the peaceful, unarmed persons they encountered. Then the Germans of Praia Vermelha did the same thing. After assassinating Major Benedito Teola, who tried to restrain them, they ran wild, attacking homes, drinking, and looting. Two days later, the Germans tried to get the Irish quartered in Campo de Santana to join them. However, before these new mutineers could leave their quarters, they were surrounded by the militia, which cut off their communications with the streets. And when the Irish soldiers who were guarding the public buildings and establishments tried to join their rioting comrades, they "were attacked by Negroes known as *capoeiras*" who engaged them in "mortal combat." The historian Pereira da Silva recounts

---

[4] Araujo: Op. cit., p. 115.
[5] *Diario de Rio Janeiro,* November 26, 1821.
[6] Idem., January 3, 1825.

that, even "though they were armed with muskets," the Irish were
unable to withstand the *capoeiras*, and, "defeated by stones, clubs,
and bodily skill," they fell in the streets and squares, many of them
wounded and a considerable number dead." [7]

If it is true that only with the help of the crews of English and
French warships anchored in the bay and of "leading citizens" who
assembled "civilians willing to fight" could the government bring the
revolt of these mercenaries under control, it is also true that the action of "Negroes known as *capoeiras*" was an important factor.

It was not that these Negroes and mulattoes were by nature lawless or bloodthirsty, as the more superficial interpreters of uprisings
such as that of "the tailors" in the eighteenth century or of the
Males [8] in the nineteenth century, in Bahía, still believe. Or the uprisings of the runaway slaves, or the revolts and riots of the colored
people like those of 1823 in Recife, or the feats of the *capoeiras* there
and in Rio de Janeiro.

What these young Negroes and half-breeds did, at times in disorderly manner, was to give release to the normal energies of strong
young men and adolescents, which the authorities did not always
allow them to express in less violent form than running away to join
the colonies of fugitive slaves, killing white overseers, revolting, instead of dancing the samba, practicing their *capoeiragem*, their cult
of Ogun, the Mohammedan religion. It was the shortsightedness of
such repression that turned their festive gatherings into sessions of
witchcraft, the cult of Ogun into a coarse imitation of Masonry,
with mysterious signals and whistles, Mohammedanism into the mortal enemy of the religion of the Christian masters of plantations and
city houses, *capoeiragem* into a criminal and bloody activity, and the
samba into a low, indecent dance. It is curious to observe today, long
years after the violent repression of such Africanisms, that the descendants of the razor- and dagger-armed dancers are becoming
sublimated into our "football dancers," as seen in players like the
Negro Leonidas; the samba is turning into a dance more Bahían than
African, winning the applause of international audiences when per-

---

[7] J. M. Pereira da Silva: *Segundo Periodo do Reinado de D. Pedro I no
Brasil* (Rio de Janeiro, 1871), p. 287.

[8] A revolt of Islamic slaves in Bahía.

formed by an artist like Carmen Miranda; the vestiges of the cult of Ogun and Allah are turning into marginal Roman Catholic practices.

Even the rebellious Negroes of patriarchal Brazil always wanted to be paternally guided and protected by their masters or persons of standing. It was when the whites fell short in their role as social fathers of their slaves and treated them like mere animals, or beasts of burden, or hired them out as human machines, that many of the Negroes forsook them.

It is said that the "revolt of the tailors" in Bahía very nearly turned the old captaincy, once the seat of the viceroys, into a "republic along the lines of Haiti." [9] This was the objective of the Negroes and mulattoes who in 1823 triumphantly swarmed through the streets of Recife, protesting against the whites who oppressed them and proclaiming themselves emulators of Henri-Christophe.[1] And from a petition of the conspirators to the governor of the captaincy it seems that the desire of the Bahíans—"nearly all of them colored, slaves, and manumitted"—was to make Dom Fernando José of Portugal the head of the government of Bahía with the title of "President of the Supreme Court of the Democracy of Bahía." A president elected by the people and not a governor named by a remote king. The young conspirators—one of whom, Manoel de Santos Lira, though grown, had the appearance of a boy of seventeen, and for that reason his lawyers advised him to allege that he was a minor—were imbued with a vague French republicanism; but a republicanism which, instead of proclaiming war on all whites or all masters, was prepared to accept the patriarchal system that prevailed in Brazil, as was evidenced by the respect of the slaves and ex-slaves for those masters who took a paternal attitude toward the Negroes and workers.

This state of affairs is not to be wondered at in late eighteenth-century Brazil, where from the sixteenth century slavery would seem to have been more benevolent than in English America. Even in southern United States, at the beginning of the nineteenth century, there was one who considered the patriarchal system "as it exists in certain regions and colonies of America and the United States under

[9] H. Cancio: *D. João V* (Bahía, 1909), p. 21.
[1] Alfredo de Carvalho: *Estudos Pernambucanos* (Recife, 1907).

the name of slavery . . . a co-operative system of society." This is the thesis upheld by an "inhabitant of Florida" in a pamphlet privately published by its author in 1829 under the title *Treatise of the Patriarchal or Co-operative System of Society*. It seemed to him that the system of slavery, when it took a patriarchal form, was not only necessary but advantageous for both master and slaves, provided they understood it and carried it out; and that it could be modified to allow the slaves a share in the profits of their work, after deducting the gains on capital investment. The slaves the author of this curious study especially had in mind were those who worked on the cotton plantations of southern United States.

Perhaps it was due to the feeling that the patriarchal system was co-operative after its own fashion that slaves in Brazil often robbed their masters of small articles, justifying themselves on the grounds that "stealing from the master is not stealing." [2] It was like a son stealing from his father. And this feeling would also account for the habit of slaves of running away from a master who used them badly to seek the protection of one from whom they might expect paternal treatment. Even today one finds descendants of slaves in Brazil who say that they cannot get used to a house where there is not an old man or woman whom they can ask to bless them every night, as children do their parents. And the mystic appeal of those politicians known as "fathers of the poor," "fathers of the humble" clearly has its origin in this remote tendency.

It is possible that some of the revolutionists of 1798 in Bahía thought along the same lines as the economist or sociologist of Florida, and believed it possible to realize the dream of a republic, co-operative and at the same time patriarchal, in which the whites or the masters, held in filial regard by slaves and former slaves, would continue to act in the role of guardians, by election or by the choice of a population politically free but patriarchal in its social structure.

There is evidence to show that the African slave or his descendants in Brazil, when paternally treated by a master whose social and cultural superiority they accepted, were more or less resigned to their status. The exceptions seem to have been rare. The Negro with

---

[2] Koster: Op. cit., p. 443.

whom Saint-Hilaire talked in Minas Gerais, and who told the Frenchman that he was satisfied with his life as a slave,[3] would seem to have been representative or typical of the slaves of his epoch, that is to say, those who received fatherly treatment at the hands of their masters.

Koster seems entirely correct when he remarks that, in contrast to those persons who made the accumulation of wealth their principal aim, the Brazilians of old stock who owned land and slaves showed themselves free of that "avaricious spirit that works a man or a brute animal until it is unfit for farther service, without any regard to the well-being of the creature, which is thus treated as mere machine, as if it was formed of wood or iron . . ."[4]

The decline of the personal relationship between masters and slaves was mainly responsible for the dissatisfaction of the majority of Africans or their descendants in Brazil with their status as slaves and bondsmen. This, which began when the early sugar mills were expanded into large factories, with hundreds and not merely dozens of slave workers, was accentuated by the development of the mines and, in the nineteenth century, by the frequent sale of slaves from Bahía and the northeast to the coffee plantations of the South or the rubber groves of the far North, where they were exploited under a system of absentee-landlordism or by men trying to get rich quickly. Negroes, who had felt themselves members of the family of the Big House—some of them had been born on the plantation—and who were accustomed to a patriarchal way of living, when sold in this way to strange masters felt themselves reduced to the state of chattels or animals. It was natural that in their new surroundings they should behave like all strangers, all the uprooted—like newly arrived Africans, or the Europeans themselves who were not yet adjusted to the Brazilian milieu, or the white or near-white Brazilians of the North in their early years in the southern provinces—for whom it is easier to fall into crime—stealing, revolt, insurrection—than for those who remain in the place where they were born or raised. This explains the frequent insurrections of Negroes brought in from the

[3] A. Saint-Hilaire: *Voyages dan l'Intérieur du Brésil. Partie I. Les Provinces de Rio de Janeiro et de Minas Geraes*, I (Paris, 1830), pp. 98–9.

[4] Koster: Op. cit., p. 390.

North to the province of São Paulo, and also the fact that the slaves who rebelled against their masters in the North were nearly always African-born Negroes—mainly from areas which had come under Mohammedan influence—and not creoles or "Brazilians."

When the Frenchman Charles Wiener was in Rio de Janeiro, after the importation of African slaves had been forbidden, he was amazed at the traffic in human beings that went on. A man was bought or sold just as animals were bought and sold, horses or sheep, ox or dog.[5] Naturally, the more frequent these sales of slaves, many of them native-born, the more difficult it became to maintain the system of master-slave relation as a relation between persons. It was living in the house, plantation, or ranch, coming to feel affection for a family or a master, that made of the slave a person of the household, one of the family, a member of the "patriarchal co-operative" to which the "inhabitant of Florida" referred. When it was not easy to sell or trade the slave as an object, an animal, then he was offered as a mere article of barter, as was the case of many a slave in Salvador who belonged to some merchant alien to the patriarchalism of the old plantation houses. Merchants who advertised that they would exchange slaves for "dried beef from Montevideo" or "onions from Porto Alegre," or "quality coral."

The thing that shocked more perceptive observers than Wiener in the second half of the nineteenth century was the fact that slaves took over the work not so much of horses or oxen, which were being superseded in a number of their duties, but of machines, which the patriarchal and slave-based economy of the Empire continued to ignore. In the first half of the century, Walsh was astonished at the limited use of machines and even animals in Brazil, where everything was still done by slave labor; pointing out, however, that many Brazilians were eager to learn about or own mechanical inventions employed in Western Europe, to which they attributed the superiority of the Northern Europeans.[6]

Mawe, visiting the plantation of Captain Ferreira in Morro Quei-mado in Rio de Janeiro, was amazed at the old-fashioned equipment of the sugar mill and distillery. The Englishman told the captain that the furnaces of the distillery could not be worse, to which the cap-

[5] Charles Wiener: *333 Jours au Brésil* (Paris, n.d.), p. 23.
[6] Walsh: Op. cit., II, p. 78.

tain answered that there were none better in the neighborhood.[7] The fact was, as the Englishman could see for himself, that white plantation owners such as Captain Ferreira left all the care of the machines in the hands of Negroes, who knew nothing about running them. When Mawe tried to convince the distillery foreman, who was a Negro, that he was wasting a vast amount of fuel and that the unpalatable flavor of the rum produced at Morro Queimado could be improved, the Negro laughed, certain that, as he had learned the process from an old distiller, there was no better way of making it, and showing complete indifference to the problem of wasting or saving fuel. The Englishman reached the conclusion that, as the owners were uninterested in introducing mechanical improvements in their establishments and homes, it was impossible for Brazil to change its old ways. And these ways could be summed up as the least possible use of the machine and the maximum use of the slave, with a little help from the ox or the mule.

Plantation, sugar-mill, ranch owners, even the residents of city dwellings were averse to technical improvements in their business enterprises or their homes. "This aversion to improvement I have often observed among the inhabitants of Brazil," says Mawe, attributing the fact to the dependence on Negro or slave which characterized the entire industrial structure of the country, and not merely agriculture: the factory of tiles as well as that of sugar, the soap factory as well as the mine. Nor was the Negro, in his slave capacity, as a rule interested in mechanical improvements, which he felt would increase, if not his work, his worries and responsibilities. Walsh made a similar observation some years later about a grist mill he saw on a ranch, an antiquated and inefficient device which wasted water. His diagnosis was: ". . . It is one of the effects of slavery."[8]

This explains why, after the foreign technician or workman, the free Negro or mulatto of the city was our most enthusiastic advocate of mechanization. He perceived in his mastery of the machine a way of bettering his social position, of improving his status, approaching that of the foreign technician or mechanic, and making himself necessary to the native whites through his knowledge of those contrap-

---

[7] John Mawe: *Travels in the Interior of Brazil* (Philadelphia, 1812), p. 191.
[8] Walsh: Op. cit., II, p. 40.

tions, which masters and slaves avoided familiarizing themselves with, fearing that they might upset the routine of their life and work, their system of patriarchal relationship.

Walsh observed in Minas Gerais that the entry of a considerable number of foreigners, mostly English, as mining technicians and workers, in a country where the preponderance of blacks was becoming, according to him, "alarming," was an important event, and its importance grew as the newcomers increased. For the highly perfected instruments of every kind which these white men brought in, the machines they set running, their great manual skill as machine operators, the lightening of labor effected by the machines they governed were "invaluable lessons for the natives." [9] The English priest had already observed that in the interior, and not only in the cities, there were many who believed that the English had secret, even magic methods of discovering wealth that the Brazilians were incapable of coming upon. They were of the opinion that the English machines could go so far as to move rivers from the plains to the mountains, and "other miraculous wonders." [1]

Mawe, struck by "the apathy of the inhabitants" of Minas Gerais, had already thought of the advantages of introducing among them English methods of caring for the land and livestock. He believed that the example of one ranch run in English fashion would do much to arouse the people from their sluggishness.[2] The same idea occurred to him as he went through Santa Catarina: a land which could have become a "perfect paradise" in the hands of the English. And in Curitiba what impressed him most was to see a region capable of producing wheat of the finest quality used like the lands of the North for raising manioc, inferior in food value to wheat. He attributed this to the fact that flour calls for a series of mechanized operations, including mills and ovens, whereas manioc, when ripe, can be converted into meal in half an hour, without any machine processes being involved.

The technical backwardness of mining (which in certain areas conferred upon the miner, like the sugar, coffee, cotton plantation on their owners in others, a superior social standing than that attained by a farmer cultivating cereals or vegetables, which was known as "or-

---

[9] Ibid., II, p. 213.   [1] Ibid., II, p. 131.   [2] Mawe: Op. cit., p. 217.

dinary farming,") was also apparent in the early years of the nineteenth century. Mawe presented Captain Ferreira with a design for a machine for washing gravel, which was superior to that in general use in the colony. And besides trying to teach the people of the interior advanced methods of making butter and cheese, he impressed many of the farmers with the English saddle he used in his travels about Brazil, and which was new to them. Mawe remarked that the introduction of sidesaddles for ladies was changing the habits of the women of the upper classes, who before had never gone out except to mass, and then in curtained sedan chairs, and were now taking to the healthy custom of horseback riding.[3]

Koster observed on his two trips to Pernambuco, the first in 1808 and the second in 1811, that "the major part of the best mechanics . . . are of mixed blood."[4] Undoubtedly a number of these were mechanics of the new type, that is to say, machinists whose numbers were growing quickly in that area, for Pernambuco was one of the first areas in Brazil where English machine shops and foundries were set up with European superintendents and many of the workmen European, too. Machine shops similar to those which began to flourish alongside the mining enterprises of Minas Gerais and, earlier, in Rio Grande do Sul and São Paulo. These European technicians and workmen gradually transmitted their knowledge of machines, instruments, gadgets, new inventions, to their Negro and, especially, their mixed-blood assistants. These were intelligent and anxious for social advancement. This took place both in Minas Gerais and in Pernambuco, which were probably the two main centers of the social and technical revolution in Brazil during the early decades of the nineteenth century.

It also took place in Rio de Janeiro, another area where this revolution had powerful effects, changing ways of living and relations between classes and races, between masters and servants, between men and animals. Debret, who was living in the capital of Brazil at this time, observed that it was what he called the *classe mulâtre* which furnished the majority of skilled workmen. The Frenchman anticipated other observers in pointing out the fact that it was, in the main, Brazilians of this "mulatto class" who most quickly learned

---

[3] Ibid., p. 370.   [4] Koster: Op. cit., p. 393.

from the new European workmen their techniques and skills. The colored apprentices of French and German shoemakers in Rio de Janeiro soon became "rivals of their masters." [5] Colored women quickly picked up from French designers and dressmakers for whom they worked not only their techniques, but also their manners, becoming in turn sought-after designers and dressmakers.

Debret recalls that a number of French technicians, on their return to France, set free the most skilled of their slaves as well as Negro women who had served them as domestics. And he goes on to say that, "trained with care and kindness as workmen and servants, these Negroes, upon receiving their freedom, were sought out and hired by the whites." Certain mulatto women even became mistresses of mansions, when their lovers were successful at their trade.

If the knowledge of the new machines and techniques increased the esteem in which the Negroes and mulattoes, to whom these techniques were transmitted by European workmen, were held, it also heightened the prestige of such Europeans, often making possible a union between them and families which had achieved aristocratic standing as owners of lands, slaves, or mines. An aristocracy which was not always based on the purity of the European racial strain, though they were nearly always white, near white, or with an admixture of Indian blood.

Burton in the second half of the nineteenth century observed that in Minas Gerais workmen or mere clerks of English mining companies established there since the early years of the century, persons of humble origins, had been marrying into some of the "first families" of the region. This led him to the conclusion that in a democratic empire such as Brazil all whites were equal. The color of the skin constituted of itself, in the presence of "an inferior race" or "a serving caste," a kind of aristocracy: the aristocracy of the whites. And this aristocracy or caste offered no real barriers to an Englishman, even if only a workman or clerk.

It is possible that in certain cases the parents of the daughters of leading families, or the girls themselves, saw in these fair-skinned Europeans the necessary guarantee against the nightmare of a

---

[5] Jean Baptiste Debret: *Voyage Pittoresque et Historique au Brésil* . . . *1816–1831*, II (Paris, 1834–9), p. 19.

"throwback" child—whose color might reveal the presence of an African strain introduced into the blood stream by some Negro or mulatto woman, beautiful or rich, whom a remote ancestor had married, some poor white seeking a fortune, or some Portuguese who had succumbed to the charms of a dark Venus. For Minas Gerais was at the time a province that was known for the admixture of African blood in a large part of its inhabitants, the result, perhaps, of the isolation in which it had lived during the eighteenth century, settled almost exclusively by unmarried or celibate Europeans who found themselves obliged to take colored women. This situation was repeated in the nineteenth century in an area similar to Minas—Goiás—when European adventurers and Brazilian *bandeirantes* began to flock there in search of gold. "All the mineowners," wrote Cunha Mattos, "were white Americans or Europeans, unmarried, and only rarely did a woman of their own color enter the province . . . Some of these unmarried men had Negro or Indian slave women in their houses in whom they begat children . . ." And when the whites left after amassing wealth, among the half-breeds who remained behind and inherited part of their property, a number distinguished themselves and even became rich.[6]

It seemed to Burton that throughout the interior of Brazil, and in the small cities, it was easy for the European technician or workman, "whatever be his speciality or trick," to make a brilliant career for himself, something that was becoming more difficult in the large cities as a result of the antipathy that was growing up there toward foreign artisans and businessmen. What happened was that, in the large cities, a considerable number of native-born Brazilians or mulattoes, who had learned to operate machines or engines, began to feel that they alone were entitled to utilize the new techniques. They came to look upon the foreign technicians as intruders who had no right to compete with them. They, the free mulattoes, should be the only machinists, the exclusive managers of the factories, the dark St. Georges of the horsepower.

If in the beginning there was a reluctance on the part of the poor, free Brazilians—mixed bloods, for the most part—to work in the ma-

---

[6] Cunha Mattos: "Corografia Historica da Provincia de Goiás," *Rev. Inst. Hist. Geog. Br.*, XXXVII (Rio de Janeiro, 1874), pp. 299–301.

chine shops and the maintenance services of the first railroads built in
Brazil, it was not long before they were intensely enthusiastic about
such work, which came to employ as many of them as the mines and
foundries. After years as superintendent of a railroad, J. J. Aubertin
pointed out that he had no grounds for complaint about the lack of
Brazilian workers, to whom the railroad afforded "livelihood and
independence." [7] Burton had already pointed out that the mines and
railroads were creating "a race of skilled and practiced hands . . ." [8]
And also a new stratum of society: that of free men, held in esteem
because they knew how to manipulate or control machines or motors
imported from Europe. Machines which replaced the slow work of
animals and slaves with a power, speed, and return which animals and
slaves could not attain.

This new type of man and this new race of mechanics was not the
product of mines and railroads alone; the foundries had a share in it.
And besides the foundries, those industrial activities which, after in-
stalling the machines, needed the machinists, that is to say, the new
kind of mechanic or expert. At first, these were foreigners, but it
was not long before many were Brazilians, mestizos and free Negroes, some of whom became highly skilled in difficult specialties and
to many of whom this brought the desired social advancement.

The technical revolution brought about by the introduction of European machines in the cities, the mines, and the plantations was soon
followed by a social revolution as the result of the new values represented by technicians, machinists, the new type of mechanic, and the
changed relations between the landholder and the technician or machinist, now a free man. In many cases the technician or machinist
took on the role of prime minister in a monarchy no longer absolute,
but limited or constitutional, a prime minister who diminished the
once all-powerful figure of the owner of lands and the master of
slaves.

Now things were different. The machine was detracting from the
importance of slave as well as master, of white landholder and black

---

[7] J. J. Aubertin: *Eleven Days' Journey in the Province of São Paulo*
(London, 1866), p. 6.

[8] Richard F. Burton: *Explorations of the Highlands of the Brazil*, I (London, 1869), pp. 262–7.

worker. And it was enhancing the status of the mestizo, the mulatto, the half-breed, as well as the poor white, whose sole patrimony or claim to standing was his technical skill, essential to the landowners, the factory owners, the community. The machine contributed to making a middle class of a middle race.

Advertisements of the new machinery which began to appear in the colonial newspapers of Brazil, and quickly multiplied in those of the Empire, were proclaiming from the housetops not only the technical, but the social revolution which was taking place. Never did a revolution come about so noisily, in sight of everyone, as this of Brazil in the first half of the nineteenth century. These advertisements shook to its foundations the entire slave-based patriarchal system. For the triumph of the machine represented the ruin of this system.

The man or youth who opened the pages of the *Gazeta do Rio de Janeiro* in the days of Dom João found the most fascinating section that of the advertisements: advertisements of machines, of carriages whose speed was combined with durability; of surgeon's instruments, cabinetmaker's tools, furnaces, boilers, plows. If during its earlier years the *Gazeta* had carried mainly advertisements of china and fabrics, butter and preserves, during this second phase machinery and pianos took priority. The carriages themselves departed more and more in manufacture and style from the palanquins and litters to become with each passing day "trains," "machines," mechanical or engineering products which, to the comfort and at times luxury of their velvet upholstery and silver lamps, added the ability to move with great speed over streets and roads.

The passion for speed took such hold of Brazilians that some of them seemed possessed of the devil. This explains the sensation caused in still drowsily colonial Rio de Janeiro by the appearance of Baron Charles de Drais with his machine "known as the Draiscene, or Velocipede." It was put through its paces before Their Royal Highnesses at the royal country house of Bôa Vista and, according to the *Diario do Rio de Janeiro*, "the baron, after having demonstrated the machine, had the satisfaction of being complimented by Their Royal Highnesses on his useful and skillful invention." According to the same newspaper, the new machine resembled a horse: "It looks like a wooden horse set upon two wheels, which are turned by the feet of the rider . . . When driven over flat dry roads, it can make nearly four leagues an hour, the same speed as a galloping horse. When going downhill, its speed exceeds that of a horse going full tilt." [9]

The light English carriage was a novelty which had the same effect on many Brazilians as a new toy on a child. Rio de Janeiro soon became famous for the speed with which, the horses at full gallop, these vehicles dashed through the streets, jolting and bumping in spite of the shock-absorbing springs. Exhibitionism or snobbishness, perhaps, on the part of the owners accustomed to rattletraps or poky palanquins, who suddenly found themselves the possessors of carriages which proclaimed their superior station. And the slaves or Negroes elevated to the post of coachman and wearing a high hat, like gentlemen of position, in all probability took advantage of the power now in their hands—wheels, whip, high hat, their preeminence over the crowds in their high coachman's seat, which was like a throne for this new type of ruffian. In the slave hierarchy the coachman came to occupy one of the most important categories.

Other novelties, besides the new swift carriages, were being advertised. Machines of every sort, including vehicles offered for sale with the necessary accompaniment of slaves and horses, as can be seen from an advertisement in the February 4, 1822, edition of the *Diario do Rio de Janeiro.* "For Sale: carriage with horse and skilled Negro driver." There were horses especially trained for carriage use, and slaves to handle horse and carriage, who could also act as butler. "A good gentleman's butler, who can be used as a carriage footman or coachman," states an advertisement in the same newspaper for March 8, 1822. And on March 15, 1825: "Young good-looking Negro . . . who knows how to handle horses and is a well-trained driver."

On January 24, 1818, Pedro José Bernardes advertised for sale, not carriages or coaches, but "a still, recently arrived from London," which called for experienced slaves to handle it. It was a type of apparatus already known in Brazil, "where several of the same kind have been installed and have proved of great use and value to their owners because of their excellent qualities."

---

[9] *Diario do Rio de Janeiro,* June 26, 1822.

On August 21, 1819, it was João Gilmour who advertised in the *Gazeta do Rio de Janeiro* that he had received from London milling machines "for the manufacture of sugar, distilling, and any other effect," in addition to having himself brought in "two complete milling machines of the latest type, to grind cane, and had set one of them up on the plantation of the Order, where anyone interested in engineering may see it; and he is prepared to take careful note of orders for milling or other machinery, and transmit them to the factory in London." And on December 8 of the same year the *Gazeta* informed its readers that "Thomas Reid, an Englishman," recently arrived from Jamaica to "improve the furnaces for boiling syrup," is ready "to undertake this change-over at once, which will make it possible for them to be fueled with bagasse or wood firing one boiler, which will heat all the others." For further details, "address the house of Ewing and Hudson, Englishmen, 3 Rua dos Pescadores."

On January 1, 1820, Ladislau do Espirito Santo was advertising "an excellent lightning rod, complete with fixtures . . . all of bronze"; and on July 12 of the same year, Costa Guimarães, at 13 Rua do Cano, "wished to make known that he had the following articles: sugar mills of different sizes, the most complete and latest models, boilers, vats, doors for mill and distillery furnaces, kettles of different sizes with covers, grates and doors for kitchen stoves which are economical of fuel and conducive to the health of cooks, ovens of different sizes that operate with the heat of the stove, iron wheels for hand carts, iron ovens to roast manioc meal, and an inexpensive portable steam stove which can also be used for baking." On August 5, Jackson and Richardson announced the arrival, by the ship *Regente* from London," of a large assortment of saddles, bridles, etc., with all appurtenances, military and other, carriage lanterns and harness of superior quality for one or four horses; binoculars; mathematical-instrument kits, combs, razors." And the issue of the *Gazeta* for November 11, 1820, advertised "opera glasses" and "geographical maps." For the most part, these were articles designed for the residents of city mansions, more ready, as a rule, than the plantation owners of the interior to adopt English kitchen stoves, iron wheels for hand carts, fine harness, machines for milling wheat, corn, manioc, and swift-moving coaches and carriages, which, driven by skilled slaves and drawn by trained animals, reduced the number of slaves needed in the city and eliminated the need for pestle and mortar and the rustic fireplace.

Ignacio Alvares Pinto de Almeida took the initiative in organizing an exposition of machinery designed to arouse the people of Rio de Janeiro to the importance of replacing slave and beast of burden by the machine, "to promote national industry." And in keeping with these ideas, he stated in the *Diario do Rio de Janeiro* [1] that, "ardently desirous of seeing the national industry of this United Kingdom stimulated . . . with the permission of His Majesty . . . I am opening an annual subscription whose product will be used for the purchase of machines or models to be put on display so they can be copied and employed for the promotion of the national industry of this United Kingdom, where unfortunately the arms of slaves are almost the only machines known and employed, which are expensive, unreliable, and also contrary to the principles of Christian humanity . . ." Among the machines to be put on display was "one for winnowing grain without having to depend on the state of the weather" and "a machine for grating, pressing, and bolting manioc, all in one operation . . ."

In 1828, a typical year in the technical, social, and not merely commercial or economic revolution Brazil had been undergoing since 1808, our main exports were rum or sugar-cane brandy, cotton from Minas Novas and Minas Gerais, indigo, rice from Santos and its surrounding area, sugar from Campos and Santos, horsehair, coffee, meat, rope, horn, hides, tallow from Rio Grande, rosewood, ipecac, shoe leather, tobacco, tapioca. We were importing in large quantities steel, iron, copper, lead in bars or in the form of hawsers, anchors, bullets, wire, harness, carriages, surgical instruments, door locks, candlesticks, copper roofing, sheet tin, nails, machinery, vats, furnaces, clocks, stoves, coal.

It was not long before we were receiving steamboats, complete or ready to be assembled. And by the middle of the century, steel rails, locomotives, railroad cars. Then came the mains: water piped into the houses; sewers to carry off the waste to the sea or rivers. Sanitary fixtures in the houses. Gas pipes.

---

[1] Idem., September 15, 1821.

This marked the end of the public fountain, of water brought in by slaves, of night soil carried away by slaves, of streets illuminated by oil, when not by private citizens preceded by slaves carrying lanterns or torches. A technical revolution which affected not only the economy but the social and cultural structure of Brazil. Even the landscape, especially in the area of mansion and shanty.

The sugar industry itself and the social and cultural patterns based on it and on cane growing—the area, par excellence, of the several-storied Big Houses and the brick slave quarters like that of the Salgado plantation in Pernambuco—underwent considerable changes as the result of the substitution of horse-drawn sweeps by steam engines, and of wood by bagasse for stoking the furnaces, even though the old-type sugar industry and cane raising did everything it could to hold out against the social consequences of such changes. Normally, under climatic conditions more favorable to whites than those of northern Brazil, and given land or property laws less favorable to the almost feudal latifundia, the technical changes would have led to a greater substitution of slave labor by that of free men, and even the introduction—which was practically non-existent in the sugar area—of European settlers as technicians and skilled laborers.[2] And even to co-operative associations of sugar-cane producers around the new mills—later known as *centrales*—for the purpose of increasing the yield and improving the quality of the crop. Apparatus or machinery to reduce the cost of milling to a minimum, thus curtailing the number of slaves and animals required.[3]

"The introduction of machines" and "the encouragement of settlers" were considered by Henrique Jorge Rebello, in a report published in 1836, inseparable, "the foundations on which Brazil should erect its new edifice of national prosperity." In his opinion, the main concern of a country deeply preoccupied over the importation of African slaves should be to "bring in machines to make up for the

[2] See G. E. Fairbanks: *Observações sobre o Commercio do Assucar e o Estado presente desta Industria en Varios Paizes, etc.* (Bahía, 1847). Also F. de P. Candido: *Clamores da Agricultura no Brasil e Indicação de Meios Facílimos de Leva-la Rapidamente a Prosperidade* (Rio de Janeiro, 1859); and J. G. de Morães Navarro: *Discurso sobre o Melhoramento da Economia Rustica do Brasil* (Lisbon, 1799).

[3] Antonio Gomes de Matto: *Esboço de Um Manual Para os Fazendeiros do Açucar* (Rio de Janeiro, 1882).

lack of manpower." [4] Dom Fernando José de Portugal reached the same conclusion at the end of the eighteenth century. In a letter of March 28, 1798, to Dom Rodrigo de Sousa Coutinho, he recommended the use in Bahía of oxen and plows to work the land, and, with a view to saving wood, "burning the cane refuse after it had been ground, as the English and French do in the Antilles," [5] in the furnaces.

For "the planter who needs a hundred Africans for his agricultural activities can dispense with sixty of them by the installation of machines." [6] And by bringing in German and Swiss settlers and settlers "from other civilized countries that can spare them, our civilization would prosper," as it was already doing in the far South and in São Paulo. In the latter province, "the cultivation of the potato commonly known as the English potato" has, thanks to the European colonists, reached a high degree of perfection, sufficient to supply the needs of the population of that province, and with a surplus for export to Minas Gerais, Goiás, and Rio de Janeiro. [7]

But it was not only the economic effects of this change of population that should interest the new Empire. There were the social and cultural consequences of the immigration of Europeans from technically advanced nations, whose importance could be seen in the new techniques of production and transportation they brought to Brazil. For example: "wagons with axle-mounted wheels which make possible the hauling of many hundredweight of merchandise of different kinds by one yoke of oxen, whereas four or six were formerly needed." Another example: "improved methods of making charcoal, which have been brought to such perfection that São Paulo, with a single layer of good immigrants from Northern Europe upon the half-breed Indian and white population, . . . could provide charcoal for the military trains, in addition to abundantly supplying its own fuel needs. [8] Not to mention the manufacture of good cheese and

---

[4] Henrique Jorge Rebello: *Memoria e Considerações sobre a População do Brasil* (Bahía, 1836), p. 43.

[5] Ms. Arquivo Historico Colonial, Lisbon, IV, 18, 170.

[6] Rebello: Op. cit., p. 36.

[7] Ibid.

[8] Ibid., p. 39.

butter, with which it has "on many occasions supplied the country when the imported product was not available." [9]

Similar advantages had been reaped in other areas to which Northern Europeans had come, some of them of the type classified as "bourgeois" by a Portuguese politician or economist sent out to Brazil in the seventeenth century to report on the state of the colonial economy. [1]

Ferdinand Denis [2] refers to the considerable immigration, which he calls Occidental, that is to say, of non-Iberian origin, which by the early nineteenth century was already making itself felt: French, English, Swiss, Germans, Irish, Swedes, Danes, Russians. Not all of them, to be sure, of bourgeois or industrial type. But the most influential were; and we owe to them the introduction of many industrial and technical values, as well as the bourgeois influence on the manners and customs of the wealthy or genteel city residents and even the plantation owners who had closer contacts with the cities. By 1830 Denis was of the opinion that the drawing room of an upper-class home in Rio de Janeiro or Bahía differed very little from its Parisian counterpart. And he looked upon the imitation by Brazilians of English manners as prejudicial to "the expression or development of the natural inclinations of a meridional people," going so far as to rejoice —as did Debret and other Europeans of the period who did not allow their artistic sensibilities to be swayed by the economic interests of French or English imperialism—over the fact that there were still people who clung to their old habits: the traditional eating habits which had been supplanted among the wealthy by the French or Italian cuisine; the rush mats plaited by Negroes; Indian hammocks; old-fashioned sofas upholstered in cowhide; lace made by the ladies, as in the sixteenth century; the women's way of walking—"completely oriental," he calls it—which the French dancing masters had not yet succeeded in changing.

It must not be assumed that all enlightened Brazilians of the first half of the nineteenth century were agreed that it was in the best interests of Brazil to substitute slave labor by machine cogs, the flesh

---

[9] Ibid.

[1] Ms. in Mss. Section, National Library of Rio de Janeiro, I, 32G, No. 17.

[2] Ferdinand Denis: *Brésil* (Paris, 1839).

and blood horse by the so-called iron horse, the colored farmer or
workman by the white. At the same time that Rebello's report appeared in Bahía, one was published in Rio de Janeiro entitled "Memoria sobre o Commercio dos Escravos em que se Pretende Mostrar
que Este Trafico he para Elles antes hum Bem do que hum Mal,
Escripta por XXX. Natural dos Campos dos Goitacazes." (*Considerations on the Slave Trade Designed to Show That This Trade Is to the
Slaves' Benefit Rather Than Their Harm*, written by XXX, an inhabitant of the countryside of Goitacá.) "Without slavery, what
would become of America's export trade?" asked the defender of
slavery. "Who would work the mines? the fields? carry on the coastwise trade?" And touching on the point under consideration here: "It
is generally held that the introduction of machines in Brazil would do
away with the need for so much manpower. In industrialized countries I have no doubt that machines reduce considerably the number
of workers; but the same does not hold true of countries that raise
sugar or coffee. For instance, the machines best adapted to sugar
mills are those of steam or water power; to provide for the steady
operation of such mills, the services of at least two hundred workers
are required; who is the owner in our present state of population who
can hire two hundred workmen for his mill? Even supposing it were
possible to find that number, he could not get them for less than
twenty thousand milreis a month, which adds up to forty-eight hundred thousand milreis annually. Just for the sake of argument, let us
suppose that he could hire them for half that amount, twenty-four
hundred thousand; this, together with the minimum expense of running such a mill, would ruin the most profitable and after the first
year make it impossible for it to continue, and it would collapse."
This advocate of slavery conceded the need for bringing in settlers.
But for purely economic reasons: ". . . so that there may be a rapid
increase in our population, for only in this way will wages drop, and
the workers can then be employed in our mills and fields, for certain
services, at least." [3] The possibility did not occur to him of various
producers of cane utilizing a central mill, from which all would bene-

---

[3] See *Memorias sobre o Commercio dos Escravos* (Rio de Janeiro, 1838),
p. 9.

fit thanks to its powerful machinery and its saving of manpower. Nor the need for farmers to learn better and cheaper methods of production from the Northern Europeans, not only cheaper but less harmful to the health of the people.

For one of the most important discoveries of the hygienists of Brazil of the early nineteenth century was that "the destruction of the vegetation of the mangrove swamps" and "the widespread burning-over of the land" was affecting to an alarming degree the conditions of human life. Not so much around the Big House and slave quarters of plantations and ranches, which kept pushing forward into the virgin forest, leaving behind the ravished and impoverished land, as in the cities of the interior close to the old or deserted plantations.

This devastation must have been responsible in large measure for epidemics and diseases previously unknown, such as the so-called Macacú epidemic in Rio de Janeiro in 1828, which spread to Magé, Guapí, Porto de Estrela, Pilar, Iguacú, and Irajá.[4] The health official assigned to study it made an intelligent ecological investigation, reaching the conclusion that the changes that area had undergone as a result of the ruthless exploitation of the land had contributed to rendering it unhealthy almost to the point of making it uninhabitable.

But it was not only the hygienists; men who had made a study of plant life and agriculture, such as Theodoro Peckolt,[5] endeavored to draw the attention of Brazilians of the mid-nineteenth century to the dangers of the wholesale clearing of woodland, with the "natural consequence of increasing the heat of the climate and lowering the rainfall." In Peckolt's opinion, "the fundamental reason for this as for so many other errors was slavery." And he went on to say: "Bearing in mind the value of the land, the capital employed in the purchase of slaves, in feeding and clothing them, and the inevitable losses from disease, death, etc., the return is small, in spite of the fertility of the land. For that reason, the planter endeavors to get all he can out of it as quickly as possible; he lacks the necessary labor force to manure it

---

[4] José Pereira do Rego: *Esboço Historico das Epidemias que tem Grassado na Cidade do Rio de Janeiro desde 1830 a 1870* (Rio de Janeiro, 1872).

[5] Theodoro Peckolt: *Historia das Plantas Alimentares e de Gozo do Brasil, Contendo Generalidades sobre o Agricultura do Brasil* (Rio de Janeiro, 1871).

properly, so he uses the system of burning it over; moreover, there is no lack of virgin forest for his needs, and those of his children and grandchildren."

The belief that coffee did well only on cleared forest land was responsible for making the climate of Rio de Janeiro what was known in the language of the time as "bastard," and the abandonment of the worn-out land by planters who went looking for new clearings left the defenseless population of cities and towns adjoining the deserted plantations exposed to epidemics and diseases fostered by the new climatic and soil conditions. Hence the deplorable sanitary conditions of the cities of the interior, which, once famous for their fine residences, quickly became ruined; famous at one time for the number of their grand pianos, they came to achieve a sad notoriety for their malignant fevers. This also explains the growing exodus of families from the cities of the interior to the provincial capitals and the Court, where they were obliged to change their former mansions for mean dwellings, and one-time owners of luxurious homes descended to the category of the "have-nots."

In spite of the badly laid-out streets and the lack of adequate drainage, Rio de Janeiro and the capitals of the wealthier provinces even in the first half of the nineteenth century were healthier than the small cities of the interior. This can be attributed, for the most part, to improvements in sanitation and provisioning, many of which were sponsored by the English and French interested in bringing to Brazil, together with their capital, their appliances, their machines, their water and sewer systems, their new methods of street paving and lighting of streets and houses, their superior manufacturing techniques. English capital especially played an important role in these urban changes. The Anglophile José da Silva Lisboa was justified in saying that "the improvement of the cities and the elegance and beauty of city buildings and country places" was due in large measure to the "active and extensive change that took place upon the establishment of trade relations between the English and Brazil." [6]

After 1808, and especially between 1835 and 1850, there was a great improvement and remarkable changes in sanitation and trans-

---

[6] José da Silva Lisboa: *Memoria dos Beneficios Politicos do Governo de El Rey Nosso Senhor D. João VI* (Rio de Janeiro, 1818).

portation, illumination and street planting in Rio de Janeiro, Recife, São Paulo, and even in Rio Grande, Pelotas, Porto Alegre, Belem. Salvador and Ouro Preto were slower in adopting certain of these improvements.

In Rio de Janeiro an effort was made to raise the level of the city, filling in the low and marshy areas. The streets began to be paved, and provisions for draining the rain water from the streets were made. New streets were opened, and new houses were built. The filling-in of the big mud flat known as Cidade Nova was begun. Water from Tijuca was piped in to supply the needs of the population, which was growing not only as a result of foreign immigration, on the increase since 1808, but also through the clandestine introduction of slaves. Gas mains were laid. The urban area expanded. Until 1830 the city's population had been crowded into a perimeter marked by a line which, beginning at one point of the shore, Praia Formosa, and following the streets of Aterrado and São Cristovão, ended at the Praia do Botafogo, with many vacant lots in streets which half a century later would become central arteries.[7]

A step which Pereira Rego pointed out as one of the most urgent for Rio de Janeiro—and the other large cities of Brazil—was taken in the first half of the century, "in the interests of mankind and science": "doing away with burials in the churches, transferring them to the Misericordia Cemetery, thanks to the activity and determination of Councilman José Clemente Pereira." The capital of Bahía took similar measures; among its ordinances for June 17, 1844, there is one absolutely forbidding "burial in churches or their environs."

In the Court, prisoners were transferred from the Calabouço to the House of Correction, "sparing the center of the city the deplorable sight of half-naked and shackled men going about the streets," some of whom were punished in public: scourged with whips of four or five strips of braided leather dipped in sand. Another great change, looked upon as equally important for public health as well as for the

[7] See José de Sousa Azevedo Pizarro Araujo: *Memorias Historicas do Rio de Janeiro* (Rio de Janeiro, 1820–2); C. Schlichthorst: *Rio de Janeiro wie es ist* (Hanover, 1829); Charles Hanbury: *Limpeza da Cidade do Rio de Janeiro* (Rio de Janeiro, 1854); Pereira Rego: *Memoria Historica das Epidemias de Febre amarela e Cólera-morbo* (Rio de Janeiro, 1873).

personal safety of the inhabitants of the capital, was the transfer of the slaughterhouse from Praia de Santa Luzia to a more remote spot. There had been a succession of "disagreeable incidents of runaway animals" racing madly through the city streets, their terror increased by the sight of machines as strange to them as to the backwoodsmen. The very horses which came from the country got out of control amidst the city hubbub, with the iron trains, the steam horses, the vehicles dashing through the streets. In Salvador, too, an ordinance of 1844 forbade "horses, cows, or sheep running loose in the streets," and they might be kept "only if fenced in." As for dangerous animals running about the streets, such as dogs who might have rabies and "attack people," they might be run "through by anybody and buried or thrown into the sea at their owner's expense . . ."

It is of maximum interest for the understanding of that transitional period which the first half of the nineteenth century represented for the main areas of our country to point out that various of the modifications our physical environment and institutions underwent were directly or indirectly connected with the end of the slave trade. With the abolition of the slave trade, the large cities had to resort to the use of machines or, at any rate, horses and dairy cows, for the needs of the rich city homes. For many years capital had been flowing into the cities without finding the necessary outlet. Business opportunities were limited, the movement of funds restricted. The greatest fortunes of the Empire were, to a large extent, in the hands of slave traders and had been used only for the purchase of slaves. With the discontinuance of the trade, such capital was freed for material improvements, especially in the capital.[8] Part of it went into urban construction, bringing to it what the hygienists of the day regarded as "better and more healthful conditions"; some into the development of transit systems; dairies to produce milk to take the place of the vanishing wet nurses; the mechanization of public or private services which had formerly depended on slave labor.

To be sure, the transition in the large cities, with their large slave population, to machine, factory, animal power, dairy cows, and urban development did not take place smoothly but with severe crises,[9]

[8] Charles Reybaud: *Le Brésil* (Paris, 1856), pp. 230–1.
[9] Victor Vianna: *O Banco do Brasil* (Rio de Janeiro, 1926).

which in areas such as Rio de Janeiro, Bahía, Pernambuco, and Maranhão affected society in its habits or ways of living, and not merely the Brazilian economy. The halting of the African slave trade was like a death blow—and not even the *coup de grâce*—to a form of economy and society that was already archaic, being both feudal and capitalist. This blow hit not only the capitalists, the traders in "living souls," and the still feudal landowners (for whom these "living souls" were life itself) but also the population of the cities, conditioned to a large extent by this same system, which for a long time had been breathing its last but was slow in giving up the ghost.

The mere transfer of capital formerly employed in slaves to the breeding and exploitation of livestock, a seemingly unimportant change whose dramatic repercussions on the social ecology of the Empire apparently escaped those who, like Victor Vianna, Roberto Simonsen, Affonso Arinos de Mello Franco, and Caio Prado Junior, have studied our economic or financial history, would of itself have produced a profound crisis. In 1858, in reply to the questionnaires which, by an Imperial order of October 9 of the previous year, had been sent out to the governors of the provinces in connection with the alarming scarcity of food supplies, the commission named by the governor of the province of Ceará to study the matter gave as its answer that the shortage of meat was due to drought and an outbreak of epizooty, but, above all, to "the existence of a powerful company in the province of Minas Gerais which for the last few years has been laying out large sums in the purchase of cattle in Piauí . . ."[1] The same thing was true of Rio Grande do Norte, according to a report from the president of that province to the Imperial government: ". . . The selling off of cattle from here to other markets."[2] And the identical phenomenon—the transfer of capital formerly employed in slaves to the purchase of animals for slaughter or hauling—was found in the province of Santa Catarina, whose president complained to the Imperial government about the "wan-

---

[1] *Relatorio Apresentado à Assambléia Legislativa no Segunda Sessão da Décima Legislatura* (Rio de Janeiro, 1858): "Parecer da Commissão encarregado . . . para consultar sobre as causas da carestia do generos alimenticios," p. 8.

[2] Op. cit.: *Informação do Rio Grande do Norte*, pp. 1–3.

dering life" a large part of the population was leading, lured by the "trade in mules and horses." [3]

This trade was, for the most part, with Rio de Janeiro, the Court, as was that of the "powerful company" of the province of Minas, seeking to supply the population of the metropolitan and neighboring areas with animals for meat, milk, and work, and employing for this purpose the capital formerly utilized in the importation of slaves from Africa for the benefit of the more feudally agrarian areas of the country. Thus an ecological, and not merely a technological, revolution was taking place: the transfer of capital from the sugar-producing North, which needed slaves for its still predominantly sugar and patriarchal economy, to the coffee-producing South, less patriarchal than commercial, in whose agrarian economy the substitution of the slave by the European immigrant was easier, as well as the substitution of the Negro by the machine, also European, in its urban economy.

The death blow to slavery by the legal prohibition of the slave trade was followed by another: the epidemic of cholera morbus, or Asiatic cholera, which swept like a Biblical plague through the slave quarters of plantations and ranches. And not only the slave quarters, but the shanties of Negroes and mulattoes in the vicinity of the city mansion, to the point where it seemed to some of the victims that it was a diabolical device of the whites to do away with the colored population.

But by way of biological, and not merely sociological, compensation, at about the same time that Asiatic cholera was ravaging the African and slave population, yellow fever made its appearance, specializing in the killing of Europeans or pure whites between the ages of sixteen and thirty, for the most part, of the better class. It was as though yellow fever had taken upon itself the task of delaying the victory over rural patriarchalism typified in men of over sixty who rarely caught the disease, by foreign capitalism or bourgeois techniques represented by foreigners who were still young: the English, French, Portuguese of city dwelling or shop, and an occasional renegade Brazilian. Or acting as a brake on the triumph of the

---

[3] Op. cit.: *Informação do Presidente de Santa Catarina*, p. 2.

liberalism of the young university graduates over the hidebound conservatism of the older men.

There are those who attribute to yellow fever the patriotic role of having protected the Empire from the cupidity of Europeans or Britons. The truth is that it would seem to have prevented the denationalization of Brazil as the result of too rapid a transfer of economic control from the hands of the slaveowners and the slave traders to the bankers and the dealers in iron or steam machinery. From the hands of the old men of the Big Houses to those of the young men of the city mansions.

Be this as it may, the fact is that under the stimulus of the two scourges hygenic and living conditions improved in the larger cities as well as in the slave quarters, in the Big Houses, and the ranches of the interior which had suffered not only the Asiatic plague but also the "white man's fever."

CHAPTER XI

THE RISE OF THE COLLEGE
GRADUATE AND THE MULATTO

IN APPRAISING the Brazil of Dom Pedro I, Dom Pedro II, and
Princess Isabel, the campaign for the abolition of slavery, the agita-
tion for the republic, the Brazil, also, of the young lady on the
verandah speaking the love language of fan, flower, or handkerchief
with the youth on the corner in high hat and frock coat, in all this,
one must take into account two great forces that were triumphantly
emerging, at times conjoined in one: the college graduate and the
mulatto.

From the closing days of the colony the college graduate ("Ba-
charal") and university graduate ("Doutor") and the mulatto had
come to symbolize elements of differentiation within a rural and
patriarchal society endeavoring to establish an equilibrium, or what
the modern sociologist would call an adjustment, between two
great opposed forces: the master and the slaves. The Big House with
its slave quarters had represented among us a veritable miracle of
adjustment, which the antagonism between mansion and shanty
came to perturb or shatter.

The urbanization of the Empire, with the ensuing shrinking of
so many spacious Big Houses into narrow city residences and later
into pinched chalets; the breaking up of so many slave quarters into

shanty towns, no longer of runaway slaves in the midst of the forest or on top of some remote hill, but of free Negroes or mulattoes within the city—a phenomenon of the year 1830 which grew with the abolition of slavery—made the old equilibrium well nigh impossible. The day of the almost absolute predominance of the slaveholders over all the other components of society, even over the viceroys themselves and the bishops, was passing.

The change in social values began to grow up around other elements: Europe, a bourgeois Europe, from which we were receiving new styles of living; tea, government by a cabinet, English beer, Clark's shoes, tinned crackers. And men's wearing apparel that was less showy, duller; a growing fondness for the theater, which was beginning to supplant the church; the four-wheeled carriage, which was substituting riding horse or palanquin; the top hat and parasol, which were taking the place of captain- or sergeant-major's sword of the old country squires. And these new values were becoming the emblems of authority of a new aristocracy, that of the city mansions. Of a new gentry, that of the professional men, the university graduates, perhaps more than that of the businessmen or industrialists. Of a new caste: that of owners of slaves and even of land too sophisticated to tolerate country life in its pristine rudeness.

These tendencies were incarnated principally in the university graduate, the legitimate—or illegitimate—son of the plantation or ranch owner who brought back new ideas from Europe—from Coimbra, Montpellier, Paris, England, Germany—where he had gone to study under the influence or at the suggestion of some liberal tutor or cosmopolitan-minded relative.

At times it was the sons of the late-come bourgeoisie of the cities who went to Europe to study. The sons or grandsons of "peddlers." With the prestige of an European education, they returned the social equals of the sons of the oldest and most important families of the landowning class. And not only their equals but often their superiors because of their better assimilation of European values, and their personal charm for the other sex, which the crossbreed, when eugenic, would seem to possess to a higher degree than the racially pure. Some of them were the natural sons of eminent white fathers and had inherited the small hands, well-shaped feet, and often the nose or lips of their well-born parent.

The rise of the white college graduate especially in the field of politics was rapid, and, in general, in the social. The reign of Pedro II marked the beginning—among other changes—of "juridical romanticism." Until that time, Brazil had been governed more by the good judgment of its elder citizens than by the juridical concepts of the young men. With Pedro II, the tradition or mystique of age was almost completely shattered. A mystique or tradition already undermined, as we have seen, by certain youthful captains-general sent out by the mother country during the colonial period almost as a taunt or challenge to the old local authorities. But it was under Pedro II that the new mystique—that of the young college or university graduate particularly the "Bacharel," or "Doutor" in jurisprudence—became the order of the day.

The university or college graduates who were returning from Coimbra, Paris, Germany, Montpellier, Edinburgh, and later from Olinda, São Paulo, Bahía, Rio de Janeiro, most of whom had studied law or medicine, a few philosophy or mathematics, and all of them bringing in with the enthusiasm of their twenty years the latest ideas of England and the latest fashions of France, came to emphasize, among their plantation fathers and grandfathers, not only the lack of prestige of the patriarchal era but its rustic backwardness. It was natural that the second Emperor, in his early years of rule a pedantic child presiding with a certain air of superiority over cabinets of old men, some having Indian blood, and even African, often profoundly sensible countrymen but lacking French culture and with only the smattering of Latin they had learned to the tune of ferule or quince switch, should have attracted, as he did, the new university graduates, not only because of the solidarity of youth, but also because of the solidarity of European academic culture. For there was no greater academician in our country than Pedro II. Nor anyone less native and more European. His reign was the reign of the college graduates.

Dom Romualdo de Seixas—a Bishop—recalls in his memoirs that "a prominent deputy, who is today a senator of the realm," suggested that there be sent out to Pará, for the purpose of more closely incorporating that predominantly Amerindian province of the far North into the Imperial system, "meat, meal, and university or college graduates." And Dom Romualdo goes on to say: "The proposed measure seemed like a witty sally; but in thinking it over, it becomes apparent that the first two proposals were those best designed to please those peoples oppressed by hunger and poverty, and the third equally valuable because of the magic virtue vested in anyone holding a university degree, which transforms those lucky enough to have it into human encyclopedias qualified for everything." [1]

It would hardly be an exaggeration to say of Dom Pedro II that he had more confidence in the law graduates who administered the provinces according to the precepts of law and justice than in giving meat and meal to the poor. Such aid was momentary and settled nothing.

But the college graduate (in keeping with a Brazilian and Portuguese custom, designated as doctor when his bachelor's degree is in law or political science or engineering) did not make his appearance with Dom Pedro II and in the shade of the royal palms planted by his grandfather the King. The Jesuits had already given the colony, still in the shadow of the jungle, its first college graduates and its first simulacra of post-graduates. And in the seventeenth and eighteenth centuries, thanks to the fathers' endeavors, to their courses in Latin, Salvador was already producing B.A.'s prepared in the Jesuit schools, like Gregorio de Mattos and his brother Euzebio,[2] Rocha Pitta,[3] and Botelho de Oliveira.[4] Some of them continued their education in Europe, to be sure; but it was in Bahía, and with the older priests, that nearly all of them studied the humanities.

However, it was during the following century that the rise of men trained in the political and social life of the colony really began. Gonzaga,[5] Claudio Manoel da Costa,[6] the two Alvarengas,[7] Basilio da Gama[8] represent the growing prestige of the college graduates in colonial society, the definite participation of the man of letters or

---

[1] Romualdo A. de Seixas: *Memorias do Marquês de Santa Cruz, Arcebispo da Bahía* (Rio de Janeiro, 1861), p. 91.

[2] Intellectuals of early colonial times.

[3] The author of an early history of Brazil written in bombastic style.

[4] An intellectual of early colonial times.

[5] Intellectual and poet who participated in the Minas Gerais uprising in the eighteenth century.

[6] Idem.

[7] Idem.

[8] Epic poet of colonial times; author of *O Uruguay*.

the cloth in politics. They also represent the political triumph of another element of Brazilian life: the refined city man. And the rise of the native-born Brazilian and even of the mulatto to public office and to the magistracy.

These college graduates of Minas were forerunners of the decadence of the rural patriarchy, a phenomenon that would become clearly evident in the nineteenth century. They represent the aristocracy of the city residences, but a new aristocracy, different from the semi-rural or the commercial. The aristocracy of cap and gown. It is significant that the schools of law and political science in Imperial Brazil were known, not as schools, but as academies, and their students as "gentlemen academicians" (*senhores academicos*). A real caste.

Even though they felt the difference between themselves and Europe, or the mother country where they had studied, and looked to an independent and republican Brazil, their European formation had taken from them their taste for nature in the raw of the tropics, and had left instead a tepid emotion with literary overtones, cultivated in the shade of suburban mango groves among monkeys tamed by the Negroes of the household and parrots which, instead of words in Tupi, repeated Latin and French phrases they had picked up from these new masters. It is told, at any rate, of Moraes, the author of the Dictionary, that he amused himself teaching the parrots Latin and French.

Certain of these university graduates, even though mulattoes, when they wrote poems in praise of the tropical scene found their inspiration in the lyricism of the European countryside:

> *The fair shepherd who stirs my burning breast*
> *Will give new spirit to my verses*

wrote Alvarenga Peixoto in his *Poem to the Nativity*.[9]

Claudio Manoel da Costa, on his return to Brazil after five years in Europe, was unable to restrain or conceal his disenchantment with the melancholy landscape. These, indeed, were not "the happy plains of Arcady" where "the sound of the waters inspired the harmony of

---

[9] Claudio Manoel da Costa, in Sylvio Romero: *Martins Pena* (Oporto, 1901), p. 142; Alvarenga Peixoto: "Canto Genetlíaco," *Obras Poeticas* (Rio de Janeiro, 1865).

the verses." After five years of voluptuous intellectual formation beside the Mondego with its crystalline waters, all he could do here, in the shade of the cashews, along the banks of muddy rivers and among people as perverted as the natural setting by the "tiresome ambition of mining the earth," was to "sink into the arms of sloth, bury himself in ignorance."

Many were the Brazilians who, like da Costa, after studying outside their native land suffered veritable torment on their return: the difficult readjustment to the milieu, the landscape, the home, the family. Adolescents who had become so Europeanized and so sophisticated that the Brazilian medium, above all, the rural, at first produced in them disgust, a physical nausea.

And in spite of being young, and consequently the most inclined to freedom of body and mind, they nevertheless became the censors of their elders and of the unabashed sexual license that existed here, especially among the plantation masters. On his return to the colony, one of these university graduates did not hide the repugnance it aroused in him to see the banks of the stream that bathes Vila Rica transformed into the site of orgies; and the African *batuque* danced not only in Negro shanties but in the fine residences of the whites:

> *Oh happy dance! Up from*
> *The lowly huts, where the Negress,*
> *The vile mulatto, cinching*
> *The long ribbon beneath her belly,*
>
> *Honored you with rogues and swamp rats,*
> *Stamping the measure with her naked foot,*
> *You now have made your way at last*
> *Into the palaces and the decent home.*[1]

When, however, the disenchanted turned patriots, they became fanatical nativists, some with a spirit of martyrdom that outdid that of certain of the student heroes in Russian novels. Once their initial revulsion had passed, these European university graduates—some, at any rate, for there were others whose disillusionment lasted a life-

---

[1] *Cartas Chilenas*, I (Rio de Janeiro, 1863), p. 183. Although the authorship of *Cartas Chilenas* is still in doubt, as authoritative a critic as Affonso Arinos de Mello Franco states that Tomaz Antonio Gonzaga was the author.

time—became a creative element of dissent in the process of Brazilian integration that was taking place, almost through inertia, around the nucleus of the patriarchal plantation. On the one hand, they were enemies of the backwoods aristocracy, to whose values and ways they had difficulty in readapting themselves; on the other, they found in it their natural allies for the revolutionary plans for political independence and even for their romantic exploits.

Alvarenga Peixoto, the very one who longed for "the fair shepherd" against the background of "these ugly and lowering plains," became the bard of this

barbarous but blessed land

and even of its slaves, the country workers, men of many colors, black, brown, swarthy, so different from the fair shepherds of Europe:

> . . . *men of many mischances,*
> *browns, blacks, copper, and bronzed*
> . . . *their strong arms wrought by work*

and José Basilio da Gama took pride in extolling in his stilted manner —though at times he attempted to make it spontaneous—the trees, the animals, the plants, the fruits most pungently Brazilian. Both he and Santa Rita Durão.[2]

This partial reconciliation with the native milieu, though "ugly and lowering," took place on the part of various of these university graduates, making it not only the object of their plans for political reform and social reconstruction, but also a means of bringing about a closer relationship between man and nature. Because the Brazilians who had been educated in Europe, especially France, in the second half of the eighteenth century, and even without leaving Brazil, the priests and Masons who kept abreast of political novelties—indulging their intellectual libertinism in secret—had read those French books which set forth in fervid tones the idyll between man and nature, erecting on this basis the new theories of Liberty, the State, Human Rights, the Social Contract. Possibly it was under the influ-

---

[2] Humanist and epic poet of colonial times; author of *Caramuru;* served as chancellor of the University of Coimbra, Portugal.

ence of this revolutionary naturalism that Alvarenga Peixoto saw in "the browns, blacks, copper, and bronzed" men, Negroes, Indians, mestizos, with "strong arms wrought by work," the real builders of Brazil, those who had been changing the course of the rivers and cutting through the mountains, "armed with heavy crowbar and ringing hammer." In our colonial literature his is probably the first voice to exalt the labor of the slave, the creative, Brazilianly creative, action of the Negro, Indian, and, above all, the mestizo population.

The Inconfidencia Mineira was a revolution of college graduates, as were the two of Pernambuco, those of 1817 and 1824, at any rate of priests who were a sort of cassocked university graduates before they were priests, some of them educated in Olinda, in the liberal seminary of Azeredo Coutinho, "in all the main fields of literature suited not only to a churchman but also to a citizen who plans to serve the State." These intellectuals, looking toward an independent and republican Brazil, found their best allies in the great land and slave owners. Aristocrats domiciled for several generations in America, some of them having Indian and even Negro blood. A republic or an independent Brazil—independent of Portugal, at any rate—was to the interest of a number of these revolutionaries. The republic, moreover, had already been attempted, according to certain of our political historians, by a plantation owner of Pernambuco in 1710, whose model, they say, was Venice. It would seem, however, that what those revolutionists, nearly all of them country-bred gentry, had lacked was the intellectual leadership of some outstanding university man or enlightened clergyman. There was no lack, but rather a superfluity, of these in the Mineira uprising and the two revolts of Pernambuco at the beginning of the nineteenth century.

But in any of these, in the event that the revolutionary ideal had triumphed, a conflict would probably have come about between the partisans of independence defending the interests of the sugar growers and the miners, and those who were moved by ideological rather than economic motives, or, at any rate, motives more psychological or sociological than economic. Among the latter were many of the college graduates, especially the mulatto or "dark-complexioned." And also those who, though possessing no university degree, like Tiradentes, had something in common with them, being "dentists," or "medicine men," and not merely shopkeepers who borrowed the college graduates' rhetoric. Half-breeds who at times played the role of the middle class.

These colored college graduates and semi-doctors felt more strongly than anyone else the need for a better social adjustment which would give the intellectuals, the men with university preparation, this new aristocracy less conscious than the others of racial purity, a greater share in the country's political guidance. A typical instance of the conflict of interests that divided the men of 1817 into at least two groups was the difference of opinion of the magistrate Andrada, who incarnated the prejudices of the white race, and the ideas of liberal social democracy of Dr. Manoel de Arruda Camara.

Arruda Camara was a man who had been strongly influenced by French ideas. According to his biographers, he was a Carmelite friar who had been relieved of his vows by a papal brief. He studied in Coimbra, and there are those who state that he later studied medicine at the University of Montpellier, though the historian Alberto Rangel says that he could find no proof of this in his investigations.

The French influence, however, did not have the effect of making him lose his awareness of Brazil's social reality—a Brazil where there were already many mulattoes and half-breeds. For him, the revolution separating Brazil from Portugal should not be merely political but the complete reform of society. And this reform should include a better adjustment in the relations between masters and oppressed, between whites and colored.

The position of Arruda Camara is in marked contrast to that of Magistrate Antonio Carlos Andrada, a supporter of independence who, however, expressed in no uncertain terms his horror, not only political but even physical, of a revolution based on a radical ideology, like that of 1817, which threatened, if successful, to topple him "from the ranks of the nobility" and put him—these are the magistrate's own words—"on an equal footing with the rabble of every hue" and even to "cut down in flower his well-founded hopes of later advancement and greater honors." In contrast to this expression of racial and class superiority, Arruda Camara, in a testamentary letter he left to Father João Ribeiro, dated October 2, 1810, reveals a different understanding of the problem of race and class relations in Brazil. "The benightedness of the colored people must be done away with," he wrote to his favorite pupil, the poor priest whose dreaming head would be rotting on a pole seven years later as an example to revolutionists; "this must come to an end so that when later men are needed to fill public positions they will be ready, for Brazil will never progress unless they can play their part in its affairs; never mind that degraded and absurd aristocracy which will always try to obstaculize. With a monarchy or without it, the colored people must share in Brazil's prosperity." [3]

The rise of the French-influenced university graduate—mulatto or white—brought in its train many a flight from reality in the shape of laws which were almost Freudian in their origins or underlying motivation. Laws copied from the English and French and which were in opposition to the Portuguese: the revolt of sons against fathers. But on the other hand, it was men like Arruda Camara who spoke out against certain artificial measures which threatened the patriarchal work of integration, such as those exaggerated sentiments of nobility typified by Andrada. [4]

When Mello Moraes, around the middle of the nineteenth century, nostalgically recalled the old men of his youthful days, their prestige, the good sense with which they ruled the colony, it was to lament, among other horrors of the new epoch, the preponderance of French-influenced and trained university graduates, and contrast their lack of experience with the practical wisdom of the old administrators. Compared to their sons and grandsons versed in law or philosophy, in mathematics or medicine, they were like many of the native healers compared to the youthful doctors turned out at Montpellier and Paris: superior to them by reason of their skill and experience; by their instinctive sense of how to deal with the diseases and maladies of a medium so different from that of Europe, knowing from use and experience the properties of gums, herbs, poisons, indigenous or brought from Africa by the Negroes. And this same relation between the healers and the doctors held true of our native guerrilla fighters and the professional soldiers of Europe. The war against the Dutch, for example, was, in the main, won by Brazilian

---

[3] In Pereira da Costa: *Dicionario Biografico de Pernambucanos Celebres* (Recife, 1882), p. 641.

[4] Antonio Carlos Ribeiro de Andrada seems to have been one of the Brazilians who shocked a French aristocrat of liberal sentiments by his family pride. (Suzannet: Op. cit., p. 411.)

guerrillas, who defeated the trained troops of Europe. By men who knew every inch of the terrain on which they were fighting forces vastly superior to them in numbers and in the theoretical art or science of warfare.

For one university-trained man like Arruda Camara, who brought to the European theories the pragmatic qualities of a healer of our social ills by Brazilian methods, there were many who overdid the theory. They were romantics or pure theoreticians, who thought they were dealing with a typically European country, and not with a multifaceted population of mulattoes, half-breeds.

In 1845, when the Second Empire was in full swing, and the law schools of Recife and São Paulo were functioning briskly, trained men began to take over the administration of the provinces and the principal political and government posts. The buildings which housed the seats of government and the more important public bureaus— some new, in the French or Italian style, others former convents or homes of rich patriarchs adapted to the Empire's bureaucratic needs —loomed large on the Brazilian scene. And at the same time, as we pointed out in an earlier chapter, the private homes began to shrink in size.

The populace did not fail to observe this transfer of power. But it had become so accustomed to the prestige of the patriarchal Big Houses that in some provinces the governor's mansion still went by the name of "the Big House of the government"; and it would seem to have been difficult for the people to accord the university graduates, even barons and bishops, the same category as the captains-major and the sergeants-major. To this very day the reverence for military titles has survived; in the imagination of the folk of Brazil their Messiah will be a captain or a general rather than some B.A. or Ph.D.

However, the prestige of university titles had been on the increase in the cities and even in the country since the beginning of the Empire. Items and advertisements in the newspapers referring to "trained college or university graduates," and even "students" began to foretell this new aristocratic force which was arising, in its frock coat or its cap and gown, often richly embroidered and imported from the Orient. Almost mandarin robes. Almost caste apparel. And this attire could make aristocrats of its wearers—colored men, mulattoes, the "dark-complexioned."

The fact of the matter is that the news items referring to the university graduates were at times tactless: tailors complaining that after years of patient waiting Mr. So-and-So, a college graduate, Mr. So-and-So, a university graduate, still owed for a frock coat or a suit made to his order in such a month or year. But tailors were always the enemies of the aristocracy. In private archives of old plantation houses which I had an opportunity to examine I found that the same thing was true of the sons of barons and viscounts: not one or two, but many letters from tailors who had grown tired of waiting for their bills to be settled. Sons and grandsons of plantation owners who had not paid for their frock coats, their fancy vests, their striped trousers, until finally the bill was sent to father viscount, or grandpa baron, or simply to the manager, who ordered it paid by their agent.

The social rise of the poor university graduate, who, left to his own resources, could wear only a faded frock coat or a threadbare suit, or suffer the humiliation of being publicly denounced as a delinquent debtor, was beset with difficulties. Having no political sponsors, he could neither reach the legislature nor receive a diplomatic appointment. Often he was able to study or receive his training thanks to the heroic efforts of his mother in a market stall or his tinker father; at times through marriage with the daughter of some rich or powerful family.

In this latter fashion a number of young men, poor or near poor, came to be legislators and ministers. Some with a good or sonorous name, who needed only the help of wealth or power to achieve nobility or prestige. Others, of commonplace name, whose children often took the mother's family name.

José da Natividade Saldanha, on the other hand, was the type of Brazilian nonconformist, the educated mulatto who preferred insubordination to the easy road to victory. The son of a priest, he studied for the church in the seminary of Olinda. But he rebelled against the seminary and went to study law in Coimbra, "filled with that native independence which must be constitutional in the children of free love." And when he was sentenced to death as a result of his revolutionary activities in Pernambuco, a comment from Caracas on the white judge, Mayer, who in passing sentence had called Saldanha a mulatto, said: "This was the same mulatto who won prizes when he, Mayer, could barely manage a passing grade, and when this mulatto refused the post of military judge in Pernambuco, Mayer secured it by boot-licking." [5]

If in the time of Koster rural landowners of the most remote and distant regions requested their agents to send them bookkeepers who were white and knew how to read and cipher [6]—thus avoiding brilliant but mulatto university graduates like Saldanha—under the Empire the situation was reversed. Mediocre white bookkeepers, once useful for the patriarchal economy and racial purity of the plantation families, no longer filled the requirements. Those who were now at a premium—even with the risk to patriarchal economy that certain sons-in-law might become complete parasites, and others, a blot on the escutcheon of some pure-blooded backwoods family—were the college and university graduates, without the question of their racial purity always being an issue.

There was more than one instance of a college graduate who married into a wealthy or powerful family—above all, powerful—of plantation or ranch, and became the political mentor of the family. This was the case of João Alfredo Correia de Oliveira, whose father-in-law was the Baron of Goiana. Everything leads us to believe that it was to further the political career of the son-in-law that the family seat was moved from the Big House of Goiana to the city residence of Recife, where the father-in-law, handsome, tall, blue-eyed, but a little countrified, played second fiddle to his educated son-in-law, with his cultivated manners, whose features bore traces of the beautiful and rustic Indian grandmother who as a child was nicknamed "Maria Jump-the-Brook." The grandson of the Indian girl became minister of the Empire when he was only some twenty years old.

Years later, disillusioned with politics, João Alfredo lamented having left the plantation house for the tiled mansion of Recife. But it was too late. We should not forget, however, that there were some

---

[5] Costa: *Folclore Pernambucano* (Rio de Janeiro, 1908).
[6] Henry Koster: *Travels in Brazil* (London, 1816), p. 196.

who, having received their education in Europe, on their return to Brazil preferred the plantation of their father or father-in-law to living in the capital or one of the large seaboard cities. This was the case of the great lexicographer Dr. Antonio de Moraes Silva, who, though a native of Rio de Janeiro, ended his days as the owner of a sugar plantation in Pernambuco.

The political rise of the university graduates of a family was not only that of sons-in-law, but principally that of sons. If we have emphasized the rise of sons-in-law it is because this is a phenomenon which reveals more clearly the transfer of power, or a considerable share of power, from the rural gentry to the intellectual aristocracy or bourgeoisie. From the Big Houses of the plantations to the city mansions. Professor Gilberto Amado, in a penetrating essay, refers to the influence acquired in the second half of the nineteenth century by "the effulgent intellectual proletariat, poor doctors, journalists, orators who arose everywhere in the land with pen, word, and action, as standard bearers of liberal thought, to control public opinion." And he goes on: "It was they who, with the eclipse of the great families ruined by the abolition of the slave trade and other long-standing ills, little by little came to take the place of the sons of the plantation owners, the viscounts, marquesses, and barons, and occupy the center of the political arena." [7]

This marks a phenomenon somewhat different from that we have attempted to set forth. Different and more recent: that of the generation which came out of the schools to achieve abolition and bring about the republic. But this generation was a prolongation of the preceding one; it emphasized the substitution of the plantation owner not only by his educated son, nor even by his son-in-law of humble origins, but by the unrelated university graduate who was taking over in a more violent manner, through conflicts and dissensions with the old rural gentry and even with the wealthy city bourgeoisie.

Sylvio Romero, a well-known cultural historian, wrote that after the first thirty years of the Empire, during which Brazil—already a country of mestizos—had been governed by what remained of the white elite—" the remains of the ruling class," he calls them, identi-

---

[7] Gilberto Amado: *Grão de Areia* (Rio de Janeiro, 1919).

fying moral superiority and the capacity for administration and government with the white race—conditions began to be modified by "the hundreds of half-breed graduates" [8] emerging from the institutions of learning, those of Recife, of São Paulo, Bahía, Rio de Janeiro. And later from the military academy, the polytechnic.

Romero seems to have grasped as clearly as Professor Amado the phenomenon we have been associating with the decline of the rural patriarchy: the transfer of power, or of a considerable share of power, from the rural and almost always white aristocracy, not only to the middle-class intellectual—the university graduate, often mulatto—but also to the military, the graduates of the military academy or polytechnic, in many instances, Negroid. But here we enter upon another aspect of the problem, which falls outside the scope of this study: the army uniform, the officers' galloons, the technical training of the soldier, the military career—especially the hybrid one of the military B.A.—was another social ladder for the Brazilian mulatto. And possibly one could develop this idea a little. The political activity, from the revolutionary standpoint, of the Brazilian militias or army—always a somewhat restless and unstable group since the days of Silva Pedroso but, especially, since the Paraguayan War—may very well have been in part another expression of the discontent or dissatisfaction of the more intelligent and sensitive mulattoes, still maladjusted to the milieu.

The navy, which, until recently, through dissimulation, subtle pretexts of a technical nature, had maintained its officer caste almost entirely closed to mulattoes, and even darker persons of Indian extraction, constituting perhaps our most perfect near-Aryan group, was almost the opposite of the army. Dominated even more than the Church—which was also affected in Brazil, although not so much as in Mexico, by the resentment of the poor or mestizo priest against the rich or well-born—by the spirit of social conformity, or the mystique of respect for authority, its only revolution was, in effect, a counterrevolution.

It is easy to understand the attraction of the glittering officer's uniform for the mestizo. It satisfied his longing to equal the white by its insignia of authority and, at the same time, served as an instrument

---

[8] Sylvio Romero: *Martins Pena* (Porto, 1901) pp. 163–4.

of power and an element of strength in his restless hands. Such insignia from the first years of the nineteenth century had appealed to individuals sociologically children or women, as the mestizos often showed themselves in their process of ascent to the positions of authority or command reserved as a caste privilege for the whites or semi-whites.

Even under the colonial regime, the Count of Valladares in Minas organized regiments of colored soldiers with mulatto or black officers. This was a slap in the face to the local aristocracy. Moreover, in the colonial era there were mulatto sergeant-majors and captain-majors; even a dark mulatto, like the one Koster knew in Pernambuco. But this handful of mulattoes who came to hold the posts of gentlemen became thereby officially whites, having achieved their position of authority through some exceptional quality or circumstance. Possibly some act of heroism against rebels. Perhaps a large fortune inherited from a vicar godfather. When the Englishman inquired in Pernambuco whether the captain-major was a mulatto —a fact which, moreover, leaped to the eye—instead of being answered, he was asked "if it was possible that a captain-major should be a mulatto?"

The title of captain-major Aryanized the darkest mulatto. Its magic power exceeded even that of the university graduate's diploma. Even that of the coronet of viscount and baron which His Majesty the Emperor set upon heads that were not always covered with soft golden or even brown hair. On heads whose origin was on occasion less than plebeian.

Similar cases occurred in the United States. In a certain old city, a distinguished gentleman was pointed out to me, years ago, who was admitted to and even sought out by the most exclusive white society of the city, and who was known to have Negro blood, though remote. In a country where the mere suspicion of such ancestry is enough to give rise to the most cruel social ostracism, the case seemed to me amazing. However, I must explain that the gentleman in question had another ancestor—or possibly it was the very one of Negro origin—who was one of the great heroes of the Revolutionary War. This Aryanized his race and made his blood aristocratic.

Other mestizos of Brazil, partly aristocratized by their military position, did not feel so comfortably white as Koster's captain-

major. This was the case of Pedroso, military commander of Recife
in 1823. Pedroso put his sword of defender of the *status quo* and the
Empire at the service of the revolution. And it was an instrument in
defense not of some political cause or some mere barracks revolt but
of one of the most unmistakable movements of social dissatisfaction
on the part of the colored people which had taken place in Brazil.
Pedroso visited the shanties, fraternizing with the Negroes and
mulattoes, eating and drinking with them. And for some days the
song that was sung everywhere in Recife was:

> *The sailors and the whitewashed,*
> *All of them to hell,*
> *For only blacks and browns*
> *In this our land should dwell.*

And the one topic of conversation was Henri-Christophe and the
uprising in Santo Domingo.[9]

This same feeling of dissatisfaction perhaps explains, on the one
hand, the participation of educated mulattoes, like Natividade
Saldanha, in revolutionary movements which may have had their
origin less in their French-acquired idealism than in their almost
physical and, certainly, psychic maladjustment to the predominant
social order of a white elite. On the other, it perhaps explains, too, the
note not so much of definite social revolt but of resentment feebly
disguised as romantic sadness, as personal sorrow, the stifled grief of
the unhappy lover to be found in some of our greatest poets of the
nineteenth century. Mulattoes who after graduating from the University of Coimbra or the Imperial academies never felt themselves
wholly adapted to the society of their day, with its racial prejudices,
less marked than in other countries, but not to be ignored.

This was the case of the great poet of Maranhão, Antonio Gonçalves Dias, one of the mulatto or "swarthy" university graduates.
The son of a Portuguese father and Negro-Indian mother, Gonçalves Dias was all his life a sad misfit in the social order of a Brazil
which had just emerged from the rank of colony, when, in contrast
to governors like the Count of Valladares, who went out of his way
to set mulattoes above the native whites, there were captains like the

---

[9] Alfredo Carvalho: *Estudos Pernambucanos* (Recife, 1907).

Marquis of Lavradio, who removed a certain Indian militiaman from his post because he married a Negro. Sensitive because of his inferior origin, the stigma of his color, his Negroid features, which from the mirror were always reminding him: "Remember that you are a mulatto," Gonçalves Dias bore an open wound beneath his frock coat. The poet was not satisfied with his literary triumph or immortality; his ambition was to triumph, too, in the elegant society of his day.

I am not the first to associate Gonçalves Dias's melancholy with his awareness of his origins. It was a classmate of his at Coimbra, and one of his most intimate friends, Rodrigues Cordeiro, who in 1872 gave this testimony: it was the knowledge that he was the son of a colored woman who had become the mistress of a Portuguese that "in sleepless nights covered his heart with clouds"[1] and found expression in poems like *O Tempo*. It does not matter that in other poems dealing with more purely African subjects, such as *Escrava*, Gonçalves Dias kept himself at a distance from the Negro, nor did his voice, with the Portuguese accent of his student days in Coimbra, speak out openly in favor of the race degraded by slavery to which he was so tragically near-born.

The literary romanticism of Brazil—masculine voices lamenting and wailing until they seemed the voices of women—was not always the same as that of other countries: the revolt of the Individual against Everything—society, epoch, species—of which a French critic speaks. In certain cases it would seem to have been less the expression of the individual in revolt than of men of mixed race feeling, like the homosexuals, the social, or perhaps psychic gulf between themselves and the definitely white or pure race, or the definitely masculine and dominant sex.

This can be seen in that extraordinary artist of ours, *O Aleijadinho*—the cripple—the mulatto sculptor of the churches of Minas. In this suffering mulatto—between whom and the white ruling class there was the gulf not only of color and origins, but also the malady which was consuming his body and withering away his fingers, leaving alive only a scrap, a fragment of a man—resentment took the form of social revolt, of the vengeance of an oppressed sub-

---

[1] *Almanack de Lembranças Luzo-Brasileiro* (Lisbon, 1872).

race, of unsatisfied sexual impulses. Thus, in the sculpture of O *Aleijadinho* the figures of the "whites," the "masters," the "Roman captains," appear deformed, less because of the sculptor's devotion to Our Lord Jesus Christ and hatred for his enemies, than because of his rage at being a mulatto and a leper; because of his rebellion against the white rulers of the colony, one of whom he portrayed, or rather, caricatured or deformed for artistic and, at the same time, mystic reasons—for he was a kind of mulatto El Greco—into a hideously ugly figure, exaggerating, above all, the nose, the greatest point of somatic or plastic differentiation between the oppressors and the oppressed in the Brazil of his day. All the figures of the Roman captains and even soldiers, not to mention the Jews, who appear in his processional floats of Congonhas do Campos have noses which are caricatures of the Semitic or Caucasian type, exaggerated in size to the point of ridicule.

The typically Brazilian quality of O *Aleijadinho's* work, or at least the non-European and even—God forgive me—the non-Catholic, has not gone entirely unnoticed by his more recent critics, among them the poets Manuel Bandeira and Mario de Andrade. The revolutionary aspect was pointed out by Affonso Arinos de Mello Franco in an article describing a trip we made together to Minas Gerais in 1934. I called attention to this same point in a paper prepared in collaboration with the painter Cicero Dias for the Afro-Brazilian Congress held in Recife in 1934, dealing with African reminiscences in the folk art of Brazil. And, above all, in the art of O *Aleijadinho*, in whose Christian figures there is a deliberate deformation in a non-European, non-Graeco-Roman sense, although it could not be called characteristically African. Marginally African, but characteristically Brazilian, that is to say, mestizo, culturally plural.

This extra-European artistic sense and expression gradually came to influence, through the mulatto, Brazilian music and, with Negro collaboration, our cuisine, so un-European today in its most typical dishes. This feeling and expression is more difficult to find in the less spontaneous, more guided, more official, so to speak, arts whose natural expression was repressed by the European, Graeco-Roman, French academic tradition in painting, sculpture, poetry, architecture.

In poetry, however, there was one convention which did not survive separation from European sources, nor hold out against the extra-European influence which miscegenation was creating in Brazil's lyric expression: that of the blond, fair-haired woman. The extra-European influences made themselves felt in this aspect as early as the seventeenth century in the "Romances" of Gregorio de Mattos, in Freudian guise, as Professor Renato Mendonça has recently pointed out. It found clear expression in our folk poetry, which exalts the amorousness of the mulatto or the charm of the brown girl; and in the work of the poets, too, whose verses make more frequent mention of winsome brown girls than of fair-haired virgins.

It was through his physical beauty and sexual attraction that, in many instances, the mulatto rose socially in our medium: by the mere prestige of this beauty, or its enhancement through intellectual gifts which proved assets in Europe, and even in Olinda, São Paulo, Bahía, or Rio de Janeiro.

Aluizio de Azevedo has left us in a novel, *O Mulato*, which is a veritable "human document," copied from the provincial life of his day and employing the realistic technique which he was one of the first to use in Brazil, a detailed picture of a mulatto educated in Europe. On his return to Maranhão "the mulatto" aroused the ardent love of a white girl of good family, a family with strong race prejudices. They wanted her to marry a Portuguese, and had already chosen one whose white ugliness and coarseness was in marked contrast to the distinction and refinement of the mulatto. Moreover, the latter was no pauper. He had inherited money from his father and was able to travel in Europe after completing his studies. The dramatic conflict is between this romantic love and the social prejudices, due perhaps not so much to the young man's color as to the fact that he was the son of a slave, a plantation Negress. A Negress who was still alive, although demented, a wanderer in the woods.

The race prejudice—the time is about the middle of the nineteenth century—was felt most strongly by the girl's grandmother, a product of the colonial epoch. "Look," she said to the girl, "if I had to see you marry a half-breed Negro, I swear by this sun which shines upon us that I would prefer a good death for you, granddaughter, because you would be the first of our family to defile our blood!" And to her son-in-law: "Know, Manoel, that if such a dishonor should happen, it would be your fault, for, when all is said and done, who ever heard of allowing a half-breed so full of fiddle-faddle as this jumped-up doctor in the house? They are like that today. You give them an inch and they take an ell. They no longer know their place, the scoundrels. Now, in my days, there was not all this hemming and hawing. Someone forgot himself? Out. What is the street door for? That is what you should do, Manoel. Don't be a fool! Send him packing once and for all, and marry your daughter to a white man like herself." [2]

If the educated mulatto, like the hero of Azevedo's novel, was received with constraint and even coolly by the distinguished families of the capital of Maranhão, he was notwithstanding "enticed by a number of women, maidens, wives, and widows, whose folly went so far as to send him flowers and messages." [3] The sexual attraction of the mulatto was felt by the highest-born white women in spite of the existing race prejudices. An attraction of which various examples could be cited, under similar, if not identical circumstances to those of Azevedo's novel.

From the psychological portrait drawn by the author—and it is said that Azevedo did not invent his hero, but portrayed him from a living model, almost without any touching up—Dr. Raymundo was no intellectual *arriviste*, trying to show off his newly acquired culture, as was often the case with educated mulattoes. On the contrary, he was a man restrained in his gestures, low-voiced, who dressed in good taste, was keenly interested in science, literature, and, to a lesser degree, in politics. In his behavior a mulatto of the stripe of Machado de Assis,[4] without his almost morbid diffidence; or of Domicio da Gama,[5] "the pink mulatto," as Eça de Queiroz privately called the discreet and polished Brazilian diplomat.

These pink mulattoes, some of them golden-haired and blue-eyed,

---

[2] Aluizio de Azevedo: *O Mulato*, 12th ed. (Rio de Janeiro, 1945), p. 113.

[3] Ibid., p. 152.

[4] Brazil's greatest novelist (1839–1908), noted for his penetrating psychological analysis of Brazilian society and his delicately satirical style.

[5] Writer and diplomat of late nineteenth and early twentieth century. He was married to a North American and was Brazilian ambassador to the United States.

who could pass for whites where their origins did not happen to be known, were not rare in nineteenth-century Brazil. Since the eighteenth century there had always been a strong trend of opinion or feeling that they should pass from the ranks of slaves to free men, and, socially, from "blacks" to whites. As early as 1773 a royal edict of the King of Portugal made mention of persons "so lacking in humanity and religion" as to keep in their homes slaves who were whiter than themselves, terming them black and Negroes. Walsh was impressed by the number of blond, blue-eyed slaves he saw in Brazil at the beginning of the nineteenth century, some of them the illegitimate offspring of foreign fathers, who sold them at a high price.[6] And Perdigão Malheiro in his essay on slavery in Brazil [7] points out the tendency on the part of more liberal slaveowners to free their lighter slaves, which were also those chosen for the more exacting and delicate household tasks. Those who had derived the most benefit from the civilizing and refining contacts with their masters and mistresses.

This probably accounts for the large number of finely bred and handsome slaves, favorites of their masters, mentioned in wills and inventories of the nineteenth century. Or listed in the advertisements of runaway slaves in the colonial and imperial newspapers. Some "with a gay air," others "with a sorrowful expression"; or, like that strange Joana, in an advertisement of 1835 in the *Diario de Pernambuco*, "very fair, with straight hair, resembling a white woman"—with something mysterious in her past which the advertiser did not venture to state publicly and would communicate only to the party who had her in his house.

It is not unusual in the descriptions of the runaway mulattoes to find that they were heavy of torso like the majority of Negroes, whereas their feet were small and their fingers long and delicate like

---

[6] Walsh mentions an Englishman "who purposely had as many children as he could by slave women because he found that his children were generally pretty men with light, curling hair, blue eyes, and a skin as light as that of a European, and he was consequently able to sell them at a good price." (Robert Walsh: *Notices of Brazil in 1828 and 1829*, I [Boston, 1831], p. 193.)

[7] A. M. Perdigão Malheiro: *A Escravidão no Brasil*, II (Rio de Janeiro, 1866–7), p. 187.

those of gentlemen. Long fingers designed for the ring of the university graduate. For the pen of the notary, the bureaucrat, and even the journalist, for the sword of the army officer, the needle of seamstress or tailor, the strings of the guitar, the rifle, the reins of a fine carriage. Professions and occupations to which some of them managed to rise, not only because of their intelligence—more alert and agile than that of the pure-blooded Negroes, confused by surroundings so different from those in which they were born and raised—and their features, which more closely resembled those of the whites, but also because of those hands with their long delicate fingers. Hands more fitted than the coarse, clumsy ones of the majority of the Negroes for genteel, refined, urban occupations.

The feet, too, played a part in the social rise of the mulatto: long, well-shaped, sinewy feet, as they are described in some of the advertisements, in marked contrast to the feet of the majority of the Negroes, broad, splayed, scaly, often deformed by bunions and sores, or lacking the big or little toe, possibly eaten away by ringworm. Negro feet must have been very refractory to shoes of European last. When slippers and shoes—whose use had been limited almost wholly to the Portuguese—became generalized among the Brazilian aristocracy, men and women, with their small feet, it can be seen how difficult it was for the African Negroes, even the pages and domestic servants, to get used to this European innovation, so ill-adapted to their broad flat feet. But not for the mulattoes: their well-turned feet more easily accommodated themselves to the use of shoes, which various European visitors remarked as being one of the signs of class distinction in nineteenth-century Brazil. And, it might be added, of race, for the good-looking Negroes who served as pages in wealthy homes and were dressed in elegant livery by their masters went about the streets and house barefoot. Thus Koster painted them in one of his vignettes of a colonial street. The Englishman saw them in the streets of Recife carrying the palanquins of aristocratic white ladies, who when they showed the tip of their foot it was unbelievably small, like that of a child. The smaller, the more delicate the foot, the more aristocratic.

When the shoemaker's craft ceased to be a semi-domestic industry and became a factory industry—English for the most part in the beginning—one of the difficulties the manufacturers must have encountered was the absence of a standard Brazilian foot. True, at this time, the foot that wore the shoe was almost exclusively that of the master of the Big House, or the city aristocrat, a small, narrow foot. This became more numerous with the social rise of the mulatto. The Portuguese of grocery store, market stall, small shop preferred the comfort of wooden shoes; I have already mentioned those who, by their success as slave traders, or through some other activity, came to be plantation owners, yet rode horseback in wooden shoes. The anecdotic history of the Empire even speaks of "wooden-shoed barons." This in contrast to the aristocrats with their girlish feet, who, even when their days of glory had been eclipsed and they went about the house in underdrawers and naked from the waist up, still wore their riding boots. Or if not, high-laced shoes.

In the newspapers of the colonial period advertisements of foreign shoes, English and French, were appearing. But it was in 1822 that a certain Clark, the owner, with his brother, of a shoe factory in Scotland, opened a shoe store in the Rua do Ouvidor to sell the products of his factory in Brazil.[8] The Scotch footwear became famous. It was used by the most refined persons, judges, lawyers, students, army officers, and even country residents, rustic in attire and tastes, but gentlemen and aristocrats when it came to their shoes. Branch stores were opened years later in Rio Grande do Sul which specialized, naturally, in riding boots, as well as in Bahía, São Paulo, and Recife, the cities par excellence of holders of university degrees, the academicians, the most aristocratic and gentlemanly landowners.

I lack the necessary information to say how the techniques of manufacturing shoes for the Scotch adapted themselves to Brazil as the use of shoes grew there in the second half of the nineteenth century. A number of changes in style and last must have been needed to accommodate factory-made shoes to the different types of feet, the aristocratic foot and the foot of the Negro, when it became necessary to supply shoes for the Negro soldier, the Negro policeman, sailor, fireman, naval gunner. The most I was able to learn when I questioned the managers of Clark in 1935 was that during the period in question they manufactured a low shoe which was extensively

---

[8] See Ernesto Senna: *O Velho Commercio do Rio de Janeiro* (Rio de Janeiro, n.d.).

used by the Negroid inhabitants of the northern seaboard. More recently, however, I learned from the same source that on the basis of a century of experience in the São Paulo factory, and knowing that "footwear should be flexible enough to adjust to the shape and movements of the feet," they decided to manufacture "thirty-six different lasts and sizes of a single model," while at the same time training their sales clerks to take "anatomical measurements" of the customers' feet to fit them with properly fitting shoes.

With the incorporation into the Brazilian bourgeoisie and proletariat of Germans, Portuguese, Italians, Spaniards, people with large feet and a high instep, the Brazilian foot must have come to approach the standard for European shoes in various areas of the seaboard. However, the typically Brazilian foot continued to exist in large parts of the country, the small and agile, yet delicate foot of the *capoeira*, the samba dancer, the player of rugby in the Brazilian manner, which is more like a Dionysiac dance than the Britishly Apollonian game.

The hat, too, must have posed problems when its industrialization demanded national sizes, shapes, and styles, and its wearers ceased to be the small elite of members of the gentry and the middle class. It was not merely a question of the predominance of brachycephalics in certain regions, and of dolichocephalics in others. By the middle of the nineteenth century there were Negroes: schoolteachers, priests, engineers, doctors, leeches—not to mention coachmen and footmen, whose masters obliged them to wear a high hat or oilcloth-covered hat—who never went out without the top hat or felt hat of the whites. But it was mainly due to the mulatto that the hat ceased to be the prerogative of the aristocrat or the white bourgeois. With the educated mulatto, the use of the high hat or the felt hat of the European bourgeoisie became generalized among us.

In the Brazil Alfred Mars knew, the hand-plaited straw hat and homemade clothes of nankeen were still the usual attire of the local aristocrats who were less bent on copying European fashions.[9] After ridding themselves of the velvets and silks of the early colonial epochs, this rustic gentry had been adapting their attire to the climatic conditions of life in the tropics. With the rise of the university

[9] Alfred Mars: *Le Brésil, Excursion à travers ses 30 Provinces* (Paris, 1890).

graduate and the mulatto, this adaptation was interrupted. Clothing, hats, footwear began to be imported from Europe in increasing number, and the use of Oriental products and even the native was substituted by the European.

This was when shops like that of old Armada sprang up in Rio de Janeiro, with hats imported from Europe taking the place of those of native or even domestic manufacture. European hats of every style and the most varied materials: plush, silk, beaver, felt, velvet, satin, English straw, Leghorn, rice straw. However, Armada made concessions to the milieu. In the hats he manufactured he endeavored to adapt European styles to the Brazilian climate. Among other innovations he is credited with the introduction of the tubular sweat band in the silk top hat, the typical headgear of the educated mulatto, which had the drawback of making the head very hot. This defect was alleviated by this new type of sweat band which let the air in. And also by using lighter materials more in keeping with the climate.

Hatter Armada went even further; he began the manufacture of straw hats for the summer and the country out of palm fiber from Pará. This Brazilianizing of the material, class, and shape of the European hat—especially the top hat of the professionals—which also happened with the style and shape of shoes, coincided with the increasing rise of the mestizo, the mulatto, and even the Negro in our social milieu. Their heads and feet could now more easily be fitted with European articles adapted to Brazilian needs.

The tailors, too, modified European styles and sizes in the frock coats and trousers designed for their new customers, for some of them, at any rate. Among our aristocratized mestizos, in addition to volumnious buttocks, the arms and legs were often disproportionately long and thick in relation to the torso.

The hairdressers and barbers were not always able to give the beard and hair of the mulatto B.A.'s, and the tight-curled, often a bit kinky hair of quadroon ladies—sometimes the daughters-in-law of viscounts—the same setting and shape as the blond beard, the chestnut or brown mustache, the golden hair, of the whites or near whites. From portraits and daguerreotypes of the nineteenth century, it can be seen that the French hairdressers and barbers, who from the beginning of the century had been opening elegant establishments in Rio de Janeiro, in Recife, and the capital of Bahía, had

developed styles of coiffure and beard adapted to the somatic characteristics of Indian and African mestizos, who by Pedro II's day were
increasing in number in the best society. There is a curious note apparent in certain of the photographs of women whose Indian hair is
dressed more in the Spanish fashion than the French, more Oriental
than European. Some of the young ladies who look out from the
portraits and daguerreotypes have a Chinese or Malay air which this
style of hairdressing accentuates. Many of the old portraits of the
Brazilian mistresses or daughters of the Big House or city mansion
leave a definite impression that we are looking not at Europeans, but
at upper-class or caste Polynesian, Melanesian, Malay, Hispano-
Arabian, or Indian women. An impression due not only to the shape
or prominence of the eyes—so marked among those of mixed blood
—but to their attire and the way in which they wear their hair. In the
latter the art of the French hairdresser may have had a hand, making
the best use of elements somewhat refractory to the European style
of hairdressing, and trying to harmonize the hair with the features.
At times utilizing Asia to come to terms with Africa.

The mulatto woman, *au naturel* or adorned by the art of the
French hairdresser, the English shoemaker, the Parisian dressmaker,
the European perfumer—and we doubt that any one ever made such
use of perfumes, possibly to cover up the so-called Negro smell,
which, incidentally, was an attraction for certain voluptuous whites
—always had her charm for the white man. And the Brazilian
mulatto for the white woman, if not in his pristine form—tradition
recalls horrible crimes which were committed because of white
women giving themselves to mulatto slaves in moments of uncon-
trollable passion—when he had become aristocratized by education,
especially a European education, as in the case of Dr. Raymundo in
Aluizio Azevedo's novel. The European fashion of hairdressing, of
attire accentuated in the mulatto that extraordinary charm which,
in Azevedo's opinion, resided in the eyes, and in that of others,
in the ingratiating smile, so typical of the mulatto. So typical
of the slave, in general, in relation to his master in slaveholding
regimes where a good adjustment has been arrived at between the
several component elements. The habit of command develops in the
masters a loud voice, and in the slaves a soft, gentle manner of
speaking, accompanied by a pleasant smile. The patriarchal slave

system which was so long in force in Brazil would seem to have developed in the slave, and in his mulatto descendant, agreeable manners which came from the desire of the slaves to win the good graces, if not the love, of the masters.

The sex appeal of the mulatto woman lay not only in her eyes, but in her way of walking and of smiling, and, in the opinion of some, even in her feet, perhaps more agile than either those of white or Negro women; her fingers, more skilled than those of the whites in head-rubbing and removing chigoes from the feet, as well as other aphrodisiac exercises; the greater terseness of her sexual organs; the odor of her flesh, which had its special appeal for some. For all these reasons, somewhat hastily and in the name of a science still as new and undeveloped as sexology, a kind of permanent "sexual super-excitation" has been attributed to her, which would make her abnormal and, from the point of view of European and Catholic morality, dangerously amoral. This attitude came to be accepted by two of our most sober thinkers, one a man of science, the other of letters: Nina Rodrigues [1] and José Verissimo. [2] Popular belief, so often right in its intuitions, but so often completely mistaken—the idea that the earth was flat and fixed, for example—continues to give credence to the concept of the diabolical mulatto woman, super-excited by nature, and not by her social environment, which incited her to amorous adventures much more than racially pure women, better defended from such stimuli by their more stable social status.

As a result of the belief in this superexcitation, true or false, the mulatto woman was sought by those looking for bizarre sexual pleasures. So this psychological aspect of the relations between men of pure blood and half-breed women was in certain cases another factor in the social rise of the mulatto. This may have been the reason for certain marriages between white men getting on in years, elderly members of distinguished families, and pretty mulatto, quadroon, or octoroon women, who dressed like white women but were surrounded by an aura of sexual ardor conferred on them by the fact that they were not pure-blooded. There were instances of this in Brazil, and it may be that Bryce had such cases in mind when he

[1] Anthropologist of the late nineteenth and early twentieth century who specialized in the study of the Negro in Brazil.

[2] Literary and social critic of the same period.

compared the social scandal occasioned by the marriage of a white gentleman to a girl who was not completely white, her features, hair, or color revealing her African blood, with that set off in England by the marriage of a "gentleman" to a servant girl.[3] The initial shock was followed by the acceptance of a union unequal from the point of view both of age and class.

In Brazil, however, if the mestiza was light-skinned and dressed well and behaved like a person of the upper class, she was white for all social effects. But always, or nearly always, carrying an aura of greater sexual ardor than other women, especially the upper-class whites, which exposed her to more liberties on the part of the fashionable Don Juans and to greater risks in her dealings with men.

The same thing was true of the male mulatto: the "bold scoundrel" of folklore, the "roistering mulatto," the "sharp mulatto," the "uninhibited mulatto." There were all sort of rumors concerning his superiority over the white in the field of love-making. Even more specific advantages than those attributed to the mulatto woman.

If it is true, as Hrdlička states in a study of comparative anthropology, that the Negro in general is superior in the size of his genital organs, this superiority has not always been borne out in regional studies of members of the black race compared with those of the white. On the contrary, there are those who hold the opposite view.[4] Léon Pales, on the basis of an investigation carried out in French Africa and summed up in his study "Contribution a l'Étude Anthropologique du Noir en Afrique Equatoriale Française," [5] disputes the asseverations of Pruner Bey (1860), Duckworth (1904), and Kopernicki (1871), the writers who probably have contributed most to the legend of "the exceptional, inordinate size of the penis among the Negroes." Pales found Negroes "du penis volumineux, hors des proportions habituelles," but they did not constitute the norm among men of their race, especially, as he points

---

[3] James Bryce: *South America. Observations and Impressions* (London, 1910), p. 212.

[4] Pires de Almeida: *Homosexualismo* (Rio de Janeiro, 1906), especially pp. 74–5.

[5] In *L'Anthropologie*, XLIV (Paris, 1934). See also Pires de Almeida: Op. cit., pp. 104–5.

out, "il y a des blancs qui n'ont rien a leur envier sous ce rapport." Davenport, in a comparative study of Negroes, mulattoes, and whites which he carried out in Jamaica, unfortunately does not touch upon this aspect, possibly out of Anglo-Saxon modesty. In Brazil a doctor of the Empire who had undertaken studies of this nature reached the conclusion, perhaps overhastily, that "the penis of the African . . . which is as a rule large and heavy even under normal circumstances, increases little in size during an orgasm, never achieving complete rigidity." Hence "the dubious fecundation of a white woman by a Negro . . ." [6]

However, the sexual attraction the white woman felt for the mulatto, and even the Negro, was based in part on the belief in his physical superiority as a male, heightened by a certain pleasure in the unusual, even the bizarre. This was a belief of long standing. In the first chapter of *The Thousand and One Nights*—Owen Berkeley Hill recalled years ago [7]—there is a clear case of the sexual attraction felt by women of high class for a man of dark, primitive race. And Lieutenant-Colonel Berkeley Hill points out the fact that the Negro plays an outstanding role in the sexual life of the Turks, Persians, Hindus, and Parisians, who seem to be drawn to beings of a darker race and possibly more elemental in their nervous reactions and more vigorous physically than themselves. According to Seneca in a letter to Lucullus, the Negro played the same role in the life of the ancient Romans, among whom there were many men given to the cult of the dusky Venus, and women to a voluptuous admiration for colored men. Which explains the large number of Negroes of both sexes brought into Rome.

In Berkeley Hill's opinion, it is plain that both men and women, and especially the white, well-bred woman—what he calls the "racially superior type"—is "capable of feeling the strongest kind of sexual attraction for a man of more primitive racial type." Hence, the great sexual jealousy or envy of the racially superior male, which, together with reasons of an economic nature, would explain certain race prejudices. To counteract the charm of the Negro male for the white woman, the civilized male has created an aura of mockery and

---

[6] *L'Anthropologie*, XLIX.
[7] "The Color Bar," *The Spectator*, London, September 15, 1931.

contempt around the black and his primitiveness and of antipathy around the mulatto, so often accused of being false or fickle in his affections, of being unequal to the white man in real gentlemanliness and masculine elegance, not to mention intelligence in its higher aspects, the qualities of balance, judgment, and power of concentration, which, according to such critics, were rarely achieved by the half-breed or full-blooded Negroes. The only asset of the half-breeds was a facile brilliance of verbal and, possibly, plastic expression.

This, however, was not the opinion of the Benedictines, those shrewd friars who, in Brazil, were always carrying on genetic experiments with their slaves, and who reached the conclusion in the eighteenth century that the best, those most endowed with intelligence and talent, were the mulattoes. Sir George Stauton, who passed through here with Lord Macartney en route to China around the middle of that century, heard from the friars of the monastery of Rio de Janeiro the highest praise of the intelligence of their mulatto pupils in the liberal arts. And they adduced the case of a mulatto who had just been selected to fill an important professorship in Lisbon.[8]

The Jesuits, too, encouraged crossbreeding of Indian with Negro in the slave quarters of their plantations. On their plantations, the historian Ribeiro Lamego points out, "the most intensive crossbreeding of Ethiopians and Amerindians took place, something very difficult in view of the repugnance of the latter for the former." [9] In this crossbreeding, which filled the Jesuit slave quarters with half-breeds, *cafusos* and *caribocas,* some critics of the Jesuits' work have thought they discerned the ill-concealed intention of increasing the slave population by an infusion of Indian blood, inasmuch as it was easier for the fathers to come by Indians than by Negroes, and less expensive. Be that as it may, there is no evidence that the Jesuits were at all interested in the intellectual or social improvement of the Negro and mulatto, either in their schools or even in their slave quarters, in contrast to the Benedictines.

To the latter, as was said, we owe experiments in genetics whose

---

[8] Sir George Stauton: *An Authentic Account of an Embassy from the King of Great Britain to the Emperor of China* (London, 1797), p. 192.

[9] Alberto Ribeiro Lamego: *Planicie do Solar e da Senzala* (Rio de Janeiro, 1933).

results have been subject to the most varied interpretations. Toward the end of the eighteenth century Stauton, on the basis of the information given him by the friars, saw evidence among the mulattoes of the monasteries—some of whom the members of the order had raised from the slave quarters to professorships and posts of intellectual responsibility in the mother country itself—of an intelligence equal to that of the whites. Years later, in a discussion of the problem of miscegenation by the doctors of the Empire, one of them, and one of the most distinguished, Dr. Nicolau Joaquim Moreira, in a study of crossbreeding considered both from the anthropological and from the ethical point of view, was to invoke in support of the downgrading of the mulatto the example of the plantation of Campos, which also belonged to the Benedictines, "as a limited instance of mixed breeding," in contrast to another plantation of theirs, Camorim, "established nearly three centuries ago" and "still having a homogeneous and strong Negro population, whose intelligence is on the increase and whose skull has become modified so that it now approaches that of the Caucasian race." [1]

The aforementioned experience, that is to say, the conservation by the friars of the Negro slave population on one of their great plantations in as pure a state as possible, in contrast to the others, where the crossbreeding of white and Negro was encouraged, is extremely interesting, and suggests the desirability of attempting a study of the pockets of Negro population. Dr. Moreira's remark about the modification of the skull in a population presented as pure and homogeneous may anticipate one of the possible interpretations of the results of Dr. Franz Boas's experiences with European immigrants in the United States.

As for the "increased intelligence," it may be that this was the result of social stimuli on the plantation of the Benedictines, perhaps the kindliest slave masters our country knew. Aside from such special cases as the Benedictines, the lighter mulattoes were more exposed to such stimuli in Brazil during slavery days than the darker Negroes. This explains, in large measure, the reputation they ac-

---

[1] Nicolau Joaquim Moreira: "Questão Etnica-Antropologica: O Cruzamento das Razas Acarreta Degradação Intelectual do Produto Hibrido Resultante?" in *Annaes Brasilienses de Medicina*, XXII, 10 (Rio de Janeiro, March, 1870), p. 265.

quired as being more intelligent, though with greater moral defects, than the Negroes. Here, as in the United States, the social rise of the mulatto slave took place not only in the plantation houses, where they were preferred as domestic servants, but also that of the free mulatto in the cities and the capital. The latter's adjustment to city living was quicker than that of the free Negro because of the fact that social selection always operated in the sense of favoring the individual of lighter color and more European appearance, of more European formation or experience.

With the growth of the cities in the nineteenth century, the larger urban centers became the "paradise of the mulattoes," as one historian of the eighteenth century had already called them. The ideal milieu for the rapid advancement of the most agreeable and most skillful, especially those with technical training or an education. A phenomenon resembling that of the Jews in cities like Rio de Janeiro; from the eighteenth century the distinction between them and the "Old Christians" had practically disappeared, as Gastão Cruls points out in his *Aparencia do Rio de Janeiro*.[2]

The Brazilian mulatto, D'Assier wrote in 1867, was the product of the cities and the seaboard plantations rather than of the interior or backlands.[3] His occupations were those which the Indian did not carry on because of his indolence, the Negro because of his lack of intelligence, and the white not to lower his dignity. Thus, for the most part, soldiers, tailors, masons were mulattoes.

From the beginning of the century mulattoes began to emerge in great numbers from the tenements and shanties where the poorer Portuguese and Italian immigrants were "shacking up" with Negro or mulatto women. Not only did these Europeans feel no sexual repugnance for colored women; on the contrary, they may have found in them a certain sexual charm, in addition to the fact that, as I mentioned earlier, they represented a considerable economic asset, with their skills as laundresses, cooks, candymakers, makers of dolls, which was of no small help to these poor immigrants in their early struggles. Thus the Portuguese and Italian immigrants, so numerous

---

[2] Rio de Janeiro, 1949, I, p. 304.

[3] Adolphe d'Assier: *Le Brésil Contemporaine. Races. Moeurs. Institutions. Paysages* (Paris, 1867).

around the middle of the nineteenth century, especially in the cities, became mighty procreators of mulattoes.

It was for mulattoes of this sort that life was hardest. They often wound up as ne'er-do-wells, guitar players, neighborhood bullies, henchmen of political leaders, water-front vagabonds, and the women as prostitutes. They lacked the facilities which smoothed the path of social and intellectual advancement for many mulattoes of rural origin who had aristocratic blood in their veins. On these mulattoes, born and raised in slums and tenements, their unfavorable social situation had a powerful effect, predisposing them to instability and unadaptability to the normal patterns of life and work, to job-shifting, to a general state of rebelliousness, all of this socially pathological, and which so many associate with the biological process of miscegenation. For these mulattoes their irregular origin was complete and all-embracing in its social effects: the illicit union of which they were the fruit; the low social status of their parents; the socially inferior surroundings in which they were born and raised.

To be sure, their more stimulating urban surroundings—"the street"—with which the city urchins were in intimate contact from an early age, youngsters who were further removed from the white boys of the city residences than those of the sugar mills from the young masters of the Big Houses, hastened the development of certain aspects of their intelligence. But in the sense of a precocious and unchanneled rebelliousness. In an anti-social sense, up to a point —the mischievous escapade, stealing fruit from the orchards of the aristocrats, or sweetmeats and cakes from the street venders' trays and the market stalls of the Portuguese, throwing stones at the windows of the fine residences, defacing walls with obscene words and drawings. The walls of the suburban homes, of the city residences were often filthy with the daubings of these young mulattoes and Negroes of the tenements, whose resentment, conscious or not, also took the form of making the portals of great mansions, the corners of fine residences, their latrines. The owners often had to resort to encircling their doorways with spiked iron fences, a prolongation of the walls topped with shards of glass, to defend them against the street rabble, against the disrespect or rancor of the "have-nots."

The free mulatto of the city, for the most part the son of Portuguese or Italian immigrant, grew up in this atmosphere of antagonism between the shanty and the mansion, between the tenement and the suburban residence—an atmosphere almost unknown to the mulatto who had spent his childhood on a plantation or ranch, favored, if he was a house servant, by a more kindly relationship between the two extremes, the masters and the slaves. Favored by selection on the basis of color and features, thanks to which from early childhood the more gifted, lively, intelligent of the slaves, even when they were not the sons of the master, received special treatment, some of them studying with the family chaplain and even the seminary teachers or at the university, their expenses paid by their masters.[4] Thus it came about that with the growing gulf between the mansions and the shanties the enmity between the colored people and the whites deepened.

Concerned over the number of Negroes and mulattoes in Brazil, especially in the cities, and the possibility that the native-born Brazilians, irritated by the Mother country, might join forces with the Negroes, thus sublimating, as can be seen today, the sense of regional difference in that of race and even of class, Araujo Carneiro wrote in 1822: ". . . The critical situation of Brazil, with the many Negroes in which it abounds," for "if the Brazilians grow exasperated" they may, "as a last and desperate measure, call upon the Negroes to assist them and reduce that vast and rich country to the state of the island of Santo Domingo." [5]

Francisco Soares Franco had already given thought to the matter in 1821: "The colored caste is the dominant one in Brazil today," [6] dominant, that is to say, in numbers. Hence his suggestion that miscegenation be encouraged and the mestizo favored, European immigration stimulated and the further importation of Negroes forbidden. The whites would take the place of the Negroes in the seaboard cities, in trades or domestic service, while the blacks could be used in the hinterland to work the mines and plantations. He

---

[4] See W. H. Webster: *Narrative of a Voyage to the South Atlantic Ocean* (London, 1834), p. 43.

[5] H. J. d'Araujo Carneiro: *Brazil e Portugal ou Reflexões sobre o Estado Actual do Brazil* (Lisbon, 1822), p. 11.

[6] Francisco Soares Franco: *Ensaio sobre os Melhoramentos de Portugal e do Brazil*, IV (Lisbon, 1821), p. 14.

called upon the legislators to forbid the marriage of mestizos except to "whites or Indians," thus promoting the "decantation" of the half-breeds into the white race. Soares Franco was also of the opinion that "Brazil should not tolerate so many bachelors," for the unmarried man was as a rule "contemptuous of his social responsibilities." Moreover, it was the duty of all to contribute to the transfer of the descendants of Africans to the white race.

In another essay of the same period, Francisco d'Alpuim de Menezes wrote that the Brazilian, "lacking machines for the heavy work of his plantations, the basic establishment of his country," found himself obliged "to employ the services of slaves, implacable enemies of their master." And superior in numbers to the latter in a proportion of at least six to one. This being the case, it was impossible for the Brazilian to live independent of "an European power which could guarantee the obedience of these slaves." [7]

Thus the attitude of a great sector of the whites in Brazil—principally the Europeans—was one of terror at the time that the political independence of that Portuguese colony was in gestation. Some of them looked upon such independence as impossible unless measures were taken to secure the protection of some European power against the African element, or a preponderance of Europeans in the new state. Perhaps the solution lay in the development of a new element, neither African nor European but a combination of both, with the addition of a third, the Indian—in a word, the mixed-breed. This had been glimpsed not only by men of the talent of José Bonifacio but by others of good common sense like Soares Franco. It was a solution, moreover, to which the social policy of the mother country and the church had been contributing for a long time (with the possible exception of the Jesuits). In this connection, certain incidents mentioned in the old historians of colonial Brazil are significant.

Mello Moraes Filho states, for example, that in colonial Rio de Janeiro a white Portuguese had been put in command of a body of colored militia, and this aroused a protest on the part of the battalion because of the fact that he was white and European. On being informed of this attitude on the part of his men, the Portuguese invited

---

[7] Francisco d'Alpuim Menezes: *Portugal e o Brazil* (Lisbon, 1822), p. 13.

the officers to a banquet and there, in an eloquent speech, stated that he was of African descent.[8] This seems to have sufficed to win him the confidence of his troops. Thus it was not only those of the "colored race" who passed over to the "white," but also the whites who passed over to the colored when the change suited their convenience.

Pedroso, who became the leader of the mulattoes and Negroes in the insurrection of Recife in 1823, did not have to declare himself "of African descent" to win the support of that large and restless part of the population. His condition of light mulatto, with military prestige, allowed him to lean toward either extreme, the ruling white class or the ruled mulattoes and blacks, who were struggling to establish themselves by strength of numbers as the true independent Brazil.

The insurgents went so far as to "behave disrespectfully to white women," and to take numerous Europeans prisoner. And to go about shouting that "all this land belongs to the mulattoes and Negroes rather than to the whites." This is the clear manifestation not only of race hostility but of class and regional revolt. The implication in such attitudes and declarations is that Brazil should belong to the mulattoes and Negroes, and not to the whites, and, least of all, to the Europeans, that is to say, the whites of another region. Pedroso was acclaimed by the insurgents as the "Father of the Country." Father of a country where the citizens were the Negroes and the mulattoes. But the father: paternalism, patriarchalism. The predominant patriarchal system of Brazil was too strong to be shaken off by the insurgents gathered around the figure, at once revolutionary and patriarchal, of the mulatto Pedroso. The truth of the matter was that to many of those rebellious Negroes and mulattoes their biological fathers were unknown, their place being taken by "uncles" or fictitious fathers, their mothers being the sole reality.

We have already mentioned maternalism as a typical feature of the social and character ("ethos") formation of the Brazilian. This was true not only of those of city residence or plantation house, that is to say, areas sociologically stamped by the almost absolute power

---

[8] Mello Moraes: *Fatos e Memorias* (Rio de Janeiro, 1904), p. 131.

of the biological father projected into the sociological father, but of those of shanty or slave quarters.

In the case of the latter, who were often ignorant of their biological father, the dominant figure of family, and, up to a point, political authority, was that of the sociological "father" or "uncle." This patriarchal expression, however, in no way detracted from the cult of the maternal figure incarnated in the biological mother, who at times became the substitute for the father, that is to say, the provider of food, clothing, education, for the child or children of the unknown or absent father. The historian Rocha Pombo, in his *History of Brazil*, recalls that among the free Negroes of Brazilian cities, those living in shanties for the most part, a type of patriarchy of African inspiration or model existed, in which the oldest Negro of the community assumed the name of "father," and the middle-aged that of "uncle," while those of the same age were "brothers" or *malungos*.[9] L. Couty, in his *L'Esclavage au Brésil*, points out the matriarchal character of families of the same social stratum he knew in Brazil: children who knew only their mother.[1] It was she who brought them up. Some even managed to give their sons a university education. They did this by selling sweetmeats or fruits in the streets or at a market stall, cooking for wealthy families, or, less puritanically, accepting the favors and gifts of white gentlemen, setting aside a part of their gains for the education of their sons, especially those who were whiter than they. Wetherell observed in the city of Salvador the pride these dark mothers took in their lighter-skinned sons.

Such contradictions between maternalism—not to be confused with matriarchalism in the strict sense of the term (as the eminent Brazilian essayist and scholar, Joaquim Ribeiro, in my opinion does)—and patriarchalism were frequent in the social development of Brazil, tinged by certain African vestiges which acted as an adjective modifying the noun, or as the ethnological content, which is volatile, in relation to the sociological form, which is enduring or constant.

This explains the Africanisms of this sort, that is to say, those re-

---

[9] Rocha Pombo: *Historia do Brasil*, II (Rio de Janeiro, 1822), p. 542.
[1] L. Couty: *L'Esclavage au Brésil* (Paris, 1881), p. 74.

lated to the family organization, observed by one of the most distinguished Africanologists of our day, Professor M. J. Herskovits, who vigorously defends the thesis of African survivals in the union of the sexes and the family organization in Brazil,[2] against his equally distinguished colleague, Professor F. Frazier.[3] Professor Frazier is of the opinion that all these rites were absorbed there into European rites. In Recife the young Brazilian Africanologist, René Ribeiro, in his study "On the *Amaziado* Relationship and Other Aspects of the Family in Recife, Brazil," [4] came upon elements which seemed to support Herskovits's thesis, that is to say, that concubinage among colored people as a rule amounts to a stable family relationship, in contrast to European concubinage. This thesis is supported by the French sociologist so familiar with Brazilian problems in general and Afro-Brazilian in particular, Professor Roger Bastide.[5] In his opinion, and this is the point which particularly interests us, the free Negro, when he left the rural slave quarters for the city, tended to reconstruct the "big family" in the African manner, with the members classified by age groups; the "big family," whose existence in typically Brazilian cities was recalled, as I observed and Professor Bastide points out, by the historian Rocha Pombo. In the opinion of the discerning French sociologist, what we must accept is that the Afro-Brazilian family, when brought together in the cities, that is to say, in the shanties and poor dwellings of free Negroes: artisans, craftsmen, greengrocers, etc., revived the African rites of the social relationship of children to "mothers," "fathers," "uncles," "brothers," reinterpreted in European terms.

It may have been in this system, at one and the same time patriarchal, maternal, and fraternal, of the African "big family," with "fathers" and "uncles" invested with authority concommitant with their age, experience, wisdom, and not economic standing, and "brothers" or *malungos* joined by the solidarity of age, and not by

---

[2] "The Negro in Bahía, Brazil: A Problem in Method," *American Sociological Review*, VIII, 4 (1943).

[3] "The Negro in Bahía, Brazil," in *American Sociological Review*, VII, 4 (1942).

[4] *American Sociological Review*, X, 1 (1945).

[5] Roger Bastide: "Dans les Amériques Noires: Afrique ou Europe?" in *Cahiers des Annales*, No. 4 (Paris, 1949).

the fact of being children of the same father, or a common mother, or both, that the movement known as the uprising or revolt of the "tailors" or "mulattoes" was, in part, inspired. The egalitarian and republican—in a word, fraternal—ideas of the French revolution also played a part in it. In his testimony one of the conspirators, the mulatto José Felix, stated that "the reason for wanting to convert this continent into a republic was to do away with the Prince's great robbing of this city"; and he added that the revolution was needed "so we can breathe freely, for we live in bondage, and because we are dark-skinned we are denied all opportunity, and being a republic there would be equality among all." [6]

Another revolutionist or conspirator, João de Deos, "a mulatto tailor with a shop on the street to the right of the Palace," to set himself apart from the Portuguese oppressors and annoy them not only by his ideas but by his attire as well, wore "low-cut, pointed slippers, and breeches so tight as to be indecent"; and when anyone remarked on his way of dressing, he would answer: "Hush, this is the French style, and you will soon see that everything is French." The ideas and attire of this anti-Portuguese revolutionary were so openly French that Anna Romana Lopez do Nascimento, a free mulatto woman who was a friend of his, was told, when she asked why he had been imprisoned, that it was "because he was mixed up in French doings." [7] It was a complex movement, as was the so-called Praieira Revolt in the city of Recife half a century later; both of them egalitarian in the sense of being opposed to the absolute power of the autocrats who, to the indignation of those who had to walk on foot in eighteenth-century Bahía, had themselves carried abroad in gilded palanquins, and in Pernambuco in the first half of the nineteenth century, driven about in carriages with silver lanterns.

The ambition of the insurgents or conspirators was to see the officers of the troops of the line and, naturally, other posts of authority filled not exclusively by Negroes or mulattoes, but "without distinction of quality but of ability." What the "republicans" of Bahía wanted was that neither class nor place of origin, which conferred "quality" on the individual, be conditions for his holding posts and

---

[6] *Anais da Biblioteca Nacional do Rio de Janeiro*, 1922–3, XLV, pp. 26ff.
[7] Loc. cit., p. 58.

positions of importance, but only his "ability." They were in a hurry to see accomplished what was slowly coming about: the rise in evaluation as the result of ability, that is to say, intelligence, knowledge, worth of the individual, regardless of his race, class, and place of origin.

"When by reason of his origin, his connections, wealth, or individual worth a mulatto aspires to a position," wrote Rugendas, "it is very rare, one might almost say it never happens, that his color or mixed blood constitute an obstacle. However dark he may be, if he is classified as white, and this is so stated in all his documents, he is qualified to hold any position." [8] And he goes on to say: "There exist in Brazil regiments of militia made up entirely of mulattoes, to which whites are not admitted; in return, the law forbids a mulatto to enter regiments of soldiers of the line. But for the reasons stated above, many mulattoes join them, even the officer corps, which happens most often when they belong to wealthy, well-regarded families, those which have been in Brazil the longest, those in which there has been the most miscegenation, without this affecting their standing, their dignity, and their right to aspire to military posts." The marriage of white men and colored women, "which is common among the middle and lower classes," also takes place at times "in the upper classes." When a white woman of wealthy, distinguished family married a very dark man, it caused a certain amount of scandal, but "astonishment" rather than "censure." And Rugendas, with a keen understanding of how race feeling was outweighed by that of class or region, states: "Other things being equal, dark color and African blood constitute a handicap; however, a white man of standing does not marry a white woman of humble origin either." [9]

If "young Europeans of good appearance and with some business experience" found it easy to "marry wealthy colored women," as Rugendas also observes, it was because the Europeans constituted a "class" in colonial Brazil and during the early years of our independence. They regarded themselves as superior to the native-born whites, even though these were economically, culturally, and so-

---

[8] Maurice Rugendas: *Voyage Pittoresque au Brésil* (Paris e Mulhouse, 1935).
[9] Ibid., p. 95.

cially superior to those Portuguese upstarts. A disdain for the "sea crabs," as they were called, had existed on the part of the Brazilian-born from early colonial days.

It cannot be denied that under cover of strict patriarchalism the rise of the half-breed encountered prejudices of an irrational nature. But neither can it be denied that there was an economic rivalry between the patriarchal system and the rise of the half-breeds, not only in the figure of the university graduate and the soldier, but principally in their capacity as mechanics and master craftsmen, owners of slaves and lands and mines, and not merely the employees of white masters. João Dornas Filho has pointed this out in a brief and pithy essay: ". . . When the mulatto or free Negro was no longer a slave, he had to be paid, and payment made no sense under the slave system." [1] And in this connection he reproduces interesting colonial documents such as the letter of Dom Lourenço de Almeida to Antonio do Vale Mello of March 17, 1732: "This wicked breed of people has worked great harm throughout the district of Minas, and especially in the vicinity of Serro Frio, because the free Negro women, with their stores and taverns, when they are the concubines of slaves, were the cause of the latter stealing the diamonds they found, giving them to these women and not to their masters; and in addition to this, they managed to steal diamonds with such skill from their owners to buy the Negroes' freedom that the Mineiros have repeatedly asked me to clear this area of all free Negroes and mulattoes for it was they who in one way or another possessed themselves of the diamonds dug by the Negro slaves . . ."

Basilio Texeira de Sa Vedra, in his "Informaçao da Capitania de Minas Geraes" (Report on the Captaincy of Minas Geraes), drawn up in Sabará on March 30, 1805, said: "The marriages, and even more, the concubinage of landowners and Negro and mulatto women, have made a third of the population free, without providing means for their maintenance, without teaching them good habits, and they have the crazy idea that free people don't have to work . . ." And he goes on to say: "I should like to see a law passed forbidding mulattoes to be recognized as the legitimate offspring of

---

[1] João Dornas Filho: "O Populario do Negro Brasileiro," *Diario de Minas,* February 19, 1950.

whites; and that, like bastards, they should receive only support from them, and this carefully administered; I should like to see them assigned a certain portion of land, certain lots, so they could not own a large tract; I should like to see many of them obliged to work at crafts and freeman's trades, at which they are, as a rule, very skillful; I should like to see them treated with care, insofar as this redounds to their usefulness, and also the free Negroes, born in this country, who are called creoles, and who are not of much account either; and above all, forbid Negroes to hold other Negroes as slaves, or mulattoes to own mulattoes, and still less for mulattoes to be the slaves of Negroes. In this connection, there are infamous cases of sons who buy their parents, brothers, and sisters, and do not give them complete freedom. All these precautions seem necessary to me to assure the greater safety of this conquest . . ."

Stubbornly determined to carry on with slaves what other economic systems were beginning to accomplish with machines, the Brazilian patriarchal system saw in the mulatto imbued with scandalous or French ideas a revolutionist to be silenced or repressed. This was a difficult task in view of the part early played by numerous half-breeds in expert occupations indispensable, if not to the development, to the rescue of Brazil from the danger of stagnating into a pathetically archaic subnation.

Felippe Nery Collaço, born in Pernambuco in 1813, a colored man who studied law at the University of Recife, was less conspicuous for his French ideas than for his interest in engineering; he was professor of English in the high school of Pernambuco and distinguished himself for the "technical council of engineering" which he established in the capital of the province.[2] His was not an isolated case. Like him, a number of gifted mulattoes appeared in the first half of the last century, whose capabilities were studied and utilized, as we earlier pointed out, by teachers of advanced ideas, such as the Benedictines.

However, the Benedictines were not the only ones in slavery days to study the effects of the Brazilian medium upon the Negroes of Africa, or the effects of crossbreeding on the mestizos. There were

---

[2] Sebastião Galvão: *Dicionario Corografico, Historico e Estatistico de Pernambuco, O-R* (Rio de Janeiro, 1921), p. 142.

doctors like Tiburtino Moreira Prates, who wrote one of the most interesting theses submitted to the School of Medicine of Bahía in the first half of the nineteenth century: *Identidade da Especie Humana (Identity of the Human Species.)*[3] Dr. Moreira took the position, based on observations carried out in Brazil as early as the first half of the nineteenth century, that: "Everyone knows that the Negroes born in Brazil differ greatly from their African progenitors in physical characteristics as well as intellectual faculties." And bearing out D'Orbigny: "In the investigation we have carried on in this province, we have found three families descended from Africans who have remained pure for three generations; these persons are not only not as dark as their parents, but in their traits they do not differ from half-breeds, which is no slight modification." He went even further: he anticipated the modern culturists when he affirmed, on the findings of his studies in Bahía, that men of all races "have the ability to assimilate the culture that develops the faculties of the spirit, to adapt themselves to the religious practices, to the habits of civilized life; in a word, they all have the same mental nature. . . . The men of the Ethiopian race, looked upon as the most degraded, can, notwithstanding, display the finest virtues and rise to the heights of learning." This was already taking place in Brazil: "Everybody knows the obstacles encountered by the Negro who attempts to devote himself to the career of letters, not to mention the lack of pecuniary means, inasmuch as this race is the poorest of our people; but in spite of this we have numerous examples of Negroes who have shown themselves highly gifted in science, letters, and fine arts; we have seen them vie for and obtain in open competition a university chair . . ." And with regard to the mulattoes: "Another class which is ridiculed by its very progenitors is the mulatto, whose intelligence has often been held in contempt by men swayed by prejudice . . ." But the intelligence of the Brazilian mulatto has become more manifest with every passing day: "In spite of a certain rivalry which still exists between whites and mulattoes, the latter, either because of the important role they played in our struggle for independence, or because of their growing number, or for whatever reason may be, are held in esteem in Brazil, and can

---

[3] Bahía, 1848.

attain high posts when fortune favors them." Especially in the province of Bahía: "Indisputable proof of the intelligence of the mulatto can be deduced from the statistics of this province: it is rare to find men here, even those considered white, in whose forebears there is not some admixture of Ethiopian blood; nevertheless, the Bahíans are outstanding by reason of their abilities and their love of letters and science, and no other province has produced such a number of learned men." Above all, in the field of medicine: "There are more than a hundred students in the medical school of this city; half of them are indisputably mulattoes; of the others, we know that many are quadroons who have 'passed'; of others, we are ignorant of their ancestry; those who are unquestionably of the Caucasian race do not number more than twenty."

The same theory was upheld during this same period by M. P. A. de Lisboa in his *"Notes sur la Race Noire et la Race Mulâtre au Brésil"*:[4] ". . . We may conclude that the weakening of intelligence among the Africans is due to the defects of the social conditions under which they lived in Africa rather than any important constitutional difference." And with regard to the mulattoes: "In Brazil, among all classes of society, jurists and doctors, the men who rule the political destinies of the country as well as men of letters, one sees mulattoes of talent, mental gifts, perspicacity, and education, which give them great importance and standing."

Nor should we forget another important testimony from the pen of a European on the situation of the mulatto "class" or "race" in nineteenth-century Brazil, that of Eliseé Reclus in a study published in the *Revue des Deux Mondes: "Le Brésil et la Colonisation, les Provinces du Littoral, les Noirs et les Colonies Allemandes."* After pointing out that no law exists in Brazil to prevent a father recognizing his son—which favored the emancipation of the mulatto— the French geographer wrote: ". . . One can foresee the not distant day when the blood of former slaves will flow in the veins of every Brazilian." And he adds: "The sons of the emancipated slaves became citizens; they entered the army and the navy . . . and could speak with the same right as their Caucasian brothers-in-arms of the

---

[4] *Nouvelles Annales des Voyages et des Sciences Geographiques,* directed by V. de Saint-Martin, II (Paris, 1847), p. 65.

national cause and the honor of the flag. Some of them rose rank by rank until they were in command of whites who were their inferiors; others took up the liberal professions and became lawyers, doctors, professors, artists." And stressing what we might call the predominance of sociological over biological whiteness in Brazil during the first half of the nineteenth century: "It is true that the law does not confer upon Negroes the right to vote or to hold office; but the more or less dark-skinned officials make no difficulty about recognizing as whites all those who wish to so style themselves, and provide them with the necessary documentation legally and indisputably to establish the purity of their origins." [5]

This points up the long-established tendency in Brazil to accept as valid the document or statement rather than the biological facts with regard to a person's race. A tendency which was to have the passive co-operation not only of written documents but of paintings and even colored photographs. These were "documents" whose purpose was to superficially Aryanize all those who were "white" because of a social status equivalent to that of the whites.

The phase of the shift of power from the rural plantations to the city, or suburban residences, was characterized among us by the transition from the painted portrait to the daguerreotype and the photograph. For a time this was marked by its faithfulness: the ugly was ugly, even if the sitter was rich and important. Later on, photography became cynically commercial and was colored "to order." Experts in the United States made a specialty of toning down into golds and pinks the new-rich, the new-powerful, the new-educated "high yellows" and even mulattoes of Brazil and other South American countries.

The vogue of "colored photographs" explains the fact that even today there are to be found in family parlors pictures of deceased forebears who, though unmistakably mulattoes or quadroons, at times give us in their apologetic, not to say angelic, photographs the impression of being examples of those "Europeans degraded by the tropics" to whom the writer Mario Pedrosa refers. In such cases the photograph is not a decisive argument but rather an accessory to a hoax.

---

[5] *Revue des Deux Mondes*, Vol. 40 (Paris, July 15), p. 388.

CHAPTER XII

REFLECTIONS
ON MISCEGENATION IN
PATRIARCHAL AND
SEMI-PATRIARCHAL BRAZIL

Raymundo José de Souza Gayoso, in his *Compedio Historico-Politico dos Principios da Lavoura no Maranhão* (*Historical-Political Compendium of the Principles of Agriculture in Maranhão*) (Paris, 1818), discusses the different strata of population in colonial Maranhão. Especially in São Luis, one of the first cities in Brazil to achieve bourgeois affluence without losing the patriarchal tenor of living or coexistence.

"The population of the city according to the latest census," he states, "did not number thirty thousand; but, inasmuch as it has increased since the year 1808, it may now have reached this figure. Its inhabitants can be divided into various classes. The most powerful, and the one most worthy of consideration, is that of the Portuguese."

Next came the descendants of Europeans who had settled in Brazil, the native-born white Brazilians.

After the native whites followed the mulattoes and half-breeds. Half-breeds who were almost white or "semi-white," as they were sometimes called.

"The third class of inhabitants of Maranhão is a mixed race, the offspring of a European and a Negro woman, or a European and an Indian woman," wrote Gayoso. And he added: "Those of the first mentioned are called mulattoes; those of the second, mestizos. At the beginning of the conquest of the New World, all the courts of Europe endeavored to create a single race of their new and old vassals, encouraging marriages between Europeans and the natives of the land. These alliances were entered upon as soon as Maranhão began to emerge from the possession of its first inhabitants; however, perhaps the laxity of customs, or the heat of the climate, were the principal stimuli to the production of inhabitants of this sort, to the point where they came to constitute a considerable part of the population." This situation was not limited in Maranhão, but existed in several subregions of Brazil.

"The Portuguese, as well as the Spaniards, classify by different names all degrees of such descent and all varieties of the human species." With a certain display of erudition, Gayoso goes on: "Robertson, in his history of America, says that the first generation of mestizos or mulattoes are looked upon as Indians or Negroes; that by the third the original color of the Indian has become extinct, and by the fifth the color of the Negro has disappeared so completely that the offspring cannot be distinguished from the European and enjoy all the latter's privileges. I have seen a trade chart of America which carries a list where these gradations are set forth in more detail.

TABLE OF MIXTURES

TO BECOME WHITE

White and Negro produces mulatto
Half white, half black
White and mulatto produces quadroon
Three-quarters white and one-quarter Negro
White and quadroon produces octoroon
Seven-eighths white and one-eighth Negro
White and octoroon produces white
Completely white

TABLE OF MIXTURES

TO BECOME NEGRO

Negro and white produces mulatto
Half Negro and half white
Negro and mulatto produces quadroon
Three-quarters Negro and one-quarter white
Negro and quadroon produces octoroon
Seven-eighths Negro and one-eighth white
Negro and octoroon produces Negro
Completely Negro

Gayoso added to Robertson's classification certain addenda on the Brazilian situation, based on his firsthand knowledge of Maranhão: "The mixture of a mulatto and quadroon or octoroon will produce other shades of color, approaching white or black, in keeping with the progression outlined above. And it is this sector of the population, which is of robust constitution, that carries out all the manual activities and tasks calling for strength and dexterity which the members of the upper class, for the most part, deem it beneath their dignity to perform, more out of vanity than laziness, or perhaps both."

As for the Negroes, they constitute "a fourth of the population." The Indians are not sufficiently integrated into the society of Maranhão—an area representative of the society or the patriarchal economy of the greater part of Brazil—to be considered an important class.

It was probably Gayoso who made the most careful effort to compile a systematic classification of miscegenation in patriarchal and semi-patriarchal Brazil. He attempted to do this by subordinating the categories of races and subraces to those of classes and subclasses. In this he was followed some years later by Abreu e Lima, who took up the problem in a study published in Rio de Janeiro in 1835, approaching it from a point of view that was almost Marxist: emphasizing the hatreds which separated these "races" or "classes," these "subraces" and "subclasses." "Our population may be divided into two groups, the freemen and the slaves, who certainly show no marked affinity for one another. Even so, we could congratulate ourselves if the group of freemen were homogeneous and in conditions of perfect equality . . ." Instead, Abreu e Lima considered it to be subdivided in four different families, as opposed and inimical to one another as the two large groups, consisting of free Negroes, free mulattoes, native-born whites, and adoptive whites, without counting the Indians, whom he looked upon as a separate "family" or "race" or "class." A rivalry existed between all of them in proportion to their "respective classes," he wrote. It seemed just to Abreu e Lima that the free mulattoes should not tolerate an attitude of superiority on the part of the whites; they were men like the whites, born of the same soil, and—a patriarchal argument in favor of the equality of races and subraces—"sons of our own fathers." Therefore, they had the same rights as the whites, the same rights as the other native-born Brazilians, the same rights as the other free Brazilians.

The denial of such rights to free mulattoes—which it should be pointed out was never systematic in Brazil—gave rise to disturbances of a social nature, at times disguised as political. And also the more obvious manifestations of what some consider the pathology of miscegenation, giving their diagnosis a purely biological character when this pathology would seem to have been the result, for the most part, of social circumstances unfavorable to the normal development of the mulattoes and dark-skinned people.

In South Africa, which today resembles the patriarchal and ethnically stratified colonial Brazil, those engaged in the study of miscegenation are beginning to recognize—as a critic of the *Journal of the African Society* in a review of a book by Ray Phillips suggests—that the results of miscegenation seem unfavorable because of "social reasons." [1] This must be recognized before the problem can be studied on a purely biological basis. The real evil lies in the "illicit connections" which constitute there, as in other countries with a half-breed population, the large percentage of unions between white men and Negro women. An illicit union of itself creates a situation of definite inferiority for the bastard, and this is even greater in the

---

[1] *Journal of the African Society*, IV (London, 1930).

case of the half-breed bastard. This is true both of Africa and the United States.

This is likewise the case of the Eurasians, the offspring of Europeans and Hindus, rejected by both English and Hindus, and who today constitute one of the most melancholy population groups in the world. A morbid midway point, less between two races than between two rigid civilizations. It is a unique situation, for neither of the two races, neither the imperial nor the—until recently—subject or dominated, and neither of the two civilizations—not even the Christian of the conquerors, whose religious doctrines so fervently proclaim humanity and gentleness—will lower itself to absorb them nor make itself elastic enough to tolerate them. And the stigma which marks them in the eyes of each civilization is the unfortunate union which brought them into existence. The fate of the Eurasian women is almost always that of prostitutes of white men. The men, as a great mark of condescension, may rise to the rank of minor public servant. But the whole population is—or was for a long time— comprised of socially unhealthy members. The "pathology of miscegenation" can be seen in this sad, suffering group of hybrids in its most crude and manifest aspects. Perhaps in its most dramatic form. They are the best example of the social problem of the rejected as well as the biological problem of the mixed-bloods. The North American mulatto can take shelter under the ever more powerful wing of the "Negro" race, more than a third of which are mestizos. The Eurasian has no refuge from the light which all day long proclaims his "infamous origin." Only in the darkness of the night can he fraternize with those of pure race, and this under cover of sexual relations.

It is not surprising that this rejected sector of society should show a physical inferiority which makes it so weakly, so unhappy, so sensual, even for Orientals. This fact has been observed among halfbreed populations in general, and is apparently due to reasons which are, in the main, social.

Without denying or ignoring the tendency of certain races toward certain morbid states—like the running amok of the Malays, for example—which some associate in absolute fashion with ethnic causes, others ascribe to climate, we must take into account the strong social forces which would seem to foster the development of tuberculosis and forms of mental illness among mestizo peoples. It is known that as a rule the Negro—at any rate, the North American, who has been the object of more study than the others—is less predisposed than the whites to spinal diseases, to obesity, deafness, visual ailments, and diseases of the nose and throat. Less susceptible to typhoid fever, malaria, bladder ailments, cancer. The mulatto, too, has a number of these fortunate predispositions of the Negro; but shows a much higher incidence of tuberculosis and venereal diseases than the whites. Tuberculosis seems to be the most frequent manifestation of physical weakness not only among the North American mulattoes but among mixed-breeds in general. Davenport points out that this may be due to the lack of resistance to civilized diseases inherited from their primitive forbears.[2]

But aside from this possibly inherited tendency, one must always bear in mind the social situation—including the economic—of the mulatto, as well as of the Negro transplanted to America. In the case of rickets, which is so frequent among North American city Negroes, a study of their social background in the United States, the darkness of the overcrowded tenements of New York and other cities during the winter, the lack of sun, of fresh air, the inadequate diet, all fostering the possible special susceptibility of the Negro to the disease, throws light on the frequent malformation of the body among colored children. The greatest enemy of children, whatever their color, is poverty, to which Professor Reuter gives the importance it warrants in his study of the health of the Negro and mulatto in the United States.[3]

The regional variations in tuberculosis mortality in the United States would seem to indicate a strong relation between the disease and social and economic conditions. Even though the malady is declining, it is still predominantly a city disease. And anyone who has ever visited the Negro tenements or the poorest Negro neighbor-

---

[2] C. B. Davenport: *Heredity in Relation to Eugenics* (New York, 1911); *Race Crossing in Jamaica*, in collaboration with M. Steggerda (Washington, 1929). See also Octavio Domingues: *Hereditariedade em Face da Educação* (São Paulo, n.d.).

[3] E. B. Reuter: *The American Race Problem* (New York, 1927). See also Roquette-Pinto: "Notas sobre os Tipos Antropologicos do Brasil," in *Anais do 1° Congresso Brasileiro de Eugenia* (Rio de Janeiro, 1929).

hoods of certain North American cities—Waco, Texas, for example—will find no exaggeration in the almost lyrical tone in which General Clement de Gradprey once referred to the shanties of Recife, and later, the writer Ribeiro Couto. The twenty thousand shanties of the Negroes, mulattoes, the dark people of Afogados, Pina, Santana de Dentro, Oiteiro, Motocolombó, which are the most typical of Brazil. Those built on dry ground should shock no one because they are made of straw. The sun comes into them like a rich, generous friend of the family. From the point of view of defense or protection of man against tuberculosis, straw is an excellent, cheap building material for the larger part of the proletarian population of the tropics.

There are, as we mentioned in an earlier chapter, the shanties built in the mud. Some, the better ones, which stand on piles above the marshes or mangrove swamps, even have a pleasant air of lacustrian huts, and are at a hygienic distance from the damp earth or the stagnant water. But others are set right in the slime, the inhabitants living in an unhealthy intimacy with the damp and decay, like the shanties of Joaneiro in the area of Recife itself. The problem is an ecological one, of uneven distribution, the rich monopolizing the good and dry sites, the poor—comprising, as a rule, the half-breeds, mulattoes, or Negroes—packed like sardines in the mud. At times in their struggle with the mud the poor eventually make the place healthfully habitable. But a dry and healthful site becomes a desirable one; the shanty dweller is ousted, and the rich come to put up their houses of stone and mortar. Valuable houses. The shanties spring up again, in other mudflats, in other swamps.

The same thing happens on the hillsides of Rio de Janeiro with the *favelas*, which resemble certain *ranchos* in Rio Grande do Sul, which have been dealt with in a study by Professor Thales de Azevedo; these are groups of shacks even more unhygienic than the shanties of the cities of the North. Shacks of rotten planks and sheets of tin, as stifling on humid nights as the slums and tenements where other sectors of the poor inhabitants of Brazilian cities are crowded almost without air and sun, that sun and air which are a luxury within easy reach of the shanty dwellers. A population in large part Negro and mulatto; though in Rio Grande do Sul the Indian admixture was greater than the Negro. I believe I was the first to point out, after a trip to that area in 1939, the wretched physical condition of the gauchos living in huts that are the equivalent of the shanties; I realized that the conventional notion of the gaucho as strong, rosy, and healthy in contrast to the sallow northerner was myth or legend.

Tuberculosis being, as it is, a plague that thrives upon poor living conditions, including, as Dr. Alvaro de Faria points out, "diet deficiencies," it is not to be wondered at that our mulatto and Negro population, badly housed and fed, should have contributed such a large number of consumptives to the cemeteries. Moreover, the blacks do not "have the defenses which the whites have been storing up during centuries of living with those suffering from the white plague," being, on the contrary, "still virgin territory" for its contagion. Therefore, the reputed susceptibility of the Negro and mulatto to tuberculosis may be practically discounted in comparing the resistance or physical strength of the whites to that of the Negroes and the mulattoes. The truth of the matter is that, brought from Africa to "a different milieu, so full of social and organic enemies," as Dr. Faria puts it,[4] the Negro in Brazil and the darker mulatto, who in four centuries have "produced more of the social wealth than they have consumed," reveal themselves today as not only full of possibilities but of proofs of physical strength and intellectual ability.

It must be pointed out once more, however, that these proofs and possibilities are to be found today in Brazil in the mulatto rather than in the pure Negro, who for almost half a century—the period of the steadiest rise of our colored population—has become rare among us. Moreover, in the United States itself, specialists in Negro studies, like Professor M. J. Herskovits, emphasize the fact that the pure Negro probably constitutes less than one quarter of the colored population, the other three quarters being mulattoes. Hence, in his opinion, the error into which Professor Reuter falls who, in his

---

[4] Alvaro de Faria: "O Problema da Tuberculose no Preto e no Branco e Relação da Resistencia Racial." Study presented at the First Afro-Brazilian Congress (Recife, 1934).

claims for the superiority of the mulatto over the pure Negro, forgets that the latter hardly exists in sufficient numbers to make a fair comparison possible.[5]

Those influences of social conditions alluded to in the case of tuberculosis, and its prevalence among half-breed populations, should be taken into account in an interpretation of mental diseases among Negroes and mulattoes. Ulysses Pernambucano de Mello verified in a statistical study of the patients of Tamarineira in Pernambuco that, in the case of toxic and infectious psychoses, alcoholism accounted for 11.81 per cent of the cases among the Negroes, whereas among the whites and mulattoes the incidence of alcoholism was only 7.01 per cent.[6] And Professor Cunha Lopes found proof in Rio de Janeiro of "the chronic alcoholism of Negro women or their low resistance to alcohol," whereas "the mulatto phenotype reveals a divergence from the Negro race, inasmuch as the mulatto woman shows a lessened reaction to this social toxin." This descending curve of alcoholism from the black woman, socially the most degraded—the alley prostitute, the companion of the soldier or the drunken sailor—to the white woman, the socially superior element, may reflect the influence of the social factor more than any other. The colored women are also the most numerous victims of cerebral syphilis in Rio de Janeiro. Cunha Lopes, observing the large number of Negroes among the idiots and mental imbeciles, reached the conclusion, on the basis of this and other observations, that, from the point of view of psychopathology, the Brazilian mestizo or mulatto is steadily assimilating the qualities of the whites. The same thing that is happening anthropologically, according to the findings of Professor Roquette-Pinto.

I find myself in disagreement with Pernambucano de Mello when he states that the living conditions of the Negroes are no different from those of the poor whites and half-breeds who constitute the

---

[5] Melville J. Herskovits: *The American Negro: A Study in Racial Crossing* (New York, 1928).

[6] Ulysses Pernambucano de Mello and his collaborators initiated in Pernambuco, under the stimulus of the organizers of the Afro-Brazilian Congress held in Recife in 1934, the study of mental illnesses and Afro-Brazilian religious activities. This study was continued by Professor René Ribeiro, a pupil of Herskovits.

majority of the patients he has examined. For it seems to me that even among the poorer classes the influences unfavorable to the Negro—unfavorable to his social acceptance or sentimental aspirations, for example—are operative, influences which may very well affect his mental health and the social normality of his life.

At the Afro-Brazilian Congress of Recife in 1934 two veteran folklorists, Alfredo Brandão of Alagoa and Rodriguez de Carvalho of Paraíba, presented a large collection of folk songs and sayings which revealed the contempt in which the dark Negro was held, even by his equals or near equals, in submerged cultural or economic living conditions—mulattoes, or Indian-Negro half-breeds. To be sure, in Brazilian folklore the country or backwoods Indian-Negro half-breed is also looked down upon by the city mulatto, who prides himself on being closer to the whites in blood and culture, including the fact of wearing shoes:

> *The mulatto is son of the white man,*
> *The white man is son of the king,*
> *The caboclo, I don't know of whom;*
> *As he is the son of the forest,*
> *He neither wears shoes*
> *Nor talks aught but nonsense.*

But it is the Negro who bears the brunt of the satire which expresses the social contempt in which he is held by the poor mulattoes and whites. Numerous sayings bear this out: "If the Negro does not dirty up the place when he comes in, he does as he goes out." "A Negro standing up is a stump; lying down, he's a pig." "All a Negro's good for is to be a white man's bodyguard." Or in the songs sung at fairs:

> *An old nigger when he dies*
> *Stinks like hell;*
> *Mother of God, don't let him*
> *Go to heaven.*

And:

> *The white man eats in the parlor,*
> *The Indian in the hall,*
> *The mulatto in the kitchen,*
> *The Negro in the privy.*

The white man drinks champagne,
The caboclo, Port wine,
The mulatto drinks rum,
And the Negro, pig piss.

The Negro was jeered at and disdained not only because of his somatic characteristics—flat nose, thick lips, kinky hair, big backside—and his reek, or "budum," but also for objects and forms of African culture which in Brazil remained typical of the blacks and were not used by half-breeds or whites. The Jews' harp, for example:

His mother is an owl
Who lives in the hole of a tree;
His father, a Negro of Angola,
The Jews' harp plays he.

In Brazilian folklore the Negro was also mocked by those of his own social class for using articles of apparel which took on, as pointed out earlier, an almost exclusive quality of race and, above all, class: shoes, top hat, sunshade, gloves, diamond rings, cane, Prince Albert. We have seen that in colonial days Negroes were forbidden by law to use jewels, sword, dagger.

Any Brazilian who is over fifty will recall having seen in his childhood days, in those areas where there was a large Negro population, people staring and street urchins jeering at any Negro women who ventured out wearing a white woman's hat, those hats covered with flowers, ribbons, feathers which were high fashion forty years ago. And that Negro or near-Negro women could enjoy the pomp of a parasol only at carnival time: those big parasols far prettier than any bourgeois umbrella, red and at times fringed with gold, parasols of the queens of the street dancers.

Such an attitude did not hold true with regard to the mulattoes; our folklore offers no proof of such disdain, nor did it jeer at their social ambitions or achievements. Naturally, we refer to the light mulatto; barring special favorable circumstances, the situation of the darker ones was much the same as that of the Negro. To be sure, there were always insinuations, even against the light ones, to the effect that they were treacherous, fickle, flighty. In this the mulatto was the object of resentment on the part of the Negro and the *cabo-clo*, as well as of feelings of rivalry on the part of the white, his privileges of caste or class, rather than race, threatened by the successful climbers.

In old family albums of the period of the Empire it is not unusual to come upon the photographs of such victors wearing frock coat, a big ring, a gold chain, with cane or sunshade at his side—all the insignia of the white aristocrat; or some lady dressed in black silk, with pleated skirt, her hair arranged in slightly un-European puffs, bejeweled, with the air of a great lady. The Count of Gobineau wrote that he had seen among the Empress's ladies-in-waiting three who were unmistakably mulattoes, and he mentions one of them by name, Dona Josefina de Fonseca Costa. Moreover, this French champion of the Aryans, exaggerating a little, wrote that "Brazilian" was with rare exceptions tantamount to "colored." There was colored or Indian blood in the veins of the best families. According to him, the Minister of Foreign Affairs at the time that Gobineau was diplomatic representative in Rio was a mulatto, the Baron of Cotegipe. As were several senators. Among the most distinguished families there were members of a mulatto cast. Of the ladies-in-waiting Gobineau mentions, one was "brown," one was "light chocolate," and the third "violet." [7] A distinguished historian, since deceased, told me, in this connection, that he had found in France among the private papers of Emperor Dom Pedro II a list of eminent mulattoes, drawn up in Dom Pedro's own handwriting, which may have served Gobineau as the basis for his generalizations.

In an epoch like the nineteenth century in Brazil, with its high mortality rate, not only of infants but of women as well, when only the husband, as a rule, lived on to a ripe old age, with three or four successive wives, and six to eight children by each, it must not have been rare to find cases of brothers on their father's side some of whom were white, some Negroid, some with an Indian admixture. The three races with the same patriarchal family name. Pure whites with a mulatto half-brother or sister. Cases of this sort make generalizations about certain families difficult. It can easily be seen how under the same roof of plantation house or city residence, or the

[7] George Readers: *Le Comte de Gobineau au Brésil* (Paris, 1934).

same family name—Cavalcanti, Argolo, Albuquerque, Breves, Wanderley—there could be brothers who differed in race, color, features, blood stream.

As a result of this, or the circumstance of the mother or grandmother of the household being a mulatto, dramatic situations often arose which are reflected in certain Brazilian novels or stories. Fair-skinned persons preventing visitors from catching sight of their fat, broad-beamed mulatto mother or grandmother. Others hiding the dark brother or sister, the "skeleton in the closet," whose features or color would give away the less illustrious or less Aryan origins of them all. And still others displaying their condition of New Whites —a variety of New Christians of the socially accepted color—not only in the jewels, sunshade, spats, cane, gold tooth, diamond rings once forbidden to Negroes and dark mulattoes by law or custom, but also in exaggeratedly Aryan concepts and prejudices. This among the more sophisticated; the more naïve alleging that they could not bear the smell of Negroes, affecting a physical horror of them, and exaggerating the use of articles which the Negro was unable to adopt without discomfort or without looking ridiculous, like pince-nez, for example. And certain styles of hair and beard.

The social climbing of the New Whites has already been mentioned. By itself, or in conjunction with other forms of social climbing—that of the new educated, the new powerful, the new rich, and, in my opinion, like these, social in origin and motive—we find it in certain of our most distinguished mulattoes, who by their economic or intellectual rise became officially white. But there is not a trace of it in Machado de Assis, for example. The restraint, the poise, the reticence of this pale mulatto, nicknamed "the English mulatto," have become classic. Nor in Baron Cotegipe,[8] so refined, so witty, so subtle, incapable of the least act or trace of snobbery. Nor in Gonçalves Dias, Juliano Moreira,[9] Domicio da Gama—for a time Brazilian ambassador in Washington—Dom Silverio Gomes Pimenta.[1] Nor in another bishop, pink and plump, loving black beans and pineapple, whom I knew as a child when, coming to the end of

---

[8] A statesman of outstanding political ability during the Empire.
[9] A distinguished Negro psychiatrist of the twentieth century.
[1] A highly respected and admired Negro archbishop of Minas Gerais.

his days, he used to ride in his carriage through the streets of Recife, Dom Luiz Raymundo da Silva Brito. However, the social climbing of the mulatto, with all its "inferiority complex," linked to that of the "newly learned," leaped to the eye in the great figure of Tobias Barreto, a mulatto who was almost a genius and who, to compensate for his Negroid ancestry vis-à-vis Brazilian, Portuguese, French or Francophiles in general, exaggerated his Germanophilism, his cult of the science of the Germans, who were even whiter than the French. And in Nilo Peçanha,[2] in whom the snobbery of the "new powerful" was unsweetened by that charm which is one of the best qualities of the Brazilian mulatto when he has triumphed or is on the road to triumph. This was the case, too, of Francisco Glycerio.[3]

The Brazilian charm we talk so much about—the man who is "ugly, yes, but attractive," and even "bad or immoral, true, but very charming"; the "cordial man" whom Ribeiro Couto and Sergio Buarque de Hollanda speak of—[4] this charm and cordiality are especially typical of the mulatto. Not so much the withdrawn, pale type as the pink, the brown, the "high yellow." Nobody is as pleasant as he, nor has such a jolly laugh, such a cordial way of offering a stranger the classic demitasse, or his hospitality, his help. Nor such an affectionate way of embracing, transforming this rite of friendship among men into a typically Brazilian expression of cordiality. The Count of Gobineau himself, who continually felt ill at ease or uncomfortable among Pedro II's subjects, seeing them all as degenerates as a result of the effects of miscegenation, nevertheless recognized the Brazilian as the cordial man par excellence: "very polite, gracious, pleasant." Evidently the Brazilian with a dash of African blood or some African trace in his formation; not the pure white or "European," often on his guard, nor the *caboclo*, who is, for the most part, wary and laughs little.

This *simpatia* of the Brazilian, clearly more pronounced in the mulatto, "in whom the Aryan lymph," Professor Gilberto Amado

---

[2] A vice-president of the republic who succeeded to the presidency on the death of the president. Though Negroid and of humble origin, he was married to an aristocrat.

[3] A politician of São Paulo during the republic.

[4] S. Buarque de Hollanda: *Raizes do Brasil*, 2nd ed. (Rio de Janeiro, 1947), p. 213.

writes, "has not yet dissolved the animal exuberance of the Negro temperament," [5] does not seem to me to be mainly ethnic in origin, nor to come from the pure "carnal delight of the first African women who showed their beautiful teeth in a smile and happily dusted themselves off in the new slave quarters after the master had come seeking them out." "The rich laughter" Professor Amado speaks of in the Brazilian mulatto seems to me rather a social development; and I completely agree with the distinguished essayist when he says of the smiling mulattoes: ". . . The habit of serving, acquired during the long submission of slavery, gives them a cooperative and obsequious character," a "resilient sweetness with which they meet obstacles." In that "rich laughter" there was undoubtedly African extroversion; perhaps greater plasticity of the muscles of the face than among the whites. But it probably developed, as has already been suggested, under the social conditions of the rise of the mulatto, his rise as a free man and not merely in the slave quarters and harems of the plantations, but with these slave quarters and harems as its point of departure.

The professionally trained mulatto competing with the white lawyer, doctor, politician sought to triumph over his competitors by making more of an effort than they to please his clients, his patients, his constituency. His easy laugh was not only one of the elements but one of the most powerful instruments in his professional, political, economic ascent; one of the most characteristic expressions of his ductility in passing from a servile state to that of command or domination or, at any rate, of equality with the white rulers, once unique, undisputed. Of his passing not only from one race to another but from one class to another. By the middle of the nineteenth century some of these triumphant mulattoes felt themselves more "Celtic" or more European in appearance, and not merely in education, than the whites of long standing in Brazil. On February 19, 1859, a collaborator of the *Diario de Pernambuco*, who concealed his identity under the initial *W*, commented on a passage in *O Liberal Pernambucano* for September 6, 1856, which he considered "a gem": ". . . We have seen grandchildren of African crossed with Europeans as light and with the oval of their face as

---

[5] Gilberto Amado: *Grão de Areia* (Rio de Janeiro, 1919), pp. 136–7.

perfect as persons of purely Celtic strain. Whereas those whose families have lived in Brazil for a longer time begin to acquire a more marked colonial type, losing the oval shape of the face (and taking on the heavy jaw of the backlands), as happens especially in the North, and their skin become darker."

The collaborator of the *Diario* interpreted this to mean that the editor-in-chief of *O Liberal*—a distinguished mestizo—was trying to prove that he was "white and not half-breed."

This is stupidity or malice on W.'s part. What *O Liberal Pernambucano* was trying to point out, it seems to me, disinterestedly or *pro domo sua,* was the action of the cultural medium on the individual: on the physical make-up of the mestizo, who, swayed by contradictory origins at times, tended toward the socially higher when social and cultural influences favored this. If we accept the results of Boas's famous investigations, nutrition, in conjunction with other forces of the milieu, affects the shape of the head and the oval of the face of the newcomers, cutting the ground from under the supposed absolute fixity of such racial characteristics as manner of walking, talking, gesticulating, laughing.

With his ready laugh, a laugh no longer servile like that of the black, but, at most, obsequious and, above all, establishing a climate of intimacy, the Brazilian mulatto, if of the extrovert type, became another creator of intimacy. That "desire to establish an intimacy," which the essayist Sergio Buarque de Hollanda considers so typical of the Brazilian, and with which he associates our tendency toward the use of diminutives, a device which helps, says he, "to familiarize us with things." [6]

In the use of the diminutive, which can become a little cloying at times, nobody outdoes the mulatto. It was he, at any rate, who strengthened and fixed this tendency of ours, who most enriched it with typically Brazilian social meanings and overtones. For the interests, the difficulties of a person in the process of transition from one class to another, almost from one race to another, the diminutive, softening his words, represented a respectful and at the same time intimate approach to former masters, and to affairs once outside his province and the sole prerogative of the whites.

---

[6] Hollanda: Op. cit., p. 217.

True, this affectation of the mulatto at times bordered on effeminacy—almost the coyness of a girl, with certain manners, gestures like those of a woman trying to please a man—in his dealings with the white man who was his social superior. It recalled, too, the adolescent vis-à-vis the sexually and socially mature man, the complete, triumphant man whom he, the adolescent, in his heart longs to outstrip, imitating, exaggerating his adult qualities—the deep voice, the strength, the intellectual and physical superiority—and with whom he makes every effort to establish a footing of intimacy. Socially insecure, the mulatto attempts to reassure himself with this gentle, unctuous, somewhat feminine approach. Until he has attained social maturity, at least outwardly, when he often becomes the social climber, the parvenu, the new cultured, at times developing that "morbid social pushing," as one Spanish-American journalist puts it.

But it would be wrong to conclude on the basis of this social ambition, difficult to explain biologically, that the mulatto is incapable of achieving stability as the social and intellectual equal of the white man. As far as intellectual capacity is concerned, the mulatto has given in Brazil, as in other countries where miscegenation exists, nearly every proof of this, even acheiving in Machado de Assis and Cotegipe the finest type of humor—pure and not contrived humor—in Auta de Souza [7] the highest poetic spirituality, and in Livio de Castro [8] the capacity for sociological analysis, later manifested by other extremely intelligent Negroids of Brazil.

We lack tests based on recent techniques which would make it possible to reach firmer conclusions arrived at, not on the basis of outstanding and isolated cases, but of whole groups which are truly representative, regarding the mental differences which the three groups may present among us. Examining the reports of teachers during the early days of the Empire, some of them very carefully kept, indicating the degree of progress of pupils classified according to color, one finds proof not of the intellectual inferiority of the mestizo—mulatto, or Indian and white, Indian and Negro half-

[7] An early twentieth-century mystic poetess of Negro origin.
[8] A Negro sociologist of the nineteenth century.

breeds, but principally mulatto—but rather of his aptitude for learning.

As we have seen, this same aptitude was found in children and adolescents of African ancestry by the Benedictine friars in colonial days. And if this aptitude seemed weaker in the Negro, we should not forget that the lighter mulattoes had freer access to situations and social contacts which favored the development of their intelligence and the flowering of their personality.

As for resistance to disease, in so far as such resistance depended on nutrition and living conditions, the poor free mulatto of slavery days, in the cities of Brazil in the nineteenth century, suffered disadvantages as compared with the Negro or mulatto slave, better fed than he in the slave quarters of the plantation houses and city residences. In resistance to disease and in life expectancy. Dr. Luiz Robalinho Cavalcanti, for some time assistant to the late Professor Antonio Austregesilo, found from statistics compiled in the Psychopathic Hospital of Rio de Janeiro, that, among 1,198 patients over the age of fifty, longevity was greater among whites and Negroes than among half-breeds (mestizos of white and Negro, white and Indian, Indian and Negro, or a cross of these). In interpreting the results of the investigation, he utilized, in part, the suggestion of Professor Roquette-Pinto: the inequality of social guarantees of longevity between Brazilian mulattoes and whites.[9] But as between mulattoes and Negroes? Possibly the better adaptation of the Negro to the tropical milieu. But, we must not forget—however much importance is attributed to this better adaptation—the difference in social conditions between Negro slaves under the patriarchal slave system and many of the free and destitute mulattoes. A difference whose favorable effects may possibly still be reflected in those Negroes of almost Biblical age whom we all know: old Negroes who carry their seventy, eighty, and even ninety years on feet that can still dance a *batuque* or a *xangó*.

At the same time, it is worth noting among the younger generations of Brazilians—who have been less affected by this difference of so-

---

[9] Luiz Robalinho Cavalcanti: "Longevidade. Sua Relação com os grupos etnicos da população." Paper presented at the First Afro-Brazilian Congress (Recife, 1934).

cial guarantees—the rise not only of the lighter mulatto, but also of the darker, among athletes, swimmers, football players, who to-day are nearly all mestizos.[1] The same is true of the bulk of the army, the navy, the air force, the police, and the firemen: among their sports champions the Negro is becoming more and more rare, with the mulatto predominating. Strong mulattoes and mestizos, who can compete advantageously with whites and blacks in games, tourna-ments, military exercises.

We should not forget the stamina of the plantation "bad men"—most of them mulattoes or Indian and Negro half-breeds—nor of the longshoremen in many of our cities, nearly all of them mulat-toes. Just as we should not forget that many a dark mulatto passes for Negro in Brazil, where today it is almost impossible to find anthro-pologically pure Africans or Negroes. Many of those regarded as such are mestizos who give the erroneous impression of being Ne-groes because of their richer melanic pigmentation. Dark, but still mulatto. As Roquette-Pinto, a distinguished anthropologist, has stated: "It is almost certain that there are no pure Negroes in Brazil today." An occasional one, perhaps, but, by and large, the Negro of Brazil is the mulatto. The negroid. Among us the Negro problem has been simplified by the long process of miscegenation which took place everywhere, with the exception of a few outlying runaway slave settlements or some group or redoubt of whites entrenched in their class or race prejudices. Even the great leaders of what our Negro has kept as most uniquely his—his religious traditions—are today mulattoes. Mulattoes, many of whom are now greatly de-Africanized in their ways of living, but who re-Africanize them-selves by going to study in Africa. As in the case of Father Adão of Recife, who made himself into a native religious leader in Lagos, speaking African as fluently as Portuguese. A situation similar to that of the so-called Brazilians of Africa: descendants of Africans who, when they became free during the nineteenth century, returned to Africa and whose grandchildren and great-grandchildren keep their Brazilian customs, including the cult of Our Lord, whom they have converted into Our Lady, of Bonfim.

But it is religious traditions, transplanted to Brazil like other forms

---

[1] See Mario Filho: *O Negro no Foot-ball Brasileiro* (Rio de Janeiro, 1945).

of Negro culture, or cultures, that show the strongest resistance to de-Africanization. Far more than blood, color, and physique. Europe will not conquer them. But they will acquire new forms through their transculturation with European and native values.

It is unlikely that Brazil will ever be, like Argentina, an almost European country; or like Mexico or Paraguay, an almost Amerindian one. The substance of African culture will remain with us throughout all our formation and consolidation as a nation.

This Africanizing influence is exerted by the mulatto nurses who still today teach the white children to talk, and with these first lessons of Portuguese, transmit to them African traditions, songs, superstitions; by the mulatto cooks who in white homes Africanize French recipes with their own special seasoning; by handsome quadroons and octoroons who by their beauty and sexual allure rise from shanty to tiled mansion—the mistresses of businessmen, officers of the police force or the army, of government officials, of rich Portuguese, of Italians, Germans, of the sons of barons and viscounts of the days of the Empire. They carry with them, as they ascend the social ladder, many vestiges of their African origins to predominantly European milieus, reviving in some and introducing in others African tastes or values.

Vieira Fazenda, in Rio de Janeiro, and Nina Rodriguez, in Bahía, found that the "saints' room" and chapels of certain patriarchal city mansions on certain days of the year were transformed into veritable voodoo shrines. A Catholic priest who entered one of them would have cried out in horror. The same candles that illuminated Our Lady with the Infant Jesus in her arms were illuminating African divinities disguised as Catholic saints: images which had come not from Portugal or Italy, or France, but some of them from Asia or made here in Brazil, whittled from cashew wood or cedar by the hand of mulatto or Negro. For this was one of the crafts in which our mulattoes, especially the effeminate type, specialized in Brazil, that of imagemaker. Sculptors of Onofres, Anthonys, Our Ladies in cashew. Makers of images for shanties and for mansions where semi-African forms of religion managed to creep in, often through those quadroons and octoroons whose beauty and sexual appeal transformed them from shanty wenches into "dark-complexioned ladies," mistresses or daughters of mansions. There they became an element of Africanization as a result of the ineradicable traces in them of their semi-African formation; at times against their will, for they would have preferred to be exactly like the white ladies. And they became the mothers—not always legitimate—of distinguished Brazilians, whose cause—that of the recognition of their civil rights as "natural offspring"—was ardently and skillfully defended in the parliament of the Empire by Brazilians of humble or African origin, elevated by their technical or intellectual gifts into political leaders.

Nobody today is so deluded as to think that we Brazilians—nearly all of us, even those of São Paulo and Rio Grande do Sul, with our Negro cousins—are a really Latin people, and, even less, strictly Christian, in the sense that the French, for example, are. (Though we should not forget, in passing, that the type of Christianity Renan encountered in the shadows of Saint-Sulpice differed not a little from that of the folk of Brittany.) We are agreed that Catholicism was a powerful factor in the integration of Brazil; but a Catholicism which in its contacts in the Iberian peninsula with African forms of religion acquired a dark or mulatto tinge. Thus it adapted itself to the conditions of life in the tropics and to our people of hybrid origin. The doors of the shrines opened wide to admit African idols disguised as St. Cosme and St. Damian; coal-black St. Benedicts, St. Iphigenias. Dark-hued Madonnas of the Rosary. Colored saints who took their place beside fair St. Anthonys and golden-locked cherubs in a fraternization that outdid that of humans. Saints and angels, traditionally blond, were forced to imitate the people, becoming, like them, the relatives of blacks and mulattoes. In the hands of our image-makers, even Our Lady took on mulatto traits: she sometimes put on flesh and acquired the breasts of a black mother. And the most popular image of Christ in Brazil is that of the dark, pale Jew, with black or at most brown hair and beard, and not blond like the historical or orthodox North European representation of the Redeemer. It may be that if the priests had insisted on imposing golden-haired or blond saints, they would have estranged a large number of Brazilians from Catholicism and there might have grown up around the altars and the saints the same atmosphere of coolness and indifference as around the throne of blond emperors and regents. There is a basis of truth in the rather far-fetched allegation that the first Emperor lost his throne because he was not a native-born Brazilian, and the second, because he was not a mulatto.

It is natural that the masses should prefer as their culture heroes figures in whom they find the truest reflection of themselves. Their features, their vices, their gestures, their laughter. This represents one of the most powerful forces of integration triumphing over differentiation: the hero, the saint, the genius differs by reason of his exceptional degree of courage, saintliness, intelligence; the masses, however, reabsorb him by reason of the much or the little they find in him of themselves. In the last analysis, there has never been a hero, a genius, or even a saint who has not drawn from the masses some part of his greatness or his virtue, who does not reveal some common trait in his superior personality. There are those who go to the lengths of looking upon the man of genius as a thief, a thief of the treasures the people have amassed and which he alone reveals. The treasure which overflowed in him but came from the others. Be that as it may, the masses tend to recapture what the hero or the genius has to a certain extent usurped from them, exaggerating the similarities and the points of contact between themselves and him. In the cult of the hero there is a touch of the affection of the cat, the classic affection of the cat for its master: when seeming to be caressing the leg of the master, what the cat is doing is voluptuously stroking its own fur. Thus, when the Negroid or *caboclo* masses find a hero or saint with Indian hair or frizzy beard they take more pleasure in him than in a blond hero; it is a way of stroking their own fur.

Nor is this limited to lands like Brazil where miscegenation exists, and where the masses discover—with certain narcissistic satisfaction—in Negroid or Indianoid individuals talent or ability equal to that of the whites, once the sole and exclusive rulers. It is the "consciousness of the species"—as Giddings would say—working from the bottom to the top. This tendency or consciousness is also to be found in countries where the blond type predominates. Figures that depart markedly from this type with difficulty achieve popularity in lands of fair people. The second Coleridge, almost as gifted as the first, never enjoyed the esteem he deserved in England. And the reason for this was, at least in part, his heavy growth of beard, which gave his face, even when shaved, an un-English, an almost Negroid shadow. His biographers point out not only the annoyances but also the antipathy this heavy beard occasioned him from his adolescent years.

In Russia, a Negroid like Pushkin could win quick popularity, and become the greatest poet of all the Russians, because the Russians, only in part blond, accepted men of genius with mestizo and markedly anti-European features: mongoloids of the type that found their fullest expression in Dostoievski, and in Gorki and Lenin in more recent days.

There is no doubt that in Brazil, "in contraposition to ethnic miscegenation," traits of the cultures "identified with the three races that have gone into our national composition" persist, as Azevedo Amaral points out.[2] Mainly the European and the Negro. (In the case of the latter, Professor Herskovits would say "cultures.") It is doubtful, however, that one can speak of these cultures as maintaining themselves "isolated and with their ethical, metaphysical, social, economic, and political values opposed to one another," as Azevedo Amaral claims. The most active characteristic of the Brazilian social milieu today would seem to be precisely the reciprocity between the cultures, and not the domination of one by the other, to the point where the lower has little or nothing to offer, remaining, as in other countries where miscegenation exists, in a state of almost permanent tension or repression.

Ours is a reciprocity between cultures which has been accompanied by intense social mobility between classes and regions. Vertical and horizontal mobility. Possibly in no country the size of ours does the person of the far North—Pará, let us say—feel so much at ease in the far South, and find, more on the basis of temperament than racial origin, so many opportunities for social and political advancement. This is the case of hundreds of professional men from Ceará, Pará, Sergipe, Bahía, Pernambuco—some of them Negroids or *caboclos*—who have had successful careers in Rio Grande, Paraná, São Paulo, and even governed those states or represented them in the national parliament or congress. Perhaps in no other country is it possible to rise so quickly from one social class to another: from shanty to mansion. From one race to another: from Negro to

---

[2] Amaral Azevedo: *O Brasil na Crise Atual* (Rio de Janeiro, 1935), Chap. VIII.

"white" or "dark-complexioned" or "caboclo." From one region to another: from Ceará to São Paulo.

On the other hand, one finds whites in Brazil—whites, near whites, and even blond persons—who have come down in the social scale and are today the "poor whites," "the yellows," "the eaters of toads with banana," so despised by those of the lower classes of darker color. Like the majority of the Negroes, the mulattoes, and the darker *caboclos*, they live in shanties, in houses made of straw or thatched with straw like those of Africa; they eat with their fingers out of gourds cut in two, like the Indians and the Negroes; they go barefoot and sleep in hammocks or palm fronds. They use banana leaves instead of plates; their children go naked; their women prefer red dresses like the Indian and Negro women. Men and women of this type of whites prefer witch doctors and forest herbs when they are sick to medicines from a drugstore or laboratory; others prefer the leader of native cults to the priest. Then where is the culture, the way of living rigidly identified with race? Azevedo Amaral's thesis seems as erroneous as the "Aryanism" of Professor Oliveira Vianna, who, moreover, after a more thoroughgoing study of the subject, has been sensibly modifyng his earlier criteria of ethnocentric interpretation of Brazilian problems of race and culture.[3]

If it is a fact that Brazilians are mobile in both directions—horizontally and vertically—it is because the psychological contours of race and class are not so rigid in our country. The Pernambucan feels himself closer to the man from Rio Grande do Sul or São Paulo than to his neighbor, the Bahían. And he has his reasons for this. The Pernambucan, like the gaucho of Rio Grande do Sul, and in contrast to the Bahían, likes fighting and is more of a rustic on horseback than a soft city dweller. Like the Paulista, he is reserved and taciturn; unlike the people of Bahía, Rio de Janeiro, or Ceará, he does not quickly make friends with strangers. On the basis of that hard and fast race psychology to which Azevedo Amaral ascribes such importance in our formation, attributing to it the psychological divergences between the different groups of Brazilians according to the amount of this or that race which predominates in each, how do we

---

[3] F. J. de Oliveira Vianna: *Instituções Politicas Brasileiras* (Rio de Janeiro, 1949). This work modifies many of the author's earlier opinions.

account for the affinity between the Pernambucans and the gauchos of Rio Grande do Sul? Assuming the repercussion of race on man's behavior to be absolute, the affinities of the Pernambucan should all, or nearly all, be with the Bahían of the Reconcavo and not with the Spanish-like gaucho of the far South or the Paulista.

Possibly the affinities are due rather to points of similarity in the social formation of those of Pernambuco, Rio Grande do Sul, and São Paulo. A less easy-going and self-indulgent formation than that of the Bahían; more warlike and more independent of the Court or the mother country; more alert by reason of the need to be always defending the country, Brazil, Portuguese America, with their efforts and their blood. As a result of this formation, there developed in these three groups habits of independence, leadership, separatism, and, at the same time, liberalism. One can today discern points of resemblance between the early nineteenth-century revolutions of Pernambuco and Rio Grande do Sul. Between the trends toward separatism, toward republicanism in the nineteenth century, of North and South [4] in regard to Rio or "the Court."

In the case of the affinity—let us call it, provisionally, psychological—of a northern group, ethnically almost the counterpart of the Bahíans, for southerners of predominantly European ethnic formation, or at any rate, almost free of African blood as compared with the Pernambucan or Bahían, the racial factor pales under the more powerful effects of similarities in social formation. Or social experience.

So much importance is no longer conceded to the oversimplified race psychology which for many years consisted in associating, in absolute fashion, qualities or defects with the race, the nation, or region of the individual. This was a simple approach, according to which the Mediterranean man was always, by inflexible racial determinism, volatile, passionate, unstable, imaginative, with a strong bent for the plastic and graphic arts, but without the pertinacity, fortitude, love of freedom, levelheadedness, governing capacity of the Nordics. Little is as yet known, indisputably or on the basis of techniques of measurement and comparison, of mental and temperamental differences between races; and even less of the superiority and inferiority

---

[4] See Manuel Duarte: *Provincia e Nacão* (Rio de Janeiro, 1949).

of such differences. Race superiorities and inferiorities have been established, some by popular consensus, others by the pseudo-science, always so dogmatic, of second-rate psychologists and third-rate sociologists. The problem of the relation of the intelligence and temperament of the half-breed or mulatto to those of the purer races is in the same situation; the idea being that the mulatto shows all the defects and none of the virtues of the white or the Negro. The idea, too, that the mulatto remains an unstable subrace, incapable of the high accomplishments of intellectual creativity and political leadership: merely of improvisations and facile brilliance.

However, one can never sufficiently stress this fact: under the system of slavocrat economy, the white, or, at most, the white-Indian, sector of the population of Brazil was the one that enjoyed the best opportunities—if the Jesuits had had their way, they would have been the only ones—for intellectual development and social advancement. Even so, some of the outstanding examples of intellectual and artistic ability in our country, in the stifling atmosphere of the privileged regime for whites and white-Indians, were men of the genius of *O Aleijadinho*—the son of a Negro woman; Antonio Vieira—the grandson of a negroid woman; mulattoes, quadroons, or octoroons like Caldas Barbosa, Silva Alvarenga, Natividade Saldanha, Gonçalvez Dias, Machado de Assis, Montezuma, the Rebouças, José Mauricio, Torres Homem, Saldanha Marinho, Juliano Moreira, Livio de Castro. All showed themselves capable of exceptional intellectual and artistic creativity; and some were examples of moral integrity, men of the probity of Machado, the Rebouças, Juliano Moreira in their private as well as in their public and artistic life.

Moreover, one aspect of the intellectual honesty of the Brazilian mestizo which does him credit should be pointed out: his ability to turn his back on the easy narcissism which would lead him, so effortlessly, to look upon himself as the ideal solution to the problem of race relations. As a matter of fact, our leading apologists of "Aryanism" have been mestizos—"mongrels" from the ethnic point of view. During a phase of his life as an intellectual guerrilla fighter, Sylvio Romero [5]—whose features revealed a strong Amerindian mixture—

---

[5] Distinguished nineteenth-century historian, folklorist, professor of logic and the philosophy of law. Elected to Congress, 1899–1902, he assisted in drawing up a new civil code.

was an "Aryanist," as were, after a fashion, Euclydes da Cunha,[6] and, more recently, Oliveira Vianna[7] and Jorge de Lima,[8] none of whom was 100 per cent Caucasian in his physical or cultural and social formation.

Nobody would venture to deny that numerous qualities and psychological attitudes are biologically conditioned by a person's race. But conditioned, not determined in exclusive or absolute fashion. Once we have discarded ethnic as well as geographic and economic determinism, and look upon race, milieu, and techniques of production as forces which condition human development without determining it rigidly and uniformly—on the contrary, exerting a reciprocal and always varied influence on one another—we are free to interpret this development in terms of its own dynamics.

One then sees that many of the qualities associated with race have developed as the result of historic or, rather, dynamic forces of culture exerted on the group and the individual. Conditioned by race and, certainly, environment, but not created by the one nor determined by the other. Race gives predispositions, conditions the special forms of human culture. But such specializations are developed by the totality of the environment—the social more than the merely physical—peculiar to the region or the class to which the individual belongs. Peculiar to his situation.

This is the case of the mulatto, a predominantly social product, with defects which at first glance seem mental or temperamental but which, on closer examination, reveal themselves as mainly social. And the mulatto is more pronouncedly what the race is more diffusely: the negation of the biologically static in the individual or the group. The clearest affirmation of the biological mobility of races. "Race is dynamics," Dixon points out. It develops and changes through the renewal of basic elements of the same race or through the introduction of elements of another race. And the half-race is even more dynamic: a kind of middle class in its attitudes when well-balanced between the two extremes.

---

[6] Early twentieth-century writer, author of *Rebellion in the Backlands* (*Os Sertoes*).

[7] Early twentieth-century Negroid sociologist with Aryanist leanings.

[8] A highly talented Catholic mystic poet (1895–1953) who wrote on African themes.

Racial mobility, in its early transitional stages—the Brazilian phase which so disturbed Count Gobineau and Professor Agassiz—has its dramatic aspects. The combinations tend, however, when miscegenation is extensive and of long standing, to give rise to relatively stable types such as can already be observed in certain regions of Brazil.

Professor Hooton—who was of the opinion that miscegenation creates new races—points out that there can be seen, in the offspring of crossbreeding between primary races, combinations and traits which recall the great secondary races.[9] Mixed-breeds of white, Negro, and Indian, for example, show a close resemblance to the Polynesians, today classified as a race. This is what is happening in Brazil in regions where the interbreeding of these three races has been more intense and of longer duration: the new type acquires features similar to those of the Polynesians and reveals a tendency toward stabilization as a race. A relative stabilization, naturally, for not even in the case of the so-called pure races is this absolute.

This relative stabilization of traits provisionally combined, so to speak, and not actually a "cultural synthesis" leading to a definitive state, is also the goal of the various cultures that have contributed to the formation of Brazil through reciprocity rather than the clash of antagonisms. The dynamism of these cultures on combining is even greater than that of the races. Therefore, much may be expected from the penetration of Brazilian culture by elements of Italian, Germanic, Polish, Syrian origin, which, though existent in our formation for many years, some from the beginning of the nineteenth century, have only recently been coming into intimate contact with the traditional elements of that culture.

Antagonisms are still frequent in Brazilian social or cultural life; they are reflected in politics, occasioning clashes and rivalries between groups and regions. Rivalries between gauchos and Bahíans; Paulistas and those of Ceará. And not merely between Brazilians of old stock and neo-Brazilians which Professor Coelho discusses in his brief, stimulating study.[1]

But these clashes cannot be interpreted on the basis of the sim-

---

[9] E. A. Hooton: *Up from the Ape* (New York, 1931), p. 429.
[1] J. P. Coelho de Sousa: *Conflito de Culturas* (Porto Alegre, 1949).

ple criterion of conflicts between races biologically or psychologically incapable of understanding or getting along with one another. Nor the equally oversimplified criterion of pure "class struggle" of the orthodox Marxists who see in the Paulista, for example, nothing but "the capitalist colonizer" and in the northern Brazilians only "the colonial masses."

The differences between subgroups in a society like the Brazilian is due more to the conflict between phases or moments of culture which, incarnated in the beginning in three different races, today are represented by purely social populations, and by regional and temporal differences in technical progress. And also by the varying ease of social and intellectual contacts with foreigners and among one another of groups or regions, subgroups and subregions.

There is also the fact of inequality due to social gulfs, which are still great and which became accentuated from colonial days with the growth of an industrial economy in certain regions which benefited powerful political and economic minorities. A growth favored by ecological conditions of soil and climate which cannot be overlooked in the interpretation of Brazilian contrasts.

Within the industrialized cities, decisively favored by these or other circumstances, on the hilltops, under the shadow of the smokestacks of factories and mills, there were the shanties and slum settlements, differing profoundly from the aristocratic sector of the population. A kind of enemy in plain view, Moors always skirting the coast. On the hills, as in Rio de Janeiro, or in the mudflats, as in Recife. Inhabitants so different from the ruling class as the result of their living conditions—which as a consequence of slavery coincided with the difference of color or race—that the group rather than the race was, at least provisionally, the determining factor among the Brazilians: those of more Europeanized areas as compared with those spots, not so much of African blood, but of a more African or, from the cultural point of view, more elementary or primitive way of living. Those of the exploited class with relation to those of the exploiting class, rather than race.

However, even during this phase of major social differentiation between mansions and shanties, which corresponds to the greatest disintegration of the patriarchal system in Brazil, elements or means of communication between the social or cultural extremes were not lacking. Hence, the antagonisms, which were never absolute, did not become so after that disintegration. And one of the most powerful elements of communication during this difficult phase, because of his racial and, above all, his cultural dynamism, was the mulatto.

The meeting of cultures, like that of races, under conditions which do not sacrifice the expression of the desires, tastes, interests of one to the exclusive domination of the other, seems to be especially favorable to the development of new and richer cultures than those called or looked upon as pure. The greatest disadvantages, from the standpoint of this development, lie precisely in the isolation or the social gulf which hampers the opportunities for contact between one group and the others, one race and the others. For this reason, Lars Ringbom sees in the mestizo the best solution to the extremes of individualism or collectivism in the great races and great cultures which he considers pure.[2]

Professor Hooton, in turn, points out that Egypt achieved its extraordinary degree of civilization as the result of profound miscegenation: the fusion of the basic Mediterranean race with Negro, Armenoid, and, possibly, Nordic elements. Greece, too: a blend of Mediterranean, Armenoid, Nordic, and, probably, Alpine stocks. Rome was the combined effort of Mediterranean, Nordic, and Alpine races.[3]

Racial purists should not forget these many examples of the enrichment of regional or national cultures through the work of miscegenation. One of these, Professor Gunther,[4] in the groups of geniuses he studied anthropologically on the theory that the capacity for invention and creativity is highest among the Nordics, admits the presence of other races, together with the Nordic, which is rarely found simon pure even among the heroes of the so-called Nordics. Luther was, in part, non-Nordic, as were Schopenhauer, Schumann, Ibsen. But the salt of the Nordic-Alpine and Nordic-Mediterranean countries was, in Gunther's opinion, the Nordic blood; the strength of those geniuses resided in the Nordic blood that flowed through their hybrid veins. This is a dangerous and feeble argument. Not

---

[2] Lars Ringbom: *The Renewal of Culture* (Tr., London, n.d.).

[3] Hooton: Op. cit., p. 458.

[4] H. F. K. Gunther: *Rassenkunde des Deutschen Volkes*, 11th ed. (Munich, 1927).

only does it recognize the advantage of crossbreeding—at any rate, between races not too disparate in their somatic characteristics and psychological trends—but it justifies Hertz's right to ask: "If it is true that the culture of Greece, Rome, Italy, Spain, the Slavs is due to the contribution of the Nordic elements that entered into the formation of these peoples, why, then, was not the beginning of all these cultures in the points of origin of the Nordics, in Scandinavia and the north of Germany? Why is it that these regions only followed, in relatively recent times, the routes opened by the hybrid peoples of the south?" [5]

Of Brazil one thing is certain: the regions or areas of greatest miscegenation are those which have been most productive of great men. Our Virginia during the monarchy, the mother of a large number of privy councilors and ministers of State, was Bahía, with its admixture not only of the best blood the slave trade brought to America but also of the highest type of culture which Africa transmitted to the American continent. Maranhão, known as the Athens of Brazil, was another subregion of intense miscegenation, with its many idealized or romanticized Indian half-breeds. Minas Gerais was still another, with the Negro predominating over the Indian as the colored element. In contrast to Rio Grande do Sul, whiter and so radical and unyielding in its political attitudes—with the exception of the half-breeds of the missions area, *caboclos* whom the Jesuit teachings had turned into a kind of introverted or Apollonian Brazilians, with their unctuous manners, their diplomatic attitudes—the men of the regions of greater and more pervasive race amalgamation brought to the administration of our country, to its politics, its diplomacy, the governing of the Catholic Church, a gift for compromise, a sense of timing, a balance which made them the greatest pacifiers, the best bishops, the most able diplomats, the most effective politicians.

And without intending the slightest reflection on the Brazilian navy, I would point out once more that, although it made itself, for long years, the greatest pool of whites or near whites in Brazil, it contributed a relatively insignificant number of great men. Not even a professor of mathematics of the stature of Benjamin Constant.

---

[5] F. Hertz: *Rasse und Kultur*. Eng. tr. by G. S. Levetus and W. Entz: *Race and Civilization* (London, 1928).

Saldanha da Gama and Jaceguay were two exemplary gentlemen rather than authentic great men. Barroso and Tamandaré were two *bourgeois gentilhommes* whose limited martial imagination was partially compensated for by their bravery. The contrast with the army's officer staff, which for years has been in large part mestizo and even Negroid, leaps to the eye. And with the contrast, the idea that, at least in the sense of corresponding more closely to the Brazilian milieu and of easier and possibly deeper adaptation to its interests, its tastes, its needs, the half-breed, the mulatto, or, to put it more delicately, the dark-complexioned person, would seem to show more capacity for leadership than the white or near white.

It is no longer a question of the advancement of mulattoes or mestizos in the shadow of the declining social domination of the whites and near whites of the patriarchal Big House and city mansion. It is the more general and less individual triumph of the mestizo and, principally, of the mulatto, of the half-breed, thanks to the closer ties between the half-breed leader and the masses, in their majority mestizos like him. Biologically or sociologically mestizos. There are considerable groups of southern Brazilians whose situation as sons of Italians, Poles, Germans, Syrians, Japanese is psychologically and sociologically—if not culturally—akin to that of the half-breed and justifies the characterization of the Brazilian masses as sociological half-breeds.

But these and other aspects of the relation between the decline of the patriarchal system in Brazil, whose power was incarnated for the most part in whites and near whites of almost exclusively Portuguese and Catholic culture, and the development of a society both mestizo and varied in its ethnic and cultural composition, and predominantly individualistic in its family organization, will be studied, or at any rate considered, in a forthcoming work. For Brazil is becoming more and more a racial democracy, characterized by an almost unique combination of diversity and unity.

Index

Index